T0372691

The Limits of Judicial Independence

This book investigates the causes and consequences of congressional attacks on the U.S. Supreme Court, arguing that the extent of public support for judicial independence constitutes the practical limit of judicial independence. First, the book presents a historical overview of Court-curbing proposals in Congress. Then, building on interviews with Supreme Court justices, members of Congress, and judicial and legislative staffers, as well as existing research, the book theorizes that congressional attacks are driven by public discontent with the Court. From this theoretical model, predictions are derived about the decision to engage in Court-curbing and judicial responsiveness to Court-curbing activity in Congress. *The Limits of Judicial Independence* draws on illustrative archival evidence, systematic analysis of an original dataset of Court-curbing proposals introduced in Congress from 1877 onward, and judicial decisions. This evidence demonstrates that Court-curbing is driven primarily by public opposition to the Court, and that the Court responds to those proposals by engaging in self-restraint and moderating its decisions.

Tom S. Clark is Assistant Professor of Political Science at Emory University. His research interests include American judicial institutions and the interaction between courts and other political actors. His research has been published in numerous journals, including the *American Journal of Political Science*, the *Journal of Politics*, the *Journal of Law, Economics & Organization*, and the *Journal of Theoretical Politics*. His dissertation, on which this book is based, was awarded the 2009 Carl Albert Award for the Best Dissertation from the Legislative Studies Section of the American Political Science Association. Clark received his Ph.D. and M.A. from Princeton University and B.A. from Rutgers University.

Political Economy of Institutions and Decisions

Series Editors

Stephen Ansolabehere, *Harvard University*
Jeffry Frieden, *Harvard University*

Founding Editors

James E. Alt, *Harvard University*
Douglass C. North, *Washington University of St. Louis*

Other Books in the Series

Alberto Alesina and Howard Rosenthal, *Partisan Politics, Divided Government, and the Economy*

Lee J. Alston, Thrainn Eggertsson, and Douglass C. North, eds., *Empirical Studies in Institutional Change*

Lee J. Alston and Joseph P. Ferrie, *Southern Paternalism and the Rise of the American Welfare State: Economics, Politics, and Institutions, 1865–1965*

James E. Alt and Kenneth Shepsle, eds., *Perspectives on Positive Political Economy*

Josephine T. Andrews, *When Majorities Fail: The Russian Parliament, 1990–1993*

Jeffrey S. Banks and Eric A. Hanushek, eds., *Modern Political Economy: Old Topics, New Directions*

Yoram Barzel, *Economic Analysis of Property Rights, 2nd edition*

Yoram Barzel, *A Theory of the State: Economic Rights, Legal Rights, and the Scope of the State*

Robert Bates, *Beyond the Miracle of the Market: The Political Economy of Agrarian Development in Kenya, new edition*

Jenna Bednar, *The Robust Federation: Principles of Design*

Charles M. Cameron, *Veto Bargaining: Presidents and the Politics of Negative Power*

Kelly H. Chang, *Appointing Central Bankers: The Politics of Monetary Policy in the United States and the European Monetary Union*

Peter Cowhey and Mathew McCubbins, eds., *Structure and Policy in Japan and the United States: An Institutionalist Approach*

Series list continues following the Index.

The Limits of Judicial Independence

TOM S. CLARK
Emory University

CAMBRIDGE
UNIVERSITY PRESS

CAMBRIDGE UNIVERSITY PRESS
Cambridge, New York, Melbourne, Madrid, Cape Town, Singapore,
São Paulo, Delhi, Dubai, Tokyo, Mexico City

Cambridge University Press
32 Avenue of the Americas, New York, NY 10013-2473, USA

www.cambridge.org
Information on this title: www.cambridge.org/9780521135054

First published 2011

Printed in the United States of America

A catalog record for this publication is available from the British Library.

Library of Congress Cataloging in Publication data

Clark, Thomas S., 1980–
The limits of judicial independence / Tom S. Clark.
    p.   cm. – (Political economy of institutions and decisions)
Includes bibliographical references and index.
ISBN 978-0-521-19488-4 (hardback) – ISBN 978-0-521-13505-4 (pbk.)
1. Judicial independence – United States.   2. United States. Supreme
Court – Public opinion.   3. Judgments – United States – Public opinion.
4. United States. Supreme Court – History.   I. Title.   II. Series.
KF8775.C58   2010
347.73'26 – dc22   2010012780

ISBN 978-0-521-19488-4 Hardback
ISBN 978-0-521-13505-4 Paperback

For Leigh Anne

Contents

List of Tables

List of Figures

Acknowledgments

Writing these acknowledgments is in many ways the most difficult part of this book. I began this project in 2005, after finishing my exams in graduate school and beginning the research that would occupy the remainder of my Ph.D. education. In the intervening years, the project has grown and improved owing to the many, many people who have been generous with their time and insights. I owe to each of these people an incredible intellectual debt and my deepest gratitude.

Chuck Cameron is perhaps the person most responsible for my intellectual and academic orientation and achievements. His guidance and training during my years in graduate school shaped the way I think about research and the approach I take to answering questions. I cannot thank Chuck enough for all he has done for me and this project. Every student should be so lucky as to have a mentor like Chuck. Keith Whittington also had a profound impact on my intellectual growth and this project. The most detailed reader this project will ever have, Keith's keen insights and sharp mind kept this project from going off the tracks more times than I care to count. Brandice Canes-Wrone also exerted considerable influence on me as a scholar and on the shape and content of this project. When I struggled early on, she suggested I inform my theoretical model by actually speaking to the subjects of my study. Her advice proved invaluable and left a lasting impression on me. Josh Clinton graciously gave of his time, offering a fresh perspective and invaluable insights to this project. He helped me better organize the project and focused me on how best to strengthen my argument.

Upon arriving at Emory with a dissertation that I wanted to revise into a book, I found a nurturing and stimulating environment. My colleagues in the political science department gave generously of their time and helped me improve this project into the book you see today. Cliff Carrubba, Michael Giles, and Tom Walker all read the book and offered detailed comments. Cliff's eye for theoretical clarity and rigor pushed me to tighten my argument and more clearly highlight my contribution to the literature. Michael brought a fresh perspective on the research design and pushed me to think carefully about my approach. Tom helped me convey my points clearly and told me when it was time to call the book "finished."

The rest of my colleagues tolerated my incessant questions and "thinking out loud." Justin Esarey and Drew Linzer, in particular, suffered sharing a hallway with me – which meant that they were responsible for telling me when a figure was crazy and uninterpretable as well as helping me when I couldn't get R to cooperate. Jeff Staton offered insightful comments about my work and listened to me while I worked out ideas, often over coffee, but sometimes (painfully) without. David Davis, Harvey Klehr, and Dani Reiter provided encouragement throughout the process of submitting the manuscript for review and working my way through the publishing process.

Beyond my colleagues and advisors, I have benefited from encouragement, criticism, guidance, and insights from a number of very smart people. John Kastellec, Jeff Lax, Adam Meirowitz, Jim Rogers, Jeff Segal, and Georg Vanberg, in particular, have made important contributions to this project. They have commented on various parts of this book – in the form of conference papers, articles, a dissertation, and even a book manuscript – over the years and have helped me shape it into the product it has become. They have given of their time simply because of their support for me and their dedication to the discipline. I have also benefited greatly from seminar participants at Princeton, Emory, Columbia, Ohio State, New York University, UC-Davis, Northwestern, Michigan State, Harvard, and the University of Illinois. The anonymous readers at Cambridge, Princeton, and Chicago offered very useful and insightful comments that improved considerably the quality of this book. For that, I cannot thank them enough.

I would also like to thank the editors at Cambridge University Press. I thank Lew Bateman and Steve Ansolabehere for their support, confidence, and guidance.

Of course, the support needed to write a book extends far beyond the intellectual and disciplinary support of one's colleagues. Since I began graduate school, I have been lucky enough to have a strong network of family and friends. Most of them do not understand what it is I do – only because I can't explain it well – but nevertheless encourage me. Sometimes they just feign interest when I talk about methodological or other research dilemmas; sometimes they seem genuinely interested in my research. I thank Dad and Pierrette, my aunts and uncles, Brian, Jenna, Vanessa, Dan, Jay, Lisa, and Rockininny, among others. While my grandfather did not live to see me go to graduate school, he has nevertheless encouraged me throughout this process, and I thank him.

Finally, my wife, Leigh Anne, has patiently dealt with long days while I work and ignore her on the couch, vacations spent with my nose in a book or working on a laptop, far too many evenings out "talking shop," and the general inconvenience associated with the unfortunate state of affairs that is being married to an academic. Through this all, she has actually read drafts of this book, talked to me about it, and kept me anchored. Together with our daughter, Madeleine, she reminds me every day of what matters most, keeps me humble, and helps make sure that I occasionally take a break from work. Without them, I might have finished this book, but I would have been a lesser person.

I

Introduction

Among all of the institutional features of the American Constitution, none is more significant than the separation of powers. Separation of powers represents perhaps the most important contribution the American experiment has made to constitutional democracy throughout the world. With its roots in Montesquieu's insight, the notion of setting power to counteract power has grown into a principle of limited self-government that motivates constitutional democracies in every corner of the globe. In the context of the American judiciary, the separation of powers is a particularly interesting and perplexing institution. Although the courts are often considered strong institutions with the power to exercise a constitutional veto over majoritarian politics, the federal judiciary has been referred to as "the least dangerous branch," following from Alexander Hamilton's famous assertion that the Court "is possessed of neither force nor will, but merely judgment."[1] These seemingly diminutive descriptions of the courts are due to their lack of constitutional authority of enforcement and their reliance on action by the elected branches to give effect to judicial decisions. That is, the judiciary has "neither purse nor sword" and relies instead on legislative or executive powers for its institutional efficacy. Indeed, the separation of powers among governing institutions is a hallmark of the American Constitution and was a guiding principle for the Framers. In this vein, James Madison observed in *The Federalist* that each of the original states had chosen to divide governing powers among multiple institutions while also providing overlap and cross-checking vetoes. He also noted that realizing the American goals of freedom and liberty

[1] *The Federalist* #78.

requires that government be self-limiting. To achieve this goal, he wrote, "ambition must be made to counteract ambition."[2]

Owing to the founding principle that the government be limited by setting power to check power, and the apparently weak institutional position of the judiciary, one might expect that the Supreme Court's decision making should be constrained by the necessity of political will to see any of its policy goals carried out. A major focus of scholarship on the role of courts in policymaking suggests they are in fact unable to bring about significant policy change without having at least political will to enforce their decisions. Gerald Rosenberg (1991) finds that a lack of political will – the willingness of political actors to take action to carry into effect judicial decisions – was the cause of delayed enforcement of the Supreme Court's order to desegregate public schools in *Brown v. Board of Education*. Despite these claims and the apparent weak institutional position in which the judiciary finds itself, both popular journalism and scholarly literature frequently claim that the Court's discretion is virtually limitless and that the Court is free to pursue its ideological and policy goals without constraint by the political system.

From an empirical perspective, popular critics bemoan an imperial Court, composed of unelected, life-tenured judges, whereas political scientists have documented evidence that the Supreme Court is primarily motivated by its own policy goals and that there does not appear to be anything in the political system that can attenuate its ability to pursue those goals (Segal and Spaeth 2002). Critics of that view, though, have observed that Congress does have tools for overcoming the Court's power. With the power to control the Court's budget, jurisdiction, and calendar – as well as the power to increase or decrease the size of the courts and the senatorial power to confirm judges nominated by the president – one might reasonably expect that Congress is able to exert some influence on how judges decide cases. Indeed, these tools, given to Congress by the Constitution, are the defining feature of the American separation of powers.[3] Nevertheless, evidence that these tools constrain

---

[2] See *The Federalist*, #47 and #51.

[3] I distinguish the American separation of powers from other separation-of-powers systems. In France, for example, the separation-of-powers is given a very different interpretation. Rather than enabling each branch of government to "check" each other, the various branches are given very specific and hard spheres of autonomy. The solution to preventing unchecked accumulation of power, under the French interpretation, is to endow each institution with a strict sphere of autonomy that no other institution can breach and that the particular institution *cannot exceed*. In my sense, then, there is very little that distinguishes separation of powers from checks and balances.

the Court and operate as effective limits on judicial power has been mixed at best.

From a more theoretical perspective, a related academic debate concerns the so-called countermajoritarian difficulty. The countermajoritarian difficulty asks how we can reconcile American norms of democracy and majority rule with the Supreme Court's constitutional veto over democratically crafted laws and has been the defining question of American constitutional theory for the past century. Because the Supreme Court is unelected and essentially unaccountable, how do we square our commitment to democracy with judicial supremacy in the realm of constitutional interpretation?[4] Responses to these questions have been numerous and come in a variety of forms. Most notably, normative constitutional theorists have developed various prescriptions for the use of judicial review by the Court (Thayer 1893; Llewellyn 1934; Wechsler 1959; Bickel 1962; Ely 1980).

Each of these lines of inquiry, though, is concerned with the same question – what is the balance of power between the courts and the elected branches of government, and what are the limits of judicial independence? In this book, I approach this debate from a different perspective and offer both theoretical and empirical insights into the countermajoritarian difficulty. Although I recognize the importance of institutional tools for interactions among the branches of government, I contend that another, perhaps more important, component of the limitations on the Court's institutional independence is a form of indirect representation on the Court. As already noted, the Court is without power to effect policy changes without political will or political "nerve" on the part of elected officials with the power to implement judicial decisions. A key determinant of political will is public will. Elected officials were reluctant to enforce desegregation following *Brown* because the public did not approve of the decisions and would punish their representatives if they were to act against segregation. Similarly, elected officials continue to work to prohibit abortion because their constituents do not respect the Court's decision in *Roe v. Wade* and want to see it evaded. We also see evidence of continued disregard for the Court's prohibition on school prayer, especially in the South. Thus, I argue that because the Court relies

---

[4] Of course, a large scholarly debate has emerged, in part in response to this question, examining the extent to which the Court does in fact have the final word on matters constitutional. In general, most scholars believe that, at least sometimes, the Court does not have the final word on constitutional meaning, either in theory or in practice. However, it is largely conceded that most often the Court does have the final say.

on political will to give effect to its decisions, and because political will is often directed by public opinion, the most relevant constraining force on judicial power is public support for the Court. In this way, the public plays a subtle yet important role in the courtroom and in interinstitutional interactions between Congress and the courts.

Scholars have long been interested in the determinants of public willingness to support divergent decisions from the Supreme Court. Political scientists and legal academics have concluded that the perception of judicial decisions as *legitimate* is a reason why the public will support enforcement of decisions with which it disagrees. Grossman (1984, 214) characterizes the scholarly interpretation of legitimacy as "essentially a normative concept, [which] questions the authority of courts to displace the value choices of elected legislative bodies by judicially fashioned policies." Because the public perceives the Court as acting on higher, constitutional authority in the capacity of a legal institution rather than on ideological grounds as a political institution, divergent decisions are perceived as more acceptable. Indeed, this is a relationship recognized by the Court. In an interview, one Supreme Court Justice commented to me, "It is important that the Court have institutional prestige in order to make decisions that the public may not like but will accept as legitimate."[5] The central argument I advance in this book is that the most effective limit on judicial independence is the need for institutional support from those who really wield power in a democracy – the people. Courts (and the U.S. Supreme Court in particular) generally benefit from a high level of diffuse public support. As a consequence, elite will is not necessarily enough to check the courts; rather the separation of powers requires a degree of public will to "rein in" the judiciary.[6]

---

[5] This book will make substantial use of evidence gleaned from interviews I conducted with Supreme Court justices, members of Congress, former law clerks, and legislative staffers. Additional details are provided in Chapter 3, and a full description of the interview methodology is provided in the appendix to this book.

[6] The reason public support for a check on the court is necessary is that public support for the court is a determinant of the court's *institutional legitimacy*. Legitimacy is a source of power for the Court – perhaps the most important source of power – because it is a resource on which it can draw to make decisions with which the public and political actors will disagree. In particular, I invoke the term to refer to what scholars have called "diffuse support." To be sure, political scientists and legal academics have studied a variety of forms of judicial legitimacy and have attributed to it a variety of meanings. I recognize this impressive and consequential area of research but confine the analysis here to a single, limited conception. Judicial legitimacy will refer throughout to diffuse support, which acts as a reservoir of good will that can induce elites to comply with decisions with which they may disagree. I will provide a fuller discussion on this point in Chapter 3.

In the remainder of this chapter, I first sketch the terms of the scholarly debate as it now stands. I then discuss the importance of diffuse public support for the judiciary and describe how concerns for such support affect interactions between courts and the other branches. In particular, I suggest that legislative attacks on the Court – what I define below as Court-curbing – are an important feature of this interaction. Finally, I conclude by providing an overview of the research that I present in subsequent chapters and preview the conclusions that I draw from that research.

1.1 POLITICS AND JUDICIAL INDEPENDENCE

In the study of the separation of powers and the judiciary, the central question of interest is one of judicial independence. How much influence do extrajudicial actors have on judicial decision making? Judicial independence has been considered in a variety of contexts and from a variety of methodological and theoretical perspectives. Indeed, the attention that the subject has received has in many ways led to considerable confusion about what we mean when we speak of judicial independence – so much so that a group of scholars recently attempted to clarify both how to study judicial independence and exactly what judicial independence is (Burbank and Friedman 2002).

In this book, I adopt the definition most commonly used by political scientists – *judicial independence* refers to a court's ability to make decisions that are unaffected by political pressure from outside of the judiciary. Judicial independence is in this sense strongly related to judicial power. To study judicial independence, I focus on structural features of the judicial system and the separation of powers. Historically, we have seen that structural features of a judicial system – such as life tenure, salary protection, and so forth – can be broken down. When this is the case, formal structural protections may be reduced to mere "parchment barriers" against political encroachments on the judiciary. The focus of the present study is to examine how breakdowns in judicial independence (or the possibility of a breakdown) influence the choices judges make.

Throughout this book, I also refer to the separation of powers; this term is one that also has been muddied throughout the course of academic debate and development. Here, I adopt a specific definition. The *separation of powers* refers to the checks and balances that enable governing institutions to impose on each other's decision-making autonomy. An exercise of the separation-of-powers, for example, is an instance in which political power is used to stop the Supreme Court from making a particular choice. A successful exercise of the separation of powers means that judicial independence, as I have defined it here, has broken down. Historically, breakdowns in judicial independence have occurred in most systems at one point or another. Substantial scholarly work has shown that formal protections of the judiciary break down in places like Argentina, Russia, and Hungary. This research also suggests in places like Japan, England, Germany, Mexico, and the European Union more informal norms and protections can easily break down.[7] For when the judiciary is out of line with a unified set of elected branches of government, the judiciary may very well find itself in a perilous position and risk significant consequences if it uses its power to thwart the elected majority's will (Ferejohn 1999).

Judicial independence, though, need not be a necessarily shaky protection for the courts. Cultural norms may create incentives for political officials to tolerate a divergent independent judiciary (Weingast 1997), and there may be other reasons why elected officials would refrain from using their power to sanction a recalcitrant judiciary. For example, an independent judiciary may be politically desirable because it can help entrench current policies and insulate them from future majorities (Landes and Posner 1975). On the other hand, precisely the opposite reason may support the political preservation of an independent judiciary – the courts may be useful because they can allow the current majority to overcome past political bargains with which the current majority disagrees (Whittington 2003, 2005). Or, perhaps an independent court may be useful for overcoming "bad" political bargains because the courts' power to review policies after implementation, combined with their legal expertise, creates a system in which judicial review of legislation helps resolve policy uncertainty (Rogers 2001). At the same time, scholars have explicitly referenced public support for the courts as a source of judicial independence (Caldeira and Gibson 1992; Gibson, Caldeira, and Baird 1998; Vanberg 2005; Staton 2010).

For whatever reason, one thing is clear: in order to preserve judicial independence, there must be incentives for those with the power to destroy the courts to maintain judicial power. This is a feature of politics that is pervasive; institutions that serve the interests of politicians are more likely

---

[7] See Helmke (2002); Iaryczower, Spiller, and Tommasi (2002); Hausmaninger (1995); Scheppele (1999); Ramseyer (1994); Ramseyer and Rasmusen (2001); Salzberger and Fenn (1999); Vanberg (2005); Staton (2010); Carrubba (2005).

to be sustained by those politicians than are institutions that frustrate their interests (Weingast 1997). In this book, I am concerned with the conditions under which the incentives for political actors to maintain judicial independence are insufficient. Under what conditions is judicial independence overcome by the separation of powers?

The intent of the current project is to examine the conditions under which one should expect to see protections of judicial independence break down. I show that waning public support for the Court manifests itself in the form of institutional signals from the elected branches of government – specifically, Congress – to the Court about the Court's standing with the public. Because the Court relies on public support in order to be an efficacious policy maker, upon observing signals of waning public support, the Court is more likely to lose judicial independence and make a decision constrained by the preferences of the elected majority.

1.1.1 Between Legal Rules and Telephone Justice

Independence and a lack of independence are not the only two possible institutional designs. Rather, judicial independence exists on a continuum. At one end, the judiciary is completely subservient to political pressure. At the other, the judiciary reigns unchecked, acting as an "imperial" court. The question is, how much political pressure is brought to bear on the judiciary, and how does the judiciary respond to that pressure? There are several ways in which political pressure can be brought to bear on the judiciary. Perhaps the most flagrant – and, to American sensibilities, disturbing – form of political control of the courts occurs by direct efforts to influence a judge, what is commonly referred to as "telephone justice." Telephone justice describes a system in which an elected official may call a judge on the telephone and direct that judge to decide a particular case in a particular way. At the other end of the spectrum fall "legal rules" or guidelines. For example, the United States Constitution sets requirements for cases that the Supreme Court may hear and gives Congress power to prescribe jurisdictional boundaries for the Court.

This book is concerned with a type of exercise of the separation of powers that falls in between legal rules and telephone justice. Specifically, I focus on institutional interactions between a legislative body and a judiciary. There exists a grey area in between blatant political pressure, such as telephone justice, and explicit legal rules, such as jurisdictional and mootness requirements. In this grey area, the Court may have the power to make a certain decision but may be constrained by long-term (or even short-term) considerations about the consequences that will follow from its decision. The question raised by this grey area is: what are the incentives created by the American institutional design and under what conditions can the Court be induced to exercise self-restraint?[8]

Students of Supreme Court–Congress interactions have suspected that ideological divergence between the Court and Congress, in and of itself, should be sufficient to induce the Court to exercise self-restraint. Although the judges of the federal judiciary may be independent in the sense that they have tenure during good behavior and protection of their salaries (among other things), the judiciary as an institution is very weak and depends heavily upon support from the elected branches of government in order to use its power (Ferejohn 1999). Therefore, when the Court and Congress disagree about policy, the court should have an incentive to "hold back" and make decisions that, while not ideal from the Court's ideological stance, will nevertheless be enforced by the relevant political actors (Marks 1989; Ferejohn and Shipan 1990). This is a theme that permeates both normative and positive studies of the judiciary and explicitly underlies much of constitutional theory scholarship. When the elected majorities are aligned against the courts and the courts exercise their power to thwart the majority's will, then the courts risk considerable consequences. The problem that motivates constitutional theorists is one of how to balance a normatively desirable judicial function of protecting minorities and enforcing their rights against equally desirable American notions of majoritarianism and democracy. This very problem has been the defining question of constitutional theory for the past century (Bickel 1962), and I will return to this theme in Chapter 7. For now, though, I note that the extent to which public support for the Court may influence judicial decision making has direct implications for normative debates about the constitutional theory of judicial power.

Particularly when empirically investigating these debates, scholars have largely distinguished between statutory decision making and constitutional decision making. Because statutory decisions can be reversed through ordinary legislation, whereas constitutional decisions require a constitutional amendment to be overridden, it is often assumed that the Court should be more responsive to congressional preferences in the context of statutory decision making. Indeed, because of the difficulty of

---

[8] Because I am concerned with judicial independence in the American context, I focus on the case in which Congress takes an action to intimidate the Supreme Court.

reversing constitutional decisions by the Court, it is on constitutional decision making that the normative literature has primarily focused. For, it is the Court's power to making "binding" constitutional law while not being held electorally accountable that troubles constitutional theorists; this is the very definition of the "countermajoritarian difficulty." By contrast, empirical scholars have focused on statutory decision making, because it is in this area of decision making, if at all, we should expect to find judicial deference to the policy preferences of the elected branches. The theoretical argument I advance, however, applies equally well to both constitutional and statutory decision making, and will have direct implications for both normative debates about the countermajoritarian difficulty and empirical scholarship on judicial independence.

1.1.2 The Separation-of-Powers Model

In political science scholarship, the paradigmatic approach to studying whether ideological divergence between the Court and the elected branches induces the Court to exercise self-restraint is known as the separation-of-powers model. Various versions of the separation-of-powers model – ranging from "soft" rational choice (Murphy 1964; Epstein and Knight 1998) to rigorous positive political theory (Ferejohn and Shipan 1990; Spiller and Gely 1992; Clinton 1994; Knight and Epstein 1996; Stephenson 2004; Carrubba 2005; Rogers 2001; Vanberg 2005) – have been proposed. Generally, though, these theories all posit a comparable set of assumptions and incentives about judicial–legislative relations. They contend that the justices of the Supreme Court may not always act independent of the elected branches – rather, the institutional arrangements of the separation of powers create an incentive for sophisticated decision making.[9] Whether acting to manipulate the opinion of the Court (Murphy 1964; Epstein and Knight 1998; Maltzman, Spriggs, and Wahlbeck 2000) or to avoid cases that may have adverse political consequences (Perry 1991; Murphy 1964; Boucher and Segal 1995), sophisticated behavior is simply a product of the institutional setting in which the justices operate.

---

[9] Sophisticated decision making refers to a strategic choice by an individual to choose something other than her most preferred option, because the ultimate consequence of choosing the most preferred option would lead to a suboptimal ultimate outcome. This is contrasted with sincere decision making in which an actor always chooses – strategically or not – her most preferred option.

In the foundational study of strategic behavior on the Supreme Court, Murphy (1964) demonstrates that under certain circumstances, the justices sometimes have to take account of the external political environment in which their decisions will be received.[10] In this respect, the justices have two considerations: securing that their decisions will be enforced and reducing the effects of hostile political reactions (Murphy 1964, 123).

> The obvious strategy open to a Justice in confronting a statute which threatens his policy objectives is the simple and direct one of attempting to sweep it into constitutional oblivion by declaring it invalid.... In some instances a Justice might be certain that such a direct course was necessary and prudent; in other circumstances he would have grave doubts about the appropriateness or effectiveness of its use.... [One reason he may have doubts is that] there is always the danger of constitutional decisions generating a counterattack, either against the particular policy which was defended from congressional opposition or against the Court itself. (Murphy 1964, 156–7)

Importantly, in each version of the separation-of-powers model, the justices actually fear political reprisal. The threat of meaningful congressional response to judicial decisions is sufficient to create incentives for the justices to engage in sophisticated decision making.

Separation-of-powers theories have generally made extensive use of spatial models of voting. Specifically, constrained court theories claim that the ideological preferences of Congress will limit the range of decisions available to the justices. In the first such model of judicial decision making, Marks (1989) proposed that a single-dimensional spatial model of institutional interactions can demonstrate that the ideological preferences of key institutional actors can either cause the Supreme Court to strategically alter the position at which it sets policy or give the Court complete freedom to set its own ideal policy. The intuition behind these models is given in Figure 1.1. This figure shows a single policy dimension, running from left to right. Each of the House of Representatives, the Senate, and the Supreme Court have ideal points in this policy dimension – their favorite policies. Because, at least in statutory cases, Congress can reverse a Supreme Court decision if both chambers can agree on a new law, the Court may sometimes have an incentive to deviate from its own

---

[10] Murphy's book is primarily concerned with strategic interactions among justices, rather than between the Court and an elected institution. However, the interaction between the Court and the external political world is an important component of judicial decision making and intra-Court negotiation, as Murphy makes clear. Indeed, in an earlier book, Murphy (1962) explicitly addresses the interaction between the Court and Congress.

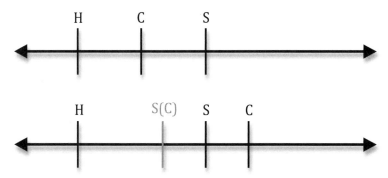

FIGURE 1.1. *Standard representation of the Court–Congress separation-of-powers model.* H, S, and C show ideal points for the House, Senate, and Court, respectively.

preferred policy. Consider the first example in Figure 1.1; in this case, the Supreme Court's ideal policy falls in between the House's and the Senate's. If the Court were to decide a case and set policy at its own ideal point, Congress would be unable to reverse that decision. Notice that if Congress were to try to move that decision closer toward the House's ideal policy, the Senate would not agree; if Congress were to try to move that decision closer to the Senate's ideal policy, the House would not agree. The veto that each chamber has over policy creates a "gridlock interval" (Krehbiel 1998) that insulates the Court's ideal policy from congressional reversal.[11]

By contrast, consider the second example in Figure 1.1. Here, the Court's ideal point is to the right of *both* the House's and Senate's. If the Court were to set its own ideal point, both the House and the Senate would agree to move the Court's decision. In particular, the Senate would agree to any policy that falls to the left of the Court's ideal point *and* to the right of the point S(C), shown in grey. The point S(C) is just as far away from the Senate's ideal point as is the Court's ideal point; thus, any policy in between S(C) and C is better for the Senate than C.[12] As a consequence, if the Court sets policy at its own ideal point, the House

---

[11] Of course, the president also has a veto, which may or may not be relevant in any given case. Inclusion of the president in this model does not significantly change the example I describe here but merely adds an additional condition that must be satisfied in order to achieve congressional reversal. Namely, the president must agree with the policy change.

[12] This result derives from the standard assumption that each player's utility from a policy is simply a function of the absolute distance between her ideal point and the relevant policy.

could propose legislation at the point S(C), which is much better for the House, and the Senate would not object. (Alternatively, the House could propose legislation just to the right of S(C), if it were concerned the Senate would side with the Court in the event it were indifferent between the House's proposal and the Court's ideal point.) A forward-looking Court then would have the incentive to set policy in the first instance not at its own ideal point but rather right at the Senate's ideal point. This decision would ensure that the Court's policy could not be reversed; it also is the best possible policy from among those that Congress cannot change.[13] This sophisticated decision to deviate from its own ideal point is motivated by the Court's foresight that there is a range of policies that will be agreeable to the Senate and the House; the Court has a first-mover advantage, though, and can select its own preferred policy from among those that cannot be reversed. If it were to disregard this incentive and simply select its own ideal policy, then Congress would surely reverse that decision, and the Court may wind up with a new policy that is worse (from its perspective) than what it could have selected in the first instance. It is this type of sophisticated decision making that the traditional separation-of-powers model predicts.

Separation-of-powers models, however theoretically sophisticated, have not found much empirical support. In fact, the bulk of the empirical evidence suggests that the Supreme Court is not at all influenced by congressional ideology. Most prominently, Segal and Spaeth (2002, ch. 8) advance the "attitudinal model" of judicial decision making, which posits that a justice's own ideology is the primary determinant of judicial decisions and that considerations about policy reversals or other backlash from Congress do not affect the justices. Advocates of the attitudinal model generally cite five features of the federal judiciary to justify their claim that the Court can operate free from political considerations. First, Supreme Court justices *control their own docket*. "While not a guarantee that the justices will vote their policy preferences, it is a requisite for their doing so" (Segal and Spaeth 2002, 93). Thus, the Supreme Court's discretionary docket enables it to select the cases that allow it to vote its preferences.[14] Second, the Supreme Court is immune to *electoral*

---

[13] The set of policies that Congress cannot change is called the Pareto optima. Any policy from H through S is a Pareto optimum. The Court's strategic goal in this example is to select the best policy – from its own perspective – from among the Pareto optima.

[14] Of course, this gives rise to the possibility that case selection may itself be a strategic process. Indeed, some evidence is suggestive of strategic case selection by the Supreme Court (Perry 1991; Cameron, Segal, and Songer 2000).

accountability, and there is no evidence of an electoral influence on life-tenured judges. Third, judges are immune from *political accountability*. Segal and Spaeth (2002, 94) note that only once has Congress impeached a Supreme Court justice, and removal was unsuccessful. Other, more subtle efforts to politically influence the justices have been rare. Fourth, Supreme Court justices lack further *ambition*. Justices of the modern Court are generally assumed to hold no aspiration for higher office. Although this was not true during the very early years of the Court's existence, it is certainly accurate today. Fifth, because the Supreme Court is *the court of last resort*, the justices do not have to worry about being reversed by a higher judicial authority. While judges of the lower federal courts (and even state supreme courts) must worry about review by the Supreme Court, the High Court itself cannot be reversed, which enables it to behave as its own principal.[15]

At bottom, the attitudinal model is one in which the justices, as in the separation-of-powers model, are in fact assumed to be forward-looking. However, as opposed to the separation-of-powers model, the attitudinal model is one of forward-looking justices who see no credible threats and therefore have no incentive to engage in behavior that incorporates congressional policy preferences (Segal and Spaeth 2002, 92–7). This interpretation of the attitudinal model is different from an interpretation in which the justices are simply not forward-looking. Unfortunately, in the scholarly debate, the subtle distinction between justices who are forward-looking but do not perceive any credible threat of retaliation and justices who are not forward-looking has been blurred. In part due to improper use of terminology and in part due to a lack of theoretical clarity about the assumptions and predictions of the attitudinal model, this distinction has not been made sufficiently prominent in the study of Court–Congress relations. In this book, I adopt what I believe is the best and clearest interpretation of the attitudinal model – one in which the justices are in fact forward-looking but do not perceive a sufficiently large credible threat of congressional response to create any incentive for sophisticated decision making.

[15] Other explanations for the inability of the separation-of-powers model to explain judicial behavior very well include the claim that Congress pays very little attention to the Court, though there is evidence that Congress does pay attention to judicial decisions on issues of salience or importance to the legislature (Pickerill 2004; Hausseger and Baum 1999; Meernik and Ignagni 1997; Ignagni and Meernik 1994; Sala and Spriggs 2004). That is, because the vast majority of cases decided by the Supreme Court are not salient, the Court is able to act on its own policy preferences without concern for potential congressional overrides.

1.1.3 Breakdowns in Judicial Independence

Even though the separation-of-powers model fails to find broad systematic evidence – and the weight of support for the attitudinal model seems
to be insurmountable – examples of breakdowns in judicial independence abound. One can point to numerous historical instances where the
Court's behavior can best – or perhaps only – be understood as evidence
of the Court's inferior institutional position. In substantively important
decisions – sometimes in dramatic fashion – the Court has occasionally
backed down from its preferred course of action to, apparently, appease
political and public sentiment. In cases involving economic regulation
during the New Deal (Leuchtenberg 1995, 1969), national security during the Cold War (Pritchett 1961; Murphy 1962), and school busing
and prayer during the Republican Revolution (Keynes and Miller 1989),
the Supreme Court has apparently capitulated to political and popular
pressure. Proponents of the separation-of-powers model have pointed to
such examples as evidence that the Court can be constrained by political
pressure (Gely and Spiller 1990, 1992; Eskridge 1991*b*; Clinton 1994;
Knight and Epstein 1996).

What is missing from these accounts, though, is an empirically mea-
surable condition that can systematically explain when the Court should
and should not be responsive to separation-of-powers constraints. Some
scholars have proposed that case salience (Hettinger and Zorn 2005) or
specific features of the law (Ferejohn and Weingast 1992) may be useful
ways to predict when the Court should be more or less constrained by
the political checks and balances. I propose, by contrast, a revision of
the assumptions that underlie the separation-of-powers model. As I have
described it, this line of research assumes that the Court is concerned
primarily – frequently only – with policy outcomes. However, I argue
that in addition to policy outcomes in individual cases, the Court is also
concerned with the institutional integrity of the Court. This is, to be sure,
not a novel claim. Other scholars have noted that the Court does act
to protect the institution and that public support for, and the prestige
of, courts can be an integral factor in separation-of-powers interactions
(Vanberg 2005; Stephenson 2004; Staton 2010).

In this vein, Murphy (1962, 62) notes that historically, the "Justices [of
the Supreme Court have been] acutely aware of the attacks against their
decisions, and they [have been] willing to make concessions when they
[feel] that danger [has] become too threatening." Exploring the opposite
side of this phenomenon, William Lasser (1988) observes that potentially

controversial Supreme Court decisions have usually been handed down during times when the political majority is sufficiently fractured as to preclude a major political backlash. In reviewing three major Supreme Court crises, Lasser (1988, 262) claims it is instructive that

> The Supreme Court lived through each of its crises not by luck, nor by statesmanship, nor by coincidence. It survived because no one was really trying to kill it. It survived because, when it suffered its "self-inflicted wounds," its opponents had neither the incentive nor the desire to take advantage of its apparently weakened condition, even when they had the power to do so. Scholars have marveled at the Court's ability to survive the fiercest of battles. What they have failed to recognize is that the Court's enemies, for the most part, were shooting blanks.

1.1.4 Judicial Legitimacy and the Separation of Powers

How is the Court able to know when its enemies are "shooting blanks"? How does the Court know when it needs to avoid "self-inflicted wounds"? In analyzing the interaction among the public, Congress, and the Court, this book seeks to demonstrate a systematic way for identifying when the Court should be sensitive to political and popular constraints on judicial power and when we should see judicial independence break down. I present a systematic way for identifying those instances when we will observe the instances of judicial self-restraint that seem to occur and argue that the Court will be more sensitive to its limitations when it is concerned about its institutional legitimacy. As discussed above, institutional legitimacy is an important resource for the Court. A growing body of research has posited that the concern for institutional legitimacy may motivate constrained behavior by courts. That is, fears about losing institutional legitimacy may attenuate the Court's ability to decide cases in isolation of external political pressure (Vanberg 2005; Stephenson 2004; Staton 2010). I explicitly adopt that proposition here. The contribution of my study to this literature will be to investigate both how the Court learns about its institutional legitimacy and how the elected branches in conflict with the courts may use their connection to the public to manipulate the courts' beliefs about their public support.

To be sure, scholars have spent considerable energy investigating judicial legitimacy. In the context of the American Supreme Court, research has mostly focused on the sources of judicial legitimacy. As we will see in greater detail in Chapter 3, this research has led to significant theoretical and empirical developments. Most important for my purposes here, the literature demonstrates that the Court is concerned about preserving its legitimacy, which involves being sensitive to how the Court is perceived by the public and members of the bar (Baum 2007; Klein and Morrisroe 1999; Epstein and Knight 1998; Staton 2006). Perhaps as a means to this end, we often see that the Court has an incentive to protect its institutional legitimacy by avoiding institutional confrontations and acts on that incentive (Caldeira 1987; Lasser 1988; Hausseger and Baum 1999; Stephenson 2004; Vanberg 2005; Staton and Vanberg 2008; Carrubba 2009; Marshall 2004, 1989*b*; Friedman 2009). That concern for institutional legitimacy, and specifically for reliance on public support to compel compliance with its decisions, can affect judicial decision making is a lesson from this research upon which this book tests. Friedman (2009, 14) summarizes the point nicely:

> In a sense, today's critics of judicial supremacy are right: the Supreme Court does exercise more power than it once did. In another sense, though, they could not be more wrong. The Court has this power only because, over time, the American people have decided to cede it to the justices ... The tools of popular control have not dissipated; they simply have not been needed.

In the comparative context, this strand of research has been particularly fruitful. Students of judicial institutions abroad have uncovered important examples of judicial behavior apparently motivated by a concern for institutional legitimacy. Some scholarship explicitly incorporates legitimacy into separation-of-powers interactions in the comparative context. Formal models of the separation of powers in other constitutional systems and the European Union incorporate institutional legitimacy into the theory of judicial efficacy (Carrubba 2009; Vanberg 2005; Gibson and Caldeira 1995). I rely directly on the insights of that research for the claim that the perception of judicial legitimacy is a necessary important condition for judicial efficacy. There is also evidence that judges will make an effort to actively shore up their institutional legitimacy by working *with* public opinion (Murphy and Tanenhaus 1990; Staton 2006). I build on these developments by explicitly incorporating institutional legitimacy into the separation-of-powers model. In particular, I demonstrate how the Supreme Court's concern for its legitimacy develops and the conditions under which the Court will be motivated to act to protect that legitimacy. I argue that when the Court is subjected to political criticism and is attacked by legislators, it will become concerned about the state – and future – of its legitimacy.

1.2 DIFFUSE SUPPORT AND JUDICIAL LEGITIMACY

The type of legitimacy about which the Court is concerned is what is known as *diffuse support*.[16] As opposed to specific support, which refers to public approval of decisions in individual cases, diffuse support refers to broad support for the Court as an institution. Judicial legitimacy, or diffuse support, is generally considered to represent a court's normative authority to make a binding decision. Competing models of diffuse support have been offered in the extant literature. According to one view, diffuse support for the Court is a belief "inculcated early in the life-cycle, perhaps even in adolescence, and change[s] little over time" (Gibson and Caldeira 2009, 4). According to another view, legitimacy is a quality that institutions earn. Importantly, just as it can be earned, legitimacy can be lost (Grosskopf and Mondak 1998). In a recent theoretical analysis, Carrubba (2009) demonstrates that by exercising proper restraint and serving the interest of those subject to their jurisdiction, courts can earn a level of legitimacy that endows them with robust institutional capacity. Although few would argue that any individual decision may itself undermine support for the Court, sustained judicial overstepping may lead to an erosion of the Court's legitimacy.

Diffuse support provides a resource on which the Court can draw in order to gain compliance with decisions for which the public may not have *specific* support. At least since Alexander Hamilton wrote in *The Federalist #78* that the judiciary "must ultimately depend upon the aid of the executive arm even for the efficacy of its judgements," students of the courts have recognized that the judiciary is a weak institution relative to the elected branches. That is, the judiciary is given no positive powers and therefore depends heavily upon political will to give effect to its decisions. The Court is therefore faced with an implementation problem, and diffuse support is a necessary resource for overcoming that institutional weakness (Caldeira 1986; Murphy and Tanenhaus 1990; Weingast 1997; Stephenson 2004; Vanberg 2005; Carrubba 2009; Staton 2010). Public support for the Constitution and the courts as an institution provides the necessary political will to give effect to potentially unpopular decisions. Indeed, this is a relationship that is recognized by the Court. In an interview, one Supreme Court justice commented, "Once the public ceases to believe that the Court is not a political institution, they will no

---

[16] I use the terms diffuse support, institutional (judicial) legitimacy, institutional support, and institutional loyalty interchangeably throughout this book.

longer support the Court."[17] Another justice observed that the Court's being "perceived as acting legitimately . . . [is] predicated on whether the public understands that we are a court and act a legitimate way."[18]

What is more, research documents evidence of such a relationship between public support for the Court and the Court's institutional efficacy. Using the rubric of rational anticipation, McGuire and Stimson (2004, 1019) suggest "a Court that strays too far from the broad boundaries imposed by public mood risks having its decisions rejected." That is, when the Court makes too many decisions that do not have *specific* support, the Court risks losing its *diffuse* support and, consequently, its institutional efficacy. The Court is therefore constantly working to maintain a balance of diffuse support that can be used to support decisions that lack specific support. Mondak and Smithey (1997, 114) summarize the point nicely: "A disgruntled public may not only refuse to cooperate with a Supreme Court decision but may also pressure elected officials to resist implementation of judicial orders."

I argue in Chapter 3 that when Congress engages in political attacks on the Court, the Court will interpret those attacks as signals about waning public support for, and confidence in, the Court. To be sure, there is good reason for the Court to interpret political attacks on the judiciary as an indicator of waning judicial legitimacy. Research has shown that when public support for the Court declines, the public will increasingly support efforts to politically sanction the Court and restrict judicial power (Caldeira and Gibson 1995; Gibson and Caldeira 1995, 1998, 2003; Gibson, Caldeira, and Baird 1998). For example, Caldeira and Gibson (1992, 638) claim that individuals who have no diffuse support, or institutional loyalty, for the Court will be willing to "accept, make, or countenance major changes in the fundamental attributes of how the high bench functions or fits into the U.S. constitutional system." It is on congressional threats to make such changes that the research in this book focuses.

1.2.1   Court-Curbing and Judicial Independence

Congress may engage in political attacks on the Court in a variety of ways. Members of Congress may make floor speeches criticizing the Court during debates, they may talk with the press or their constituents, or they

---

[17] Personal interview with "Justice C."
[18] Personal interview with "Justice A."

may introduce legislation threatening to affect the Court's power and hold hearings on that legislation. I focus explicitly on the introduction of legislation that threatens to restrict, remove, or otherwise limit the Court's power, which I call *Court-curbing* legislation.

In Chapter 3, I present a detailed argument for why a focus on Court-curbing, as opposed to other types of political attacks on the Court, is appropriate. Briefly, though, I focus on Court-curbing legislation for several reasons. First, Court-curbing legislation is a very visible form of political attack. As I demonstrate in subsequent chapters, the justices do pay very close attention to Court-curbing proposals in Congress. Second, because I assume that the Court is concerned about its relationship to the public, the best signal for the Court to pay attention to is one that is plausibly tied to public opinion. Introducing legislation – and especially Court-curbing legislation – is a primary way in which legislators can position-take and credit claim in front of their constituents (Mayhew 1974). That is, introducing legislation, such as Court-curbing legislation, can be electorally beneficial to legislators. They can point to the bills they sponsored to credibly signal to their constituents that they have made an effort to "rein in" the Court. Third, the Constitution gives Congress very specific, and powerful, tools for affecting the Court. These tools include setting the Court's jurisdiction, altering the size and term of the Court, or even impeaching members of the Court. Critical speeches and other activities may be significant political attacks on the Court, but the introduction of Court-curbing legislation also carries the potential of actually affecting the Court's institutional power (which in turn bolsters the bills' credit-claiming function).

To be sure, Court-curbing is not a new phenomenon; since the earliest days of the American Constitution, there has been a tension between the elected branches and the judiciary; that tension frequently produced heated conflicts between the branches. From changes to the federal judiciary's jurisdiction to alterations in the size of the Supreme Court to impeachment of Supreme Court justices to procedural constraints on the Court to proposed constitutional amendments, Congress has responded, at times with vigor, to perceptions of misguided judicial encroachments on political will.

Political scientists, for their part, have made considerable effort to understand Court-curbing, its causes, and its consequences. However, most studies of Court-curbing have focused on explaining when

Court-curbing is most likely to be enacted and documenting the historical trends in legislative efforts to curb the judiciary's power (Nagel 1965; Rosenberg 1992; Keynes and Miller 1989; Murphy 1962; Pritchett 1961). These studies place an emphasis on the threat of enactment and the consideration of Court-curbing as a legislative endeavor. In particular, the focus has been on whether Court-curbing can either reverse a judicial policy or induce the Court to reverse itself. Although policy-specific reversals are surely an important element of Court-curbing, I focus in this study on the position-taking element of Court-curbing rather than on the legislative enactment element. As opposed to most previous work on Court-curbing, I do not focus on the probability of enactment, but instead on the electoral function served by Court-curbing in Congress and the *meaning* that the justices ascribe to the legislative proposals.[19] That is, Court-curbing is important not so much because it attempts to restrict the Court's power but instead primarily because it signifies a loss of public support and *threatens* to do so in a way that is publicly visible and politically attractive. More specifically, I argue in Chapter 3 that the justices interpret Court-curbing threats as signals about the nature of its public support. Of course, I do not rule out the possibility that the potential of Court-curbing enactment may be a significant concern for the Court. My argument is simply that, short of its potential to be enacted, Court-curbing can serve as an important signal to the justices about the currents of public opinion and support for the Court.

Of course, Court-curbing may be even more general than this claim suggests. In particular, it may be the case that Court-curbing, as I define and use it throughout this book, may simply be a proxy for a number of elements in the political environment. Other forms of information come to the Court about its public support, types of information that are less easily quantifiable. In other words, measures of legislation proposed in Congress may be simply capturing other political developments that are harder to systematically measure, such as the tone or content of political debates and discussions involving the Court. The key to the theoretical argument I advance is that the Court is concerned about its institutional legitimacy and learns about its public support by observing developments in the political environment. The justices may learn about changes in the

---

[19] It is important to emphasize that my argument should not be construed to imply that Court-curbing is not at all about securing policy reversals from the Court. Rather, I simply intend to highlight the fact that Court-curbing is often introduced by members of Congress who are under pressure from their constituents and hope to garner an electoral benefit from "position-taking" on the Court.

Court's institutional legitimacy in many ways. Simply being part of the Washington political elite surely clues them in to what their status is as an institution. The justices also read papers and are exposed to the same current of media as are most people. Moreover, because of the nature of the Supreme Court's term, which does not last all year long, the justices have the opportunity to return to their homes for regular, extended periods of time. Finally, many of the justices have professional networks, such as former colleagues, who may provide feedback to the justice's about the professional bar's estimation of the Court.

I do not make the assertion that Court-curbing is the *only* mechanism by which the Court learns about its institutional legitimacy. I simply make the assertion that Court-curbing serves as one medium through which the Court learns about its relationship with the public. The reason I focus on this particular medium here is that this research is concerned with Court–Congress relations. I make the point in this book that an important, and previously overlooked, component of the relationship between the Court and Congress is Congress' ability to use its electoral connection to signal information to the Court about its legitimacy and public support for the institution. This component of the Court–Congress relationship, I argue, is an integral part of the system of separation of powers. In Chapter 7, I will return to this point and discuss both the positive and normative implications of this relationship.

1.2.2 The Politics–Legitimacy Paradox

To preview, the argument I advance here reveals an intriguing paradox in American government, which I call the *politics-legitimacy paradox*. I argue here that a first principle for the Supreme Court is the maintenance of judicial legitimacy, which in part consists of the maintenance of the image of the courts as apolitical, legal institutions. The courts' legitimacy as unelected, unaccountable actors with a constitutional veto hinges on the perception that their decisions are made in light of neutral legal arguments. Judgments about public policy based on ideology or politics from the courts might reasonably be considered illegitimate from a democratic theory perspective, because democracy requires that policy decisions be made by accountable representatives. The loss of public support – judicial legitimacy – undermines courts' capacity to enforce constitutional limits on government, among other things.

In order to protect this legitimacy, we will see, the courts – the Supreme Court in particular – often have an incentive to engage in a deeply political calculation. Because the Supreme Court wants to preserve public support for the institution, it will be unwilling to stray too far from the broad contours of what will be accepted by the American public. The irony is that in order to protect its image as a neutral, independent decision-making body, the Court must in fact pay close attention to what will be deemed acceptable by the populace and sometimes yield from any neutral perspective to avoid overstepping the bounds imposed by perceptions of what is legitimate. Therein lies the limits of judicial independence and the politics–legitimacy paradox. In order to guard its image as an apolitical decision-maker, and with it its institutional legitimacy, the Court must engage in deeply political behavior.

The politics–legitimacy paradox underscores a question of democratic theory: how much independence should be afforded to courts? Constitutional theorists must wrestle with competing goals that require finding an appropriate balance of power. For example, constitutional designers may want to ensure minority rights while maintaining a strong national government. The politics–legitimacy paradox demonstrates that courts may be an important component of the solution to that problem, but precisely what function they can serve depends on the extent of judicial independence and the source of judicial power. Although this book does not focus directly on normative questions about constitutional theory, it does have implications for positive questions of constitutional design. We will return to those normative questions in Chapter 7.

1.3   A ROADMAP TO THE BOOK

In the remainder of this book, I develop and evaluate this argument in detail. In Chapter 2, I present a political history of Court-curbing. In doing so, I introduce an original dataset of Court-curbing since Reconstruction. In presenting the data, I will describe the contours and trends in Court-curbing activity. The analysis reveals that there have been seven major periods of Court-curbing since Reconstruction and that these periods have been marked by both conservative and liberal hostility toward the Supreme Court. These data will provide the foundations for later empirical analyses in the book.

In Chapter 3, we then move to a more systematical investigation of Court-curbing and judicial independence. I develop a model of conditional self-restraint in which the Court has an interest in protecting its institutional legitimacy. The theoretical argument builds directly from recent developments in the comparative study of judicial independence.

A key insight made by Vanberg (2005) is that when a court is likely to have public support, it can act against those with political power; when the Court is unlikely to have public support, it will defer to the elected branches of government. Chapter 3 develops a model concerned with the conditions under which legislative action can serve as an informative signal to the Court about that very public support. Court-curbing, in the model, is a position-taking endeavor for legislators hoping to gain an electoral benefit. The chapter begins by outlining a set of assumptions about judicial and legislative preferences. These assumptions deviate in several important ways from previous separation-of-powers models and are supported with evidence from interviews with Supreme Court justices, former law clerks, members of Congress, and legislative staffers, as well as evidence from scholarly literature. I then formalize the theory. The formalization begins with a simple decision-theoretic problem and then presents two game-theoretic extensions to the model. From these models, I derive a set of empirically testable predictions that will motivate the rest of the book.

Chapter 4 tests the model's predictions concerning the introduction of Court-curbing. This chapter assesses whether the introduction of Court-curbing by members of Congress follows the patterns predicted by the model. The analysis reveals that, as predicted, decreases in public support for the Court motivate Court-curbing legislation, as does ideological divergence between the public and political elite and the Supreme Court.

In Chapters 5 and 6, I examine judicial responses to Court-curbing. Specifically, Chapter 5 analyzes the incidence of judicial invalidations of federal legislation. The evidence presented demonstrates that the Court responds to Court-curbing legislation by refraining from exercising its constitutional veto over federal legislation. Specifically, the evidence suggests that increases in Court-curbing signal a lack of public support for the Court, which in turn creates an incentive for the Court to exercise self-restraint. These patterns are detected in aggregate- and micro-level statistical analyses. Qualitative and archival evidence from the New Deal era is then offered to provide an illustration of the systematic patterns in the context of one notable historical episode.

Chapter 6 then presents a complementary analysis of the Court's decision making in statutory cases. Using data on the Court's cases of statutory construction since 1953, the analysis demonstrates that the ideological orientation of the Court's decisions responds to the ideological orientation of Court-curbing. This evidence is interpreted to imply that Court-curbing can affect not only constitutional decisions by the Court but may be an efficient wholesale way for Congress to respond to multiple retail-level statutory decisions by the Court.

Finally, in Chapter 7, I provide some concluding remarks as well as some anecdotal evidence from political and judicial elites about the implications of Court-curbing and the relationship between the Court and Congress. These concluding remarks help contextualize the findings reported here and suggest several policy implications regarding the checks and balances and constitutional design. Among others, one implication to which I return is the countermajoritarian difficulty. The arguments and evidence offered in this book provide insight into both theoretical and empirical efforts to reconcile judicial power with democratic theory.

2

A Political History of Court-Curbing

To best understand the nature of conflict between the legislative and judicial branches, we begin with a political history of confrontations between Congress and the Court. In this chapter, I present a historical overview of the introduction of Court-curbing legislation. As I noted in the preceding chapter, Court-curbing refers to legislative attempts to limit or remove the Supreme Court's power (Stumpf 1965). Here I provide a detailed overview of the frequency with which Congress has engaged in Court-curbing, the types of legislation that have been proposed, and the partisan and ideological forces behind Court-curbing over time. I also identify several periods during which Court-curbing was particularly forceful and briefly describe the substantive disputes at issue. With this background in hand, subsequent chapters in this book develop a theoretical framework for understanding the causes and consequences of these periods of conflict.

2.1 THE POLITICS OF COURT-CURBING

Scholarship on the relationship between Congress, public opinion, and the Supreme Court suggests a connection between major political developments, shifts in public opinion, and judicial decision making. This work has focused most directly on the ability of governing coalitions to affect appointments to and the political leanings of the Court (Dahl 1957). For example, Adamany (1973) notes that major realigning elections – elections that have left the Court and the "lawmaking majority" out of step with each other – have historically been followed by periods of particular tension between the Court and Congress. More broadly,

studies of the "macro-polity" have investigated how governing institutions respond to variation in public preferences. These studies have
documented evidence of Supreme Court responsiveness to variation in
public policy preferences (Erikson, MacKuen, and Stimson 2002, ch. 8;
Stimson, MacKuen, and Erikson 1995; Taylor 1992) as well as a relationship between public policy preferences and legislative attempts to
reverse Supreme Court decisions (Pickerill 2004; Ignagni and Meernik
1994; Meernik and Ignagni 1997; Clark and McGuire 1996; Marshall
1989*b*,*a*, 2004). However, most empirical evidence suggests that efforts
to reverse unpopular Supreme Court decisions are not generally successful
(Stumpf 1965; Henschen 1983; Marshall 1989*b*; Ross 2002; Cross and
Nelson 2001) and that unpopular opinions do not generally influence
public approval of the Court (Marshall 2004; but see Durr, Martin, and
Wolbrecht 2000). Nevertheless, members of Congress do consider legislation to reverse the Court or restrict its powers with considerable regularity
(Paschal 1992; Martin 2001; Devins 2006; Bell and Scott 2006).

   As distinguished from legislative attempts to reverse Supreme Court
decisions – the mechanism that is at play in traditional separation-of-
powers models – it is helpful to conceive of Court-curbing as electoral
posturing in response to public opinion (or efforts to galvanize public
opinion), or to create an issue constituency and politicize the judiciary.
Seen this way, congressional responses to Court decisions may be significant not because they threaten to overturn decisions but because they
signal public discontent with the Court. I refer to Court-curbing throughout this book as "position-taking," by which I mean that Court-curbing
is a symbolic activity taken in response to public opinion in a member's
constituency or to galvanize political supporters.[1] Interested constituents
often contact their representatives to voice their displeasure with the
Court (or courts in general), and a way in which members respond to
such constituency pressure is to introduce Court-curbing bills. Representatives and senators may hope to gain some electoral benefit by introducing these bills. On this point, it is instructive that 78% of the Court-
curbing bills introduced since Reconstruction have been introduced in the
House of Representatives, while only 22% have been introduced in the
Senate. Given that the House of Representatives is generally thought to

---

[1] It may be, of course, that the causal arrow runs in the other direction – that Court-
curbing is undertaken to affect public opinion about the Court. I deal with this possibility
theoretically in Chapter 3 and empirically in Chapter 4. For now, though, I note this
possibility and acknowledge that both mechanisms may be at work.

be more closely tied to public sentiment, we might expect that members of the House will more reflexively respond to changes in public support for the judiciary or moments of great public discontent.[2] Thus, to the extent Court-curbing is primarily a position-taking tool, we should indeed expect these bills to originate disproportionately in the House.

There is considerable anecdotal evidence demonstrating the position-taking benefit of Court-curbing. For example, interest groups central in Court-curbing movements often seek to publicize legislative activity and create constituent pressure for legislators. Groups such as Eagle Forum's Court Watch regularly post synopses of Court decisions and summarize legislative attempts to curb judicial behavior. Further, Court Watch encourages citizens to pray for the "activist" judges and to pressure their legislators to take affirmative steps to "rein in" the courts. For example, Court Watch's Web site defines its goals as follows:

> Court Watch is dedicated to building in America a federal judiciary respectful of, and responsible to, the U.S. Constitution. Court Watch pursues its mission through the Courting Justice Campaign, which is now entering its Phase Two. In Phase One, we focused our efforts on opposing Bill Clinton's activist/liberal judicial appointments and on beginning to raise America's awareness of the damage and danger of activist/liberal judging. Our objectives for Phase Two further the cause of federal judicial reform – the effort to create a judiciary which is truly committed to courting justice. Phase Two is outlined in our "Five for the Future Plan": (1) To promote the confirmation of constitutionalist judges; (2) To eliminate any and all judicial power to tax; (3) To reduce the size of the bloated judiciary; (4) To defederalize the bulk of America's criminal law; (5) To require, as a minimum, a unanimous vote of a three-judge federal panel to invalidate citizen-passed initiatives.[3]

Court Watch is not alone among groups that make Court-curbing and "judicial reform" a central electoral topic. Other groups at the federal level include the Traditional Values Coalition, the Family Research Council, the Moral Majority, People for the American Way, and Judicial Watch, while myriad other groups focus on limiting the power of state judges. The majority of these groups have a conservative political ideology, perhaps as a consequence of the rapid and substantial development

---

[2] The House is in fact specifically designed to foster a more direct connection between the public and the legislature than the Senate. The shorter terms and smaller constituencies are examples of this institutional design.

[3] Eagle Forum's Court Watch homepage, http://www.eagleforum.org/court_watch/index .html (accessed June 1, 2007).

of conservative legal activism during the late twentieth century.[4] But, recently, liberal groups concerned about the conservative shift in the federal courts have begun to call for legislative efforts to limit judicial power. What is more, speaking with congressional staff members reveals such groups' high salience among legislators.

Despite the political salience and potential substantive significance of Court-curbing, there is a dearth of systematic analysis of the causes and consequences of legislative attacks on the courts. This is in large part due to the unavailability of data on Court-curbing proposals for any significant period of time. However, there do exist several scholarly works examining the causes and consequences of Court-curbing. In particular, detailed case studies have been written, focusing on specific periods of Court-curbing. Numerous studies have examined the so-called Court-Packing Plan proposed by Franklin Roosevelt in order to overcome the Supreme Court's frustration of the New Deal legislative program during the mid- to late 1930s.[5] In addition, the confrontation between Congress and the Supreme Court over national security, McCarthyism, and race relations during the mid-twentieth century has been examined in at least two detailed case studies (Pritchett 1961; Murphy 1962).

Broader, systematic studies of Court-curbing, by contrast, have been limited in number and depth. However, two notable studies stand out. Independently, but using the same data, Stuart Nagel and Gerald Rosenberg have examined the volume of Court-curbing legislation introduced in Congress since the Founding.[6] Nagel, writing in 1965, identified seven distinct periods of Court-curbing; writing in 1992, Rosenberg identified nine such periods. Rosenberg's primary claim is that during six of these nine periods, the Supreme Court failed to "exhibit independence." That is, the Court changed its jurisprudence to comport with the ideological preferences of Congress. The six periods of judicial "subservience" are 1893–1897, 1922–1924, 1963–1965, 1823–1831, 1955–1959, and 1977–1982. To explain why the Court does not express independence during confrontations with Congress, Rosenberg identifies four variables

---

[4] Steven Teles (2008), for example, demonstrates the rising prominence and sophistication of the conservative legal movement during the late twentieth century. While part of that development involves the generation and nurturing of nuanced and strong legal arguments, another front in the conservative movement has been the criticism of the courts being too liberal and "activist."

[5] For example, William Leuchtenberg (1969, 1995) has authored several studies examining the development of Roosevelt's legislative proposal.

[6] Rosenberg, writing later, extended the Nagel dataset forward in time.

that affect whether or not the Court will be responsive to Court-curbing activity. In particular, he cites the election of court opponents, the number of court opponents, the intensity of opposition, and the likelihood of coalitions forming as central factors that determine whether the Court will respond to congressional hostility.[7]

The data used by Nagel and Rosenberg are, unfortunately, no longer available and must be recollected. However, this provides an excellent opportunity to replicate their data collection and correct for two particular problems in their data. The first difficulty occurs because Nagel and Rosenberg conduct an underinclusive search for Court-curbing bills. They exclude from their analyses the proposal of constitutional amendments and joint resolutions. They do so because, for their purposes – namely, measuring the risk of enactment of consequential Court-curbing legislation – constitutional amendments are sufficiently remote possibilities, while resolutions are sufficiently inconsequential. However, as I demonstrate below, the inclusion of constitutional amendments and joint resolutions dramatically changes the landscape of Court-curbing for the post-Reconstruction period. What is more, for the analyses in this book, constitutional amendments and resolutions are just as important as other measures, because they signal public opinion, just as do ordinary statutes. Simply because they have less likelihood of enactment or less legal significance does not mean that they are any less credible signals about legislators' constituents' discontent with the Court. Indeed, as a position-taking measure, one might expect a constitutional amendment is more useful to a legislator than an ordinary statute. The second difficulty occurs because Rosenberg and Nagel do not control for the ideological orientation of Court-curbing. In later sections, I demonstrate below that the ideological orientation of Court-curbing is an important feature of congressional

---

[7] Nagel (1965, 944) also identifies several variables that he claims have an "affirmative correlation" with whether or not Court-curbing is successful. The nine factors that Nagel identifies are: 1) judicial review of federal, and to a lesser extent, state statutes; 2) cases involving economic issues; 3) a low level of unanimity on the Court; 4) a liberal or Democratic Congress confronting a conservative Court; 5) a conservative or Republican Congress confronting a liberal Court; 6) a "crisis"; 7) public opinion and pressure groups in favor of the attack; 8) more bills are introduced in the House than in the Senate; and 9) a low level of congressional cohesion. Notice, incidentally, these two studies, and the analysis of Court-curbing, focus directly on the elite-level interactions behind Court-curbing. These confrontations are primarily, if not exclusively, about policy disagreements between the Court and Congress and the risk of the enactment of Court-curbing legislation. Chapter 3 examines Court-curbing not as an institutional threat but rather as a conduit through which public support for judicial institutions is communicated to the Court.

hostility. In light of these difficulties (and the fact that their data are no longer available), I have undertaken an entirely new data collection.

2.2   ANTEBELLUM COURT-CURBING

Through both constitutional amendment and ordinary statutes, Congress has considered legislation that would restrict or remove judicial power regularly throughout American history. It is important to remember that the Constitution gives Congress explicit power to regulate the jurisdiction of the federal courts and to change the size of the courts (as well as to propose constitutional amendments).[8] While the focus in this book is on Court-curbing since the end of Reconstruction in 1877, there were several notable periods of intense conflict between the Court and the elected branches during the early and mid-nineteenth century, and the focus here should not be interpreted to undermine or minimize the importance of Court-curbing during the earlier years of American history. Rather, I focus on Court-curbing post-Reconstruction because I believe it is in that context that the theoretical argument I advance is most applicable. However, it is instructive to understand the basic contours of early periods of Court-curbing to more fully appreciate the context in which modern Court-curbing takes place. The early episodes of Court–Congress conflict defined the boundaries and context within which future power struggles would take place. Indeed, the nature and meaning of Court-curbing in the modern Republic can only best be understood in light of the several, significant episodes of Court–Congress conflict during the first 100 years of American constitutional history.

2.2.1   *Marbury* and Confrontations in the Early Republic

Perhaps the most well-known instance of conflict between the judiciary and the elected branches took place very early in the Republic's history, in the context of a case known as *Marbury v. Madison*. When Thomas Jefferson was sworn into office in March 1801, he was immediately confronted with a judiciary staffed by Federalist appointees of Presidents

---

[8] Despite the clear constitutional grant of authority, there has been considerable debate and uncertainty about the extent to which Congress can use these powers ever since the Constitutional Convention. See Keynes and Miller (1989) for an analysis of the theoretical, political, and academic debate.

George Washington and John Adams. To make matters worse, an enactment by the lame-duck Congress, the Judiciary Act of 1801, attempted to insulate the federal judiciary from the influence of Jeffersonian Republicans. For example, in an attempt to deny Jefferson the opportunity to appoint a new justice in the event of a vacancy, the Act reduced the number of seats on the Supreme Court by one, effective with the next vacancy.

Perhaps more dramatically, the Act created seven new circuit court judgeships – federal judges with lifetime appointments. President Adams, between the passage of the Act and the expiration of his term of office, attempted to fill as many of those judgeships as possible. At the same time, another Act of Congress created other judgeships in the District of Columbia, which Adams tried to fill. One commission for such a judgeship, signed but not delivered before Adams left office, was for William Marbury. When he did not receive his commission, Marbury went to the Supreme Court to ask for a writ of mandamus – an order directing an administration official (in this case, Secretary of State James Madison) to execute his duty (in this case, deliver the commission to Marbury). The Judiciary Act had given the Supreme Court original jurisdiction over writs of mandamus.[9]

The case created a considerable political controversy, as it was unclear exactly what would happen if the Supreme Court, staffed by Federalist appointees and led by Chief Justice John Marshall (who was a cousin of Jefferson and one of his greatest antagonists), ordered the Administration to deliver Marbury's commission. The Republicans, however, had a solution. Being in control of Congress and the White House, in March 1802, they repealed the Judiciary Act of 1801 and enacted the Judiciary Act of 1802. The Judiciary Act of 1802 reorganized the circuit courts and, importantly, abolished the Supreme Court's August Term.[10] As a consequence, when the then-current term of the Supreme Court ended in June 1802, the next term of the Court would not start until February 1803.

When the Court reconvened in February 1803, it immediately decided *Marbury v. Madison*. In a deft political move, the Court held that the 1789 legislative provision giving the Court jurisdiction over the case was itself unconstitutional and that the Court therefore lacked the authority

---

[9] Numerous accounts of these events exist (see, for example, Warren 1926; Stites 1981; Clinton 1994; Knight and Epstein 1996; Nelson 2000).

[10] Under the Judiciary Act of 1801, the Court was to have a single term from the first Monday of August until the beginning of the following June. There had previously been a February Term for the Court.

to decide the case. (Jurisdiction is the authority of a court to hear a particular case.) That is, the Court, led by Marshall, conveniently side-stepped having to issue a writ of mandamus to Madison by deciding that, under the Constitution, the Court did not constitutionally possess the authority to do so. While the Court noted in its opinion that Marbury was entitled to his commission, it ruled that he would have to go to a different court to compel Madison to deliver it.

The Court's decision has been widely examined throughout history and is generally cited as the primary source of authority for judicial review in the American context. However, the decision is not just a source of judicial power, it is also a strategic decision by the Court made in the context of a very hostile political environment. While asserting the power to declare Acts of Congress unconstitutional, the decision is a very delicate attempt by the Court to *avoid* making a decision that would further provoke the elected majority. The specific decision made by the Court allowed the justices to hold their ground by maintaining that Marbury was entitled to his commission. At the same time, by declaring that it did not constitutionally have the power to issue the writ of mandamus, the Court avoided ordering Jefferson to deliver the commission, an order that would surely have been ignored and likely undermined the Court's efficacy. Then, just twelve days later, the Supreme Court struck a fatal blow to the effort to have Adams' last-minute appointments commissioned, when it decided *Stuart v. Laird*.[11] In *Stuart*, the Court upheld the repeal of the Judiciary Act of 1801, observing that Congress had the constitutional authority to abolish federal courts.[12]

It may appear at first glance that the Court capitulated to the will of the elected branches – especially, Congress – in *Marbury* and *Stuart*. However, the Court may have actually won the metaphorical battle. The Court's power and influence grew considerably over the subsequent 30 years. In landmark cases, including *McCulloch v. Maryland*, *Cohens v. Virginia*, and *Osborn v. Bank of the United States*, the Supreme Court deftly interpreted the Constitution to establish precedents that national power was supreme to state power.[13] There was, to be sure, frequent political backlash against the Court's decisions affirming national power. For example, in 1821 there was a proposal to give the Senate appellate

[11] 1 Cranch 299 (1803).
[12] Indeed, this case has been cited as a significant step by the Court to accommodate the Jeffersonian majority (Ackerman 1998).
[13] See, for example, Keynes and Miller (1989, 107–9) for a discussion of the politics of these cases.

jurisdiction over Supreme Court cases in which a state is a party (Murphy 1962, 21). At the same time, there were other proposals to limit the Court's power by, for example, requiring a supermajority of justices to concur in order to invalidate a law on constitutional grounds (Murphy 1962, 22). Nevertheless, the justices reacted negatively to these proposals, none saw enactment, and the Court weathered the storm without seeing its power legislatively curtailed.

2.2.2 Conflicts from Jackson through the Civil War

By the mid-1820s it was becoming apparent that the Court was pushing the limits of what would be tolerated by the people. Indeed, the late 1820s would be marked by significant conflict between the Marshall Court and Jacksonian Democrats. The most well-known conflict during this era arose in the context of the Supreme Court case *Worcester v. Georgia*.[14] That case arose after a pair of conflicts between the Supreme Court and the State of Georgia over the rights of Cherokee Native Americans living within that state in which the Court declined to provide extra protection for Native Americans.[15] However, in *Worcester* the Court held that the Cherokee nation was a sovereign entity. In doing so, it overturned the conviction of two missionaries for living on Cherokee territory without the state's permission (contrary to Georgia state law) and declared the missionaries must be set free. Georgia resisted, and the state legislature ordered the governor to disregard the Court's decision.

The conflict came to a head when President Andrew Jackson refused to enforce the Supreme Court's order. It is in the context of this decision that Andrew Jackson reputedly stated, "John Marshall has made his decision, now let him enforce it." While it is almost surely apocryphal (Murphy 1962, 26), the spirit of Jackson's statement is instructive – the president refused to use his executive power to enforce the decision on Georgia. The delicate balance that Jackson was at that time trying to strike between national power and states' rights – in the context of the nullification crisis in South Carolina – suggests that Jackson's refusal to intervene was much more complicated than his disdain for a strong national judiciary. Nevertheless, the point remains that in refusing to enforce the Court's decision in *Worcester*, a clear message was sent to the Court that there

---

[14] 31 U.S. (6 Pet.) 515 (1832).
[15] *Johnson v. M'Intosh* 21 U.S. (8 Wheat.) 543 (1823); *Cherokee Nation v. Georgia* 30 U.S. 1 (1831).

were limits to how far it could exercise its power. In response to the Court's strong exercise of national power over the states, states' rights Democrats from the South and West launched a Court-curbing campaign in Congress.[16] None of these efforts was terribly successful, however. Scholars have observed that the legislative failure of these proposals was likely due in part to the strategic withdrawal by the Court, which eased political pressure (Murphy 1962; Lasser 1988).

Throughout the early 1830s, the Court would exercise considerable self-restraint, giving rise to a period of relative peace between the Court and the elected branches. In part as a consequence of deep divisions on the Bench, this period of calm was furthered by the appointment of Chief Justice Taney following Marshall's death. Unfortunately, that peace would be interrupted by the slavery issue. When the Court decided *Dred Scott v. Sandford*[17] in 1857, it had already been the subject of criticism from abolitionists (Murphy 1962, 28–29). In *Dred Scott*, the Court declared that slaves were indeed property and that slaves and their descendants could never be citizens. The Court also held that Congress could not prohibit slavery in the territories. The decision unleashed a bitter and strong attack on the Court, especially from Northern abolitionists. While none of the proposed Court-curbing legislation was actually enacted, animosity toward the Court and Chief Justice Taney was only fed by the Court's opposition to federal power. Both during and immediately after the Civil War, the Court continued to oppose national power, and it was feared that the justices would invalidate key components of Reconstruction. Members of Congress sought to expand the size of the Court and allow President Lincoln to appoint Republicans to the Bench; others wanted to abolish the Supreme Court and establish an entirely new one (Murphy 1962, 31–32).[18]

Following the Civil War, a brief period of strife occurred, as the Radical Republicans in Congress sought to solidify the affirmation of federal supremacy in the face of opposition from the Court. In *ex parte Milligan*,[19] the Supreme Court held that Lincoln's suspension of habeas corpus and establishment of military tribunals while the federal courts were operating was unconstitutional. The *Milligan* decision, then, implicitly questioned the military rule on the South following the Civil War.

---

[16] Nagel (1965, 928–931) describes this episode in detail.
[17] 60 U.S. (19 How.) 393 (1857).
[18] Notably, President Lincoln did not take part in any of these attacks.
[19] 71 U.S. 2 (1866).

Once again, Congress tried to impose a supermajority requirement for the Court's use of judicial review to invalidate an Act of Congress, though this was ultimately unsuccessful. Congress did manage, however, to remove the Court's jurisdiction over habeas corpus claims, even over a veto by President Andrew Johnson. The Habeas Corpus Act of 1867 had the effect of preventing the Court from hearing a habeas petition from William McCardle – a newspaper editor who had been arrested and held for trial before a military commission. The Court conceded that the Act meant it would have to dismiss McCardle's case. The Court's move in this case diffused the tension, as the Court appeared prepared to recognize the supremacy of the federal government in the wake of the Union victory in the Civil War.

2.3   COURT-CURBING SINCE RECONSTRUCTION

It is in the context of the federal supremacy established following the Civil War that we turn in the remainder of this book to an examination of Court-curbing since Reconstruction. A focus on this period makes sense because of important changes in the political system that took place during the Civil War and Reconstruction. During the antebellum era, there was a genuine question about whether the states were sovereign over the national government or vice-versa. Most agree, though, that the Civil War answered that question in favor of national government sovereignty over the states, and the Fourteenth Amendment to the Constitution serves as one indicator of that deep change in the nature of our federal system. In this spirit, since the conclusion of the Civil War and Reconstruction, the role that the Supreme Court plays in regulating legislative activity – at both the state and federal levels – has grown. What is more, the institutional strength and capacity of the Supreme Court grew significantly during this period, and the Court from Reconstruction forward looks like an altogether different institution than the Court before the Civil War. In addition, Congress increased the strength and capacity of the Court in the aftermath of the Civil War with various pieces of legislation, culminating in The Jurisdiction and Removal Act of 1875, which gave the Court full federal jurisdiction.[20] For these reasons, we may expect that the fundamental nature of the relationship between the

---

[20] Later, with the creation of the Courts of Appeals in 1891 and subsequent legislative enactments, the Court was further insulated as the justices were no longer obliged to "ride circuit" and gained increased discretion over their docket.

Supreme Court and the public and their elected representatives during the postbellum period is qualitatively different than it was before the Civil War and Reconstruction.

2.3.1   Court-Curbing Bills

To create a dataset of all Court-curbing bills introduced in Congress since Reconstruction, I have undertaken an extensive data collection process. Specifically, I have used three different sources to identify Court-curbing bills. First, for the period 1877–1937, I read the indices of the House and Senate Journals. I identified all bills introduced in Congress indexed under an extensive set of terms.[21] For the period 1937–1989, I read the *Digest of Public General Bills and Resolutions*, which includes a synopsis of all bills introduced in Congress. The synopsis of each bill referred to the Judiciary Committee of either chamber of Congress was read to assess whether it was possibly a Court-curbing bill. Finally, for the period 1989 through 2008, I used the online THOMAS search engine to identify all bills indexed under the same exhaustive set of terms used for the House and Senate Journals. I then read each bill, from each of the three sources, to determine whether it constituted a Court-curbing bill. I also "double-coded" each year from 1981 through 1989 using each of the search methodologies; no discrepancies among the three search methods were uncovered. A list of the bills identified as Court-curbing bills is included in Appendix B.

2.3.2   Types of Proposals

The Court-curbing bills that have been introduced in Congress since Reconstruction can be divided into six substantive categories: Composition; Jurisdiction; Judicial Review; Remedy; Procedural; and Resolutions/Miscellaneous. Within each category, bills can also be divided between those that are ordinary statutes and those that are constitutional amendments. Table 2.1 summarizes the distribution of bills collected. The method of curbing the Court invoked in Court-curbing bills has varied considerably over time. As Keynes and Miller (1989, 152) note, "rhetorical threats, statutory revision, constitutional amendments, and jurisdictional legislation" all seem to be considered as appropriate

---

[21] Specifically I identified all bills indexed under "Courts," "Judges," "Justices," "Judiciary," "Judicial Power," "Constitution," and "Constitutional Amendments."

TABLE 2.1. *Distribution of Different Types of Court-Curbing Proposals in Congress, 1877–2008*

Type of Measure	Statutes	Amendments	Total	Proportion
Composition	74	234	308	34%
Jurisdiction	179	6	185	21%
Judicial Review	86	55	141	16%
Resolutions/Misc.	103	0	103	11%
Remedy	85	9	94	10%
Procedural	61	5	66	7%

means of reining in the Court. What determines the particular method of Court-curbing at any given time is in some sense idiosyncratic, however. Intellectual movements are sometimes behind specific proposals, such as the movement to exercise Congress' constitutional power over appellate jurisdiction during the late 1970s. During most periods of Court-curbing, though, the method invoked in the legislation is often designed to be as broad as possible. For example, in an interview, one member of Congress described the difference between narrowly tailored legislation, which might pass and actually reverse a judicial policy, and broad legislation that rarely ever passes. "One is a scalpel; the other, a B-2 bomber. A scalpel is usually more effective, but the B-2 bomber gets all the attention."[22] The congressperson's analogy is suggestive evidence of the significance of Court-curbing as a position-taking endeavor. By introducing highly salient bills, members of Congress can rouse their constituents and create a political controversy. This type of legislative activity, although it may potentially have policy consequences by way of creating a political controversy, is distinct from legislative activity directly focused on policy change. To the extent a member is primarily concerned with policy change, she will prefer to use the "scalpel." However, to the extent the member wants to attract attention and create an issue on which she can position-take, she will prefer to use the "B-2 bomber."

COMPOSITION BILLS. Legislation aimed at affecting the composition of the Court constitutes more than one-third of the Court-curbing bills considered by Congress since Reconstruction, most of which have been in the form of constitutional amendments. Because jurisdiction-stripping

---

[22] Throughout this book, I make extensive use of evidence obtained through personal interviews I conducted with Supreme Court justices, members of Congress, former law clerks from the Supreme Court, and legislative staffers. Full details in the interview procedures are provided in the appendix to the book.

is generally regarded as the main mechanism by which Congress attacks the Court, it is interesting to observe that composition-oriented measures are a plurality of all Court-curbing bills. Even while the justices' tenure is constitutionally protected and can only be altered by an amendment, proposals to impose limitations on the justices' tenure have been by far the most frequent example of composition-oriented Court-curbing. For example, during the late 1960s, there was a significant push to restrict judicial tenure, and at least ten such amendments were introduced in the first two months of 1969 alone. Many constitutional amendments were introduced that would have limited the service of federal judges, including the justices, to a fixed number of years (frequently either eight or twelve years). It is notable that at the same time, Justice Douglas, who was considered by many to be an ideologically driven justice with extremist viewpoints, had been serving on the Court for thirty years. There were widespread calls for him to retire and Republicans in Congress attempted to impeach him.

What is more although the justices' tenure can only be changed by a constitutional amendment, members of Congress have introduced bills that would attempt to do so through ordinary statute. One bill, introduced by Senator Samuel Nunn (D-GA), was titled

> To Establish a Council on Judicial Tenure in the Judicial Branch of the Government, to establish a procedure in addition to impeachment for the retirement of disabled Justices and judges of the United States, and the removal of Justices and judges whose behavior is or has been inconsistent with the good behavior required by article III, section 1 of the Constitution, and for other purposes.[23]

This bill, if enacted, would have sought to create a method to remove judges from the federal bench without impeaching them. Specifically, it sought to create a "Council" that would determine whether a judge should be removed. Clearly prohibited by the Constitution, the idea of creating a method outside of impeachment had been proposed previously and attracted some public and political attention. Other measures that have been considered with some regularity over time include different selection methods (election, by committee, from among the state supreme courts) or alterations to the size of the Court. Less common examples include statutes prescribing qualifications for nominees, providing for

[23] S.4153, 93rd Congress, 2d Session.

mandatory retirement, or prohibiting justices from continuing on the bench upon the conviction of a felony.[24]

JURISDICTION BILLS. Bills designed to limit or remove the Court's jurisdiction over areas of the law or types of cases constitute the next largest class of Court-curbing bills. These bills, which mainly take the form of statutes, attempt to remove the Supreme Court's jurisdiction over specific substantive issues. Article III, Section 2 of the United States Constitution, which establishes the Supreme Court, reads in part, "[Except for the few cases in which it has original jurisdiction], the Supreme Court shall have appellate jurisdiction, both as to law and fact, with such exceptions, and under such regulations as the Congress shall make." Precisely what the consequence of removing the Court's jurisdiction over an area of law would mean generally depends on the context. When, for example, the federal courts have jurisdiction over a dispute, such a bill would leave the dispute to be resolved by the lower federal courts. By contrast, when the state courts have jurisdiction, then the dispute would remain in the state courts and could not be appealed to the U.S. Supreme Court. This power creates a powerful tool that Congress may use to pressure the Court. Jurisdiction-stripping, which is frequently described as the Supreme Court's Achilles' heel (Burton 1955, 175), was a very popular method of Court-curbing at the beginning of the twentieth century but then faded from congressional activity until the mid-1950s. From 1955 through the late 1980s, jurisdiction-stripping again became the most prominent form of Court-curbing. In particular, during the late 1970s, a sustained campaign was waged in Congress to remove the Court's jurisdiction over particular controversial issues such as school busing and prayer, abortion, reapportionment, and flag burning – issues in which the Court had involved itself during the 1970s. During the late 1980s and

---

[24] These figures suggest that by not including constitutional amendments in their analyses, Nagel and Rosenberg underestimate the frequency of a major component of Court-curbing activity. As noted, alterations to the size of the Court have been less common during the period of study. However, it should be noted that prior to Reconstruction, the Supreme Court's size was subject to alteration on several occasions. In particular, Congress' displeasure with President Andrew Johnson led to abolishment of several seats on the Court in order to prevent him from making any appointments to the bench. Because these measures – the bulk of which come in the form of constitutional amendment – are largely excluded from the Nagel/Rosenberg data, there is some reason to expect their data may paint an incomplete picture of the trends in Court-curbing over time. Specifically, the exclusion of constitutional amendments and resolutions presents a picture of Court-curbing that overemphasizes legislation introduced with a primarily policy focus.

1990s, jurisdiction-stripping efforts in Congress again waned. The beginning of the twenty-first century, however, has witnessed a slight uptick in the prominence of jurisdiction-stripping activity. For example, the Military Commissions Act of 2006, enacted by the 109th Congress, removes federal court jurisdiction over habeas corpus petitions by enemy combatants held in the military detention facility in Guantánamo Bay. Another recent example of note is the Illegal Immigration Reform and Immigrant Responsibility Act of 1996, which stripped federal courts of jurisdiction over a series of administrative agency decisions in immigration cases.

JUDICIAL REVIEW BILLS. Judicial review-oriented Court-curbing generally purports to accomplish one of three ends: removing the power of judicial review, prescribing requirements for the use of judicial review, or limiting the application of judicial review. Efforts to remove judicial review have been both statutory and constitutional and generally provide that the Court shall not have the power to declare Acts of Congress unconstitutional. Attempts to provide requirements for judicial review require a minimum number of justices who must concur in an act of judicial review; measures that seek to limit the applicability of judicial review subject declarations of unconstitutionality to either congressional override or popular referendum. This type of Court-curbing legislation has been fairly frequent, constituting 141 out of the 897 bills introduced in Congress between 1877 and 2008, although no such bills were introduced into Congress before 1907, and the frequency remained relatively low until 1935. However, the well-documented frustration of the New Deal legislative program by the Court highlighted the "countermajoritarian" difficulty associated with giving a constitutional veto to an unelected institution. Likely as a consequence, following the New Deal and the tension between the Court and the elected branches during that time, Congress has been especially sensitive to the Court's power to declare legislation unconstitutional. The Court's countermajoritarian function has become at times a salient topic of political and public criticism of the Court.

As a consequence, there was a series of Court-curbing bills introduced in the mid-1930s aimed at the Court's use of judicial review, whereas some of the earliest Gallup public opinion polls asked questions about public support for constitutionally prohibiting the Court from declaring Acts of Congress unconstitutional. Another period of increased Court-curbing directed at the Court's use of judicial review occurred in the late 1960s. Substantively this period was motivated by the Warren and Burger Courts' invalidation of state legislation, in cases ranging from race relations to the rights of criminal defendants. More recently, criticism of "judicial activism" – from both the political left and right – highlights the democratic difficulty of judicial review with charges that judges insert their own political preferences into public policy, in lieu of majoritarian preferences. I will discuss each of these periods of Court-curbing in greater detail below.

REMEDY BILLS. Remedy-oriented bills are the type of Court-curbing perhaps most narrowly tailored to a specific substantive issue. These bills generally seek to restrict the Court from issuing some specific type of order or using a particular means to resolve a dispute. Further underscoring the general pattern that Court-curbing is broad in nature and rarely issue-specific, these bills have been relatively rare historically. Representing only 11% of all Court-curbing introduced since Reconstruction, remedy-oriented Court-curbing has been popular during only two specific periods. First, during the early 1900s, Congress considered, and nearly achieved, limitations on the federal courts' power to issue injunctions in labor disputes. As I describe in greater detail below, with labor–business disputes at the forefront of contemporary politics, the Court became a major campaign issue for both political parties in 1912.[25] Limitations on relief would become fashionable again during the 1970s. Primarily in response to reapportionment and busing decisions, Congress attempted to prohibit the Court from ordering specific relief to racially based disputes (Keynes and Miller 1989). Often employed in conjunction with jurisdiction-stripping legislation, these bills sought to prohibit the federal courts from ordering forced busing to racially integrate public schools. I return to this example below and again in Chapter 6, where I discuss the details of the confrontation over school busing in greater detail.

PROCEDURE BILLS. Legislative proposals to alter judicial procedures constitute a much smaller proportion of the Court-curbing legislation.[26] Representing less than 8% of the bills introduced since Reconstruction, procedure-oriented Court-curbing has sought to set rules for constituting a quorum on the Court, require recusal under certain circumstances, or provide procedures for following stare decisis. These measures were most

[25] Stephenson (1999) provides an excellent discussion of the role the Court has played in various presidential elections. Indeed, Stephenson even suggests that the entanglement of the judiciary in the dialogue of presidential elections may have been evidence of a robust political process, though he also suggests it could be reason for concern.

[26] I specifically exclude from this category bills that seek to impose rules for the use of judicial review, which are classified separately in the "judicial review" category.

frequently considered during the late nineteenth century and witnessed a minor resurgence during the 1965–1971 period. Often, procedure-oriented Court-curbing seeks to affect the methods or mechanisms by which decisions from administrative agencies may be appealed, and these legislative efforts can be a particularly potent form of political control of the courts (Smith 1999). What is more, whereas most Court-curbing legislation rarely emerges from the committee to which it is referred, procedure-oriented Court-curbing during the late nineteenth century tended to make it very far through the legislative process, perhaps due in part to the low profile of procedure-oriented Court-curbing. However, it is interesting to note that procedure-oriented Court-curbing may potentially have the greatest impact among other types of Court-curbing, as it proposes to limit the Court's own internal operations.

OTHER BILLS. A final category of Court-curbing includes resolutions and miscellaneous proposals. These bills have appeared very sporadically throughout history and generally reflect congressional displeasure with a specific decision and rarely make substantial efforts to limit judicial power. Most recently, resolutions have expressed the sentiment that Congress does not approve of the citation of foreign law by the Court and that the Court should follow the legislatively created sentencing guidelines.

There are several important ways in which these different categories of Court-curbing vary. Among these are the ease of enactment and the constitutional validity. First, certain measures are more easily enacted than others, such as the removal of jurisdiction or limitations on remedy. These types of measures may generally be enacted by simple legislation and therefore pose a greater threat of actually being written into law than do limitations on the use of judicial review or changes to the tenure of the justices. It is not clear whether Congress can impose limitations on the use of judicial review without a constitutional amendment, and any legislative effort to do so would surely spark a lively political battle. Similarly, changes to Supreme Court tenure would most definitely require a constitutional amendment, which is necessarily harder to enact than ordinary legislation. Second, certain measures pose more dubious constitutional questions than others. For example, it is readily apparent from the Constitution that Congress may alter the size of the Court or may enact enticing retirement benefits, whereas it is less clear that Congress has the power to limit the use of specific remedies or impose quorum requirements on the Court. What is important to note here is that the vast majority of these measures have no real chance of being enacted;

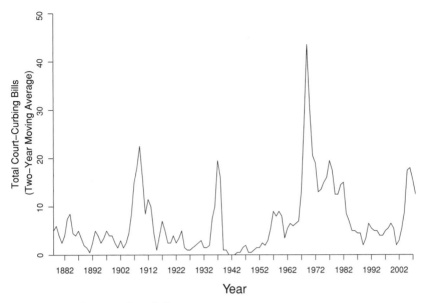

FIGURE 2.1. *Court-curbing bills, 1877–2008.*

they are simply position-taking efforts by members of Congress and have only symbolic value.

2.3.3 Historical Trends

The sheer number of Court-curbing bills introduced in Congress has oscillated over time, though several distinct periods of heightened Court-curbing can be identified. Figure 2.1 shows the total number of Court-curbing bills each year between 1877 and 2008. Roughly speaking, the years can be divided into periods of "high" Court-curbing and periods of "low" Court-curbing. The major periods of "high" Court-curbing are the early 1880s, 1906–1911, the mid-1930s, the mid-1950s, the late 1960s, 1975–1982, and 2001–2008. I identify the periods by first performing a visual inspection on the pattern of Court-curbing activity. After identifying peaks and valleys in the trend, I performed a more careful substantive analysis of the content of the bills to assess when the substantive issues motivating Court-curbing in one period seem to have resolved. Because it is very difficult to systematically link Court-curbing bills to particular substantive debates, I instead consulted a variety of secondary materials. I considered first the articles written by Nagel (1965) and Rosenberg

(1992) as well as historical accounts of tensions between the Court and Congress.[27] With initial guidance from these sources, I then return to the data to identify when key sponsors began to engage in Court-curbing activity. Finally, I consulted newspaper accounts and law reviews for evidence of growing tension between the Court and Congress. The volume and substance of the bills were then used in conjunction to identify specific start and end points for the periods of Court-curbing.[28]

Table 2.2 shows the distribution of types of Court-curbing during each of these periods. The table illustrates the prevalence of each type of Court-curbing during the seven major periods of Court-curbing and provides an overview of the patterns on legislative attempts to "rein in" the Court. Attacks on jurisdiction and remedy were primary components of the 1906–1911 period, whereas judicial review and Court composition were the primary targets of Court-curbing during the New Deal era and the late 1960s. Jurisdiction and Court-composition played a major role during both the mid-1950s and the 1975–1982 periods, while the 1975–1982 periods also witnessed a volume of efforts to limit the remedy the Court may impose. This variation is interesting but is not surprising, given the specific substantive issues at stake during each of these periods. Notably, though jurisdiction-stripping has traditionally been thought of as the main form of Court-curbing, these data indicate that although

---

[27] For example, the case studies written by Pritchett (1961) and Murphy (1962) as well as Keynes and Miller's (1989) study of school busing, prayer, and abortion provided insights into the substantive issues of dispute during specific years. Further, Stephenson's (1999) analysis of the role the Court has played in presidential campaigns provided guidance.

[28] Although there is some overlap, the periods identified here differ from the Nagel/Rosenberg data in their particular beginning and ending points. Generally, there are two reasons why my periodization differs from the Nagel/Rosenberg periodization. First, because they do not consider proposed constitutional amendments, Nagel and Rosenberg overlook a considerable amount of Court-curbing, and this often changes when a period begins or ends. For example, much of the Court-curbing legislation considered during the late 1960s was in the form of a proposed amendment, the inclusion of which makes the years 1966–1969 – my period of "high" Court-curbing – overshadow the years 1963–1965 – the Nagel/Rosenberg period – in terms of the intensity of Court-curbing. Second, in some instances, the data I have assembled portray a different pattern than those reported by Nagel and Rosenberg. For example, they identify the years 1922–1924 as a period of high Court-curbing, with eleven bills introduced during those years. I have also identified eleven bills introduced during those years. However, this compares with ninety-two bills that were introduced between 1906 and 1911. That is, I identify a period of six years with about fifteen bills introduced on average each year, whereas they identify three years with fewer than three bills introduced on average each year. These two types of discrepancies, then, reveal a slightly different periodization of Court-curbing than the previous scholarship has documented.

TABLE 2.2. *Types of Legislation during the Seven Periods of Court-Curbing*

Total court-curbing bills introduced each period and percentage of bill by type in each period shown (percentages may not total to 100 due to rounding)

	Judicial Review	Composition	Procedural	Jurisdiction	Remedy	Other	Total
1882–1887	5 (15%)	7 (21%)	20 (59%)	1 (3%)	0 (0%)	1 (3%)	34
1906–1911	11 (12%)	14 (15%)	5 (5%)	26 (28%)	30 (33%)	6 (7%)	92
1932–1937	28 (49%)	23 (40%)	2 (4%)	4 (7%)	0 (0%)	0 (0%)	57
1953–1959	11 (24%)	19 (41%)	1 (2%)	15 (33%)	0 (0%)	0 (0%)	46
1965–1969	29 (24%)	58 (48%)	3 (2%)	11 (9%)	16 (13%)	5 (4%)	122
1975–1982	5 (3%)	44 (36%)	4 (3%)	43 (35%)	21 (17%)	5 (4%)	122
2001–2008	6 (7%)	0 (0%)	0 (0%)	20 (24%)	0 (0%)	58 (69%)	84

jurisdiction may be an extremely potent and important tool at the disposal of Congress, Court-curbing has made use of a variety of legislative and political tools to rein in the Court.

2.3.4   Who Court-Curbs?

The various types of Court-curbing bills, appearing with varying frequency through history, have been at one point or another supported by both liberals and conservatives alike. Figure 2.2(a) shows the conservatism of Court-curbing sponsors over time. The solid black bars represent the median Court-curber each year, and the vertical bars show the distribution of sponsors' ideal points. This figure reveals that there have been two distinct ideological periods of Court-curbing. From 1877 through 1940, Court-curbing was very clearly a weapon utilized by liberals to attack the Court. During the postwar era, however, Court-curbing has become primarily the province of ideological conservatives. This is not surprising, because during the late nineteenth and early twentieth centuries, government was controlled by the Republican Party, and the federal bench moved in a decidedly conservative direction. However, with the arrival of FDR and the New Deal Democrats in Washington (followed by an extreme conflict with the Court and nine subsequent appointments by FDR to the Supreme Court), the bench became much more liberal. As a consequence, liberals became less hostile toward the bench, whereas conservatives became increasingly so. In fact, it is in large part due to the liberal takeover of the bench by the mid-twentieth century that a growing conservative legal movement began to build its own infrastructure and, ultimately, came to dominate the courts, if not the law schools (Teles 2008).

Interestingly, although the Court has moved in a conservative direction during the late twentieth and early twenty-first centuries, conservatives have continued to assail the judiciary. Figure 2.2(b) makes this pattern particularly clear. As the density plots show, Court-curbing was primarily liberal during the pre-1950 period (although it appears to be more moderate than during the first two periods), whereas Court-curbing has been overwhelmingly (and increasingly) conservative since. It is notable, though, that Figure 2.2(b) reveals an increase in liberally oriented Court-curbing during the most recent period.[29]

---

[29] Note also that, although it is difficult to tell from Figure 2.2(a), the variance in Court-curbing ideology is fairly constant. With the exception of the mid-1950s, Court-curbing ideology during all eras is distributed around a mean with a standard error of about 0.30.

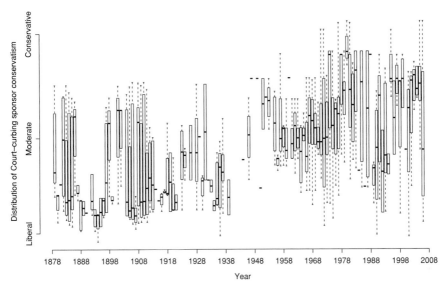

(a) Distribution of sponsors' ideal points, 1877–2008

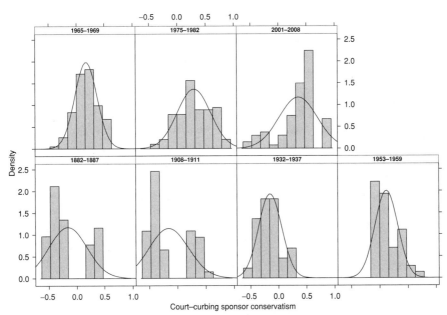

(b) Distribution of sponsors' ideal points during seven periods

FIGURE 2.2. *Conservatism of Court-curbing sponsors, 1877–2008.* Top panel
(a) shows distribution of conservatism (ideal points) among Court-curbing sponsor each year; bottom panel (b) shows distribution of all Court-curbing sponsors
during each of the seven periods of Court-curbing identified above.

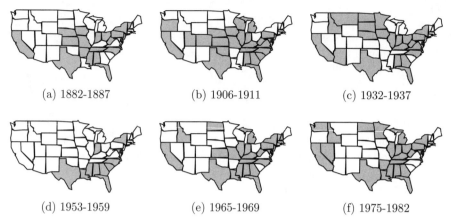

(a) 1882-1887   (b) 1906-1911   (c) 1932-1937

(d) 1953-1959   (e) 1965-1969   (f) 1975-1982

FIGURE 2.3. *Geographic distribution of Court-curbing sponsors during six of the periods of "high" Court-curbing.*

One might imagine there is considerable geographic variation in who sponsors Court-curbing. Was Court-curbing primarily driven by Midwestern progressives during the early twentieth century? Were Southerners the primary critiques of the Court during the civil rights era? Figure 2.3 summarizes the geographical distribution of Court-curbing during six of the seven periods of high Court-curbing volume. In this figure, the shaded states are states from which at least one representative or senator sponsored Court-curbing legislation during the period. As the figure shows, Court-curbing has at various times come from different regions of the country. Court-curbing during the 1953–1959 period was most tightly concentrated in the Southeast, at most other times it has been fairly widespread. With the exception of the Southwest, most regions are represented by Court-curbers during these periods of "high" Court-curbing. This further underscores the claim that the introduction of more Court-curbing bills is indicative of broader discontent with the Court. Indeed, as we will see in the next chapter, the number of Court-curbing bills introduced is highly correlated with the number of unique Court-curbing sponsors ($r = 0.99$).

A final note should be made regarding the "seriousness" of these measures. A legitimate concern may be voiced that there is not much variation in how "far" these bills go through the legislative process. It is true that most bills never make it out of committee; indeed, most never receive a hearing in committee. In this vein, the quality of Court-curbing bills as a true signal about congressional hostility may be suspect. However, there is some reason to believe the Court does interpret Court-curbing bills as a serious signal, without regard for their legislative seriousness. For example, Friedman (2009, 4) notes that the debate over Roosevelt's Court-Packing Plan was seen by the Court (and others) as implicitly a debate about what "sort of government [the people] preferred." Moreover, my argument is that Court-curbing is a signal to the Court about public – not elite – support for the Court because these bills are position-taking measures. That is, seen as the product of an interaction between members of Congress and their constituents – rather than as the product of an interaction among legislators – Court-curbing bills may be informative even in the absence of significant legislative success. The purpose of Court-curbing proposals is to signal public discontent, politicize the Court, and erode public confidence in the judiciary. Of course, a bill's degree of legislative significance could be an additional cue to the Court (and the public) about the extent to which Congress is reacting to public opinion about the Court. But the introduction of those bills at the very least indicates some level of public discontent with the Court.

Seen in this light, the possibility that Court-curbing bills are "mere" position-taking as opposed to serious pieces of legislation is not, in and of itself, problematic. What is more, variation in how "far" Court-curbing makes it through the legislative process is very highly correlated with the volume of Court-curbing legislation being considered in Congress. In any event, because of the difficulty associated with systematically distinguishing "serious" Court-curbing from legislative position-taking, I have devoted considerable effort here to identify the ideological orientation and volume of Court-curbing as proxies for the seriousness of Court-curbing.

2.4 SEVEN PERIODS OF COURT-CURBING

We now turn to a brief overview of the major substantive issues motivating Court-curbing during each of the seven periods of heightened Court-curbing identified above. There is a great deal of historical nuance behind each of these episodes that cannot be treated here. However, it is instructive to consider the ways in which specific substantive issues motivate various types of Court-curbing; these brief historical accounts also help illuminate the motivation for Court-curbing, which will be explored more fully in the following two chapters. This discussion reveals that the introduction of Court-curbing bills in Congress does in fact represent the degree of concern in Congress with the Court and Congress' willingness to engage in a political battle with the court.

The particular substantive focus of individual Court-curbing bills is often difficult to identify. Indeed, this is often intentionally so, as Court-curbing is frequently motivated by broad discontent with the Court, and Court-curbing bills serve as wholesale-level responses to a series of retail-level problems. Nevertheless, a qualitative examination of each of the seven periods of "high" Court-curbing allows for us to more carefully examine the broad substantive contours of these periods of hostility between the Court and Congress. The periods on which I focus here are the early 1880s, 1906–1911, the mid-1930s, the mid-1950s, the late 1960s, 1975–1982, and the post-2001 era. In light of the politics during these years, the periods identified as "high" Court-curbing are intuitive. Indeed, the judiciary has played a major role in the elections and political rhetoric of these times (see, e.g., Stephenson 1999). Here, I will briefly describe the political circumstances that characterize each of these periods.

1882–1887. Between 1882 and 1887, a period of tension between the Court and Congress was marked by the first major onslaught of Court-curbing since Reconstruction. As we saw previously in Figure 2.1, most of the Court-curbing during these years took place between 1882 and 1884. Similarly, we see in Figure 2.2(b) the sponsors of these bills were decidedly liberal in ideological persuasion. This era was marked by a sustained effort by liberal and progressive members of Congress to place procedural restrictions on the Supreme Court. Indeed, the 1880s followed a period of relative judicial activity during the 1870s, and the Democrats who dominated the House during the 48th, 49th, and 50th Congresses were particularly hostile toward the conservative Supreme Court. Although the Democrats were the minority party in the Senate during the 49th and 50th Congresses, they were so by only two seats.

Substantively, a good deal of the Court-curbing that took place during this era was related to the Supreme Court's adjudication of cases involving railroad regulation. During the fifteen preceding years, Republicans in Congress (most forcefully in the Senate) undertook to greatly expand the Supreme Court's jurisdiction in many areas, including diversity cases (Kutler 1968). Indeed, historian William Wiecek (1969, 333) notes, "In no comparable period of our nation's history have the federal courts, lower and Supreme, enjoyed as great an expansion of their jurisdiction as they did in the years of Reconstruction, 1863 to 1876." As a consequence of the expansion of jurisdiction, the overwhelmingly conservative courts of the immediate post-Reconstruction era were deciding many more cases than they had previously, touching directly on the issues that mattered most to liberals, including railroads. In response, liberal members of Congress during this period considered creating a commission to regulate railroad rates, as the Supreme Court had been very active in preventing government regulation of the railroads. However, the Democrats' efforts were generally stymied by political pressure brought to bear by the railroad corporations and their lobbying efforts.

Moreover, because Democrats were the minority party during this period, their efforts at Court-curbing were less successful than they were to be when they would later gain control of government. Indeed, throughout the last two decades of the nineteenth century, the conservative Supreme Court continued to strike down state regulations. As Keynes and Miller (1989, 127) note, "While the Waite and Fuller courts legitimized laissez-faire capitalism, overturning state legislation regulating business and industry, in the 1880s, the Supreme Court generally sustained the congressional exercise of the commerce power vis-à-vis the states."[30]

1906–1911. The battle during the late nineteenth century led directly into the second period of Court-curbing, 1906–1911, which was marked by a distinct attack on the Court's jurisdiction and its capacity to intervene in labor disputes. The use of judicial injunctions in labor disputes had become a significant political issue as early as the 1890s (see, e.g., Gregory 1898), and by the early years of the twentieth century, it became a central cleavage between liberals and progressives on one hand and conservatives on the other (Frankfurter and Greene 1963). However, the period was also marked by more general Court-curbing, which included efforts to limit the use of judicial review, alter the Court's composition, and otherwise curtail the independence of the federal judiciary. For example, during this era, several bills were introduced seeking to forbid the members of the Supreme Court from accepting gifts of any sort from public figures or from giving public speeches.[31] Interestingly, Court-curbing during this period was sponsored by progressive members of both parties, revealing a deep political division over how to respond to the Court's labor jurisprudence (Ross 1994). Both parties made the issue of judicial interventions in labor disputes a major component of the 1908 presidential election, and the issue occupied a prominent position in both parties' platforms.

[30] To be sure, the Court's role in legitimizing laissez-faire capitalism during this era (against the wishes of the Democrats) was extremely important (see, e.g., Bensel 2000).
[31] See, for example, H.R. 13830 (60th Cong.), H.R. 11775 (61st Cong.), H.R. 5179 (61st Cong.).

During this era, the Democrats remained a minority in Congress but grew in power until they won control of the House of Representatives in the election of 1910 and the Senate and White House in the election of 1912. Indeed, the Progressives fielded their own presidential candidate in 1912.[32] In fact, upon gaining control of the House and the Senate in the election of 1912, the Democrats quickly enacted reform legislation to aid the labor movement, but it was vetoed by the lame-duck President Taft (Frankfurter and Greene 1963, 140–1). This period, then, reflects the initial Progressive backlash against the Court's laissez-faire jurisprudence and the judicial stance against regulation and the first steps toward a national welfare state. Indeed, the tension between labor and business and the consequences of this struggle for the political economy have been the subject of several studies of legal development (Kersch 2004; Ross 1994; Hattam 1993). Figures 2.1 and 2.2(b) together demonstrate that Court-curbing during this era peaked between 1906 and 1909 and was decidedly liberal in ideological orientation.

Court-curbing during this period eventually waned, following passage of the Judicial Code of 1911 and the enactment of the Clayton Anti-Trust Act of 1914 (Frankfurter and Greene 1963). The Judicial Code represented a major legislative reorganization of the courts. Friends of labor in both the House and the Senate sought to attach amendments to the legislation that would restrict the issuance of injunctions. With the failure of these amendments to pass, the issue seems to have resolved. On the other hand, the section of the Clayton Act that addressed injunctions (Section 20) was not as strong as the previous Court-curbing bills, but it represented an important compromise between labor and antilabor interests in Congress.[33]

1932–1937. The volume of Court-curbing that marked the years between 1906 and 1911 would be overshadowed by the intensity of Court-curbing some twenty-five years later. Indeed, the mid-1930s have become probably the most infamous period of Court-curbing in American history. Although most students of judicial–congressional relations are highly familiar with FDR's Court-packing plan and the "switch-in-time-that-saved-nine" in 1937, few historical accounts have focused directly on conflict between the Democrats and the Court that existed during the years leading up to 1937.

[32] Stephenson (1999, 112) notes that when the "Old Guard" Republicans renominated Taft in 1912, moderate Republicans left the party and nominated Teddy Roosevelt as a Progressive candidate, which paved the way for the Democrats to elect Woodrow Wilson.

[33] For a discussion of the compromise, see Gompers (1984).

Conventional wisdom suggests that the confrontation between the Court and New Deal Democrats, spurred by a series of Court decisions hostile to the New Deal legislative program, really began after the Democrats were reelected in 1936. Indeed, only after he was reelected in 1936 did FDR openly criticize the Court (Leuchtenberg 1995). However, as Figure 2.1 shows, there was a growing Court-curbing movement in Congress *before* the Court-packing plan in early 1937, as thirty-three Court-curbing measures were introduced in Congress between January 1935 and March 9, 1937, when FDR announced the legislative proposal (Leuchtenberg 1995).[34] What is more, Figure 2.2(b) demonstrates that these bills were overwhelmingly liberal in ideological orientation. This finding comports with the theoretical model's claim that Court-curbing can serve as a signal to the Court about Congress preferences and in turn precipitate changes in jurisprudence. To be sure, many historians have demonstrated that the Supreme Court's change in jurisprudence in 1937 could not have been due to the 1937 Court-packing plan,[35] while conceding that a fundamental shift in Supreme Court jurisprudence did take place (Leuchtenberg 1995). However, the empirical evidence presented in this chapter, in conjunction with the theoretical argument I advance in the next chapter, offers an assessment of the Court's "switch-in-time-that-saved-nine," which attributes causality to Court-curbing.

The mythical story of the 1937 confrontation between the New Deal Democrats and the Supreme Court contends that Justice Roberts famously switched his position in a key New Deal case in order to avoid further angering the Congress and ensuring enactment of the so-called Court-Packing Plan. Indeed, the focus has largely been on the Court-Packing Plan, most surely because it was very politically salient and served as the focal point of contemporary political debates. More recently, scholars have debated the validity of a causal attribution to Roosevelt's proposal (see, e.g., Cushman 1998; White 2005). I will return to this point and discuss the debate in greater detail in Chapter 5. The point remains,

---

[34] While I identify 1932 as the beginning of this period, Nagel (1965) identifies 1935 as the beginning. The primary reason why I use 1932 as a starting point is because 1932 was when the New Deal Democrats were elected, and, beginning in 1933, they considered Court-curbing bills to rein in the conservative courts. Nagel does not include those bills in his set because they were almost uniformly proposed amendments aimed at restricting the tenure of federal judges or limiting the power of judicial review. Indeed, the number of Court-curbing bills increased from one in 1932 to two in each of 1933 and 1934 and then jumped dramatically to thirteen in 1935, when the recently elected (and reelected) New Deal Democrats returned to Washington.

[35] See Cushman (1998, ch. 1) for an excellent summary of the competing historical accounts of this change in the Court's jurisprudence.

though, that the historical focus on the Court-Packing Plan overshadows the fact that a considerable amount of Court-curbing legislation was introduced in the years and months leading up to February 1937 and the Court-Packing Plan itself really marked the end of legislative attempts to curb the Court.

In this sense, although it may not have anticipated FDR's specific plan, a politically savvy Court would have been aware that Congress and the public were displeased with the Court and that further adverse decisions in key New Deal cases would surely provoke significant political consequences. Indeed, some historians and scholars of the Court have noted the political environment in which the Court was deciding cases during the mid-1930s and suggested as much (Ackerman 1998; Kalman 2005). To the general political climate, I add the (previously overlooked), great deal of anti-Court legislation being considered by Congress during the years and months preceding the unveiling of FDR's plan.[36] To be sure, some historical and political science analyses have attempted to attribute the Court's change in jurisprudence to various factors, such as public opinion or judicial concern for the Court's public prestige (Murphy 1962; Mason 1956; Levinson and McCloskey 2000; Leuchtenberg 1995). However, others have criticized this line of reasoning by noting that criticism of judicial decisions is a routine part of the political process and that the Court does not respond to such routine criticism (pars. 33–35 White 2005). Whereas the first component of this criticism is an empirical point, the latter is an assumption. In subsequent chapters of this book, I demonstrate that this assumption is not supported by the evidence – that the Court does in fact respond to routine criticism.

1953–1959. The fourth period of Court-curbing occurs during the late 1950s. This period, which has been the subject of careful scholarly attention (Murphy 1962; Pritchett 1961), was precipitated by several key decisions by the Court in cases involving national security, race relations, and criminal defendants. During its October 1955 and October 1956 Terms, for example, the Supreme Court decided several cases that restricted the government's power to persecute Communists. Among these cases were *Pennsylvania v. Nelson*,[37] in which the Court held that the State of Pennsylvania could not proscribe sedition, because the federal

---

[36] See Gely and Spiller (1992) for one notable exception. Gely and Spiller note that the confrontation over the Court-packing plan was really the culmination of a growing Court-curbing movement in Congress in the months immediately preceding FDR's announcement of the plan.

[37] 350 U.S. 497 (1956).

Smith Act already proscribed the activity; *Peters v. Hobby,*[38] in which the Court held that the loyalty board of the Civil Service Commission could not bar a special consultant from federal service because it doubted his "loyalty" and remove him from his position; and, perhaps most notably, *Yates v. United States,*[39] in which the Court declared an individual does not violate the Smith Act (a federal law prohibiting sedition) merely by believing or stating that the government should be overthrown.[40] Reaction to these decisions was immediate and divided. The media were split, as was Congress. Interestingly, the issues of the day united some liberals with some conservatives while dividing others. Numerous Court-curbing bills were introduced by Democrats and Republicans alike, while President Eisenhower avoided weighing in on the confrontation. Indeed, the reaction in Congress was so significant that several Court-curbing bills passed the House and were very nearly successful in the Senate (Murphy 1962, ch. 9; Pritchett 1961, ch. 10).[41] At the same time, state officials waged their own attacks on the Court, including the Conference of Chief Justices (comprised of the chief justice of each state), which issued a report urging the Supreme Court to exercise "self-restraint" (Schmidhauser 1963, 32; Ross 2002, 515). Even the American Bar Association failed to voice support for the Court (Murphy 1962, 118).

This period, more so than the other six periods of "high" Court-curbing, is marked by a particularly moderate ideological orientation. Whereas the earlier periods were primarily driven by liberal interests, and the latter periods by conservative interests, the Court-curbing that took place during the mid-1950s was supported by both ends of the political spectrum. The distribution of Court-curbing sponsors during this period is relatively tight and centered around a moderate mean. Figure 2.2(a) reveals with greater detail that indeed the distribution during this period was unusually tight and that the median Court-curbing sponsors were generally fairly moderate, although there is a slight conservative skew.

1965–1969. The fifth period of Court-curbing sets the high water mark for anti-Court activity in Congress. During the five-year span

[38] 349 U.S. 331 (1955).

[39] 354 U.S. 298 (1957).

[40] There were, in addition, several other cases in these points decided around the same time (Murphy 1962, ch. 5).

[41] Indeed, the story of the bills' failure to pass the Senate is complicated and full of political intrigue. The details are too many to recount here, but the reader is referred to Murphy (1962).

between 1965 and 1969, 122 Court-curbing bills were introduced, 53 of which were introduced in 1969 alone.[42] The volume and ideological intensity of Court-curbing during this period is in line with other social movements and cultural struggles of the time. It was both loud and ideologically pointed. Figure 2.2(b) reveals that the 1966–1968 period witnessed extremely conservative Court-curbing. Driven largely by reactions to the liberal social movements of the 1960s, the growing conservative movement, and the increasing political power of the religious right, Court-curbing during this period sought to put an end to the Court's focus on individual liberties that had marked its jurisprudence for the preceding twenty years. At its height during this era, the Warren Court made many important but controversial decisions regarding criminal procedure, civil liberties, and race relations (Powe 2000).

In response to a liberal Court in an era of increasingly conservative politics, the majority of bills during this period focused on either the use of judicial review or the composition of the Court, though a substantial amount of legislation also targeted the Court's jurisdiction and the remedies available to the Court. It was during this era that Congress attempted to impeach Justice William O. Douglas, and the Republicans successfully defeated the nomination of Abe Fortas to be elevated to Chief Justice (Epstein and Segal 2005; Abraham 1999). With many New Deal appointees still on the bench, a strong conservative wing of the Democratic Party, the resurgence of the Republican Party, and the election of Richard Nixon on a platform that included the appointment of "law and order judges," the reconstitution of the bench in a more conservative direction occupied a central place in the political agenda. To be sure, Nixon did make several appointments to the Bench that moved the Court in the conservative direction, replacing Chief Justice Earl Warren with Warren Burger and Justice John Marshall Harlan with William Rehnquist. However, the remaking of the Court was not complete, as Nixon also appointed Lewis Powell, an ideological moderate, and Harry Blackmun, the majority opinion author in *Roe v. Wade*. Indeed, it was

---

[42] I noted above that the years identified as the beginning and ending of this period of high Court-curbing differ from those reported by Rosenberg (1992). This is due in large part to the inclusion of constitutional amendments in my data, which were not included by Rosenberg. Including those bills suggests that the real increase in Court-curbing took place between 1965 and 1969. In particular, 1969 saw the most Court-curbing bills introduced of any year in this study, a year that is not included in Rosenberg's definition of high-frequency Court-curbing.

just after William Douglas was replaced by John Paul Stevens that the next period of Court-curbing would begin.

1975–1982. The sixth period of Court-curbing identified earlier occurs during the late 1970s. Between the years 1975 and 1982, 122 Court-curbing bills were introduced in Congress. Most of these bills were aimed at either altering the selection method for the justices or at jurisdiction-stripping (see, for example, Keynes and Miller 1989). Recall from Table 2.2 that more than half of the Court-curbing bills introduced during this period were either composition or jurisdiction oriented. The composition bills were generally borne of congressional displeasure with justices who were perceived as extreme liberals as well as the extremely long tenure of justices such as William O. Douglas and Hugo Black. Jurisdiction-stripping bills and efforts to limit judicial remedies were very common during the late 1970s and early 1980s and were frequently supported in the Senate by Republican leaders such as Jesse Helms (Weicker and Sussman 1995, 124). Primarily motivated by the Court's decisions regarding school busing, school prayer, and abortion, the jurisdiction bills represented a general continuation of some of the issues raised during the preceding era of Court–Congress tension but were never resolved (Keynes and Miller 1989). Although most of these proposals served merely as rallying points for conservatives, some were taken very seriously. In December 1980, a group of Southern Democrats worked with Republicans to attach an amendment to the Department of Justice's appropriations bill that would have restricted the federal government's ability to enforce desegregation through forced busing, had it not been vetoed by Jimmy Carter. I will return to this example in greater detail in Chapter 6.

In addition, a host of other issues made their way onto the agenda of Court-curbers, including reapportionment and flag burning. During this period, the volume of bills introduced was not as high as during the previous period, but the ideological orientation of the Court-curbers was much more conservatively extreme. Figure 2.1 reveals that the Court-curbing period beginning in 1975 was smaller in magnitude than during the late 1960s. In addition, the figure demonstrates an interesting saw-tooth pattern not present during other periods of Court-curbing. The up-and-down pattern suggests that beginning with the 1975–1982 period, Court-curbing began to cycle with the electoral calendar. What is more, we saw in Figure 2.2(b) that the ideological orientation of the Court-curbing sponsors during the 1975–1982 period was much more ideologically conservative than during the 1962–1969 period.

Writing contemporaneously, Senator Charles Mathias, Jr. (1982, 27) commented,

> In more than 20 years, I have never seen such a concerted assault on the federal courts as has been mounted so far in the 97th Congress. We already have before us some 30 court-curbing bills. Several of them would drastically curtail federal court jurisdiction. The sponsors of these bills make no bones about their purpose: They want to abolish federal court jurisdiction over some very specific and controversial areas of the law. Abortion, school prayer, busing, and the all-male draft are among the issues they would remove from lower court and Supreme Court jurisdiction.[43]

Indeed, Senator Mathias' claim is supported by an overview of the substance of the Court-curbing bills introduced during this period. These issues represented major issues for ideological conservatives and occupied a central role in the conservative Republican Party's 1980 presidential election. To be sure, an important component of the Reagan Revolution was to fully accomplish the remaking of the judiciary in a conservative image, which was begun but never completed during the Nixon Administration. Winning both the presidency and the Senate in 1980, the Republicans were finally poised to undertake a massive reorientation of the federal bench, and by introducing considerable Court-curbing legislation, the conservatives in the party were able to convey the seriousness with which they were going to work to reverse what they perceived as forty years of liberal tyranny from the bench. In Chapter 6, I explore this episode in greater detail.

2001–2008. Finally, there is some evidence that the United States has recently begun to enter a new period of "high" Court-curbing. Figure 2.1 demonstrates the increasing volume of Court-curbing between 2001 and 2008 and shows that the sponsors have remained very conservative. Since the turn of the century, there has been considerable hostility between Congress and the Court. Issues ranging from religion in the public sphere, same-sex marriage, the right to die, and other social issues, as well as several idiosyncratic issues, have all been the subject of considerable legislative animosity toward the Court. What is more, as the figures reported

---

[43] Senator Charles Mathias (R-MD) should not be confused with Representative Robert Mathias (R-CA), who himself sponsored a Court-curbing bill during the 91st Congress (H.R. 7739, which sought to impose mandatory retirement ages for Supreme Court justices).

above indicate (see, e.g., Table 2.1), legislative responses to the Court during this period have been unlike other periods. More so than during other periods of Court-curbing, Congress has been very proactive during recent years, using new legislative techniques that have been designed to publicly condemn the Court and side-step the possibility of judicial review.

One way in which recent Court-curbing legislation has been different from previous legislative responses to the Court is that legislators have tried to command the states to do things that the Supreme Court seems unlikely to do. For example, in response to the Court's decision in *Kelo v. City of New London*, Congress has tried to force states to provide property rights protections that the Court refused to read into the Constitution.[44] One congressional staffer commented that "the real way to get at the Supreme Court is through appropriations – that is Congress' real power; that is why we have national speed limits and a national drinking age. Congress can tie funding to requirements on the states to get around the Court."[45] At the same time, though, Congress has also tried to force the Court to intervene in other areas. For example, during the summer of 2005 a national controversy erupted when Michael Schiavo sought to have the feeding tube removed from his wife, Terri, who was in a persistent vegetative state. Mrs. Schiavo's family opposed the husband's efforts and sought to block him in court from removing the tube. The episode attracted considerable attention, and Congress, led by House Majority Leader Tom Delay and Senate Majority Leader Bill Frist, became involved. Congress tried to force the federal courts to get involved and prevent the Florida state courts from allowing Mr. Schiavo to have his wife's feeding tube removed. Congress passed a law removing the case from the Florida state courts to the federal courts, and President Bush flew back to Washington, DC, from his vacation in Texas, to sign the bill. Ultimately, though, the federal courts denied Mrs. Schiavo's family's request, and the Supreme Court declined to intervene. This episode, however, generated considerable public attention and was thought of as a useful political stunt by Republican strategists.[46]

---

[44] Several bills were introduced in Congress that would have tied federal funds for education or transportation to a state's guarantee of stricter standards for eminent domain actions by the State.

[45] Personal interview with "Staffer 4."

[46] A story ran in the *Washington Post* on April 4, 2005, reporting on a memorandum written by then-Senator Mel Martinez of Florida. The memorandum suggested that the issue could be used against Democratic Senator Bill Nelson, as he refused to cosponsor

Although Court-curbing during the first few years of the twenty-first century has been primarily a conservative undertaking, there are some reasons to expect that liberals are poised to begin an assault on the courts. First and foremost, the courts moved in a conservative direction during the Bush Administration. George Bush's nominations to the Supreme Court have drawn heated criticism from liberals, while recent public opinion polls show a growing proportion of the public thinks the Supreme Court is too conservative in its decisions. In addition, liberal interest groups concerned with the judiciary – such as People for the American Way and the American Constitution Society – have begun to mobilize activists and citizens to urge Congress to use its Court-curbing powers to rein in the Supreme Court.[47] Finally, recall from Figure 2.2(b) above that there appears to be a growing liberal contingent among Court-curbing during the early years of the twenty-first century. Taken together, these developments suggest that America may be on the verge of a period of liberal hostility toward the judiciary.

2.5 CONCLUSION

The data utilized here consist of a new dataset that identifies every Court-curbing bill introduced into Congress between 1877 and 2008. These data reveal a pattern of variation in the volume of Court-curbing legislation considered in Congress. From the data, I have identified seven distinct periods of "major" Court-curbing activity in Congress. In addition, I have identified variation in the types of Court-curbing legislation that have been considered since Reconstruction. These types are judicial review, composition, procedure, jurisdiction, remedy, and other. These types of measures take the form of both statutes and constitutional amendments. Because such a large proportion of Court-curbing activity does take the form of constitutional amendments, these findings further suggest that the Court-curbing data previously reported by Nagel (1965) and updated by Rosenberg (1992) missed an important element of the use of congressional

the legislation. Nelson won reelection the following year, when the Democrats took over Congress. One may speculate, moreover, that the Schiavo case did not have the intended consequence, as Republicans suffered considerably in the wake of their efforts.

[47] "Democrats Attack Gonzales, Supreme Court," *New York Times*, 15 July 2007; Robert Barnes and Jon Cohen, "Fewer See Balance in Court's Decisions," *Washington Post* 29 July 2007, A3; Edward Lazarus, "Under John Roberts, Court Re-rights Itself," *Washington Post* 1 July 2007, B1; Emily Bazelon, "Throw Restraint to the Wind," *Slate*, 25 July 2007, available online at http://www.slate.com.

power to limit the judiciary. In addition, these data reveal that the periods of most intense Court-curbing do not exactly coincide with the findings reported by Nagel and Rosenberg.

For each of the seven periods of Court-curbing identified here, I have provided some brief historical context for the major issues and political divides that motivated the period. During two of the periods, 1906–1911 and 1932–1937, the charge against the Court was led by liberals in Congress; during the two most recent periods, 1965–1969 and 1975–1982, the conservatives in Congress were the Court's opponents. Finally, during the 1953–1957 period of Court-curbing, anti-Court hostility came from both sides of the political spectrum and was marked by a decidedly moderate ideology. For this reason, although the volume of Court-curbing legislation was less than some of the other periods, the Court was particularly sensitive to congressional hostility.

In the remainder of this book, I provide a theory for understanding Court-curbing and its role in interbranch relations. In the next chapter, I develop a theory of Court–Congress interactions in which Court-curbing is modeled as a position-taking endeavor for members of Congress. The significance of that position-taking, however, is its potential to serve as an informative signal to the Court about public opinion. The model yields empirically testable predictions about both congressional and judicial decision making, and in subsequent chapters, I use the data described in this chapter to systematically test those predictions. For now, though, it is important to note the systematic nature of Court-curbing that has been surveyed here and the cursory evidence of a relationship between Court-curbing and judicial decision making.

3

Conditional Self-Restraint

Why do members of Congress introduce Court-curbing bills? Do the justices of the Supreme Court care about those bills? How might the introduction of Court-curbing bills affect the Court's decision making? What role does Court-curbing play in understanding the balance of power among the branches of government? The political history of Court-curbing in the preceding chapter provides a useful starting point for thinking about these questions. In this chapter, I develop a theoretical argument that provides a framework for answering these and other questions. The key to the theoretical argument advanced here is understanding the motivation driving Court-curbing.

In Chapter 1, I described the scholarly debate about the degree to which Congress' power to reverse Supreme Court decisions constrains judicial decision making. In doing so, I suggested that a more explicit connection may be drawn between the separation of powers and judicial legitimacy than has been previously recognized. That connection can be made by considering the connection between elected representatives in government – especially, members of Congress – and the public. This chapter develops a theory of Court–Congress interaction in which judicial legitimacy is explicitly incorporated. To develop the theory, I explore the importance of judicial legitimacy for judicial independence. Building on evidence from interviews with Supreme Court justices, members of Congress, former law clerks, and legislative staffers, I establish a set of assumptions about judicial legitimacy and its relationship to the Court's decision-making process. I then formalize an interaction between the Court and Congress that rests on those assumptions.

As noted in Chapter 1, previous scholarship on judicial–congressional relations has been marked by two dominant theories of judicial decision making: the attitudinal model and the separation-of-powers model. These two theories conflict as to whether the Supreme Court should have an incentive to deviate from its own preferred policy position in order to avoid statutory reversals by Congress.[1] The threat of statutory reversals, though, may not be the only, or even the primary, constraint on the Court. Instead, it has been argued that public support – or a lack thereof – can be a consequential limit on judicial power. From this perspective, the crucial question is whether the public will side with the Court in a confrontation between the judiciary and the elected branches of government. Because the Court does not have the power to enforce its own decisions, it relies on political will – an incentive for those with enforcement powers to comply with the Court's decision – to give effect to its rulings. However, if the public perceives the Court's decisions as illegitimate, then elected officials will be reluctant to enforce those decisions. For this reason, support from the public and the political branches is an important concern for courts because it is an instrumental means to their own institutional efficacy. In a canonical model, Georg Vanberg (2005) argues that when the public is likely to support the Court, the judiciary will dominate the legislature in the law-making process; when the public is unlikely to support the Court, legislature will dominate. Jeffrey Staton (2010) extends Vanberg's model to consider how a court might be able to increase the chances of public support for the judiciary by publicizing its decisions.[2]

In this and other research, a general theme has been that when the public believes a court is acting in the public's interest, the public will force elected officials to defer to the Court (Stephenson 2004; Carrubba 2009). With its power to hold elected officials accountable and remove them

[1] This line of reasoning has its foundations in Marks' (1989) unpublished dissertation. However, the breadth and depth of theoretical and empirical investigation of the effect of separation-of-powers mechanisms, and statutory overrides in particular, is represented by a lively and sustained body of research. Some notable examples include Ferejohn and Shipan (1990); Eskridge (1991*b*); Eskridge (1991*a*); Gely and Spiller (1992); Clinton (1994); Knight and Epstein (1996); Segal (1997); Segal and Spaeth (2002); and Harvey and Friedman (2006).

[2] In Vanberg's (2005) model, the relevant question is whether the issue decided by the court is "transparent," which means that the public can understand the issue decided and the Court's decision. Staton (2010) argues we can understand judicial efforts to publicize decisions in Mexico as attempts to maximize transparency.

from office, the public can punish those officials for failing to comply with a judicial decision perceived to be legitimate. A crucial feature of the previous research is that neither the Court nor the elected branches contending with the Court is sure whether the public will support the Court. In this chapter, I build directly from the insights of Vanberg, Staton, Stephenson, and Carrubba to ask how a court might learn about whether the public is likely to side with the Court over the elected branches. A key difference between their models and mine is that I assume that the elected branches of government – specifically Congress – have better information about public opinion than the Court. I then ask whether the Court can learn about public opinion by observing position-taking in Congress. Specifically, I ask whether Court-curbing legislation can be a meaningful indicator of public discontent with the Court and create an incentive for judicial self-restraint.[3]

This chapter proceeds as follows. First, I develop a set of assumptions about institutional preferences and beliefs. Relying on evidence from interviews with three Supreme Court justices, ten former clerks, two members of Congress, and seven congressional staffers, I describe a preference structure for judicial and legislative actors that departs from previous theories of judicial preferences employed by separation-of-powers models. Second, relying on these assumptions, I formalize an interaction between the Court and Congress. I present three formal models of judicial-legislative interactions and show that Court–Congress relations can be described as a process in which the legislature signals information to the Court about public support for the judiciary. The first is a simple decision-theoretic model, which serves to illustrate the mechanism driving judicial responsiveness to congressional hostility. I then present two game-theoretic models that isolate and demonstrate the causal mechanism driving judicial-legislative interactions in separation-of-powers interactions. From the formal analysis, I derive several theoretical expectations about the expected patterns of congressional attacks on the Court and judicial responses to those attacks. In the end, the theoretical results will show that, given a reasonable set of assumptions about institutional

---

[3] Many other scholars have noted Congress' capacity to use Court-curbing legislation to attack the Court and respond to divergent decisions (Nagel 1965; Handberg and Hill 1980; Rosenberg 1992; Cross and Nelson 2001). However, these studies have largely focused on whether periods of great tension between the Court and Congress are resolved in favor of Congress or the Court. I argue, by contrast, that Court-curbing serves primarily to signal the Court about its level of institutional legitimacy.

preferences, Court-curbing in Congress can create an incentive for judicial self-restraint.

3.1 BUILDING A THEORY OF COURT–CONGRESS INTERACTIONS

Throughout this book, I adopt a rational choice institutionalism approach to studying Court–Congress interactions. Essentially, rational choice institutionalism is the method of studying the effect of institutional structures on decision making by postulating goals for the relevant actors and assuming that the actors pursue those goals through a series of interactions among each other. The first step in developing a rational choice model of institutional interactions is to establish the goals of each actor. That is, we need to specify the *preferences* of both the Supreme Court and Congress. With these preferences in hand, we can then seek to develop a theory that explains judicial and congressional behavior as motivated by those preferences.

To develop a theory of judicial and congressional preferences, I look to both existing research and interviews I conducted with Supreme Court justices, members of Congress, former law clerks from the Supreme Court, and legislative staffers. These interview subjects provide unique and valuable insights into the interaction between the Court and Congress as perceived by the individuals actually involved in the interaction. Some interviews took place in person, and some took place by telephone; most interviews lasted around thirty minutes in length and focused directly on this research. As a condition to their access, however, I agreed to maintain the confidentiality of the interview subjects. Fuller details of the interview procedures are provided in Appendix A.

3.1.1 The Court

Courts, and the Supreme Court in particular, have preferences for legal policy – for example, case outcomes or doctrine – and for judicial legitimacy and prestige – for example, respect for the courts, law, or judicial power. In rational choice terms, the Court derives *utility* from seeing policy reflect its ideological preferences and from maintaining or accruing judicial legitimacy. Although students of the courts have long recognized these two goals in judicial behavior, only recently has the scholarship begun to develop theories in which these two goals can be either complementary or at times inapposite. In order to sustain the argument here, it must be the case that (a) the Court does in fact have an interest in preserving its legitimacy, and (b) it perceives Court-curbing as a signal about its diffuse support (legitimacy).[4] I take up each of these points in turn.

Judicial Preferences for Institutional Legitimacy

Research on judicial legitimacy and the Court's relationship to the public has demonstrated that the Court cares about how it is perceived by other legal and political actors and the public (Baum 2007; Gibson, Caldeira, and Spence 2003; Gibson and Caldeira 2003; Hausseger and Baum 1999). In particular, the Court cares a great deal about its institutional legitimacy, loyalty, and prestige.

The Court cares about its institutional legitimacy for at least two reasons. First, legitimacy is the key to the Court's institutional capacity – without a positive perception as a legitimate and prestigious institution, the Court cannot be an efficacious branch of the government. It is because of the Court's lack of direct institutional power that Alexander Hamilton famously referred to the judiciary as "the least dangerous" branch. A wealth of scholarship observes that because courts are incapable of enforcing their own decisions, they rely on the support of the political bodies to give weight to their order (Rosenberg 1991; McNollgast 1995). Indeed, reliance on the political bodies for enforcement of their decisions is an important weakness of the judiciary that has been highlighted during several important moments in history. (Recall the discussion of the conflict between the Court and Andrew Jackson discussed in Chapter 2.) Elected officials will be under much greater pressure to enforce a decision with which they disagree if the public believes in the Court's legitimacy than if the public regards the Court as illegitimate. Second, the Court may prefer to protect its legitimacy simply for the sake of having a positive public image. Evidence from interviews with legal elites suggests that the justices desire to be positively evaluated by their primary audiences (as well as the public), whereas research in the field of social psychology suggests that individuals generally desire to be positively evaluated.

MOTIVATIONS FOR INSTITUTIONAL CAPACITY. The first (and primary) reason why the Court benefits from institutional legitimacy is that institutional legitimacy provides the Court with a "reservoir of good will."

---

[4] Note I am not assuming it perceives Court-curbing as a credible signal; the theoretical analysis discussed later will ask under what conditions the Court will perceive these bills as credible signals.

This "reservoir" is a source from which the Court can draw to maintain public support in the face of unpopular decisions. Legitimacy theory suggests this source of support is necessary for a nonmajoritarian institution to make decisions that thwart the will of the majority.[5] The argument here is as follows. The Court has a peculiar enforcement problem; it has the power to make potentially consequential decisions in the name of the Constitution. These decisions often imply limits on the authority or discretion of the government – Congress and the president in particular. However, the Court itself has no enforcement powers; rather it relies on Congress and the president – those actors whose power its decisions may limit – to carry into effect those decisions. This feature of the judiciary is in fact an intentional component of the separation-of-powers system. Indeed, at least since Alexander Hamilton wrote in *Federalist #78* that the Court is "possessed of neither force nor will, but merely judgment," students of American government have recognized that the Court is limited in its efficacy by the necessity of public and political will to give its decisions force. That is, because they generally do not have their own powers of enforcement, courts must draw on the legitimacy of their decisions in order to incentivize political actors to enforce them (Carrubba 2003, 2009; Stephenson 2004; Vanberg 2005; Staton 2006; Staton and Vanberg 2008; Epstein and Knight 1998, 48). A key insight made most explicitly by Vanberg (2005) is that one way in which the Court can create those incentives is to ensure public support for the Court's decision – at least the Court's legitimacy and authority to make the decision. Because those actors with enforcement power are held accountable to the public and may be punished for disregarding a judicial decision regarded by the public as legitimate, ensuring public support for the Court's decisions is one method for holding the enforcers' proverbial feet to the fire.

The importance of public and political support for the Court's institutional integrity and efficacy has been well documented. Research shows that when popular support for the Court declines, the public will increasingly support efforts to politically sanction the Court by curtailing its formal powers. For example, Caldeira and Gibson (1992, 638) claim that individuals who have no diffuse support or institutional loyalty for the Court will be willing to "accept, make, or countenance major changes in the fundamental attributes of how the high bench functions or

---

[5] This argument has been made in a variety of contexts and from a variety of perspectives (see, e.g., Carrubba 2009; Stephenson 2004; Gibson, Caldeira, and Spence 2003; Gibson and Caldeira 2003; Tsebelis 2000; Alivizatos 1995).

fits into the U.S. constitutional system." However, when support for an institution's particular action at a given time – specific support – declines, the institution can retain its governing efficacy by drawing on its diffuse support (Easton 1965). Therefore, while one might expect that the Court may suffer if it loses specific support because it makes a bad decision, the Court may draw on its diffuse support to protect it from political backlash. The diffuse support allows the Court to say, "You may not like this decision today, but, on balance you do like the Court enough to make up for this one unfavorable decision." However, the capacity to make such a claim is predicated upon maintaining a sufficient balance of diffuse support. Indeed, one dominant definition of "policy legitimacy" is that a policy is legitimate if the public perceives that the decision-maker is acting on proper authority (Jaros and Roper 1980; Johnson and Canon 1984).[6]

Judges and legal elites openly acknowledge this link between public will and judicial efficacy. For example, the Judicial Conference of the United States reported in 1995 that "[i]f the federal courts alienate the public and lose its support and participation, they cannot carry out their appropriate role." Likewise, speaking at a conference on judicial independence, then-Chief Justice William Rehnquist (2003) noted that past preservation of the independence and integrity of the Court has been "dependent upon the public's respect for the judiciary" and that "[t]he degree to which that independence will be preserved will depend again in some measure on the public's respect for the judiciary."

What is more, speaking with judicial "insiders" reveals further evidence of the importance of judicial legitimacy. The following quotes are excerpts from interviews I conducted with Supreme Court justices and former law clerks.

> *Justice B*: Certainly, in some of the most controversial areas, [public legitimacy] is in our minds. It is important that we act within the proper institutional constraints.

---

[6] This is what Adamany (1973) refers to as "symbolic legitimacy." Mondak (1994) draws a distinction between two different ways in which the Supreme Court's institutional legitimacy may influence the legitimacy of a policy outcome. First, he suggests that the Supreme Court's institutional legitimacy may directly affect the legitimacy of a policy, a process he dubs "symbolic legitimation." Second, he argues that the Supreme Court's institutional legitimacy may influence policy by causing the public to be more likely to agree with a policy and therefore be more willing to accept the policy as legitimate, a process he dubs "persuasive legitimation." In this way, the court's institutional legitimacy affects the legitimacy of its policies both directly and indirectly. Here, I do not draw this distinction but simply argue that the Supreme Court's legitimacy leads affects its ability to see its policy decisions carried into effect.

Justice C: It is important that the Court have institutional prestige in order to make decisions that the public may not like but will accept as legitimate.

Clerk 5: They are concerned with how they are perceived by the public. The justices are aware that they have no purse and no sword. They are very careful not to screw it up; they are very aware of how the public views the Court... The public is willing to accept decisions that are overwhelmingly unpopular because of faith in the Court.

Clerk 2: There is also a sense that the Court understands that the only way the Court's decrees will be carried out is that there is a sense of legitimacy. They know that they don't have an army or any purse – well, only a small purse.

Clerk 3: It is important that your output is treated with a presumption of credibility; it may be attacked, but it is important that your decisions have a presumption of credibility.

In other words, public confidence in the Supreme Court is much like a checking account – public confidence in the Court represents the account's balance, and unpopular decisions represent debits against that balance. If too many debits are made, then the account will be overdrawn, and there will be no public support for the Court and no capacity for making further unpopular decisions. One strategy for the Court to protect its institutional legitimacy and diffuse support, then, is to avoid straying too far from majority will. This incentive may induce the Court to alter its decision in ways contemplated by standard separation-of-powers models or in other, more nuanced ways.[7] The point is made perhaps most succinctly by Kevin McGuire and James Stimson (2004, 1019), who note

> [A] Court that cares about its perceived legitimacy must rationally antic-ipate whether its preferred outcomes will be respected and faithfully followed by relevant publics. Consequently, a Court that strays too far from the broad boundaries imposed by public mood risks having its decisions rejected. Naturally, in individual cases, the justices can and do buck the trends of public sentiment. In the aggregate, however, popular opinion should still shape the broad contours of judicial policymaking.

---

[7] Examples of sophisticated judicial decision making driven by a concern for judicial legiti-macy can be found in a variety of recent formal-theoretic work. Stephenson (2004) shows that in a separation-of-powers system, public support for the judiciary can induce elected officials to cede power to the courts. Vanberg (2005) similarly shows that in Germany, diffuse support for the high court can create an incentive for the legislature to not chal-lenge a divergent judicial decision. Carrubba (2009) similarly shows that by remaining within the bounds of its diffuse support, courts in federal systems can incrementally grow their power and, as a consequence, even expand the bounds of that diffuse support.

NONINSTRUMENTAL MOTIVATIONS. Beyond protecting institutional legitimacy as a means to preserving its own power, the Court also has an interest in having a positive image among its audiences. For example, Baum (2007) argues that judges' interest in being positively perceived by their primary audiences is an integral component of the judicial process that has been long overlooked by political scientists. To be sure, social psychologists have developed concepts such as *self-presentation* and *impression management*, which contend that individuals prefer to be positively evaluated, especially among their peers (Goffman 1959; Tetlock and Manstead 1985; Leary 1996; Schlencker and Pontari 2000; Leary 2007).

The justices are not unlike other people; they are clearly aware of how they are perceived by legal professionals as well as the public. One former clerk observed, "I think they do care about it [public approval]. That's a reason for the tradition and ceremony of the Court... To some degree it affects their decision-making; they say that. They are careful not to reach too far," to which she added, "these are political figures; I mean they are judicial figures, but they are public figures; like all, they are aware."[8] Another former clerk observed, "The Court does think about that issue, its public image... They take some pride and concern with their image among lawyers and legal academics and court watchers and that they maintain a reputation, both through them [the lawyers and academics and court watchers] and with the public at large."[9]

Consider also these observations from Supreme Court justices and former clerks in response to the question, "To what extent, if at all, does the Court worry about maintaining a positive image and confidence among the public and legal professionals?"

> *Clerk 6*: My sense is that the Court pays a great deal of attention to that, that they are very careful of not getting too far out ahead of the public in enforcing the Constitution.

> *Justice C*: We are always worried about [losing public support]; nobody wants to bring the Court into disrepute.

> *Clerk 2*: Yeah, I think so. Part of it is human nature – people want to be respected.

> *Justice A*: We do worry about what the public thinks at some level, yes.

[8] Personal interview with "Clerk 1."
[9] Personal interview with "Clerk 7."

> *Clerk 1*: Yes. I don't think they perceive any great public disenchant-
> ment, but there is always that risk ... They do take into account public
> views of the court and how they behave.

We see, then, that independent of an instrumental incentive to protect
its legitimacy, the Court may also have an incentive to foster a positive
image of the Court for noninstrumental reasons.

Judicial Perceptions about Court-Curbing

If the justices care about the Court's legitimacy and public prestige –
for either instrumental or noninstrumental reasons – how do they track
trends in that support? One way in which they might do so is to pay
attention to the political climate and gauge the judiciary's standing with
the public. Court-curbing is one source of elite-level behavior that may
serve as an informative signal to the Court about its "reservoir of good
will." I do not assume that the justices believe that Court-curbing is a
credible signal about its public support. Rather, in the theoretical analysis
below, I ask under what conditions Court-curbing bills can be a credible
signal of public discontent with the Court? The evidence does suggest, at
the least, that the justices of the Supreme Court do believe that Court-
curbing is driven by public discontent with the Court. In particular, the
justices perceive Court-curbing as serving three purposes. Court-curbing
may sometimes be an elite-level reaction to public opinion. Other times,
Court-curbing may be an effort by political elites to influence public
opinion by attacking the Court. Finally, Court-curbing may sometimes
be in fact a credible threat by Congress to curtail the Court's institutional
powers.

COURT-CURBING AS A REFLECTION OF PUBLIC OPINION. In the justices' view, one interpretation of Court-curbing is that it may be a reflection of waning public confidence in the judiciary. For example, "Justice
C" commented, "The Court is pretty good at knowing how far it can
go ... Congress is better than we are, especially the House. They really
have their finger on the pulse of the public." To the extent that the
Court believes that Court-curbing reflects public disenchantment with the
institution, the Court will believe that Court-curbing indicates popular
support for limiting or removing judicial power. Research demonstrates
that public approval of the Court is highly contingent upon ideological congruence with the Court's decisions.[10] Considering the European

---

[10] A long tradition of research by political scientists and legal academics has examined
the correlation between public approval of courts and congruence between public

Court of Justice, Caldeira and Gibson (1995, 358–9) note "a strong connection between approval or disapproval of decisions and diffuse support for the Court; those who, on balance, favor the Court's decisions
will, over time, accord it high levels of diffuse support," reflecting one
clerk's assessment that congressional attacks on the Court are "harm-
ful in the sense that [they] usually [represent] disenchantment with some
particular decision . . . inevitably, that is a possible threat to the Court's
independence."[11] Indeed, Grosskopf and Mondak (1998, 650) note that
reminding people of unpopular decisions makes them less likely to state
that they have "confidence" in the Supreme Court, whereas Caldeira and
Gibson (1992, 638) note that individuals who have no diffuse support
or institutional loyalty for the Court will be willing to "accept, make, or
countenance major changes in the fundamental attributes of how the high
bench functions or fits into the U.S. constitutional system." Moreover, to
the extent that Court decisions affect people in particular locations, the
local media tends to cover those decisions carefully, and public reaction
to the decisions affects support for the Court (Hoekstra 2003). To the
extent the public becomes disenchanted with the Court, one of the few –
if not the most natural and efficient – recourses the public has is to contact
representatives in Congress. As we will see below, members of Congress
often treat these instances as opportunities to position-take on the Court
by introducing Court-curbing bills, even if they do so without the intent
of pursuing the legislation to enactment.

Interviews with congressional staffers strongly corroborate the claim
that Court-curbing is often a response to pressure from constituents and
represents the district's response to the judiciary. For example, one staffer
observed, "There is some constituency pressure. When the courts make a
bad decision, we get constituents calling telling us to do something about
these activist judges,"[12] whereas another observed that "constituents
called up a lot and asked what kind of atheist country do we live in,"[13]
after the Ninth Circuit Court of Appeals declared the Pledge of Allegiance
unconstitutional. Thus, to the extent that Court-curbing reflects unfavorable public opinion toward the courts and that unfavorable opinion

---

policy preferences and judicial decisions. Notable examples include Durr, Martin, and
Wolbrecht (2000); Hoekstra (2000); Grosskopf and Mondak (1998); Caldeira (1986);
Caldeira and Gibson (1992); Tanenhaus and Murphy (1981); Casey (1976); Murphy
(1964); Dolbeare and Hammond (1968).

[11] Personal interview with "Clerk 1."
[12] Personal interview with "Staffer 1."
[13] Personal interview with "Staffer 2."

reflects popular support for limiting or removing judicial power, Court-curbing indicates an erosion of judicial legitimacy.

COURT-CURBING AS A DETERMINANT OF PUBLIC OPINION. Another view the justices sometimes have is that Court-curbing can potentially affect judicial legitimacy. These legislative proposals may influence public opinion and generate popular support for limiting or removing judicial power. In particular, congressional attacks on the Court *politicize the Court in a way that the justices believe undermines the Court's integrity and legitimacy.* One former law clerk commented that congressional hostility "may undermine the Court in two ways: It could affect the Court by making the Court seem out of line with general preferences; the second way is that besides focusing attention on a particular issue, it also associates the Court in people's minds with rough and tumble politics. Because they see the legislature legislating on the Court, it makes the Court seem political and susceptible to all of the criticism that goes on with respect to elected politicians."[14]

Similarly, testifying before the American Bar Association's Commission on Separation of Powers and Judicial Independence, United States District Judge Joseph H. Rodriguez of the District of New Jersey commented, "[w]hile principled criticism of judges and judicial decisions may serve a constructive purpose, partisan attacks on judges are a threat to judicial independence," and observed, "public denunciations and statements of lack of confidence in the judiciary can have unintended consequences for the functioning of our society. Such statements may inevitably undermine public confidence that the exercise of judicial power is being applied properly and objectively."[15] In its final report, that committee similarly noted that, "[w]hen a judicial decision is criticized, . . . the author of that decision is often prohibited by the rules of judicial ethics from entering the debate. As a consequence, the exchange of ideas and information on the case in question is less than open, which increases the risk that misinformation . . . will emerge, to the ultimate detriment of public confidence in the judiciary" (Commission on Separation of Powers and Judicial Independence 1997, 50).

Indeed, evidence from interviews with Supreme Court justices and former clerks clearly suggests that the Court believes that Court-curbing

---

[14] Personal interview with "Clerk 4."

[15] United States District Judge Joseph H. Rodriguez, Testimony Before the American Bar Associations Committee on Separation of Powers and Judicial Independence, February 21, 1997.

activity leads to lower public opinion about the Court and as a consequence delegitimizes the Court. During interviews, I asked, "Do you think that Court-curbing affects public perceptions about the Court?" Most of my interviewees responded affirmatively.

Justice A: People pay attention to what members [of Congress] say.

Justice B: For the people who do pay attention, if they are inclined to agree with the criticism, then it probably fortifies their dislike for the Court... Certainly, members of the bar and people who pay attention to the Court closely follow this.

Justice C: I find it curious that those who bemoan the Court at the same time push the Court into political issues... Once the public ceases to believe that the Court is not a political institution, they will no longer support the Court.

Clerk 2: I think it has got to have an effect. We all say we tune this stuff out, but we don't. It's just like advertising; we say we don't listen to advertising, but we do. The drum beat is powerful....The reason why the Court can decide a case like *Brown*, a decision that Congress could not have made at the time, is people still believe that the law has some independent legitimacy. Now, this is being undermined dramatically by attacks on the Court.

Clerk 6: I think there is a sense that if the Congress over responds it would be bad for the system... Another thing is a broad assault on judicial independence... I think that Court-curbing legislation is perceived as part of a broader phenomenon and the justices are really finding that quite troubling.

Clerk 1: Well, it is not totally inconsequential. It takes a lot to get through to the public; but to the extent the public is aware of it, it injects the Court into the political process; it makes it more subject to those kinds of attitudes.

Clerk 3: There is definitely a concern about the institutional response toward the Court.

Clerk 5: I think yes, which is why you saw [Justice] Sandra Day O'Connor speak out against it. When I say yes, there is not a unitary body. [Chief Justice] Rehnquist did not care when people attacked him personally. [Justice] Sandra Day O'Connor thought this was a threat to the institution.

Clerk 7: I do think it's dangerous, because it [political attacks on the Court] chips away at the legitimacy of the court. Congress and politicians have much greater access and savvyness with the media; politicians can very often make it appear that all [the justices] care about is the result and not the rationale or reasoning behind it.

Finally, in *Republican Party of Minnesota v. White*,[16] an important case concerning free speech and candidates for elected judicial offices, the Supreme Court acknowledged that political statements by judges can have a deleterious effect on judicial legitimacy and public confidence in the judiciary. In this vein, Court-curbing – to the extent that it is a politicization of the Court – runs the risk of undermining public confidence in the Court. Indeed, recent research suggests that attack ads focused on state judicial candidates lead to a diminution of judicial legitimacy (Gibson 2008). Court-curbing, which can be considered the federal analogue of judicial campaign attack ads, may therefore be expected to have a similar effect on the Supreme Court.

This evidence provides the final, crucial piece of the theory of judicial preferences that I construct here. As "Clerk 2" notes, "Now, [public support for the Court] is being undermined dramatically by all of the attacks on the court. But there is still a level of resiliency of the law among the public."[17] Perhaps more important, the evidence from both interviews with judicial elites and from public statements by legal professionals suggests that damage to public confidence in the Court inhibits its capacity to decide cases independent of political pressure. This is the very definition of judicial independence offered in Chapter 1.

COURT-CURBING AS AN INSTITUTIONAL THREAT. Beyond its function as an intermediary between the public and the Court, a final interpretation the justices may have of Court-curbing bills is that they pose a risk of actually affecting the Court's fundamental institutional powers. This is a function of Court-curbing on which I do not focus here but is nevertheless important to acknowledge. "Justice C" commented, for example, that "if the Court is perceived as a political institution, the constitutional checks will work to make the decisions look like the decisions that the public and majority want."

As I described in Chapter 2, Court-curbing proposals generally aim to accomplish broad, substantive changes to the balance of power among governing institutions by shifting power away from the judiciary in favor of Congress, the executive, or the states. Although this legislation is rarely enacted, that fact does not in and of itself demonstrate that Court-curbing cannot achieve fundamental changes in the Court's power.

[16] 536 U.S. 765 (2002).
[17] Personal interview with "Clerk 2."

For example, the Military Commissions Act of 2006, which created a system by which detainees in the Guantánamo Bay military camp are to be tried removes from the federal courts jurisdiction over habeas corpus claims by those detainees. This feature of the legislation is a clear response to the Supreme Court's decision in *Rasul v. Bush* and represents a typical example of the use of Court-curbing legislation to directly undermine judicial power. More important, the Military Commissions Act significantly alters the Court's power in these disputes and is a consequential shift of power away from the judiciary toward the executive. Thus, Court-curbing undermines judicial legitimacy and power because it poses the risk of directly undermining the Court's institutional capacity. However, Court-curbing can undermine judicial power in other, indirect ways.

JUDICIAL AWARENESS OF COURT-CURBING. Implicit in the assumption that the Court perceives Court-curbing as a signal about its standing with the public is an additional assumption that the Court is aware of Court-curbing. For one might reasonably expect that the Court is sufficiently insulated that it does not pay attention to political attacks, especially Court-curbing attacks that rarely gain sufficiently broad support to pose any risk of enactment.

However, the Court is well aware of Court-curbing activity in Congress. In fact, precisely because the justices are concerned about their legitimacy and recognize that Court-curbing is an indicator of public discontent with the institution, they do remain aware of legislative hostility toward the Court. For example, in a speech delivered at the University of Nebraska College of Law, Justice Ruth Bader Ginsburg (2006) spoke about recent congressional attacks on the Court, citing several recent Court-curbing bills considered by Congress. Justice Ginsburg (2006, 7) noted that "in some political circles, it is fashionable to criticize and even threaten federal judges who decide cases without regard to what the 'home crowd' wants" and other justices have recently made similar public comments (O'Connor 2006*b*, *a*; Breyer 2006; Roberts 2006).

In addition, many of the papers of former justices contain memoranda circulated to the Conference[18] summarizing legislation before Congress concerned with the Court, indicating that justices during previous eras similarly paid attention to legislative and political attacks on the Court.

---

[18] The "Conference" refers to the nine justices sitting on the Court at any given time. A memorandum addressed to all of the justices is generally addressed to the "Conference."

For example, on February 11, 1975, Chief Justice Burger circulated to the Conference a memorandum, which read in part,

> I read that some Senator had introduced a Bill, along the lines of one introduced by Senator Tydings six or seven years ago, to "disqualify" judges short of impeachment.
>
> I have secured copies so as to keep you advised. If so vigorous an advocate as Senator Tydings could not gain support, it may be that this proposal will not attract support. However, I venture no predictions in light of the first weeks' activities in the present Congress.
>
> I have not read the bill but will do so before the next Conference and if anyone is so disposed we can discuss it.[19]

This memorandum, which is shown in Figure 3.1, demonstrates several points central to my argument. First, the memorandum demonstrates that the justices are aware of (and discuss) Court-curbing proposals in Congress. Second, it demonstrates that the justices remember Court-curbing bills and anti-Court movements in Congress. Third, the memorandum suggests that the justices worry about Court-curbing movements "attracting support" and becoming popular political *causes célèbres*. Of course, it is possible that the justices were worried about the bill being enacted. However, it is fairly obvious that the bill, if enacted, would not pass constitutional muster. The bill in question sought to create a council on judicial tenure that would allow judges to be removed from the bench without being impeached. The Constitution clearly prescribes impeachment as the only mechanism for removing a judge. Thus, although the justices may have been worried the legislation would be enacted, it is doubtful they were worried that the enactment itself would lead to a diminution of their authority. Rather, it seems more likely they were worried about what increasing congressional support for such legislation would imply for their standing with the public.

Moreover, in personal interviews with justices and former clerks, Court insiders have explicitly acknowledged that the Court is aware of congressional hostility. "Clerk 2" observed that "Burger was very concerned about the Court's legitimacy. I think he appreciated the way in which politicians were tearing down the Court," while "Clerk 5" commented,

---

[19] Memo from Chief Justice Burger to The Conference, dated February 11, 1975, Papers of Harry A. Blackmun, Library of Congress, Box 1375, Folder 6, Congressional Matters, 1970–1978.

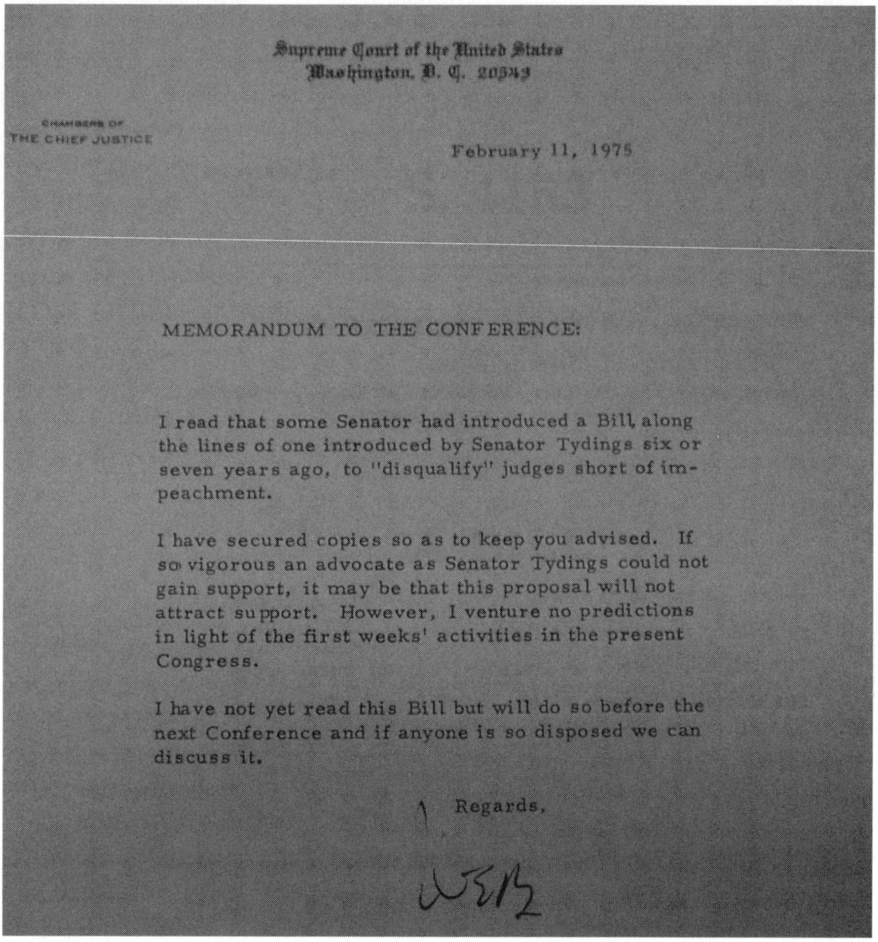

FIGURE 3.1. *Memorandum from Chief Justice Burger to the Conference regarding a Court-curbing bill that had recently been introduced.* Source: Papers of Harry A. Blackmun, Library of Congress, Box 1375, Folder 6, Congressional Matters, 1970–1978.

"Oh yeah, they are clearly aware of it and they clearly talk about it inside of the Court. There are, though, different views. There are views that they should ignore it; there are views that they should deal with it and try to prevent it. Harry Blackmun read all of the hate mail that came to him. There are others who have screeners who remove all non-procedural mail." Consider the following excerpts from personal interviews during which I asked justices and former clerks about the Court's awareness of specific legislative responses to Court decisions and Court-curbing proposals:

Justice B: We read the newspapers and see what is being said – probably more than most people do.

Clerk 8: Now that [Court-curbing legislation], the Court does pay attention to!

Clerk 1: Yes, absolutely. These are political figures; I mean they are judicial figures, but they are public figures; like all, they are aware.

Clerk 6: My judgment would be that they are very aware of it; they pay a great deal of attention to this, and they are aware of other political criticism. You know, they live in Washington, DC, and read the *Washington Post*; it's all in there.

Clerk 4: They are aware of it, certainly. For example, the justices are always aware of the March for Life on the anniversary of *Roe*. It was always a reminder on January 22nd to the justices that there was this lively popular and legislative concern with one of their decisions.

Clerk 2: When I was there I think it was clear that justices were aware of what was going on in the outside world. When there is a big demonstration on the outside steps and you could not get to your office – I mean they are aware of this. I also think it is part of their understanding to get rid of it. But, they are keenly aware of their own perception and legitimacy.

Clerk 10: Yes, they know; they all know. Some of the justices have spoken out. It would be hard for them to not know about it . . . But they certainly know when people are mad at them. My term, they were aware of it.

Finally, it is noteworthy that some scholarship has also demonstrated that the Court is aware of congressional criticism of its decisions and may seek to avoid that criticism because the cumulative effects of such attacks may create an incentive for sophisticated decision making by the Court (Hausseger and Baum 1999; Cross and Nelson 2001; Rogers 2001). This research, however, has focused precisely on elite-level institutional threats and not on the role of those threats as signals about public opinion and judicial legitimacy.

Summary

We may summarize the above argument as follows. The justices do in fact care a great deal about the public image and *they believe that congressional attacks are an indicator of declining support for the Court.* That the Court has an interest in protecting its legitimacy and may do so when faced with an institutional confrontation is not a new concept among scholars of courts, and previous research has demonstrated that expectations about public support for the Court in a confrontation with the elected branches is an integral part of a court's decision to exercise self-restraint (Stephenson 2004; Vanberg 2005; Staton 2010; Caldeira 1987; Lasser 1988). For these scholars, judicial legitimacy is central, if not the be-all-and-end-all, of judicial power. Thus, in order to overcome its peculiar enforcement problem, the Court must protect its institutional legitimacy.

Court-curbing can serve several purposes. One function it serves is to signal waning public support for the Court; another function may be to influence public support for the Court by politicizing the judiciary. Further, Court-curbing may simply be a real institutional threat to curtail judicial power. In any case, Court-curbing represents a movement by the Court away from its apolitical role in which it benefits from diffuse public support and institutional legitimacy to another role in which it is politicized and lacking the authority to make decisions by which the public will be willing to bind itself.

3.1.2 Congress

We now turn from the Court to Congress' preferences and goals. Legislators pursue two broad goals. First, they seek to see law reflect their preferred policies as closely as possible. Second, they seek to maintain their base of political support. Indeed, the significance of maintaining political and electoral support is a feature of congressional behavior that has long been recognized by political scientists.[20] In order to maintain their base of

---

[20] In perhaps the most widely cited analysis of congressional motivation, Mayhew (1974) argues that securing reelection is an overriding concern for legislators, as keeping their jobs is essential for pursuing any other goal. Mayhew argues that in order to pursue their electoral goals, members of Congress engage in three types of activities: position-taking, advertising, and credit claiming. Position-taking refers to taking a public stance on a particular policy issue; advertising refers to campaigning to make one's name more recognizable and spreading information about a legislator's activities; credit-claiming refers to publicly arguing that a legislator is personally responsible for some accomplishment.

political support, one activity legislators undertake is "position-taking." Although there are varying definitions of position-taking in the literature, I adopt a specific definition here. By position-taking, I specifically refer to a public action by a legislator designed to reflect constituent opinion. Legislators' constituents care about different issues at different times, and they may therefore have varying interests with respect to how much effort to spend attacking the Court. Thus, as distinct from a legislator's preference to see particular policies enacted, she may also have an interest in publicly taking a position on the Court – perhaps by introducing a Court-curbing bill – not with the intention of enacting that bill but simply in order to claim credit just for having taken some public action.

Ideological Policy Preferences

Legislators have preferences over policy outcomes. In particular, legislative policy preferences have two components – one, a substantive, ideological component; the other, an institutional, forward-looking component. That is, legislators care about specific policy outcomes, such as whether a given law is upheld or struck down. That legislators care about individual policies and case outcomes is widely accepted and represents the foundation of almost all political science scholarship on legislative behavior, at least since Fenno's (1973) seminal work on legislative motivations. More conservative members prefer more conservative policies, and more liberal members prefer more liberal policies. Indeed, a wealth of scholarship demonstrates that legislators divide along ideological grounds when they cast their votes and that a single ideological dimension can explain most of the variation in legislators' behavior (e.g., Poole and Rosenthal 1997).

Moreover, legislators may also care about the balance of power among the political institutions, the independence of the judiciary, and the separation of powers (Whittington 2005, 2007; Landes and Posner 1975; Rogers 2001). A legislative preference for judicial independence attenuates the cost associated with an adverse policy outcome, and such preferences are completely compatible with the argument advanced below. It is important to keep in mind, though, that policy divergence between the Court and Congress may not be simply a matter of ideological divergence but may include institutional preferences that can attenuate ideological disagreements.

Position-Taking

Because the public can hold legislators accountable for misrepresenting their preferences (Canes-Wrone, Brady, and Cogan 2002), members of

Congress will generally have an interest in correctly position-taking in line with public opinion, which is a central activity in the pursuit of reelection (Mayhew 1974). A primary way in which legislators position-take is to place their opinions on key issues on the record. Scholars have long studied the connection between constituent preferences and legislators' voting,[21] but there are ways in which members of Congress position-take other than their voting. Bill sponsorship in particular is a very efficient and visible way of position-taking.[22] Engaging in Court-curbing and other political attacks on the Court can be considered a position-taking endeavor for several reasons. Chief among these is that Court-curbing is an effective way to help build support from an issue constituency. Interest groups such as Court Watch, the American Constitutional Society, Eagle Forum, Judicial Watch, the Traditional Values Coalition, and People for the American Way closely monitor legislative activity concerning the Courts and draw their supporters' attention to legislators' actions and positions. Indeed, major Supreme Court decisions have frequently occupied central positions in presidential campaigns (Stephenson 1999). What is more, the sheer number of Court-curbing proposals introduced in Congress with great regularity but that never earn so much as a committee hearing is consistent with the claims that constituent pressure is a primary determinant of these attacks on the judiciary.[23]

---

[21] See, for example, Miller and Stokes (1963); Fiorina (1974); Achen (1977, 1978); Erikson (1978); Bartels (1991); Ansolabehere, Snyder, and Stewart (2001); Canes-Wrone, Brady, and Cogan (2002); Highton and Rocca (2005).

[22] It is worth noting here that the type of position-taking to which I refer throughout this book has a particular meaning that departs in an important way from modal interpretations of the term. Scholars often use position-taking to refer to activities by members of Congress that have no direct policy consequences. When I refer to position-taking here, I specifically mean to invoke the image of a member of Congress taking a public stance on an issue. The type of position-taking with which I am concerned here is the introduction of Court-curbing bills that their sponsors doubt will ever even receive a committee hearing, let alone be enacted. Nevertheless, members of Congress can claim credit for having introduced these bills. It is in this sense that sponsoring Court-curbing is a form of position-taking. In this book, however, I focus on an additional function served by position-taking – the possibility that position-taking can serve as an informative signal to other elites about public opinion.

[23] A critical point here is that legislators may be able to "credit claim" for bills that they introduce, even though those bills never make any progress legislatively. Ever since Fenno (1978, 168) observed that "Members of Congress run for Congress by running against Congress," it has been recognized that responsibility for legislative failures can be blamed on the complexities of congressional decision making, allowing members to blame the institution for failures while taking credit for their individual initiative. Indeed, this dynamic must explain in part why the public often holds higher views of

In general, legislators see Court-curbing as a primarily position-taking enterprise that is an important part of garnering support from a base constituency; indeed, position-taking consumes a large proportion of most legislators' time.[24] Considerable evidence suggests that congressional attacks on and responses to Court decisions are primarily driven by constituent interests (Clark and McGuire 1996). For example, one congressional staffer for a member who does not represent a state within the Ninth Circuit commented, "When the courts make a bad decision, we get constituents calling telling us to do something about these activist federal judges... After a decision from the Ninth Circuit declaring the Pledge of Allegiance unconstitutional, we get a lot of calls, telling us to rein in these activist judges."[25] Indeed, several interview subjects indicated that they believe Court-curbing is a position-taking endeavor:

> *Congressman B*: I have sponsored legislation to... prohibit the Supreme Court from reviewing state court decisions about obscenity... Obscenity is very important to my constituents... It is not so much that there is anger with the courts [among legislators]; it is a concern by their constituents that they have to meet. If I ask Congressman X if he wants to cosponsor a bill, he may not care, but he may have to do it just to make his constituents happy. It may not matter so much what Congressman X's view is, as that his constituents don't like pornography.

> *Staffer 5*: Clearly some members support it who know [it will never be enacted]. There is genuine hostility toward the Court when it does something unpopular... It is not terribly productive. Proposals that were at one time dismissed with a chuckle became leadership issues for the Republicans.

> *Congressman A*: Judges look at these things [Court-curbing bills] and say, "Oh, that's nice," and then they ignore them... They think they can do whatever they want and are not accountable to anyone... but, these attacks get a lot of attention.

> *Staffer 2*: These issues and bills rally the base every year; they also create an issue and a constituency.

> *Clerk 3*: Some actors use attacks primarily as instrumental means to a particular end, such as shoring up your political base... so, when you

their representatives than they do of Congress as an institution (Parker and Davidson 1979).
[24] Fiorina (1974, 1977); Mayhew (1974); Fenno (1978); Cain, Ferejohn, and Fiorina (1987); Snyder and Ting (2005).
[25] Personal interview with "Staffer 1."

protest outside of the Court, your audience is the public, to shore up public support, the legislature is your audience; maybe the Court, but you really don't expect that.

Thus, we see that Court-curbing can be used to position-take and respond to constituent pressure as well as to position-take to *rally* constituents and *create* an electoral benefit. What is more, interest and advocacy groups can create position-taking incentives for legislators. One former law clerk noted that interest group propaganda can be very effective in drawing attention to the Supreme Court as a political issue.[26] Such a legislative goal complements the alternative interpretation of Court-curbing – as a means to undermine public support for the Court – outlined above.

To illustrate, consider the interest group Court Watch, which is a subdivision of the conservative interest group Eagle Forum, founded in 1972 by the conservative activist Phyllis Schlafly. Court Watch maintains an extensive Web site with statistics on Supreme Court decisions and the composition of the federal judiciary[27] in a section called "Court College." What is more, the Court Watch Web site provides extensive information on Court-curbing legislation in Congress, advocates support for the legislation, and provides information on becoming an activist in favor of "judicial reform."[28]

On their Web pages, these groups keep track of Court-curbing bills and report how individual legislators vote on each of them. In July 2006, Court Watch reported that the House had passed H.R. 2389, a bill that sought to remove federal court jurisdiction over the Pledge of Allegiance. Though the bill never emerged from the Senate Judiciary Committee, Court Watch referred to this as a "double victory," because the same bill had passed the House during the previous Congress.

Groups like Court Watch, the Traditional Values Coalition, People for the American Way, and the American Constitution Society exemplify the types of organizations that create position-taking benefits for legislators. They also help explain why some legislators may sponsor Court-curbing

[26] Personal interview with "Clerk 10."

[27] For example, the Web site tracks the proportion of decisions decided by 5-4 votes and the proportion of Democratic v. Republican appointees.

[28] The Web site also urges its supporters to pray for federal officials and judges, noting "For fifty years, federal judges have been devastating the American constitutional system." (http://www.eagleforum.org/court_watch/people.shtml; accessed February 20, 2007). The Web site even provides sample prayers for individuals to say. On the Web page for the parent organization, Eagle Forum, Schlafly writes a regular column on issues pertaining to the group's interests. In January 2006, Schlafly wrote an extensive column on congressional power to alter Supreme Court jurisdiction.

bills that have little chance of being enacted and why yet others feel compelled to bring them up for a vote on the floor. Advocacy groups such as Eagle Forum, focusing on legislative remedies to their causes, attract attention to the Court and create the conditions under which members of Congress are likely to spend resources position-taking.

When the judiciary is very politically salient, then attacking the Court (either by sponsoring a bill or just voting for one) should generate a large and positive electoral benefit for legislators. However, when the judiciary is less politically salient, then the magnitude of that electoral benefit should be smaller. If the public cares less about the courts than another political issue, then the electoral fortunes visited upon a legislator from taking a position on the Supreme Court will be less than if she were to focus her attention on the more salient issue. Thus, depending upon the degree of ideological divergence between the Court and Congress and the Court's salience as an electoral issue, Congress may face a trade-off between pursuing policy goals and securing electoral benefits.

3.1.3 Two Objections

Before proceeding to consider the empirical implications of the theoretical argument and deriving testable hypotheses, I first consider two possible objections to the argument I have advanced thus far. First, it has been argued that judicial legitimacy is high, stable, and invulnerable. If so, might the theoretical model's proposition that institutional legitimacy changes be untenable? To be sure, the foundational scholarship on judicial legitimacy posited that legitimacy – or, diffuse support or institutional loyalty – are values learned by children while young and remain stable over time (Caldeira and Gibson 1992). However, more recently, research has demonstrated that judicial legitimacy is in fact vulnerable and specifically can be undermined by sustained objectionable decision making.[29] Indeed, these developments have led the foremost defenders of

---

[29] This research comes in a variety of flavors. From a primarily empirical standpoint, research has demonstrated that displeasing decisions from the Court can undermine diffuse support – institutional legitimacy – for the Court (Grosskopf and Mondak 1998; Gibson, Caldeira, and Spence 2003; Hoekstra 2003). From a primarily theoretical perspective, research has argued, as I do here, that institutional legitimacy is simply a condition of public fidelity to the Court that is earned through observing positive judicial outcomes and can be undermined by sustained decision making that cuts against popular wishes. Perhaps the most significant work in this vein is Carrubba (2009). Other recent theories of judicial decision making that incorporate the need for public support for judicial efficacy adopt (at least implicitly) a similar view of judicial legitimacy

the view that judicial legitimacy is stable and invulnerable to concede that "[t]he understanding that public attitudes toward institutional legitimacy are highly resistant to change . . . seems no longer tenable" (Gibson and Caldeira 2009, 4). Thus, we are left to believe that judicial legitimacy may, at least theoretically, be variable. Whether it has in fact changed much and can explain Court-curbing in Congress remains an open empirical question to be explored in Chapter 4.

Second, one may object that Court-curbing is not necessarily a reflection of waning diffuse support for the Court. Alternatively, Court-curbing may be either a knee-jerk reaction to unpopular Court decisions (signaling a lack of specific support for the Court's recent decisions) or an indicator of a more legislatively active Congress (indicating a greater risk of Court-curbing enactment). These objections, although reasonable, do not undermine the argument here, and the empirical analyses presented in Chapters 4 through 6 directly address these alternative accounts. First, it may very well be the case that Court-curbing represents a lack of specific support for the Court's decisions. However, given the model of judicial legitimacy I have posited – one in which institutional legitimacy is predicated on minimal instances of lacking specific support – such institutional signals would serve the same purpose of communicating to the Court that its diffuse support is in jeopardy. Second, although it is possible that the Court responds to Court-curbing not because of its informative value concerning diffuse support but instead because it signals legislative hostility and activism, it is unlikely. To be sure, the theoretical model developed here does not allow for Court-curbing enactment to take place and therefore cannot make any discriminating predictions about the effect of legislative activism on the Court's behavior. However, the empirical analyses in the following chapters account for legislative activism and demonstrate that Court-curbing is not itself part of increased legislative activity and that the Court responds specifically to Court-curbing bills rather than increased legislative activism. Thus, although I do not rule out the possibility that the threat of Court-curbing enactment affects the Court, the evidence presented in the following chapters is inconsistent with an argument that the Court *only* responds when it is concerned that the legislation will actually be enacted.

(Vanberg 2005) and provide empirical support for the claim that support for the judiciary is conditioned by the political context in which the public interacts with the courts (Staton 2010).

3.2 FORMALIZING THE ARGUMENT

Having sketched out a set of judicial and legislative goals – or, *preferences* – we are now ready to develop a theoretical framework for analyzing the causes and consequences of Court-curbing and congressional-judicial interactions. I propose here a formal-theoretic framework. Formal-theoretic analysis offers several benefits that are particularly useful for the questions I ask here. First, formal-theoretic models allow one to simplify often complex interactions and distill relationships with clarity. The simplifications engendered by a formalization are generally due to assumptions invoked by the theorist. In fact, almost every theory – formal or otherwise – can be seen this way (theories always involve some sort of simplification by assumption). However, formal theories require the theorist to clearly and carefully articulate the assumptions motivating the analysis, and interpretation of the resulting predictions can be interpreted in light of those assumptions. Second, formal analysis is particularly well suited to studying the conditions under which one actor is willing to believe signals sent from another, better-informed actor. In this case, the Supreme Court, although it has beliefs about public opinion, is less well informed about public support for the Court than is Congress. Several questions naturally arise, then. When will Congress have an incentive to be honest about public opinion? When will Congress have an incentive to "bluff" and try to trick the Supreme Court into exercising self-restraint? When might the Court be willing to adjust its behavior as a consequence of information it receives from Congress about public opinion? An entire class of formal models – known as "signaling models" – is designed precisely to address such questions.

The very purpose of employing a model, however, is to make decisions about what factors are most important to an interaction and to abstract away from the nuance of the "real world" to a more tractable theoretical setting in which the interaction in question can be studied. Models are not intended to capture every dynamic involved in a particular situation but rather to focus on a particular dynamic. Thus, although I choose to ignore certain factors in my model, I believe the exclusion of those factors from the theoretical model does not affect the relationships analyzed here.[30]

---

[30] To be sure, there may be other factors one might believe matter for this interaction, and they may have effects on the *magnitude* of particular effects. However, for the purposes of this model, it is not the magnitude of the effects in which I am interested but rather the direction of those effects.

I remain open to the claim, and readily acknowledge that there is more to the interaction among the public, Congress, and the Court than is contemplated by this model. Nevertheless, the choices I have made in this model have been made with those supplemental forces in mind.

In what remains of this chapter, I describe my theory of Court–Congress relations. Although I model this interaction formally, I relegate the technical details of the analysis to the appendix to this chapter. Through the chapter, I make every effort to present and discuss the theoretical analysis in a way accessible to the nontechnical reader. The analysis proceeds in three stages. First, I describe the basic mechanics of the Court–Congress interaction. To do so, I employ an admittedly crude model – a decision-theoretic model in which Congress behavior is fixed. This model serves to illuminate the causal mechanism driving judicial responses to Court-curbing. Second, I move to a more flexible game-theoretic model in which Congress takes an active role. This model allows us to examine simultaneously the decision to introduce Court-curbing and judicial responses to proposed Court-curbing. Third, I further extend the model to allow for public opinion to change after Congress has decided whether to introduce Court-curbing. This model allows us to consider how potential changes in public opinion may affect congressional behavior.

3.2.1   Model 1: Decision-Theoretic Setting

Consider a simple setting in which the Court faces a decision-theoretic problem. That is, congressional action does not depend on the Court's decisions but is rather assumed parametrically. Although this may seem an overly restrictive assumption, there are many ways in which Court-curbing can be driven by forces other than the Supreme Court's decisions, such as decisions by state or lower federal courts,[31] tides in political moods, electoral pressures and calendars, as well as resource and other institutional constraints.[32]

---

[31] Several staffers whom I interviewed indicated that their members frequently respond to decisions by the Ninth Circuit, for example, by using Court-curbing aimed at the Supreme Court.

[32] As "Clerk 7" commented, "A little bit of what Congress is doing when they talk about the Supreme Court is that they are setting the tone for the next nomination, for example."

Elements of the Model

PLAYERS AND SEQUENCE OF PLAY. The model begins with Nature determining whether the public supports the Court or not.[33] If the public does not support the Court, political actors and the public will reject a decision by the Court that is "unconstrained." By contrast, if the public does support the Court, then the Court has a "reservoir of good will" – or, legitimacy – on which to draw, and political actors and the public will enforce, follow, and respect an "unconstrained" decision by the Court. Next, the Court observes a "signal" about its public support. Substantively, this signal takes the form of Court-curbing bills introduced in Congress, political speeches against the Court, newspaper stories attacking the judiciary, and so forth. As this model is a limited, decision-theoretic one, I do not allow actors to choose which signal to send to the Court. Rather, I simply assume there is a fixed probability of seeing a signal of no public support – that is, Court-curbing – when the public does not support the Court. Similarly, there is a (identical) fixed probability of seeing a signal of public support – that is, no Court-curbing – when the public does support the Court. I call this probability q and assume that it is greater than 0.5. That is, the probability of seeing a signal of no support when the public does not support the Court is greater than the probability of seeing a signal of no support when the public *does* support the Court. Similarly, the probability of seeing a signal of public support when the public does support the Court is q – it is more likely that the Court will see a signal of public support than a signal of no public support when it has public support. After observing a signal – either of support or no support – the Court updates its beliefs about its level of public support. Then, it must decide a case. In doing so, it can either make a constrained decision or an unconstrained decision. All else being equal, the Court prefers to make an unconstrained decision – that is, it prefers to do what it wants without regard for public or political preferences.

BELIEFS. In setting up the model, we must next specify the Court's "beliefs." The Court's beliefs refer to what it thinks about its level of public support *ex ante* – that is, before it observes an institutional signal such as Court-curbing. Specifying the Court's beliefs is crucial, because its expectations about its level of public support will depend not only

---

33 "Nature" refers to the idea that there are forces exogenous to the model that determine a player's "type." Here, Nature chooses the type of world – either it is a world in which the Court enjoys a high level of public support or a world in which the Court does not have a high level of public support.

on what kind of congressional action it observes but also on what it believed beforehand. That is, observing a lot of congressional criticism of the Court may mean something different to the Court if the justices had a prior expectation that the public would not support the Court than if they had a prior expectation that the public would support the Court. Here, the Court's prior expectation is that with some probability – which I call p – the public does not support the Court. The sources of this prior belief may be numerous. For example, just as Court-watchers know whether Congress is hostile toward the Court and which cases will create considerable controversy, so too do the justices have anticipations regarding which issues will be important for Congress. Moreover, briefs submitted to the Court often describe the political and social implications of the case and highlight the extent to which the case is a politically controversial one. Thus, in light of these contextual sources of information, the Court has some prior expectation about its level of institutional legitimacy – its reservoir of good will.

STRATEGIES AND PAYOFFS. The final steps in setting up the model are to specify the Court's payoffs and strategies. *Payoffs* refer to how much the Court likes any particular outcome. *Strategies* refer to the various choices the Court can make at each stage of the game. Here, the strategies are simple. The Court has one choice to make – to make an unconstrained decision or a constrained decision – and it need make this choice only once. The Court's payoffs depend upon whether it makes an unconstrained or a constrained decision and its underlying level of public support, or institutional legitimacy. In particular, I assume the Court prefers to make an unconstrained decision if it has public support but prefers to make a constrained decision if it has lost its legitimacy and support. That is, an unconstrained decision with public support is better than a constrained decision, but a constrained decision is better than an unconstrained decision without public support. The motivation for these payoffs was described above, but to recap, the Court does not want to overstep the broad boundaries of its institutional legitimacy. Thus, when the political environment is too treacherous, the Court prefers to exercise self-restraint.

Analysis

Analysis of the model identifies predictions concerning the Court's choice – to make a constrained or unconstrained decision. To solve the model, I seek an optimal strategy for the Court, which is an optimal decision, conditional on the Court's posterior belief about its level of public support.[34] The formal details of the analysis, including proofs, are all reserved to the technical appendix to this chapter. Depending upon the Court's prior belief about its level of public support and institutional legitimacy, p, there will be an optimal strategy for the Court that may or may not be conditional on the observed institutional signal. In particular, there are three cases that may obtain. In one case, the Court may prefer to make a constrained decision regardless of what type of signal it observes. In another case, the Court may prefer to make an unconstrained decision regardless of what type of signal it observes. Finally, in a third case, the Court may prefer to make an unconstrained decision if and only if it observes a positive institutional signal and make a constrained decision if and only if it observes a negative institutional signal.

Proposition 1 *In a decision-theoretic model, the Court will make an unconstrained decision, regardless of what type of institutional signal it observes, if it is sufficiently optimistic about its level of public support. If the Court is sufficiently pessimistic about its level of public support, it will make a constrained decision regardless of what type of institutional signal it observes. Otherwise, the Court will make an unconstrained decision if and only if it observes a signal of public support and will make a constrained decision if and only if it observes a signal of no public support.*

Interpretation

The analysis of this simple, decision-theoretic model helps illustrate the mechanism that will underlie the more complicated theoretical analyses below. In this model, the Court has a prior expectation about whether its decisions will be rejected or followed by public and political actors. The Court will then observe a signal about its reservoir of good will – its public support or institutional legitimacy – and, using that signal and that signal's accuracy, it will update its belief about whether the public will accept or reject an unconstrained decision. With those updated beliefs, the Court can then evaluate the benefit of making an unconstrained decision, in light of the risk that it will not be supported, against the value of exercising self-restraint. This relationship reflects a comment of one former clerk, "The argument is basically that the Court is going to spend

---

34 Formally, the Court's posterior belief is given by its prior belief updated according to Bayes' rule upon observing an institutional signal – that is, Court-curbing or no Court-curbing. I leave the formal definitions of the Court's beliefs throughout this chapter to the appendix.

its capital if it is on a major issue of social justice; however, if the cost is going to be too high, then the Court will 'knuckle under.'"[35]

Moreover, the model also highlights an important interaction inherent in the Court's decision making. The Court must consider simultaneously its prior expectation about its institutional legitimacy *and* the accuracy of the signal it observes. The analysis demonstrated that, when the Court is either sufficiently pessimistic or sufficiently optimistic, the particular signal it observes will not affect the type of decision it will make. Thus, as the Court's prior expectation about its public support becomes more and more certain – either it has public support or not – the Court will be less responsive to the institutional signals it observes. However, and this point is crucial, the definition of "sufficiently" is relative to the accuracy of the signal it observes. In particular, as the quality (or accuracy) of the signal it observes increases – as q becomes greater – the Court will be more responsive to the institutional signal. In particular, the Court's prior belief that an unconstrained decision will be rejected and the quality of the signal the Court observes interact to identify two different types of regimes – one in which the signal about the state of the world does not affect the Court's behavior and one in which the signal does affect the Court's behavior.

The subtle point is that the court will be more willing to modify its behavior in light of the institutional signal it observes when either (a) the Court becomes more uncertain about its level of public support or (b) the signal becomes an increasingly accurate indicator of the Court's base of support. Therefore, when a signal is a completely credible indication about the state of the world, the Court will always follow the signal; however, as the quality of the signal decreases, the Court will be more willing to follow its prior and ignore the signal. In the game-theoretic models developed below, a similar relationship will hold. However, because in the game-theoretic model Congress can choose which signal to send, the Court will be forced to infer the quality of the signal by referencing what it knows about the incentives facing Congress. The Court will have to determine whether congressional signals are credible or, more accurately, how credible is a congressional signal.

3.2.2   Model 2: Fixed Public Opinion

The game-theoretic analysis begins by relaxing the assumption that congressional signals are exogenously determined; rather we explicitly

---

[35] Personal interview with "Clerk 8."

incorporate Congress into this model. Specifically, I consider an interaction in which Congress observes public opinion and can choose which of the two signals to send to the Court. In the next model, I further extend the analysis to an interaction where Congress has (limited) capacity to affect public opinion. The simple analysis presented in the preceding section will be useful here because it provides the intuition that motivates this model. In particular, we will see how the Court can determine whether a congressional signal is of sufficient credibility (quality) that the Court will be willing to believe the signal. To preview the result, the analysis will show that under precisely those conditions where the Court is willing to alter its behavior upon observing an institutional signal from Congress, Congress will have an incentive to be (at least somewhat) honest about constituent opinion about the Court.

Elements of the Model

PLAYERS AND SEQUENCE OF PLAY. The basic structure of this model flows naturally from the preceding, decision-theoretic model. The model begins with Nature again determining whether the public supports the Court or not. In this model, as contrasted with the decision-theoretic model, Congress moves next. First, Congress observes public opinion – it learns whether the public supports the Court or not. Following from the discussion above, one can think of this taking place as a process by which constituents call their representatives and voice their opinions, representatives visit their districts and talk with constituents, or via other mechanisms that provide direct feedback from constituents to their elected representatives. After observing public opinion, Congress sends an institutional signal to the Court. Substantively, this can be thought of as a decision to either engage in Court-curbing activity or not. Next, the Court observes the institutional signal from Congress, and it must then choose to make either a constrained decision or an unconstrained decision.

It is important to note here the ways in which this model is distinct from the models in previous literature. In Vanberg (2005) and Stephenson (2004), neither the legislature nor the court is perfectly informed about public opinion. In Staton (2010), both the legislature and the court are perfectly informed about public opinion. In contrast to each of these models, I assume the legislature has an informational advantage with respect to public support for the Court – that legislators are better informed about public opinion than the Court. As a consequence, the model developed here provides insight into the consequences of an informational asymmetry for the interaction between the judiciary and the elected branches.

BELIEFS. As in the decision-theoretic model, we must next specify the Court's beliefs about its institutional legitimacy and public support. In this model, I simply adopt the same set of beliefs for the Court as above. That is, the Court believes *ex ante* that the public does *not* support the Court (that it has lost its institutional legitimacy) with a given probability, which I will call p. Above I provided some discussion of where this belief might come from, but, to recap, recall that this belief comes from the various sources of information available to the Court, such as newspaper accounts, daily news shows, interactions with the public, and Court proceedings, such as briefs and oral arguments, which occasionally make references to public opinion and popular sentiment.

STRATEGIES AND PAYOFFS. Finally, we specify strategies and payoffs for the Court *and* Congress. To reiterate, a strategy is a set of options before a decision-maker at each point where that actor must make a choice. Congress must make a single decision – upon observing public opinion about the Court, it can choose to signal either public support for the Court or no public support for the Court. That is, Congress must either engage in Court-curbing or not.[36] The Court's strategies are identical to those above. After observing the institutional signal from Congress – Court-curbing or no Court-curbing – it must decide between making a constrained decision or an unconstrained decision.

Similarly, the payoffs follow from those in the decision-theoretic model. As before, the Court prefers to make an unconstrained decision if and only if it has public support. Making an unconstrained decision that will be rejected (i.e., when the Court lacks public support and institutional legitimacy) is the worst possible outcome for the Court. The value of making a constrained decision (i.e., exercising self-restraint) does not depend on the Court's level of public support.

---

[36] As I make clearer in the following, there is nothing particularly unique about Court-curbing that makes it the only possible institutional signal about public opinion that Congress may send to the Court. However, there are several important characteristics about Court-curbing that are theoretically relevant. First, and foremost, it is a publicly observable signal. In the analysis below, we will see that a crucial feature of the equilibria is that the public can observe the signals its representatives send to the Court. In a model where the Congress may privately communicate information to the justices – for example, by talking to them at cocktail parties or private events – no information from Congress can be a credible signal. Second, as opposed to other possible signals that may be sent to the Court, there is a plausible electoral connection behind Court-curbing – its position-taking benefit. Thus, although I leave open the possibility that other signals may exist and be communicated between Congress and the Court, Court-curbing is nearly unique in its theoretical relevance here.

Congress' payoffs similarly depend on the type of signal it sends to the Court and public opinion. However, Congress also receives a payoff that depends on the Court's decision. First, Congress receives a positive benefit if its signal matches the public's support for the Court. That is, if the public does not support the Court and Congress signals no public support to the Court (e.g., Court-curbing), then Congress receives a benefit. Similarly, Congress receives a benefit from signaling public support when the public does support the Court. By contrast, Congress pays a cost whenever its signal does not match public opinion. If Congress engages in Court-curbing, but the public supports the Court, then Congress pays a cost; if Congress does not engage in Court-curbing and the public does not support the Court, Congress pays a cost. These payoffs reflect the position-taking interest for Congress. Elected representatives receive a benefit from accurately reflecting their constituents' preferences in their official actions and pay a cost for going against their constituents' preferences. Indeed, attacking a popular Court or refusing to do something about an unpopular Court may have significant electoral consequences for a legislator. Second, Congress receives a payoff from the Court's decision. Specifically, Congress prefers the Court make a constrained decision rather than an unconstrained decision.[37] Thus, when the Court makes a constrained decision, Congress receives a policy benefit; when the Court makes an unconstrained decision, Congress pays a policy cost.

Analysis
Analysis of this model departs from the preceding model in an important way. Whereas in the decision-theoretic model, we needed only to identify the best decision for the Court to make, here we must simultaneously determine the best decision for the Court to make *and* the best signal for Congress to send, keeping in mind the Court's best decision may depend on which signal Congress sends. This type of problem – identifying the best action for one actor to take, contingent upon the other actor making the best decsion for herself, contingent upon the first actor knowing the second actor will behave that way, and so forth – is precisely what is meant by game-theoretic analysis.

[37] There is a notable literature that examines when elected officials, such as Congress or the president, may prefer for the Court to exercise its power aggressively (e.g., Lovell 2003; Whittington 2007). To be sure, this may sometimes be the case. However, in this case, there is no conflict between Congress and the Court, and the interaction analyzed here becomes uninteresting. I focus here exclusively on the case where there is some degree of policy disagreement between Congress and the Court.

In analyzing this model, I focus on *equilibria* – stable situations in which no player (i.e., Congress or the Court) has an incentive to *unilaterally* change its behavior.[38] That is, an equilibrium exists when, conditional on Congress taking the optimal action for itself, the Court has no incentive to change its behavior, *and* when conditional on the Court taking the optimal action for itself, Congress has no incentive to change its behavior. In the game-theoretic model here, there are three equilibria that can exist – a "separating" equilibrium, a "hybrid" equilibrium, and a "pooling" equilibrium. I will discuss each of these in turn.

SEPARATING EQUILIBRIUM. The first equilibrium I consider is a separating equilibrium. In this equilibrium, Congress always directly reflects public opinion about the Court. If the Court has lost its legitimacy and public support, Congress signals a lack of public support, for example, by introducing Court-curbing legislation. However, if the Court has public support, Congress signals public support for the Court – that is, no Court-curbing. It is this behavior that gives this equilibrium the name "separating." Congressional behavior is strictly separated by the state of the Court's legitimacy and public support. In this equilibrium, the Court always conditions its behavior strictly upon which type of signal it observes. In particular, if the Court observes Court-curbing – that is, a signal that it has lost public support – then it will always exercise self-restraint and make a constrained decision. By contrast, if the Court does not observe Court-curbing – that is, a signal of public support – then it will never exercise self-restraint and will make an unconstrained decision. Importantly, this equilibrium can only exist when the position-taking benefit to Congress from accurately reflecting constituent opinion outweighs any policy benefit Congress might derive from constraining Court behavior. I call this equilibrium the Constrained Congress equilibrium, because under these conditions, Congress is constrained by the electoral pressures from the public.

Proposition 2 *(**Constrained Congress**) When the electoral benefit of position-taking outweighs policy disagreement between the Court and Congress, the only equilibrium that can exist is a separating equilibrium in which Congress always accurately reflects public opinion. In this equilibrium, the Court's decisions are perfectly correlated with the institutional signals it observes from Congress. Upon observing Court-curbing, the*

---

[38] Specifically, in analyzing the model, I seek perfect Bayesian equilibria. Fuller technical details are given in the appendix to this chapter.

Court will always exercise self-restraint. When Congress does not signal a lack of public support, judicial decision making will be unconstrained.

POOLING EQUILIBRIUM. When, by contrast, the electoral benefit of position-taking does not outweigh the policy disagreement between the Court and Congress, a separating equilibrium cannot exist. The type of equilibrium that will exist depends then upon the Court's prior belief about its level of public support. In particular, two cases may obtain. In the first case, the Court is pessimistic about its level of legitimacy and public support. That is, the Court thinks it is more likely than not the public will reject an unconstrained decision by the Court. When this is the case – that is, when there is sufficient policy disagreement between the Court and Congress and the Court is pessimistic about its public support – the only type of equilibrium that can exist is a pooling equilibrium. In this equilibrium, Congress always engages in Court-curbing, and the Court always makes constrained decisions. I call this equilibrium the Constrained Court equilibrium.

Proposition 3 *(**Constrained Court**) When the policy disagreement between Congress and the Court outweighs Congress' position-taking, electoral interest, and the Court is pessimistic about its level of public support, the only type of equilibrium that can exist is a pooling equilibrium. In this equilibrium, Congress always introduces Court-curbing bills, signaling no public support for the Court. The Court always exercises self-restraint and makes a constrained decision.*

This equilibrium captures an interesting and striking dynamic. When the Court believes *ex ante* that it is sufficiently likely that the public will reject an unconstrained decision, then there will be an incentive for the Court to make a constrained decision upon observing a negative signal, even though it knows Congress may be "bluffing" and falsely representing a lack of public support for the Court. That is, the Court thinks it is likely it has lost its diffuse support; it need not be *certain*, only sufficiently pessimistic. However, the risk that the Congress is misrepresenting public opinion is not great enough to justify the Court making an unconstrained decision. Because it knows this, Congress will always prefer to misrepresent a supportive public and introduce Court-curbing bills. The key to this equilibrium is that the Court's prior belief about its level of public support is sufficiently pessimistic.

SEMI-SEPARATING EQUILIBRIUM. When the Court is, on the other hand, optimistic about its institutional legitimacy – when it believes it

is more likely than not the public will support an unconstrained decision – a pooling equilibrium cannot be supported. This is so because the
Court will not be sufficiently pessimistic to always back down in the face
of a negative institutional signal. At the same time, a separating equilibrium cannot exist. This is so because Congress, facing the potential
of a large policy benefit if it successfully bluffs the Court into making
a constrained decision, will have an incentive to sometimes sacrifice its
position-taking interests and introduce Court-curbing legislation when
the public does support the Court. Thus, the only type of equilibrium
that can exist under these conditions is a semi-separating equilibrium.
In this equilibrium, Congress always signals no public support whenever
the public has lost confidence in the Court. And, even when the public does have confidence in the Court, Congress sometimes "bluffs" and
introduces Court-curbing. The Court, for its part, makes a constrained
decision sometimes when it sees Court-curbing, but sometimes it makes
an unconstrained decision despite a signal of no public support. By contrast, the Court never makes a constrained decision in the absence of
Court-curbing. I call this equilibrium the Sparring Equilibrium.

Proposition 4 *(Sparring) When there is a sufficient degree of policy disagreement between the Court and Congress, but when the Court is sufficiently optimistic about its level of public support, only a semi-separating
equilibrium can exist. In this case, Congress always introduces Court-
curbing bills when the public has lost confidence in the Court. When
the public does support the Court, however, Congress will sometimes
"bluff" and introduce Court-curbing bills. The Court will never make a
constrained decision in the absence of Court-curbing. Upon observing a
Court-curbing, however, the Court will sometimes make a constrained
decision but will sometimes make an unconstrained decision.*

This equilibrium reveals a dynamic that complements the pooling equilibrium. In particular, in the Constrained Court Equilibrium, the Court
is willing to constrain itself upon observing Court-curbing, even though
it believes that there is a chance that Congress would be bluffing and
misrepresenting the true level of public support for the Court. That equilibrium, it was shown, can only be supported when the Court was *ex
ante* pessimistic about its public support. However, when the Court
is not sufficiently pessimistic, the Constrained Court Equilibrium cannot be supported. Congress cannot bluff whenever the public supports
the Court; instead, there must be some chance that Congress is being
honest about the Court's institutional legitimacy. That is, Congress can

only bluff probabilistically. This behavior characterizes a hybrid, semi-separating equilibrium. Under this condition, the Court still is willing to constrain itself only probabilistically whenever it observes Court-curbing; thus there is a back-and-forth between Congress and the Court. The key to this equilibrium is that in order to maintain the Court's incentive to exercise self-restraint (at least probabilistically) upon observing a signal of no public support, Congress must be sufficiently honest about public opinion. That is, Congress must only signal a lack of public support when in fact the public does support the Court with a low enough probability that the Court expects that the probability it is being misled is small enough, relative to the risk of not believing Congress and making an unconstrained decision in the absence of public support. At the same time, the Court must be willing to exercise self-restraint upon observing Court-curbing with a large enough probability that Congress is willing to play its bluffing strategy, probabilistically losing the electoral benefit in exchange for a probabilistic policy benefit.[39]

Interpretation and Comparative Statics

The three equilibria characterized previously identify the conditions that give rise to constrained decision making by the Court. Moreover, the analysis demonstrates that, under a wide range of conditions, there can be separation – the Congress will be (at least somewhat) honest about public opinion regarding the Court. Importantly, the analysis demonstrates that Congress will be willing to be honest about public opinion regarding the Court precisely under those conditions where the Court is willing to respond to institutional signals about public opinion. When, however, the Court is willing to exercise self-restraint in the face of a congressional bluff, then Congress will be willing to take advantage of that situation and bluff. This result is not necessarily obvious; indeed, it is notable that the Congress sometimes will be willing to accept divergent policy decisions in order to establish an expectation by the Court that a negative congressional signal is a credible indicator about the state of public opinion. Figure 3.2 provides a visual interpretation of the theoretical results.

---

[39] Technically, this requires that both the Court and Congress are *indifferent* between their two possible strategies. Indifference implies that the Court is willing to play either strategy – constrained or unconstrained decision – and therefore can play either strategy with any probability. The precise probability the Court chooses, in equilibrium, will be the probability that makes Congress indifferent between its two strategies – negative or positive signal about public support. In turn, the precise probability Congress chooses

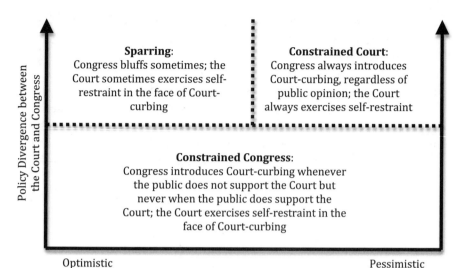

FIGURE 3.2. *Three equilibria from game-theoretic model with fixed public opinion.*

What is more, the analysis reveals several interesting comparative statics from which I will derive empirical hypotheses. First, we see that regardless of the degree of policy divergence between the Court and Congress, and regardless of the Court's prior expectation about its level of public support, the Court's decision making should be at least weakly related to institutional signals. That is, in each equilibrium, upon observing a negative institutional signal – that is, Court-curbing – the Court should be more likely to make a constrained decision than an unconstrained decision.

Observation 1 *Upon observing Court-curbing in Congress, the Court should be weakly more likely to make a constrained decision than when it does not observe Court-curbing.*

At first blush, this result seems to comport perfectly with the standard separation-of-powers model. Indeed, the basic insight of that model is that when the Court fears adverse consequences, it will be more constrained in its decision making. However, the difference here is in the underlying factors that motivate a fear of adverse consequences. In the standard model,

will be, in equilibrium, the probability that sustains the Court's indifference. Further details and a formal proof are provided in the technical appendix to this chapter.

adverse consequences are one-and-the-same with ideological divergence. Here, the focus is on nonideological indicators of adverse consequences. Nevertheless, this result does not necessarily contrast with the standard model.

In addition, the model also yields a secondary result about the Court's responsiveness to Court-curbing. As the Court's prior expectation that it has lost public support decreases, the Court will be less likely to find itself in the Constrained Court (pooling) Equilibrium – in which it always constrains itself upon observing Court-curbing – and more likely to find itself in the Sparring (semi-separating) Equilibrium – in which it constrains itself only probabilistically upon observing Court-curbing. However, when there is a low level of policy divergence between the Court and Congress, the Court's responsiveness to Court-curbing should not vary with its prior. Thus, the degree to which the Court responds to Court-curbing should be weakly increasing in its prior expectation that it has lost public support.

Observation 2 *As the Court's prior expectation that it has lost public support increases, it will be weakly more likely to make a constrained decision upon observing Court-curbing.*

Finally, notice the model predicts that the effect of Court-curbing on judicial decision making will be conditional. That is, in the separating equilibrium, there will be a strong correlation between Court-curbing and the probability of a constrained decision by the Court. By contrast, that correlation will be weaker in the semi-separating equilibrium. That is, when the Court is relatively optimistic and faces a divergent Congress, the Court will be more likely to make an unconstrained decision in the face of Court-curbing than it would otherwise. It is this result that most clearly discriminates between the theoretical mechanism posited by the model developed here and alternative accounts of judicial responsiveness to congressional pressure.

Observation 3 *The correlation between Court-curbing and constrained decision making by the Court will be weaker when the Court is optimistic about its public support and when it faces an ideologically divergent Congress.*

These comparative statics will provide the basis for the empirical hypotheses I derive below. However, before doing so, I first present the results of a simple extension to the model, in which I relax the assumption that public opinion is fixed. Instead, I consider the theoretical consequence of allowing congressional attacks on the Court to affect public opinion about the Court.

3.2.3 Model 3: Variable Public Opinion

The game-theoretic model just described illustrates the conditions under which Congress should engage in Court-curbing and the conditions under which the Court should respond to Court-curbing by exercising self-restraint. However, the model imposed the potentially strong assumption that public opinion remains fixed throughout the course of a confrontation between Congress and the Court. However, one might imagine that public opinion itself is affected by Court-curbing, and as much was suggested in Chapter 2 as we described the function of Court-curbing as a congressional activity. Suppose an alternative world in which Congress tries to affect public opinion by introducing Court-curbing and politicizing the Court. What would that mean for this model? How would a congressional ability to affect public opinion affect the relationships identified above? One might expect that Congress would simply engage in Court-curbing whenever it disagrees with the Court about policy, hoping to politicize the Court and undermine judicial legitimacy.

To address this possibility, I extend the game-theoretic model and relax the assumption of fixed public opinion. I still assume that the initial level of public support for the Court is exogenously determined, but in this model, I allow some congressional influence on public opinion. In particular, I consider the case where congressional attacks on the Court can (probabilistically) change public opinion about the Court. I therefore simply extend Model 2 to allow the state of the world to change after Congress sends a signal to the Court as a function of the signal sent. This extension to the model yields comparative statics that are comparable to those of Model 2 and provide a more nuanced understanding of the relationship between public support for the Court and legislative-judicial interactions. It is again important to note here how this extension relates to some existing research. In particular, Staton's (2010) extension to Vanberg (2005) allows the public to be influenced by the Court's decisions. This model complements that analysis by allowing congressional decisions to influence public opinion.

Elements of the Model

This model is set up identically to Model 2 – the game-theoretic model with fixed public opinion. The only difference is that in this model, a public that has confidence in the Court may not have confidence in the Court at the end of the model, if Congress has introduced Court-curbing. Congress' position-taking benefit, then, is determined by the congruence between its institutional signal – did it send a positive or a negative signal, Court-curbing or no Court-curbing – and public opinion *at the end of the game*. Thus, if Congress bluffs and introduces Court-curbing when the Court remains popular, the electoral consequences for Congress will depend on whether public opinion changes and turns against the Court.[40] For the Court, the model remains very much the same, except it must now consider the possibility that a congressional bluff might actually influence public opinion.

Analysis

Analysis of this model demonstrates a behavioral pattern parallel to that discovered in Model 2. Specifically, for sufficiently low levels of policy divergence between the Court and Congress, there exists a separating equilibrium. For sufficiently high levels of policy divergence, on the other hand, there will exist two equilibria, which depend on the underlying prior probability that the public does not support the Court. Notably, the range of prior expectations that can sustain a pooling equilibrium is larger in this model than in the model in which public opinion cannot change. In addition, in this model, a separating equilibrium can only be sustained for smaller degrees of policy divergence than in the model where public opinion is fixed. That is, in a model where Congress can lead public opinion, it will be able to bluff under a wider range of the parameters.

SEPARATING EQUILIBRIUM. In this model, there exists a separating equilibrium much like the one that existed in the model with fixed public opinion. In particular, when there is a sufficiently low degree of policy divergence between the Court and Congress, there can exist a separating equilibrium. As before, in this equilibrium, Congress always signals a lack of public support for the Court – for example, Court-curbing – whenever the public has lost confidence in the Court. However, whenever the public remains supportive of the Court, Congress will signal public support – for example, it will not introduce Court-curbing. Because it knows that

---

[40] Note that I do not allow public opinion to endogenously change. Rather, I model public opinion probabilistically. An interesting avenue for future research, though, is to explicitly model and examine how public opinion responds to congressional activity, such as Court-curbing.

Court-curbing only occurs when the public does not support the Court, the Court exercises self-restraint whenever it sees Court-curbing.

Proposition 5 *(Constrained Congress) For sufficiently small levels of policy divergence between the Court and Congress, there exists a separating equilibrium in which Congress introduces Court-curbing whenever the Court is unpopular. The Court exercises self-restraint whenever it sees Court-curbing but makes unconstrained decisions in the absence of negative institutional signals.*

While this equilibrium looks similar to the Constrained Congress Equilibrium in the preceding model, there is an important difference. Specifically, separation can be supported here only for smaller degrees of policy divergence between the Court and Congress. In both cases, Congress needs to ensure itself a certain level of policy benefits from bluffing and introducing Court-curbing when the public supports the Court, because Congress will suffer electoral consequences from inaccurately reflecting public opinion. The intuition for why smaller degrees of policy divergence warrant separation here is that because public opinion *may* change in response to Court-curbing, Congress may sometimes be willing to forgo its electoral interests in favor of ensuring a better policy outcome and (probabilistically) affecting public opinion. Therefore, for a given electoral benefit, as Congress' ability to lead public opinion increases, it will be less likely that separation can be supported and increasingly likely that either pooling or semi-separation will be supported.

POOLING EQUILIBRIUM. As in the model with fixed public opinion, the separating equilibrium breaks down when there is sufficient policy divergence between the Court and Congress. When this is the case, the type of equilibrium again depends on the Court's prior expectation about its level of public support. When the Court is sufficiently pessimistic about its public support – when it believes it is likely the public will not support an unconstrained decision – a pooling equilibrium exists. In this case, as above, Congress always signals a lack of public support (e.g., Court-curbing), and the Court always responds to those negative signals by exercising self-restraint (i.e., making a constrained decision).

Proposition 6 *(Constrained Court) When there is a sufficient degree of policy divergence between the Court and Congress, and when the Court has a pessimistic outlook about its public support, there will exist a pooling equilibrium in which Congress always introduces Court-curbing bills and the Court always responds to Court-curbing bills by exercising self-restraint.*

There are two technical details of this equilibrium that are worth noting. First, when the probability that Court-curbing will turn a supportive public against the Court is great enough, then the pooling equilibrium can exist regardless of how optimistic the Court is about its public support. That is, policy divergence between the Court and Congress is sufficient to sustain the pooling equilibrium. Second, and as a consequence of the first point, pooling will be supported for a larger range of all of the model's parameters than the pooling equilibrium in the model with fixed public opinion. However, as in Model 2, when the Court's prior falls below a critical threshold (if it exists),[41] then there will exist a semi-separating equilibrium.

SEMI-SEPARATING EQUILIBRIUM. As with the other two equilibria in this model, the semi-separating equilibrium parallels its counterpart in the model with fixed public opinion. When there is a sufficient degree of policy divergence between the Court and Congress, but when the Court is relatively optimistic about its level of public support, then there exists an equilibrium in which Congress engages in Court-curbing whenever the public does not support the Court *and* sometimes when the public does support the Court. In this equilibrium, the Court sometimes exercises self-restraint upon observing Court-curbing, though sometimes it will nevertheless make an unconstrained decision. The Court always makes an unconstrained decision when it observes a signal of public support.

Proposition 7 *(Sparring) When there is sufficient policy divergence between the Court and Congress, but when the Court is sufficiently optimistic about its level of public support, there exists an equilibrium in which Congress sometimes bluffs and sends a negative institutional signal despite a supportive public. The Court responds to Court-curbing by sometimes exercising self-restraint but sometimes does not. As the Court becomes more pessimistic, it responds more to Court-curbing than when it is more optimistic.*

It is important to note that this equilibrium cannot exist if the probability that Court-curbing turns a supportive public against the Court is high enough. The intuition here is direct. As the likelihood that Court-curbing turns a supportive public against the Court increases, the Court will be more willing to respond to Court-curbing, because, even if Congress is

[41] Recall that such a threshold might not exist, because if the probability that Court-curbing can turn a supportive public against the Court is large enough, then the pooling equilibrium can be supported *regardless* of the Court's prior belief about its public support.

"bluffing," the probability that the public will not support the Court is itself increased by the fact that Court-curbing can affect public opinion. Thus, for a more optimistic Court, Congress is more willing to bluff – because it has less to fear from misrepresenting public opinion, because public opinion may change. Because the Court is more willing to respond to potential bluffs, and Congress is more willing to bluff, the pooling equilibrium begins to take over in ranges of the Court's optimism that previously deterred too much congressional bluffing. This interactive relationship between the ability to affect public opinion and congressional behavior suggests that congressional leadership of public opinion strengthens congressional power over the Court. This is because in the pooling equilibrium, the Court always makes constrained decisions – as Congress would prefer – whereas in the semi-separating equilibrium, the Court sometimes makes unconstrained decisions.

Interpretation and Comparative Statics

Perhaps the most notable finding in this analysis is the fact that the behavioral pattern and types of equilibria that this model yields parallels that found in the analysis of the model in which public opinion is fixed. That Congress' ability to affect public opinion does not affect the fundamental comparative statics of the model is instructive, because it suggests that the model provides a general, robust description of the incentives created for institutional behavior by the preferences posited here.

Figure 3.3 shows the relationship between the equilibria from this model to those from Model 2. The most important point to note is that the basic relationships between the model's parameters – the Court's expectation about its public support and the degree of policy divergence between the Court and Congress – and congressional and judicial behavior remain the same. That is, none of the comparative statics change. The main difference is simply that the relative ranges of particular parameters supporting each type of behavior have changed. In this sense, the predictions derived from the model with fixed public opinion are robust to an alternative assumption by which public opinion can be affected by Court-curbing in Congress.[42]

---

[42] Unfortunately, though, because the comparative statics are the same (e.g., separation breaks down as policy divergence grows, Congress "bluffs" more as the Court becomes increasingly pessimistic) it will be hard to distinguish between these worlds with observational data below.

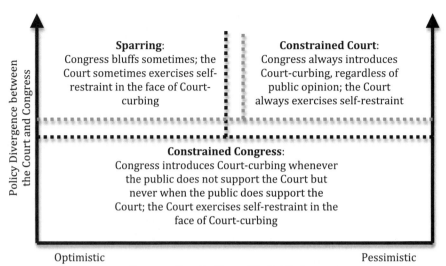

FIGURE 3.3. *Three equilibria from model with varying public opinion.*

3.3 EMPIRICAL IMPLICATIONS

The formal analysis in the preceding section helps illuminate the incentives created by the interaction posited in the first part of this chapter. From the formal analyses of legislative-judicial interactions, I derive several empirical implications about systematic patterns that one should expect to observe in the context of Court–Congress relations. This section first discusses the nature of the theoretical relationship between congressional and judicial behavior and then describes the specific functional form that these relationships should take on. Together, the expected relationships will lay the theoretical groundwork for the empirical analyses in the following chapters.

3.3.1 Hypotheses

From the model of Conditional Self-Restraint, I derive a set of empirically testable predictions. Specifically, the model makes predictions about both when Congress will engage in Court-curbing and how the Court will respond to Court-curbing.

CONGRESSIONAL ATTACKS. The theoretical models yield three predictions about the determinants of Court-curbing, which I recap here and present as empirical hypotheses. First, in each model, Congress engages in political attacks on the Court *whenever* the public has lost confidence in the Court. Therefore, we should expect to see that decreases in public support for the Court should lead to more Court-curbing and political attacks on the Court. Indeed, this prediction derives directly from the models analyzed above and closely reflects the sentiments articulated in many of my interviews with congressional staffers.

Hypothesis 1 *A decrease in public support will be associated with an increase in Court-curbing in Congress.*

Second, one should expect that Congress will be more likely to attack the Court when there is a greater policy benefit associated with constraining the Court's behavior. This is because Congress will have a greater incentive to misrepresent public opinion in the hope the Court will exercise self-restraint. Policy benefits may be affected by the degree of ideological divergence between the Court and Congress or the level of "judicial activism" on the Court. Thus, we should expect to see a positive relationship between the number of Court-curbing bills introduced and the divergence between congressional conservatism and judicial output liberalism.

Hypothesis 2 *An increase in ideological divergence between the Court and Congress will be associated with an increase in Court-curbing in Congress.*

Third, the model makes an interactive prediction about the introduction of Court-curbing. When the Court is most pessimistic about its level of public support, ideologically divergent Congresses should introduce more Court-curbing than ideologically aligned Congresses. This is because when the Court is pessimistic, an ideologically divergent Congress will have an incentive to always bluff about public opinion – this is the Constrained Court (pooling) Equilibrium. By contrast, as the Court becomes more optimistic, the excessive introduction of Court-curbing by ideologically divergent Congresses should decrease. When the Court is most optimistic, introduction by ideologically divergent Congresses should be similar to the introduction of Court-curbing by ideologically aligned Congresses. This is because as the Court becomes more optimistic, an ideologically divergent Congress will have to bluff less often to ensure judicial responsiveness to Court-curbing – this is the Sparring (semi-separating) Equilibrium. Thus, the effect of ideological divergence should be greatest when the Court is pessimistic about its public support and least when the Court is optimistic about its public support.

Hypothesis 3 *As the Court becomes increasingly pessimistic about its public support, there will be an increase in the effect of ideological divergence between the Court and Congress on the decision to introduce Court-curbing legislation.*

This third hypothesis is particularly important, because it provides a nonintuitive prediction that can help discriminate among competing causal stories. In particular, if Court-curbing is primarily an elite-level confrontation, then there is no reason to expect that the Court's beliefs about its public support will condition the effect of policy divergence on bill sponsorship. The intuition that derives from the Conditional Self-Restraint model, by contrast, clearly articulates a reason for this relationship. We will turn to an empirical analysis of this prediction in Chapter 4.

JUDICIAL RESPONSIVENESS TO COURT-CURBING. The second set of empirical predictions that can be derived from the Conditional Self-Restraint model concern judicial responses to the introduction of Court-curbing, which I also recap here and present as empirical hypotheses. The first prediction is simply that an increase in Court-curbing should be associated with an increase in constrained decision making by the Court – or, self-restraint. In each equilibrium, the Court is (weakly) more likely to make a constrained decision when it observes Court-curbing than when it observes no Court-curbing. The greater the number of Court-curbing bills introduced, for example, the fewer laws the Court should invalidate; the more conservative attacks on the Court, the fewer liberal decisions we should expect. This result reflects the sentiment articulated by several interview subjects, such as "Clerk 8," who commented, "The argument is basically that the Court is going to spend its capital if it is on a major issue of social justice; however, if the cost is going to be too high, then the Court will knuckle under."

Hypothesis 4 *The introduction of more Court-curbing bills in Congress will be associated with an increase in judicial self-restraint.*

Second, as the Court's outlook about its public support becomes increasingly pessimistic, the Court should be more likely to exercise self-restraint. In each equilibrium, the Court is (weakly) more likely to make a constrained decision as it becomes more likely that the public will not accept a divergent decision from the Court. Therefore, when the Court is a salient political topic and is out of line with public opinion, then we may expect that the Court will be more likely to exercise self-constraint than when it is a less salient political issue.

Hypothesis 5 *As the Court becomes more pessimistic about its level of public support, the Court will exercise greater self-restraint.*

Third, the model predicts an interactive relationship between Court-curbing and the degree of policy divergence between the Court and Congress. In particular, as the Court and Congress become increasingly ideologically divergent, Congress has an increased incentive to "bluff" and misrepresent public opinion. As a consequence, Court-curbing bills become less credible indicators of public support for the Court, and the Court will be more willing to disregard those signals and make an unconstrained decision.

Hypothesis 6 *The marginal effect of Court-curbing on judicial self-restraint will decrease as the Court and Congress become more ideologically divergent.*

Notice that this prediction runs against the intuition that follows from an alternative theory in which Court-curbing is constraining because of the threat of enactment. That is, if the Court is worried about Court-curbing bills actually being enacted, then it does not follow that the Court would be less responsive when it is facing its ideological opponents. Indeed, one would likely expect that under these conditions, the Court would be even more responsive to Court-curbing. A reasonable expectation is that the Court's ideological allies have a greater interest in preserving the Court's independence. Weakening the Court will undermine any influence the Court will have in the event its political allies lose power in the elected branches.[43] Thus, the threat of enacting Court-curbing legislation should be less serious when the Court's allies control the legislative process than when its ideological opponents control the legislative process. Attenuation of any judicial responsiveness to Court-curbing by ideological divergence between the Court and Congress, then, is suggestive of the

---

[43] We may think of the elected branches as maintaining judicial independence as a means of insurance against future adverse political circumstances. That is, when the Court's ideological allies are in power, they will have an interest in preserving the integrity and independence of the Court because the justices will likely outlast the current political officeholders and therefore can continue to represent the current majority's preferences in policy making. For an examination of this logic, see Whittington (2007) and Landes and Posner (1975).

role of Court-curbing as a signal about public opinion and *not* the role of Court-curbing as a direct threat to the Court's institutional powers.

Fourth, and finally, the model predicts an interactive relationship between Court-curbing and the Court's outlook about its public support. In particular, the model predicts that as the Court becomes increasingly pessimistic about its public support, the Court should be (weakly) more willing to exercise self-restraint upon observing Court-curbing. That is, as the Court becomes increasingly pessimistic, the Court will be (weakly) more likely to find itself in the equilibrium in which it is always willing to make a constrained decision (exercise self-restraint) upon observing Court-curbing. Thus, we should observe that Court-curbing bills are (weakly) more strongly correlated with judicial self-restraint when the Court is more pessimistic than when it is more optimistic.

Hypothesis 7 *The marginal effect of Court-curbing on judicial self-restraint will increase as the Court becomes more pessimistic about its level of public support.*

3.3.2 Empirical Tests

In the remainder of this book, I bring new empirical evidence to bear on these claims, contrast the findings with those from traditional separation-of-powers analyses, and provide considerable support for the claims advanced here. Specifically, I look at two ways in which Court-curbing varies and two types of judicial decision making. These empirical tests are summarized in Table 3.1. First, I examine the volume, or intensity, of Court-curbing. That is, I examine the number of Court-curbing bills introduced in Congress to assess whether this pattern systematically comports with the theoretical predictions outlined here. The hypothesis offered above predicts that as public confidence in the Court decreases, more Court-curbing bills will be introduced in Congress. Second, I examine the ideological content of Court-curbing. To do this, I measure the conservatism or liberalism of the bills' sponsors. The Conditional Self-Restraint model makes two predictions concerning the ideological content of Court-curbing. On one hand, the model predicts that as the Court becomes more ideologically divergent from the public, more Court-curbing bills will be introduced. On the other hand, the model predicts that as the Court becomes more ideologically divergent from Congress, the number of Court-curbing bills introduced should not decrease. Both of these analyses are presented in Chapter 4.

TABLE 3.1. *Summary of Empirical Predictions and Tests of Predictions from the Conditional Self-Restraint Model*

Behavior	Prediction	Analysis
Court-curbing intensity	A decrease in public support for the Court will lead to an increase in Court-curbing	Chapter 4
Court-curbing ideology	An increase in ideological divergence between the Court and the public will lead to an increase in Court-curbing	Chapter 4
Constitutional decisions	An increase in Court-curbing will lead to a decrease in the use of judicial review	Chapter 5
Statutory decisions	An increase in Court-curbing will lead to a shift in judicial liberalism toward the public's policy preferences	Chapter 6

Next, I consider the Court's responsiveness to Court-curbing. To do this, I examine the Court's decision making in constitutional cases as well as in statutory cases. In the context of constitutional decision making, the model makes a very clear and direct prediction. As the intensity of Court-curbing increases, the Court will be more likely to exercise self-restraint. Thus, we should observe that increases in Court-curbing are associated with decreases in the use of judicial review. In Chapter 5, I examine both the aggregate patterns on judicial review – that is, how many laws does the Court hold unconstitutional in a given year – as well as the Court's decision making in individual cases – that is, what is the probability that the Court will hold a law unconstitutional in a given case.

In Chapter 6, I turn to an examination of the Court's statutory deci-sion making. In the context of statutory cases, however, the model's predictions are a little less direct. The model predicts that an increase in Court-curbing will lead to more constrained decision making by the Court. The standard method in the literature for investigating whether judicial decision making in statutory cases is "constrained" is to exam-ine whether external forces are correlated with how liberally (or con-servatively) a justice votes. In the context of my argument, then, we should expect to see that more conservative Court-curbing is associated with more conservative voting, even once controlling for a justice's own policy preferences. By contrast, we should expect to observe that an increase in liberal Court-curbing will lead to more liberal voting by a justice.

To preview, I demonstrate in these subsequent chapters broad sup-port for each prediction. Although the tests draw primarily on statistical analyses of aggregate patterns in congressional and judicial behavior, I supplement the tests throughout the book with qualitative examples to help provide context for understanding the patterns documented in the aggregate data. In Chapter 7, I return to the more substantive discussion of these findings and their implications for the theoretical debate set out in this and the preceding chapters.

3.4 CONCLUSION

This chapter has developed a theoretical model for understanding the political function served by Court-curbing and the consequences such bills have for judicial independence and judicial behavior. Existing research has demonstrated that a concern for institutional legitimacy can create an incentive for a court to exercise self-restraint (Vanberg 2005; Staton 2010). I have argued here that Court-curbing bills are primarily a position-taking endeavor and that the electoral and political posturing function they serve can allow the Court to learn from such position-taking about public opinion. Interviews with Supreme Court justices, former law clerks, members of Congress, and legislative staffers serve to bolster the claim that Court-curbing is primarily a position-taking activity and that these bills are understood by the justices to be motivated by public discontent with the Court. In addition, these bills could be intended to manipulate public opinion about the Court, by politicizing it and undermining its apolitical, mythical image. In either event, Court-curbing bills are an important indicator of the Court's diffuse support and, as a consequence, its institutional efficacy.

A formalization of the decision to introduce Court-curbing, and the Court's response to Court-curbing, reveals both intuitive relationships among public opinion, Court-curbing sponsorship in Congress, and the Court's responsiveness to Court-curbing as well as counterintuitive conditional relationships among Court-curbing, Court–Congress ideological divergence, and public opinion. These conditional relationships help distinguish the predictions made here from those that would be derived from a competing argument in which public opinion about the Court does not influence the introduction of, or the Court's reaction to, Court-curbing bills. To be clear, I have not ruled out the possibility that the threat of enactment of Court-curbing might be an important part of the reason why the court responds to Court-curbing. However, the claim I make here is that, net of such an effect, the Court nevertheless responds to Court-curbing because it signals waning diffuse support for the Court. Thus, although the threat of enactment may be important, enactment alone cannot explain the extent to which the Court responds to

Court-curbing. In the remaining chapters of this book, I subject these pre-dictions to empirical scrutiny.

MATHEMATICAL APPENDIX

In this appendix, I provide formal proofs of the propositions offered in this chapter. First, however, I must introduce some notation. Let $\Omega \in \{H, L\}$ represent the state of the world, with $\Omega = H$ representing the state of the world where the public will not support an unconstrained decision and $\Omega = L$ representing the state of the world where the public will support an unconstrained decision. Let $\omega \in \{h, l\}$ represent Congress' signal to the Court. Let $d \in \{u, c\}$ represent the Court's decision in a case, with $d = u$ representing an unconstrained decision and $d = c$ representing a constrained decision. The Court's payoffs in the model are given by b_j, o, and $-b_j$. The Court receives o whenever it plays $d = c$. It receievs b_j if it plays $d = u$ and $\Omega = L$; it receives $-b_j$ if it plays $d = u$ and $\Omega = H$. Congress receives b_c if $d = c$ and $-b_c$ if $d = u$. Congress also receives ε if $\omega = \Omega$ and receives $-\varepsilon$ if $\omega \neq \Omega$. The Court's prior belief about Ω is given by $p = Pr(\Omega = H)$. In the model where public opinion is variable (Model 3), let Ω be subscripted by t, with $t \in \{1, 2\}$. Let the probability that Ω changes from L to H if $\omega = h$ be given by $r = Pr(\Omega_2 = H | \omega = h, \Omega_1 = L)$. Finally, let J represent the Court and C represent Congress.

Proof. *Proof of Proposition 1.* Upon observing $\omega = h$, the Court's poste-rior belief that $\Omega = H$ is given by $Pr(\Omega = H | \omega = h) = \frac{Pr(\omega=h|\Omega=H)|(\Omega=H)}{Pr(\omega=h)} = \frac{q \cdot p}{q \cdot p + (1-q) \cdot (1-p)}$. Therefore, upon observing $\omega = h$, the Court's expected utility from playing $d = u$ is given by $b \cdot \left(1 - \frac{q \cdot p}{q \cdot p + (1-q) \cdot (1-p)}\right) - b \cdot \left(\frac{q \cdot p}{q \cdot p + (1-q) \cdot (1-p)}\right)$. If the Court plays $d = c$, it guarantees itself a payoff of o. Thus, upon observing $\omega = h$, the Court prefers to make a con-strained decision if $p \geq 1 - q$. Now, suppose the Court observes $\omega = l$. The Court's posterior belief about the state of the world is given by $Pr(\Omega = H | \omega = l) = \frac{Pr(\omega=l|\Omega=H)|(\Omega=H)}{Pr(\omega=l)} = \frac{(1-q) \cdot p}{p \cdot (1-q) + q \cdot (1-p)}$. Thus, upon observ-ing $\omega = l$, the Court's expected utility from playing $d = u$ is given by $b \cdot \left(1 - \frac{(1-q) \cdot p}{p \cdot (1-q) + q \cdot (1-p)}\right) - b\left(\frac{(1-q) \cdot p}{p \cdot (1-q) + q \cdot (1-p)}\right)$. Because the Court can ensure itself a payoff of o by playing $d = c$, the Court will prefer to play $d = c$ if $p > q$. Notice that $q > \frac{1}{2} \Rightarrow q > (1 - q)$. Therefore, when $p > q$, the Court will prefer to play $d = c$, regardless of which signal it observes.

However, when $(1 - q) \leq p \leq q$, the Court's optimal strategy will depend on which signal it receives. Specifically, it will prefer to play $d = u$ if it observes $\omega = l$ but will prefer to play $d = c$ if it observes $\omega = h$. Finally, consider the case where $p < (1 - q)$. The Court, in this case, will prefer to play $d = u$, regardless of which signal it observes. ∎

Proof. *Proof of Proposition 2.* Suppose C plays a separating strategy. J's posterior beliefs are given by $\Pr(\Omega = H | \omega = h) = 1$ and $\Pr(\Omega = L | \omega = l) = 1$. J's expected utility from playing $d = c$ is 0. J's expected utility from playing $d = u$ upon observing $\omega = h$ is $\Pr(\Omega = H | \omega = h) \cdot (-b_c) + (1 - \Pr(\Omega = H | \omega = h)) \cdot (b_c) = -b_c$, and upon observing $\omega = l$ is $\Pr(\Omega = H | \omega = l) \cdot (-b_c) + (1 - \Pr(\Omega = H | \omega = l)) \cdot (b_c) = b_c$. Therefore, upon observing $\omega = h$, the Court strictly prefers to play $d = c$, and upon observing $\omega = l$, the Court strictly prefers to play $d = u$. Now, consider the Congress. If the state of the world is $\Omega = H$, if the Court plays $\omega = l$, it expects to receive $-b_c - \varepsilon$; if it plays $\omega = h$, it expects to receive $b_c + \varepsilon$. If the state of the world is $\Omega = L$, if the Court plays $\omega = l$, it expects to receive $\varepsilon - b_c$; if the Court plays $\omega = h$, it expects to receive $b_c - \varepsilon$. Thus, when $b_c < \varepsilon$, the Congress strictly prefers to play a separating strategy.

To see that this equilibrium is unique, consider the following. First, suppose there is a pooling equilibrium. In this case, the J's posterior belief is equal to its prior. Therefore, its expected utility from playing $d = u$ is $b_j \cdot (1 - 2p)$, while its expected utility from playing $d = c$ is 0. Thus, the J prefers to play $d = u$ iff $p \leq \frac{1}{2}$. Consider next C. Let ω_p be the signal C sends in a pooling equilibrium. Now suppose that $\Omega \neq \omega_p$. If $p \leq \frac{1}{2}$, then C's expected utility from playing ω_p is $-b_c - \varepsilon$. If $p > \frac{1}{2}$, then C's expected utility from playing ω_p is $b_c - \varepsilon$. $\varepsilon > b_c$ implies that C has an incentive to deviate from ω_p whenever $\Omega \neq \omega_p$. Thus, a pooling equilibrium cannot be supported when $\varepsilon > b_c$.

Second, suppose there is a partial-pooling equilibrium in which C plays

$$\omega(\Omega) = \begin{cases} h & \text{if } \Omega = H \\ h & \text{with probability } q \in (0, 1) \text{ if } \Omega = L \\ l & \text{else} \end{cases}$$

J's posterior belief is $\Pr(\Omega = H | \omega = h) = \frac{p}{p + q \cdot (1 - p)}$. Therefore, J's expected utility from playing $d(\omega = h) = u$ is $b_j \cdot (1 - \frac{2p}{p + q \cdot (1 - p)})$. J's expected utility from playing $d(\omega = l) = u$ is b_j. As always, its expected utility from playing $d = c$ is 0. Notice that there is no value of q that makes J indifferent between $d = u$ and $d = c$. Thus, J will play a pure strategy. Specifically, J will play $d(\omega = h) = u$ iff $p \leq \frac{q}{1+q}$. Now, suppose that $p \leq \frac{q}{1+q}$ and $\Omega = L$. C's expected utility from playing its assigned strategy is $(1 - q) \cdot \varepsilon - q \cdot \varepsilon - b_c$. If it deviates and plays $\omega = l$, then its expected utility is $\varepsilon - b_c$. $q \in (0, 1)$ implies that C will have an incentive to deviate. Now, suppose that $p > \frac{q}{1+q}$ and $\Omega = L$. C's expected utility from playing its assigned strategy is $(1 - q) \cdot (\varepsilon - b_c) + q \cdot (b_c - \varepsilon)$. If it deviates and plays $\omega = l$, then its expected utility is $\varepsilon - b_c$. $q \in (0, 1)$ implies that C will have an incentive to deviate. Thus, C will have an incentive to deviate whenever $\Omega = L$ and the partial-pooling equilibrium cannot be supported.

Third, consider a semi-separating equilibrium in which C plays

$$\omega(\Omega) = \begin{cases} l & \text{if } \Omega = L \\ l & \text{with probability } q \in (0, 1) \text{ if } \Omega = H \\ h & \text{else} \end{cases}$$

J's posterior belief is $\Pr(\Omega = H | \omega = l) = \frac{q \cdot p}{1 + p \cdot (q-1)}$. J's expected utility from playing $d(\omega = l) = u$ is $(1 - \frac{q \cdot p}{1 + p \cdot (q-1)}) \cdot b_j - \frac{q \cdot p}{1 + p \cdot (q-1)} \cdot b_j$. As always, its expected utility from playing $d = c$ is 0. For J to be indifferent between $d(\omega = l) = c$ and $d(\omega = l) = u$, C must play $q(p)^* = \frac{1-p}{p}$. However, in order for C to be willing to play $q(p)^*$, J must play $d(\omega = l) = c$ with some probability m. There is no value $m \in [0, 1]$ that makes C indifferent between $\omega(\Omega = H) = l$ and $\omega(\Omega = H) = h$. Therefore, C always has an incentive to deviate and play $\omega(\Omega = H) = h$.

Finally, consider an alternative separating equilibrium in which $\omega(\Omega) \neq \Omega$. J will play $d = u$ iff $\omega = l$ and $d = c$ otherwise. Therefore, whenever $\Omega = H$, J will make a constrained decision. Therefore, whenever $\Omega = H$, C's expected utility is $b_c - \varepsilon$. By deviating and playing $\omega = h$, C expects to receive $\varepsilon - b_c$. $\varepsilon > b_c$ implies that C will have an incentive to deviate, and this separating equilibrium cannot be supported.

Thus, whenever $\varepsilon > b_c$, no pooling, semi-separating, or partial-pooling equilibrium can be supported. The separating equilibrium is therefore the unique perfect Bayesian equilibrium when the electoral benefit of position-taking outweighs the policy benefit associated with constraining the Court. ∎

Proof. *Proof of Proposition 3.* Suppose that $b_C \geq \varepsilon$ and $p > \frac{1}{2}$ and that Congress is playing a pooling strategy. Upon observing $\omega = h$, the Court's posterior belief is that $\Pr(\Omega = H | \omega = h) = p$. Therefore, the Court's expected utility from playing $d = u$ is given by $(-b_j) \cdot (p) + (b_j) \cdot (1 - p) = b_j \cdot (1 - 2p)$. The Court's expected utility from playing $d = c$ is 0.

$p \geq \frac{1}{2}$ implies that the Court prefers to play $d = c$. Now, to see that this is an equilibrium, consider the Congress. Congress' expected utility from playing $\omega = h$ when $\Omega = H$ is given by $b_c + \varepsilon$; if it plays $\omega = l$, it expects $b_c - \varepsilon$. Therefore, when $\Omega = H$, Congress prefers to play $\omega = h$. Now, suppose that $\Omega = L$. If Congress plays $\omega = h$, it expects to receive $b_c - \varepsilon$. If it plays $\omega = l$, it expects to receive $\varepsilon - b_c$. $\varepsilon < b_c$ implies that Congress will strictly prefer to play $\omega = h$ regardless of Ω whenever $\varepsilon < b_c$ and $p > \frac{1}{2}$.

To see that this is the unique equilibrium, consider the following. First, suppose there is a separating equilibrium, such that C plays $\omega_s = \Omega$. J's expected utility from playing $d(\omega = h) = u$ is $-b_j < 0$; from playing $d(\omega = l) = u$ is $b_j > 0$. As always, its expected utility from playing $d = c$ is 0. Therefore, J will play $d = u$ iff $\omega = l$. Thus, C's expected utility from playing

$$\omega(\Omega) = \begin{cases} h & \text{if } \Omega = H \\ h & \text{with probability } q \in (0, 1) \text{ if } \Omega = L \\ l & \text{else} \end{cases}$$

when $\Omega = L$ is $q \cdot (b_c - \varepsilon) + (1 - q) \cdot (\varepsilon - b_c)$. When $\Omega = L$, if C plays its assigned separating strategy, its expected utility is $\varepsilon - b_c$. Thus, C will have an incentive to deviate and play $\omega = \Omega$ with any probability $q > 0$ whenever $\Omega = L$ and $b_c > \varepsilon$.

Now, consider an alternative separating equilibrium in which C plays $\omega - s \neq \Omega$. It is immediate that this equilibrium similarly cannot be supported. This is because the policy outcomes from this separating equilibrium are identical to those from the previous separating equilibrium. However, now J faces an additional disincentive from separation – namely, it loses position-taking utility whenever it separates.

Thus, an intermediate result:

Lemma 1 *There can be no separating equilibrium whenever $b_c > \varepsilon$.*

Now, consider the semi-separating equilibrium in which C plays

$$\omega(\Omega) = \begin{cases} h & \text{if } \Omega = H \\ h & \text{with probability } q \in (0, 1) \text{ if } \Omega = L \\ l & \text{else} \end{cases}$$

In this case, J's posterior belief is that $\Pr(\Omega = H | \omega = h) = \frac{p}{p + q \cdot (1 - p)}$ and $\Pr(\Omega = H | \omega = h) = 0$. J will therefore prefer to play $d(\omega = h) = c$ iff $p \geq \frac{q}{1+q}$. Thus, J will play $d(\omega = h) = c$ iff $q \leq \frac{p}{1-p}$. By assumption, $p \geq \frac{1}{2}$; therefore, only $q \geq 1$ satisfies this condition. C's expected utility from playing $\omega(\Omega = L) = h$ is $b_c - \varepsilon$ when $p \geq \frac{1}{2}$. Playing $\omega(\Omega = L) = h$ with any probability $q < 1$ leads to a strictly lesser expected utility whenever $p \geq \frac{1}{2}$, because whenever J observes $\omega = l$, it will play $d = u$. Therefore, semi-separation cannot be supported whenever $p \geq \frac{1}{2}$.

Finally, consider a partial-pooling equilibrium in which C plays

$$\omega(\Omega) = \begin{cases} h & \text{if } \Omega = H \\ l & \text{with probability } q \in (0, 1) \text{ if } \Omega = H \\ l & \text{else} \end{cases}$$

To see that this strategy cannot be supported in equilibrium, consider first J. J's posterior belief is $\Pr(\Omega = H|\omega = h) = 1$ and $\Pr(\Omega = H|\omega = l) = \frac{q \cdot p}{q \cdot p + (1-p)}$. Therefore, J prefers to play $d(\omega = l) = u$ iff $p < \frac{1}{q+1}$. Now suppose that $\Omega = H$. If $p < \frac{1}{q+1}$, then C's expected utility from playing its prescribed strategy is $q \cdot (b_c - \varepsilon + (1 - q) \cdot (b_c + \varepsilon)$. If $p \geq \frac{1}{q+1}$, then C's expected utility from playing its prescribed strategy is $q \cdot (-b_c - \varepsilon + (1 - q) \cdot (b_c + \varepsilon)$. In each case, if C deviates and plays $\omega = H$, then its expected utility is $b_c + \varepsilon$. Thus, regardless of p, C has an incentive to deviate and play $\omega = h$ whenever $b_c > \varepsilon$. Thus, an intermediate result:

Lemma 2 *There can be no partial-pooling separating equilibrium in which C plays $\omega(\Omega = H) = l$ with any probability $q > 0$ whenever $b_c > \varepsilon$.*

We see then that there can be no separating, partial-pooling, or semi-separating equilibrium whenever $b_c > \varepsilon$ and $p \geq \frac{1}{2}$. Thus, the pooling equilibrium is the unique perfect Bayesian equilibrium. ∎

Proof. *Proof of Proposition 4.* Suppose the C is playing a semi-separating strategy, in which it sends message $\omega = h$ whenever $\Omega = H$ and plays $\omega = h$ with probability q if $\Omega = L$ and $\omega = l$ otherwise. Further assume that J plays its prescribed strategy,

$$d(\omega) = \begin{cases} u & \text{if } \omega = l \\ u & \text{with probability } \frac{b_c - \varepsilon}{b_c} \text{ if } \omega = h \\ c & \text{else} \end{cases}$$

The Court's posterior beliefs are given by $\Pr(\Omega = H|\omega = h) = \frac{\Pr(\omega=h|\Omega=H)\cdot\Pr(\Omega=H)}{\Pr(\omega=h)} = \frac{p}{p+q\cdot(1-p)}$. Therefore, $EU_J(d_2 = u|\omega = h; q) = \frac{p}{p+q\cdot(1-p)} \cdot (-b_J) + \left(1 - \frac{p}{p+q\cdot(1-p)}\right) \cdot (b_j)$, and $EU_J(d_2 = c) = 0$. Thus, the Court is indifferent between $d = u$ and $d = c$ when $q = \frac{p}{1-p}$. Notice that for $q \in (0, 1)$, it must be the case that $p < \frac{1}{2}$, which is true by assumption.

Now, to see that $q = \frac{p}{1-p}$ is an optimal strategy for C, consider two possible deviations by C. First, C may deviate and play $\omega = h$ with probability 1 when $\Omega = L$. The C's expected payoff then is $(1 - m) \cdot b_c - m \cdot b_c - \varepsilon$. If it plays $q = \frac{p}{1-p}$, then its expected utility is $q \cdot ((1 - m) \cdot b_c - m \cdot b_c - \varepsilon) + (1 - q) \cdot (\varepsilon - b_c)$. Therefore, C prefers to play its prescribed strategy rather than deviate and play $\omega = h$ whenever $b_c < \varepsilon$, $p < \frac{1}{2}$ and J plays its prescribed strategy, $m = \frac{b_c - \varepsilon}{b_c}$. Now, consider the deviation where C plays $\omega = l$ whenever $\Omega = L$. C's expected utility is given by $\varepsilon - b_c$. Thus, it prefers to play q whenever $b_c > \varepsilon$, $p < \frac{1}{2}$ and J plays its prescribed strategy, $m = \frac{b_c - \varepsilon}{b_c}$. Therefore, C has no incentive to deviate.

To see that this equilibrium is unique, consider the following. By Lemma 1, there can be no separating equilibrium when $b_c > \varepsilon$. Suppose there is a pooling equilibrium. Let ω_p represent C's signal in the pooling equilibrium. In this case, the J's posterior is equal to its prior, p. J's expected utility from playing $d = u$ is therefore $b_j \cdot (1 - 2p)$. As always, J's expected utility from playing $d = c$ is 0. Therefore, J prefers to play $d = u$ iff $p \leq \frac{1}{2}$. This is true by assumption. Therefore, $d(\omega_p)^* = u$. Thus, C's expected utility from playing $\omega(\Omega) = \omega_p$ is

$$EU_C(\omega_p) = \begin{cases} -b_c + \varepsilon & \text{if } \Omega = \omega_p \\ -b_c - \varepsilon & \text{if } \Omega \neq \omega_p \end{cases}$$

If C deviates and plays $\hat{\omega} = \Omega$, then it ensures itself at least $-b_c + \varepsilon$. Thus, C will have an incentive to deviate whenever $\Omega \neq \omega_p$.

Finally, consider a partial-pooling equilibrium in which C plays the following strategy:

$$\omega(\Omega) = \begin{cases} h & \text{if } \Omega = H \\ l & \text{with probability } q \in (0, 1) \text{ if } \Omega = H \\ l & \text{else} \end{cases}$$

By Lemma 2, this equilibrium cannot be supported whenever $b_c > \varepsilon$. Thus, no separating, pooling, or partial-pooling equilibrium can be supported when $b_c > \varepsilon$ and $p \leq \frac{1}{2}$. Thus, the semi-separating equilibrium is the unique equilibrium. ∎

Proof. *Proof of Proposition 5.* Assume that $b_c \leq \varepsilon(1 - r)$ and suppose a separating strategy. J's posterior beliefs are, by construction, $\Pr(\Omega_2 = H|\omega = h) = 1$ and $\Pr(\Omega_2 = L|\omega = l) = 1$. J strictly prefers to play $d = c$ whenever $\Omega_2 = H$ and $d = u$ whenever $\Omega_2 = L$. Therefore, J's strategy will be $d_2(\omega = h)^* = c$ and $d_2(\omega = l)^* = u$. Now, to see that this is an equilibrium, it must be shown that C does not have an incentive to deviate. Suppose first $\Omega = H$. C's expected utility from playing $\omega = h$ is $b_c + \varepsilon$ and from playing $\omega = l$ is $-b_c - \varepsilon$. Therefore, C has no incentive to deviate from its separating strategy when $\Omega = H$. Now, suppose $\Omega = L$. J's expected utility from playing $\omega = l$ is $\varepsilon - b_c$. If it plays $\omega = h$, C expects to receive $b_c + r \cdot \varepsilon - (1 - q) \cdot \varepsilon$, because with probability r, $\Omega_2 = H$ when $\omega = h$ and $\Omega_1 = L$. Therefore, C will not have an incentive to deviate from its separating strategy when $\varepsilon \geq \frac{b_c}{1-r}$. By assumption, this is true. Therefore, C has no incentive to deviate from the separating strategy, and the behavior is an equilibrium. ■

Proof. *Proof of Proposition 6.* Assume that $b_c > \varepsilon(1 - r)$, $p \geq \frac{\frac{1}{2}-r}{1-r}$, and suppose a pooling equilibrium. Upon observing $\omega = h$, J believes that $\Pr(\Omega_2 = H) = p + r \cdot (1 - p)$ – the probability that the initial state of the world is $\Omega_1 = H$ plus the probability that the initial state of the world is $\Omega_1 = L$, multiplied by the probability that a high signal changes the state of the world. Therefore, J's expected utility from playing $d_2 = u$ is given by $-b_C \cdot (p + r \cdot (1 - p)) + b_C \cdot [(1 - q) \cdot (1 - p)]$. J expects to receive $-b_C$ if it plays $d = c$. Therefore, J prefers to play $d = c$ if and only if $p \geq \frac{\frac{1}{2}-r}{1-r}$.

Now, consider C. If C observes $\Omega_1 = H$, its expected utility from playing $\omega = h$ is $b_c + \varepsilon$; if it plays $\omega = l$, then its expected utility is $-b_c - \varepsilon$. Therefore, C strictly prefers $\omega = h$ whenever it observes $\Omega_1 = H$. Now, suppose it observes $\Omega_1 = L$. C's expected utility from playing $\omega = l$ is $\varepsilon - b_c$; if it plays $\omega = h$, it expects to receive $b_c + r \cdot \varepsilon - (1 - r) \cdot \varepsilon$. Therefore, it prefers to play $\omega = h$ whenever $\varepsilon < \frac{b_c}{1-r}$. By assumption, this is true. ■

Proof. *Proof of Proposition 7.* Assume that $b_c > \varepsilon(1 - r)$, $p < \frac{\frac{1}{2}-r}{1-r}$, and that C is playing a semi-separating strategy as follows:

$$\omega(\Omega) = \begin{cases} h & \text{if } \Omega = H \\ h & \text{with probability } q(p) = \frac{p}{1-p-2r+2pr} \text{ if } \Omega = L \\ l & \text{else} \end{cases}$$

and that J plays a mixed strategy as follows:

$$d(\omega) = \begin{cases} u & \text{if } \omega = l \\ u & \text{with probability } m = \frac{b+\varepsilon(1-r)}{b} \text{ if } \omega = h \\ c & \text{else} \end{cases}$$

C must play $q(p)$ such that J is indifferent between playing $d = u$ and $d = c$, upon observing a high signal. Therefore, $q(p)$ must satisfy the following condition $EU_J(d = u; \omega = h) = EU_J(d = c; \omega = h)$. $EU_J(d = c) = 0$. Conditional on observing $\omega = h$, J's posterior belief that $\Omega_2 = H$ is given by $\Pr(\Omega_2 = H | \omega = h) = \frac{\Pr(\Omega_2 = H \wedge \omega = h)}{\Pr(\omega = h)} = \frac{p + (1-p) \cdot r \cdot q}{p + (1-p) \cdot q}$, when C sends message $\omega = h$ with probability $q(p)$ whenever $\Omega_1 = L$. Thus, in order to be indifferent, C must play the strategy $q(p; r) = \frac{p}{1 - p - 2r + 2pr}$. Upon observing $\omega = l$, J's posterior is $\Pr(\Omega = L | \omega = l) = 1$. Thus, J always prefers to play $d(\omega = l) = u$.

Now, to see that this is an equilibrium, consider two possible deviations by C. First, C may deviate and play $\omega(\Omega = L) = l$. In this case, C's expected utility is given by $\varepsilon - b_c$. However, if it plays $q(p)$, it expects $q(p) \cdot (r \cdot \varepsilon - (1 - r) \cdot \varepsilon + (1 - m) \cdot b_c - m \cdot b_c) + (1 - q(p)) \cdot (\varepsilon - b_c)$. C will prefer to play $q(p)$ iff $m \le \frac{b + \varepsilon(1 - r)}{b}$. Second, C may deviate and play $\omega(\omega = L) = h$. In this case, C's expected utility is given by $r \cdot \varepsilon - (1 - r) \cdot \varepsilon - m \cdot b_c + (1 - m) \cdot b_c$. C prefers to play $q(p)$ iff $m \ge \frac{b + \varepsilon(1 - r)}{b}$. Thus, C will not have an incentive to deviate to either pure strategy whenever $\Omega = L$ iff $m = \frac{b + \varepsilon(1 - r)}{b}$. ∎

4

Court-Curbing and the Electoral Connection

In 1954, during a period of relative harmony in Washington,[1] no Court-curbing bills were introduced in Congress. In fact, during the ten preceding years, only fourteen Court-curbing bills had been introduced. However, 1955 and 1956 would witness a slight increase in the introduction of anti-Court bills (six and five, respectively), and in 1957, thirteen such bills would be introduced, and fifteen bills were introduced in 1959. A decade later, in 1969, at least fifty-three Court-curbing bills were introduced. What explains the decision to introduce Court-curbing legislation in Congress? What is the source of anti-Court sentiment among legislators? The theory developed in the preceding chapter suggested a number of factors that should determine the extent of Court-curbing in Congress, and in this chapter, we ask whether the historical patterns support those predictions.[2]

The Conditional Self-Restraint Model predicts that the introduction of Court-curbing bills will be driven by both public opinion and policy

---

[1] Standard measures of ideological polarization, for example, indicate that congressional polarization was at an all-time low during the 1950s (see, for example, McCarty, Poole, and Rosenthal 2006).

[2] Despite apparent interest among political scientists and legal academics alike, there has been little scholarly attention paid to systematic patterns in Court-curbing. Several notable exceptions stand out (Nagel 1965; Rosenberg 1992; Hansford and Damore 2000), though there remains a significant dearth of systematic study of Court-curbing. Of course, this may be in large part due to the difficulty of acquiring data on Court-curbing proposals (Segal, Westerland, and Lindquist, Forthcoming), but the data presented in Chapter 2 overcome that obstacle. Moreover, the theoretical focus offered in the preceding chapter represents a break with previous approaches to Court-curbing, which focus almost exclusively on Congress and the Court, while disregarding the public's role in such elite-level interactions. For a notable exception, see Bell and Scott (2006).

disagreements between Congress and the Supreme Court. Importantly, it is the public opinion motivation behind Court-curbing that allows it to be a credible signal about the Court's institutional legitimacy and diffuse support. In subsequent chapters, we will consider whether the Court responds to the introduction of Court-curbing bills, but here we first establish the determinants of Court-curbing. In the end, the analysis will demonstrate that public discontent with the Court is the primary determinant of Court-curbing, while policy divergence between the Court and Congress also influences Court-curbing. In addition, the analysis will also show simple decreases in "specific" support for the Court – public disagreements with individual decisions – does not seem to drive Court-curbing; rather Court-curbing seems to be affected by decreases in "diffuse" support for the Court. First, I present a "first cut" at the data and examine the simple patterns in Court-curbing, public support for the judiciary, and Court–Congress ideological divergence. Then, I present two statistical analyses that examine the effect of public opinion and Court–Congress divergence on (a) the intensity or frequency of Court-curbing and (b) the ideological content of Court-curbing. Taken together, the evidence provides support for the claim that Court-curbing is primarily a position-taking endeavor.

4.1 EXAMINING THE PATTERNS

We saw in Chapter 2 that Court-curbing during each of the seven periods of heightened congressional hostility toward the Court was motivated by distinct substantive problems. However, what are the systematic determinants of Court-curbing that we may use to study the macro-level patterns of congressional attacks on the Court? What are the strongest predictors of Court-curbing? Does Congress introduce Court-curbing in response to public opinion or instead to engage in a conflict with an ideologically divergent Court? Hypotheses 1–3 derived from the Conditional Self-Restraint model provide the basis for an empirical examination of these questions. There are two ways in which Court-curbing varies – the volume (intensity) of bills introduced and the ideology of the proposers. During some periods, there is very little hostility between the Court and Congress; during others, the relationship between the branches is much more strained. At some points in time, liberals are hostile toward the Court; at others, conservatives. Indeed, the political history of Court-curbing offered in Chapter 2 outlined these two trends over the past 130 years. However, we now ask whether the patterns themselves provide empirical support for the Conditional Self-Restraint model. In this section, we consider a first cut at the data to assess whether the basic patterns appear.

4.1.1 Public Opinion and Bill Introduction: Aggregate Patterns

The first, and primary, prediction derived from the model is that Congress should be more likely to introduce Court-curbing bills as the Court's prestige wanes (Hypothesis 1). That is, there ought to be an inverse relationship between the Court's legitimacy – its diffuse support – and the intensity of Court-curbing in Congress. This question raises a difficult measurement problem that will be an issue throughout the empirical sections of this book. How does one measure the Court's legitimacy? As I have described it, the Court's legitimacy is an indicator of its standing with the public – its diffuse support. This legitimacy, or diffuse support, refers to the Court's "reservoir of good will" that motivates the public (and political actors) to accept and enforce decisions with which they may disagree. In the theoretical model, the relevant concept is the Court's belief about public support for the Court. Perhaps the best measure of this concept, then, would be a measure of the justices' own perceptions of the Court's diffuse support. Unfortunately, such a measure does not exist. Moreover, it is not clear how one would go about developing such a measure, especially over any considerable period of time.[3]

Given we cannot directly measure the justices' beliefs about their institutional legitimacy and diffuse support, we must rely on other measures – reasonable proxies. The most natural such proxy measure is a public opinion poll. Indeed, direct measures of public opinion seem a natural way to measure legitimacy. Of course, it is important to note this measure necessarily captures *actual* public support for the Court, rather than *perceived* public support. An ideal public opinion poll would regularly ask the public whether they would support a Supreme Court decision with which they disagreed. Or, we might have a public opinion poll that asks the public how much respect they have for the Supreme Court's decisions.

---

[3] Such a measure would necessarily require responses by the justices, which would surely be difficult to acquire. What is more, in order to construct a measure that covers any period of time, one would have to conduct a survey of the justices each year. This essentially precludes the construction of such a measure back through time.

Such a measure of public opinion would allow us to directly capture the Court's diffuse support. Unfortunately, such data are very difficult to come by and are generally plagued with significant measurement and conceptual issues (Gibson, Caldeira, and Spence 2003; Durr, Martin, and Wolbrecht 2000; Marshall 1989*b*; Caldeira 1987). One measure that is widely used, though, is a survey question I will call the *confidence question*. The confidence question is asked in a variety of formats on a variety of surveys and usually asks respondents how much confidence they have in the Supreme Court. This survey item is the most reliable and consistent way to capture public support for the Court for two reasons. First, the question is asked regularly in nationally representative samples. Second, several surveys have asked the question over a period of time without changing the question wording.[4]

To measure the Court's diffuse support, I use these public opinion polls to assess the level of *explicit* lack of confidence in the Court. Because respondents are usually given multiple options to respond to the survey question, one must decide which responses will be counted as indicating a lack of support. As noted in Chapter 3, diffuse support for the Court is resilient. The justices are concerned not about making mildly unpopular decisions but rather about undermining their base of legitimacy, and explicit disapproval is the best way to measure the Court's diffuse support. More mild fluctuations in confidence in the Court, although important, are not the variation in which I have argued the Court has an interest.

Figure 4.1 shows the relationship between the number of Court-curbing bills introduced in Congress and the level of expressed explicit lack of confidence in the Supreme Court.[5] As the figure makes clear, there is a noisy but positive correlation. That is, as the public becomes less confident in the Court, members of Congress introduce more Court-curbing

---

[4] Despite the ubiquity of this measure in scholarly work, though, the item has been the subject of critical scholarly analysis. Notably, Gibson, Caldeira, and Spence (2003) argue that this measure does not tap into "diffuse" support for the Court but rather captures "specific" support for recent decisions. Thus, if we are interested in the Court's "reservoir of good will" and its underlying legitimacy, then this measure may be misleading.

[5] I measure explicit lack of confidence as the proportion of respondents who, on the General Social Survey, indicate they have "hardly any" confidence in the U.S. Supreme Court. Thus, respondents who refuse to answer or have no opinion are counted as respondents with confidence in the Supreme Court. Alternative operationalizations, such as discarding those respondents or including respondents with "little" confidence in the Court does not affect the patterns described here. In years during which the GSS did not ask this question, I use the average of the preceding and following years.

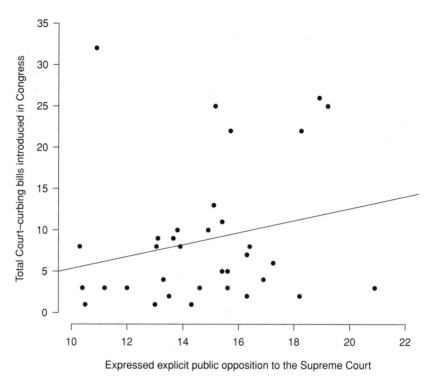

FIGURE 4.1. *Correlation between total Court-curbing bills introduced and public opposition to the Supreme Court, 1972–2008.* Public opposition is measured as the proportion of respondents on the General Social Survey who indicate they have "hardly any" confidence in the Supreme Court.

bills. This relationship is suggestive of the claim that Court-curbing is driven by constituent preferences. To the extent that the confidence question is measuring institutional legitimacy, this correlation indicates that there is more Court-curbing when the Court lacks public support than when it has public support. This finding is, in and of itself, notable, given that previous research on Court-curbing and Court–Congress relations has not generally focused on the role of the public in these elite-level interactions. That we find in this preliminary cut evidence of a correlation between public opinion and congressional behavior provides the first insight (of this analysis) into the role of representation as a determinant of separation-of-powers interactions. As we move forward through the remainder of the analyses in this book, it will be important to keep in mind this initial point of departure – the electoral connection between legislators and the public provides the conduit through which the people are represented in seemingly elite-level interactions.

4.1.2 Public Opinion and Bill Introduction: Individual Patterns

The aggregate-level, yearly patterns provide some initial evidence of a relationship between public opinion about the Supreme Court and the introduction of Court-curbing bills. However, as noted, aggregate analyses can only tell us a limited amount about the relationships. To more carefully consider the relationship between public opinion and the introduction of Court-curbing, we can push the data even further. Specifically, using the public opinion poll data, we can develop estimated levels of confidence in the Supreme Court *within each state*. Using those data, we can assess the effect of public opinion on individual legislators' decisions to sponsor Court-curbing legislation. To the extent we find that constituent opinion drives Court-curbing sponsorship, we have further evidence to support the claim that Court-curbing is driven primarily by public opinion about the Court.

ESTIMATING STATE-LEVEL OPINION. Of course, measuring state-level opinion about the Supreme Court is a difficult task. Indeed, measuring state-level opinion about any topic has been a frustrating undertaking for students of public opinion (see Lax and Phillips 2009 for a review). The most significant limitation has been that any given survey does not usually include a large enough random sample of people from each state to estimate a reliable measure of state-level opinion. Perhaps the most widely implemented method to overcome this limitation has been to aggregate all respondents within a state over a ten-year period to calculate state-level opinion (Erikson, Wright, and McIver 1993). More recently, scholars have demonstrated that state-level opinion can be estimated reliably using all individual responses, demographic and geographic correlations among the respondents, and each state's demographic breakdown (Lax and Phillips 2009; Park, Gelman, and Bafumi 2005).

Using this method, known as multilevel regression with poststratification (MRP), I estimate state-level confidence in the U.S. Supreme Court, during each Congress from the 94th through 109th (1975 through 2006). To do this, I identify every public opinion poll asked during each Congress for which individual-level responses are available and for which respondents were offered four responses. MRP is used to model the probability that any individual reports having no confidence in the Supreme Court as a function of his or her demographic and geographic characteristics.

We then have a prediction for how the probability of reporting having no confidence in the Court for each type of person for a given combination of demographic and geographic characteristics. Those responses are then poststratified according to Census data for each state, yielding a predicted state-level of confidence in the Court. Applying MRP, I estimate the level of confidence in each state during each congressional session. These estimates are shown in Figure 4.2. The figure makes clear that there is a common pattern across the states (a high level of confidence during the early period with a more pronounced increase in opposition during recent years). Nevertheless, these data also reveal considerable cross-state variation. For example, the increase in opposition to the Court has been more pronounced in some states, such as Mississippi and Nebraska, and less dramatic in other states, such as Michigan and Virginia.

With these data in hand, we are now prepared to ask a more exacting question than in the aggregate-level analysis. Are *individual* representatives' bill sponsorship decisions correlated with state-level confidence in the Court? To answer this question, I identify whether each member of the House of Representatives sponsored, or cosponsored, at least one Court-curbing bill during each session of Congress. Figure 4.3 shows the raw correlation between each legislator's sponsorship decision during each Congress and state-level opposition to the Supreme Court during that Congress. The pattern revealed here is striking – at the highest level of confidence in the Court (lowest level of opposition), less than 10% of all House members (co-)sponsor at least one Court-curbing bill. By contrast, at the lowest level of confidence (highest level of opposition), about 50% of all House members (co-)sponsor a bill. That is, moving from the highest level of confidence in the Court to the lowest level is associated with a nearly fivefold increase in the propensity to introduce a Court-curbing bill.

Of course, we can only draw limited conclusions from these data. There are other important factors that may be influencing the decision to sponsor Court-curbing legislation for which this analysis does not control. However, what these data do indicate, in conjunction with the aggregate-level data, is that there is a pronounced association between public opinion about the Supreme Court and the introduction of Court-curbing bills. Below, we consider a series of empirical models that allow us to assess the strength of that potentially causal relationship in the face of other possible explanations. First, however, we turn to a brief inspection of the relationship between public policy preferences and the ideological content of Court-curbing bills.

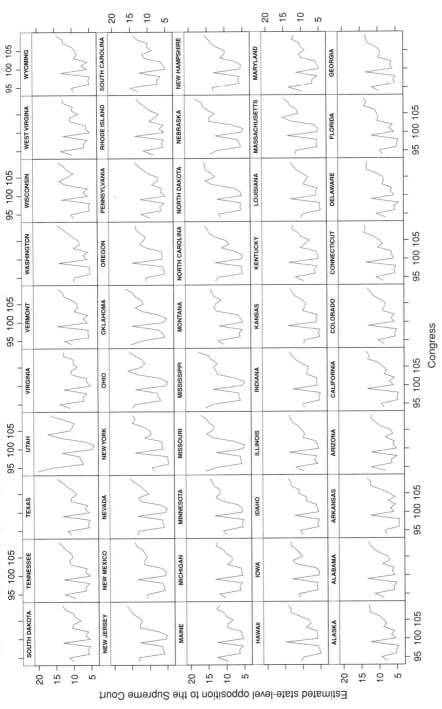

FIGURE 4.2. *Estimated state-level opposition to the Court in each state during each Congress, 1975–2005.* Opposition is measured as an "explicit lack of confidence"; the level of opposition confidence therefore corresponds to proportion of state that chooses the lowest (of four) levels of confidence in the Court.

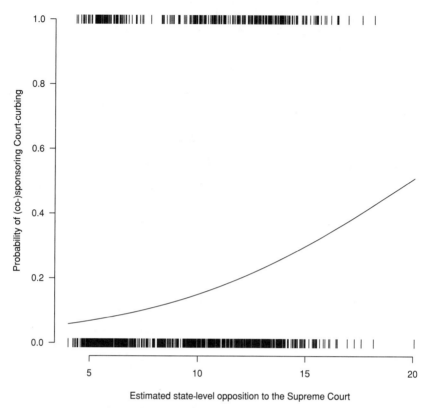

FIGURE 4.3. *Correlation between estimated state-level confidence in the Supreme Court and the sponsorship of Court-curbing bills.* The x-axis shows estimated confidence in the Supreme Court for each member of Congress during each of the 94th through 109th Congresses (points are jittered); y-axis shows whether each member sponsored or cosponsored a Court-curbing bill during each of the Congresses; line is a fit from a logit model regressing bill sponsorship on estimated state-level opposition to the Court.

4.1.3 Ideology and Court-Curbing

In addition to the relationship between judicial legitimacy and the intensity of Court-curbing, we can derive from the Conditional Self-Restraint model predictions about the content of Court-curbing. In particular, the model predicts that public discontent with the judiciary should lead to Court-curbing. Because Court-curbing is driven primarily by public perceptions about the Court's legitimacy, we should expect to find a relationship between public policy preferences and the ideology of the Court-curbers in Congress. Thus, if the public thinks the Court is too liberal, then we should expect to see conservative members of Congress engaging in Court-curbing; if the public thinks the Court is too conservative, then we should see liberal members of Congress engaging in Court-curbing.

To assess the support for this prediction, I examine the relationship between "public mood" and the ideology of the median Court-curber in Congress. "Public mood" refers to the overall liberalism of the public, as measured by Stimson (1991, 1999). I provide further details on this measure below; for now it is important to note simply that this measure is an index of the overall liberalism of the public and is derived by indexing public opinion from surveys across a range of policy issues during the postwar era. Figure 4.4 shows the relationship between how liberal the public is and how liberal the Court-curbers are in Congress. The upward-sloping relationship in the left-hand panel indicates that as the public becomes more liberal, so too do the Court-curbers in Congress. That is, in years where the public has more conservative policy views, the average Court-curbing bill is introduced by a more conservative member of Congress. Similarly, in years where the public has more liberal policy views, the average Court-curbing bill is introduced by a more liberal member of Congress. This indicates that the ideological content of Court-curbing is related to public policy preferences and is suggestive of the public–electoral motivation behind Court-curbing.

Beyond the electoral motivation for Court-curbing, Hypothesis 2 predicts that policy divergence between Congress and the Court should affect Court-curbing. One such effect is that as the Court becomes more liberal relative to Congress, Court-curbing should become more conservative. That is, conservative members of Congress should be more inclined to introduce Court-curbing when the Court is more liberal, and vice-versa. The question, then, is whether the median Court-curber's ideology is related to the ideological composition of the Court. As the Court becomes more conservative, do more liberal members of Congress introduce Court-curbing legislation? To answer this question, I consider how liberal or conservative the Court is relative to Congress. I construct a measure that equals the ideological distance between the Court median and the nearest of either the House or Senate median.[6]

---

[6] To examine this relationship, I measure the ideology of each Court-curbing sponsor each year, using the NOMINATE Common Space scores developed by Poole (1998; Poole and Rosenthal 1997). This measure runs from a lower bound of -1 (the most liberal position) to an upper bound of $+1$ (the most conservative position). Because of limitations in the availability of data, this analysis will be restricted to the period from 1953 forward.

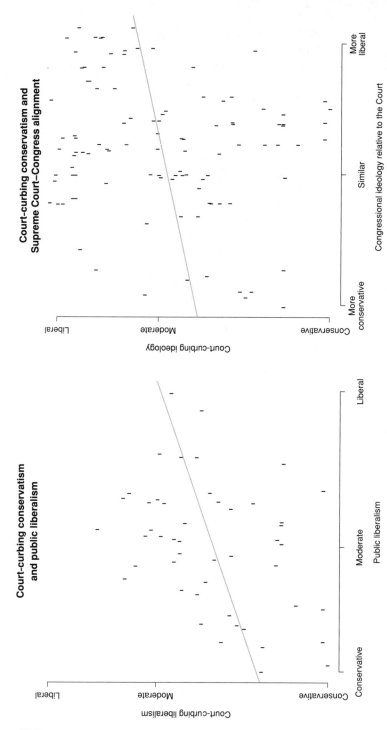

FIGURE 4.4. *Correlates of Court-curbing conservatism.* Left-hand panel shows correlation between conservatism of median Court-curbing sponsor and public mood; right-hand panel shows correlation between conservatism of median Court-curbing sponsor and Supreme Court liberalism relative to Congress.

The relationship between congressional liberalism relative to the Court and liberalism of the Court-curbers is shown in the right-hand panel of Figure 4.4. This figure shows an interesting and intuitive pattern. When Congress is more liberal than the Court, we see that the average Court-curber is very liberal. On the other hand, when Congress is very conservative relative to the Court, the median Court-curber is very conservative. However, when the Court and Congress are relatively closely aligned, then Court-curbing is not necessarily either conservative or liberal. That is, when the Court's ideological preferences are similar to the ideological preferences of Congress, we find both liberal and conservative Court-curbing. Importantly, though, as the Court moves to one end of the ideological spectrum, Court-curbing only comes from its ideological adversaries. This evidence is suggestive of the relationship outlined by Hypothesis 2, which predicts that ideological divergence between the Court and Congress should be a determinant of Court-curbing.

Hypothesis 2 also predicts, however, that ideological divergence between the Court and Congress affects not only *who* introduces Court-curbing, but *how much* Court-curbing will be introduced. As divergence in policy preferences between the Court and Congress grows, more Court-curbing bills will be introduced in Congress. There is, to be sure, such a relationship, though it is weak. The correlation between the ideological distance from the Court to Congress is positive, but it is not very strong $(r = 0.50)$.[7] What does this tell us? Simply put, the evidence indicates there is some support for the claim increases in ideological divergence between the Court and Congress are somewhat associated with increases in Court-curbing (as predicted by Hypothesis 2). Of course, the strength and magnitude of this relationship is not overpowering; the statistical analyses presented in the following further illuminate the strength of the relationship. Because the Conditional Self-Restraint model predicts that

[7] Measuring ideological divergence between Congress and the Court is a significant problem in the study of interbranch relations, as we will see throughout this book. I treat this measurement more fully in Chapter 6. For now, I simply use the *Judicial Common Space* estimates of institutional ideology developed by Epstein, Martin, Segal, and Westerland (2007). These estimates place the Supreme Court, the president, the House, and the Senate all on a common scale. The estimates are all derived from the justices, legislators, and executive voting behavior. As with many of the estimates of institutional ideology that we will encounter throughout this book, they are only available for a limited period of time – essentially the post–World War II era. Despite this limitation, the *Judicial Common Space* estimates nevertheless enable the study of a longer period of time than was possible above in the analysis of public opinion and Court-curbing. Here, I use these estimates to compare the relationship between ideological divergence and Court-curbing.

the effect of ideological divergence will be conditioned by public support for the Court, we can use a statistical analysis to ask whether that weak correlation is in fact evidence of a relationship that is conditional on public opinion.

4.2 TESTING THE PREDICTIONS

The patterns in the data we just saw are certainly suggestive of the relationships predicted by the theoretical model. But, a question remains: are the suggestive patterns we saw above meaningful indicators of a systematic relationship? If the posited relationships do in fact exist, then they should become stronger when we employ statistical methods to control for other confounding factors. To assess the strength of the relationships reported above, I employ three statistical analyses. The first two examine the number of Court-curbing bills introduced in Congress. One considers aggregate sponsorship – that is, how many bills are introduced each year. The other considers individual legislators' decisions to (co-)sponsor Court Curbing legislation. The third statistical analysis asks who Court-curbs, and considers the ideological orientation of Court-curbing proposals.

4.2.1 The Introduction of Court-Curbing: Aggregate Patterns

Measurement of Key Variables
In the first two statistical analyses, I seek to explain variation in the number of Court-curbing bills introduced in Congress. More Court-curbing bills indicate a stronger signal to the Court about waning public support. One might be concerned, though, that an increase in the number of bills introduced does not necessarily imply a substantively significant decline in public support for the Court. Perhaps a few legislators, representing outlier districts, are sponsoring many Court-curbing bills. In this case, a better measure would be the number of individuals who sponsor Court-curbing bills. These two measures are highly correlated, suggesting the number of Court-curbing bills is an accurate measure of the breadth of public discontent with the Court. Indeed, recall Figure 2.3 from Chapter 2, where we saw that, during periods of heightened Court-curbing, there is fairly broad geographic representation of Court-curbing sponsors. That periods of increased Court-curbing are associated with broader and deeper discontent with the Court means that the number of Court-curbing bills introduced is the best measure of the theoretical concept of interest – the intensity of the negative message sent to the Court from Congress.

Nevertheless, each of the analyses below shows the results that use both the number of bills and the number of sponsors as the source of variation in Court-curbing. As we will see, the two measures yield nearly identical results.

To explain variation in the number of Court-curbing bills introduced, I reference a set of factors that the theoretical model predicts should drive Court-curbing as well as a set of variables representing alternative explanations. First and foremost, the model predicts that the Court's institutional legitimacy should be the primary determinant of Court-curbing (Hypothesis 1). The first, and most important, explanatory variable is then the measure of public opposition to the Court described previously. Second, I include a measure of the ideological distance between the Court and Congress.[8] Hypothesis 2 predicts that as the Court and Congress become more ideologically divergent, Congress should introduce more Court-curbing bills. Thus, we expect to see that as the distance between the Court and Congress increases, more Court-curbing bills will be introduced (presumably, by more members of Congress). Third, Hypothesis 3 predicts an interactive effect between public opposition to the Court and ideological divergence between the Court and Congress. When the Court is most pessimistic – that is, when public opposition is at its highest – the effect of ideological divergence should be greatest. Thus, I include an interaction between public opposition and Court-Congress divergence.

---

[8] In particular, I employ the Judicial Common Space measure developed by Epstein, Martin, Segal, and Westerland (2007) and described previously to identify how far the Supreme Court is from the closer of either the House of Representatives or the Senate. Throughout this chapter, I measure Court-Congress ideological alignment by referencing the median member of the House of Representatives. Of course, there is a variety of alternative models of congressional policymaking that one might adopt, such as the party caucus model (Cox and McCubbins 1993), the committee gate-keeping model (Denzau and Mackay 1983), or the pivotal politics model (Krehbiel 1998). I have performed each of the analyses in this book using each of the various models of congressional policy making and found largely comparable results. The effect of Court-Congress alignment on Court-curbing is strongest in the floor median model (reported here), weaker in the party caucus model and committee gatekeeping model, and weakest in the pivotal politics model. Of course, it is important to note here that my measure explicitly captures the liberalism or conservatism of the Court's output as measured by the median justice's ideal point. Moreover, this measure is not necessarily based on any measure of the Court's policy content. Another possible measure would be the proportion of the Supreme Court's cases decided in a "liberal" direction, though that measure would not be comparable to congressional preferences, as these ideal point estimates are. Though, again, the distribution of liberal dispositions need not be well correlated with opinion content. Thus, one might alternatively be interested in measuring the policy content of the Court's opinions, though there do not currently exist direct measures of the Court's opinion content that are comparable to measures of legislative preferences (but, see Clark and Lauderdale, Forthcoming).

Fourth, I control for the number of laws held unconstitutional by the Supreme Court. As noted in Chapter 3, a possible alternative explanation for Court-curbing is that it is simply a knee-jerk reaction to the exercise of judicial power. When more laws are struck down by the Court, Congress introduces Court-curbing bills. Thus, I include controls for the number of federal laws and state laws struck down by the Court, by referencing the list of state and federal laws held unconstitutional each year maintained by the Congressional Research Services ("CRS list").[9] Because data on state court invalidations are not currently available beyond 2002, I also estimate the empirical model excluding that control variable. One might be concerned, however, that these measures are endogenous to the number of Court-curbing bills introduced. Indeed, my argument is that Court-curbing affects the Court's decision making. However, I also claim that Court-curbing is not necessarily driven by judicial decisions. Nevertheless, because of the potential endogeneity between Court-curbing and judicial review, I include these measures at a one-year lag. That is, the measure of laws invalidated is the number of laws invalidated the previous year. This helps account for the endogeneity and demonstrate a causal link because it is unlikely that judicial decisions in one year are affected by the subsequent year's Court-curbing.[10]

Finally, I also include a measure of legislative activism. As noted in Chapter 3, it could be the case that Court-curbing rises and falls with the general ride of legislative activism. If this were true, then judicial reactions to Court-curbing may be motivated by fear of legislative sanction, rather than judicial learning about public opinion. Thus, I include a measure of how many public laws were enacted during the relevant year.[11]

Each of these variables has been standardized; they have been centered on zero and divided by two standard deviations. Thus, a one-unit change in any variable represents a two-standard-deviation change in the predictor. This transformation is linear and thus does not change any of the substantive interpretations of the results. However, the transformation

---

[9] Moreover, the results from this analysis will be important in the next chapter, where I examine the relationship between Court-curbing and the use of judicial review to hold laws unconstitutional. There, we will want to know whether the use of judicial review drives Court-curbing in order to best assess the causal relationship between these two phenomena.

[10] I note, though, that the results reported here all hold when the model is specified without a lag.

[11] Alternatively, one could include a measure of how many bills were introduced that year. In that case, similar substantive results follow.

does allow the predictors to be on roughly the same scale (Gelman 2008) and thus for easy comparison of the magnitude of estimated coefficients.

Empirical Model

With these variables in hand, I estimate an empirical model, where the number of Court-curbing bills introduced each year (or, the number of unique Court-curbing sponsors) is a function of public support for the Court, ideological divergence between the Court and Congress, and the extent of judicial activism.[12] The empirical model is given by:

$$
\begin{aligned}
Court\ Curbing_t = f(&Public\ Opposition_t, \\
&Court\text{-}Congress\ Ideological\ Distance_t, \\
&State\ Laws\ Struck\ Down_{t-1}, \\
&Federal\ Laws\ Struck\ Down_{t-1} \\
&Legislative\ Activism_{t-1})
\end{aligned} \tag{4.1}
$$

I estimate the model with a negative binomial specification. The results are reported in Table 4.1; the table shows the results of the estimation using both the total number of Court-curbing bills introduced and the total number of sponsors as the dependent variable.

These results reveal an interesting pattern. First, we find evidence that public support for the Court is a meaningful predictor of Court-curbing. The positive estimated coefficients in the first row of Table 4.1 indicate that as public opposition for the Court increases, more Court-curbing bills are introduced. That is, even while controlling for other factors, the less confidence the public has in the Court, the more Court-curbing bills are introduced in Congress. Thus, these data provide direct support for the claim that as the Court's legitimacy and public prestige declines, Congress considers more Court-curbing legislation (Hypothesis 1).

---

[12] The dependent variable in the following analyses is the number of Court-curbing bills or the number of Court-curbing sponsors each year. These data are therefore event-count data (i.e., data that can only take on nonnegative integer values), but they are also time-series data. Although the primary empirical model used to model event-count data is the Poisson regression model, there is an ongoing debate in the literature about the best way to treat count data that are also time-series data (King 1989; Cameron and Trivedi 1998, 227–228; Brandt, Williams, Fordham, and Pollins 2000). To assess how best to model the data here, I have performed several diagnostic tests. Details of these diagnostics are reserved to the Technical Appendix to this chapter. I simply note here that the data are overdispersed but do not exhibit other time-series dynamics such as serial correlation. In light of these diagnostics, I model the data with a negative binomial regression model.

TABLE 4.1. *Determinants of the Amount of Court-Curbing in Congress*

Negative binomial coefficients (standard errors in parentheses, clustered on chief justice); dependent variables are number of Court-curbing bills introduced and number of unique sponsors in year t; all continuous predictors have been normalized by centering on zero and dividing by two standard deviations

	Total Bills Introduced				Total Bill Sponsors			
Public Opposition$_t$	0.45**	0.39**	0.59**	0.59**	0.44**	0.39**	0.42**	0.40**
	(0.05)	(0.12)	(0.17)	(0.11)	(0.05)	(0.10)	(0.06)	(0.06)
Court-Congress Ideological Distance$_t$	-0.01	-0.08	0.36*	0.36**	0.06	-0.02	0.13	0.10
	(0.24)	(0.06)	(0.20)	(0.11)	(0.26)	(0.09)	(0.16)	(0.11)
Public Opposition$_t$ × Court-Congress Ideological Distance$_t$	—	0.40*	—	0.02	—	0.37***	—	0.15
		(0.16)		(0.52)		(0.14)		(0.10)
Federal Laws Struck Down$_t$	0.11	0.06	0.23	0.23	0.10	0.05	0.11	0.09
	(0.17)	(0.09)	(0.22)	(0.29)	(0.20)	(0.12)	(0.36)	(0.35)
State Laws Struck Down$_t$	0.60	0.60	—	—	0.44	0.47	—	—
	(0.43)	(0.63)			(0.45)	(0.46)		
Legislative Activism$_t$	0.45	0.42	—	—	0.42	0.40	—	—
	(0.55)	(0.53)			(0.56)	(0.53)		
Constant	1.93**	1.98**	2.05**	2.05**	1.79**	1.83**	1.85**	1.87**
	(0.18)	(0.14)	(0.19)	(0.11)	(0.21)	(0.17)	(0.19)	(0.18)
α	0.55	0.56	0.59	0.59	0.46	0.45	0.55	0.55
N	29	29	36	36	29	29	36	36

*** $p \leq 0.01$; ** $p \leq 0.05$; * $p \leq 0.10$.

138

Indeed, the substantive effect of these results is considerable. On average, about six Court-curbing bills are introduced each year. Decreasing public support from its average one standard deviation below its mean is associated with an increase of about three bills per year being introduced. Decreasing public support to two standard deviations below its mean is associated with about seven additional bills being introduced – an over 100% increase in the number of bills introduced in Congress. The volume, or intensity, of Court-curbing, then, is very sensitive to public opinion about the Court. As the Court wanes in public prestige and legitimacy, members of Congress engage in Court-curbing with increasing frequency. By the time over ten bills have been introduced in Congress, the Court has begun to reach the lower bounds of public support for the judiciary.

A recent example of this relationship concerns the decline in the Court's public prestige during the early 2000s. In 2002, according to the General Social Survey, only 11.2% of Americans reported having "hardly any" confidence in the U.S. Supreme Court. In 2004, that figure climbed to 14.9% and again climbed to 15.4% in both 2006 and 2008. During those same years, the number of Court-curbing bills introduced in Congress climbed from only three in 2002 to ten in 2004, twenty-five in 2005 and eleven in each of 2006 and 2007. Indeed, as we saw in Chapter 2, the latter half of the first decade of the twenty-first century has witnessed a marked increase in Court-curbing activity in Congress. The evidence from the statistical analysis suggests that the increase in Court-curbing is precisely what one would expect during a period of waning public confidence in the Court. Decreases in public support for the Court are met by notable increases in congressional attacks on the Court.

At the same time, though, we find mixed support for the claim that Congress introduces more Court-curbing bills when it is ideologically distant from the Court than when it is aligned with the Court. The coefficients associated with *Court-Congress Ideological Distance$_t$* in Table 4.1 are inconsistently signed, and only two are statistically distinguishable from zero. These weak results do not provide much confidence for the claim that increased policy divergence between the Court and Congress should increase the level of Court-curbing (Hypothesis 2). However, the estimates here provide some support for the interactive effect of public opposition and Court-Congress alignment. All four estimated coefficients are positive, and two of the four are statistically distinguishable from zero. However, these models are estimated using an admittedly small number of observations (between twenty-nine and thirty-six).[13] Notably, though, when we do not control for legislative activism and invalidations of state laws, the interactive effect decreases in magnitude considerably and is not statistically significant. Moreover, one might expect that the effect of ideological distance is more subtle – perhaps this effect occurs mostly at an individual level, and crude measures of aggregate congressional ideology miss much of the important variation. In the following section, we address both of these possible limitations. In either event, though, these interactive effects are suggestive of the interactive relationship between public and elite opposition to the Court in influencing the decision to sponsor Court-curbing bills.

Finally, we find no evidence in support of either of the two alternative claims: that Court-curbing is primarily a knee-jerk reaction to the use of judicial review to invalidate legislation or Court-curbing simply rises and falls with the normal ebb and flow of legislative activism. While each of the estimated coefficients from these predictors is positive, none of them is significantly distinguishable from zero. What is more, in the case of federal law invalidations, the magnitude of the estimated coefficients is quite small. A recent example of this relationship comes from the 1990s. Beginning in 1995, the Supreme Court struck down federal legislation with increased frequency. During each year from 1995 through 2001, the Court invalidated at least four federal laws on constitutional grounds; in 2001, the Court invalidated eight such laws. The average number of laws struck down during the period studied here is only two. Nevertheless, public confidence in the Court remained high, and there was no notable increase in the introduction of Court-curbing. In 1999, ten bills were introduced, but during all other years during this period, the number of bills fluctuated between only one and six. Notably, the average number of bills introduced each year across the entire time period is only six. By the time Congress began to engage in Court-curbing (in tandem with the decrease in public confidence in the Court), the Court had already begun to move away from the increased hostility toward federal legislation. What is more, given the pace at which issues arise in politics, it seems unlikely that the increased Court-curbing from 2005 forward is attributable to a reaction to judicial review ten years earlier.

[13] Importantly, the negative binomial regression model is fitted using maximum likelihood (ML), and the small sample properties of ML estimators are unknown. However, fitting the model as a linear model using OLS, one finds substantively comparable results, which provides some confidence that the estimation reported here is estimating valid relationships.

Taken in conjunction, the significance of public opinion as a predictor of Court-curbing in Congress, and the insignificance of a primary alternative explanation – judicial activism – provide initial support for the main claim derived from the Conditional Self-Restraint model. Court-curbing activity is a reflection of public support for the Court (Hypothesis 1). At the same time, we find here weak evidence that policy divergence between the Court and Congress motivates congressional criticism of the Court (Hypotheses 2 and 3), though the test of that proposition is admittedly weak. In the next section, we consider a more powerful test – one that examines *individual* legislators' decisions to sponsor Court-curbing legislation.

4.2.2   The Introduction of Court-Curbing: Individual Patterns

Moving from an aggregate analysis of patterns of Court-curbing to an analysis of individual members' sponsorship decisions allows for more powerful statistical analysis of the determinants of Court-curbing in Congress. While informative, the aggregate analysis above is limited in two ways. First, it treats Congress as a unitary actor. While the Conditional Self-Restraint model itself treats Congress as a single decision-maker, there is clearly great variation within Congress regarding both constituent opinion and policy disagreements with the Court. Second, the aggregate analysis is limited by the availability of data. With only about thirty years worth of data, there is a significant limit to how much we can learn from statistical analysis of yearly data. The individual-level analysis here helps overcome those limitations by exploiting variation both across time and across members of Congress.

Measurement of Key Variables
This analysis seeks to explain an individual member of Congress' decision to (co-)sponsor a Court-curbing bill. I thus identify for each member of the House of Representatives how many Court-curbing bills (s)he (co-)sponsored during each Congress, from the 94th through the 109th Congress (1975 through 2006). In the analyses below, I use both the total number of bills introduced by each member as well as a simpler indicator of whether or not each member sponsored at least one Court-curbing bill during the Congress.

The Conditional Self-Restraint model predicts that a legislator will be more likely to introduce a Court-curbing bill as opposition to the Court among her constituents increases. Thus, using the data previously described, I model the sponsorship of Court-curbing first as a function of public opposition to the Supreme Court in the legislator's state during the current Congress. We saw in Figure 4.3 that as state-level support for (confidence in) the Supreme Court increases, individual legislators are less likely to introduce a Court-curbing bill. In the statistical analysis below, we assess the explanatory power of public opinion while controlling for other factors that might affect Court-curbing.

Chief among those other factors is the degree of policy disagreement between the Court and Congress. The second empirical prediction derived from the Conditional Self-Restraint model is that members of Congress should be more likely to introduce Court-curbing as they become more ideologically divided from the Court. The aggregate analysis above did not provide much evidence in support of this relationship. Here, we provide a more powerful test by examining each legislator individually. Thus, the second explanatory variable in this model is a measure of ideological distance between the individual legislator and the median member of the Supreme Court.[14] Third, the Conditional Self-Restraint model predicts an interactive of public opposition and Court–Congress alignment on Court-curbing sponsorship. I therefore include an interaction between the first two predictors.

In addition, macro-level factors may influence the introduction of Court-curbing, such as the Court's specific decisions, legislative activism, or other macro-level events. In the aggregate analysis above, I employed proxy measures for judicial and legislative activism. In the individual-level analysis here, though, we can employ a more powerful control that does not rely on those proxies; instead, I estimate a model with modeled intercepts for each individual legislator and each Congress. These modeled intercepts account for idiosyncrasies across individual legislators in their proclivity to introduce Court-curbing bills. The intercepts also account for idiosyncrasies across time, such that exogenous shocks may increase the baseline level of Court-curbing during a given period. The modeled intercepts therefore allow us to assess the effect of public opinion on bill sponsorship net of individual and temporal variation. Alternatively, one

---

[14] Specifically, I measure this distance as the absolute difference between the legislator's Common Space score (Poole 1998) and the median justice's Judicial Common Space score (Epstein, Martin, Segal, and Westerland 2007). While median justice theories of Supreme Court decision making have recently come under attack, the median justice nevertheless represents a reasonable approximation of the Supreme Court's ideological location.

could employ the same proxy measures used in the aggregate analysis above; in that case, we find the same substantive results.

Empirical Model

I estimate two empirical models. In each model, the unit of analysis is an individual legislator during a given Congress; the dependent variable is a measure of individual-level Court-curbing activity. In the first model, the dependent variable is simply an indicator for whether the legislator (co-)sponsored any Court-curbing bills during the Congress. In the second model, the dependent variable is a count of *how many* Court-curbing bills the legislator sponsored during the Congress. Full details of the empirical specification are provided in the appendix to this chapter.[15] The empirical model is given by:

$$CourtCurbing_{ic} = f(Public\ Opposition_{s[i]c}, \qquad (4.2)$$
$$Court\text{-}Legislator\ Ideological\ Distance_{ic},$$
$$Legislator\ Intercept_i,$$
$$Congress\ Intercept_c)$$

The results of the estimation are reported in Table 4.2. We find here striking evidence that both constituent support for the Supreme Court and ideological divergence from the Court affect the sponsorship of Court-curbing legislation. In the first row of Table 4.2, we estimate in each model a positive and statistically significant coefficient associated with public opposition to the Court – as support for the Court declines, a given legislator is more likely to (co-)sponsor a Court-curbing bill or to sponsor more bills. Importantly, we estimate this effect while controlling for the legislator's ideological alignment with the Court. Holding constant a legislator's policy divergence from the Court, state-level public support for the Court is a powerful determinant of Court-curbing. At the same time, in the second row of Table 4.2, we estimate a positive and statistically significant coefficient associated with ideological distance

---

[15] I estimate here a hierarchical model with modeled intercepts for the legislator and Congress. I could alternatively estimate an empirical model with modeled slopes, allowing the correlation between public opinion and Court-curbing to vary across Congresses. Such an estimation reveals some variation from Congress to Congress in the effect of public opinion on Court-curbing, though none of the variation is statistically significant. In addition, one could estimate the model excluding in turn each of the modeled intercepts included in the model. None of the results changes either statistically or substantively.

TABLE 4.2. *Effect of Public Opinion and Legislative Policy Preferences on Decision to (Co-)sponsor a Court-Curbing Bill, 1975–2006*

Estimated coefficients from empirical model (4.2); logit and Poisson coefficients (standard errors in parentheses); dependent variable in first column is whether congressman i (co-)sponsored any Court-curbing bill during Congress c; dependent variable in right column is how many Court-curbing bills congressman i sponsored during Congress c; Public Opposition$_{s[i]c}$ is estimated confidence in the Supreme Court in state s represented by legislator i during Congress c; Distance$_{ic}$ is absolute distance between legislator i and Court median during Congress c; all continuous predictors have been normalized by centering on zero and dividing by two standard deviations; $N = 7003$ for all models

	Any Bill Sponsored		Total Bills Sponsored	
Public Opposition$_{s[i]c}$	0.53**	0.51**	0.68***	0.61***
	(0.26)	(0.26)	(0.03)	(0.03)
Distance$_{ic}$	1.64***	1.25***	1.09***	0.95***
	(0.11)	(0.12)	(0.01)	(0.01)
Public Opposition$_{s[i]c}$ ×	–	1.79***	–	0.46***
Distance$_{ic}$	–	(0.21)	–	(0.02)
Constant	−2.84***	−2.86***	−2.58***	−2.57***
	(0.36)	(0.35)	(0.05)	(0.05)

*** $p \leq 0.01$;** $p \leq 0.05$;* $p \leq 0.10$.

between the legislator and the Court. Legislators more ideologically distant from the Court will be more likely to introduce Court-curbing bills than legislators less ideologically distant. Again, we estimate this effect while controlling for state-level public support for the Court.

What is more, we also find here evidence of an interactive effect between public opposition to the Court and ideological alignment. When the Court is most pessimistic about its public support – when it is the lowest in the public opinion polls – the effect of ideological divergence between the Court and a legislator on the introduction of Court-curbing is the greatest. Indeed, the substantive magnitude of this relationship is considerable. For an average legislator, moving from the lowest to the highest level of opposition to the Court increases the probability of sponsoring a Court-curbing bill from about 10% to about 30% – a threefold increase. More important, though, while increasing public opposition is associated with a greater propensity to sponsor Court-curbing for all legislators, this effect is exacerbated for the Court's ideological opponents. To see the substantive significance of this effect, consider Figure 4.5, which shows the difference between the predicted probability a Court

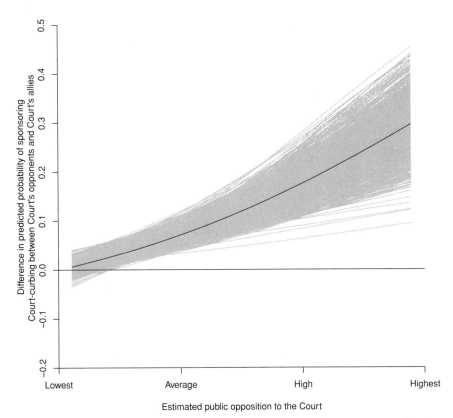

FIGURE 4.5. *Difference between Court's opponents' and Court's allies' predicted probability of sponsoring a Court-curbing bill as a function of estimated public opposition to the Court.* Figure shows net difference between the probability that a Court opponent sponsors a Court-curbing bill and the probability a Court ally sponsors a Court-curbing bill. Black line shows point estimate and grey lines show uncertainty; predictions calculated using estimated coefficients from model 4.2.

opponent will sponsor a Court-curbing bill and the predicted probability a Court ally will sponsor a Court-curbing bill.[16]

The figure reveals that, as predicted by Hypothesis 2, for most levels of public opposition to the Court, its legislative opponents are more likely to sponsor Court-curbing than are its ideological allies. Further, we also see clear evidence of the interactive effect predicted by Hypothesis 3 – as things become worse for the Court – as it falls in public opinion polls,

---

[16] Specifically, the ideological distance of the opponent is assumed to be at the 75th percentile.

the Court's ideological enemies respond more quickly. As its popularity wanes – as it becomes more pessimistic about its diffuse support – the Court's ideological opponents take advantage of its pessimistic outlook and introduce more Court-curbing.

The results of this analysis provide direct support for the Conditional Self-Restraint model's three predictions about the introduction of Court-curbing. First, constituent opinion is a powerful predictor of Court-curbing. When a legislator introduces Court-curbing, we should expect that his constituents have become displeased with the Court. At the same time, legislators who are more ideologically divergent from the Court are more likely to introduce Court-curbing bills than are the Court's ideological allies. Finally, the effect of ideological divergence appears to be conditioned by the Court's outlook concerning its diffuse support. Together, these findings support the first component of the theoretical argument advanced in Chapter 3 – they demonstrate the correlation between public support for the Court and Court-curbing – and lay the groundwork for the analysis in the next chapter of the Court's responsiveness to Court-curbing. Before moving to that inquiry, though, we turn to a second analysis of Court-curbing to examine not *how much* Court-curbing is taking place but rather *who* is Court-curbing.

4.2.3   Court-Curbing Ideology

In moving from an examination of the intensity – or volume – of Court-curbing to an analysis of the ideological content of the Court-curbing, we consider a different aspect of Court-curbing. The question asked here is whether we find support for Hypotheses 1 through 3 in not just the frequency of Court-curbing but also in the ideological content of Court-curbing. Applying the hypotheses outlined in Chapter 3 to this question suggests the following relationships. First, public policy liberalism or conservatism should be a primary determinant of Court-curbing. As the public becomes more liberal, we should see more liberal Court-curbing; as the public becomes more conservative, we should see more conservative Court-curbing. Second, policy divergence between the Court and Congress should be a determinant of Court-curbing. Thus, as Congress becomes more conservative, we should see more conservative Court-curbing from Congress. Third, there should be an interactive relationship between the ideological distance between the Court and Congress and the effect of public opinion on Court-curbing. In particular, an increase in the degree of policy ideological divergence between the Court and

Congress should attenuate the correlation between public liberalism and Court-curbing ideology.

Measurement of Key Variables

These predictions implicate three concepts that need to be measured empirically. The first concept is the ideological content of Court-curbing. Although one might imagine several ways to do so, I adopt a simple measure. I identify who sponsored each Court-curbing bill and then assign to that bill a score equal to the relative conservatism of the sponsor.[17] I then identify the median Court-curbing sponsor each year and use that person's conservatism as the measure of how liberal or conservative Court-curbing is in that year. Figure 2.2(a) in Chapter 2 shows the distribution of Court-curbing sponsor conservatism from 1877 through 2006. In the analysis that follows, I divide the bills into those sponsored by members of the House and those sponsored by members of the Senate. The two measures are positively correlated, though not necessarily strongly ($r = 0.42$). Because one of the key predictions tested here concerns the ideological relationship between the (potential) bill sponsors and the Court, I treat these two sets of bills separately.[18]

The second key concept is public support for the Court. Earlier, I considered public opinion polls asking about public "confidence" in the Court as well as a series of proxy measure for the Court's "politicization." Here, though, public support for the Court has a slightly different interpretation. In particular, we are interested in whether the ideological content of Court-curbing bills is a reflection of overall public conservatism. How, then, should we measure public conservatism? Stimson (1991, 1999) develops a measure of *public mood*; this measure is essentially a composite of many public opinion surveys and captures an underlying public liberalism across a broad range of policy issues. It is available for the years 1953 through 2002. I use this index to measure *public conservatism*. The variable *Public Conservatism$_t$* becomes larger when the public is more conservative and smaller when the public is more liberal.[19] If public opinion is in fact a primary determinant of Court-curbing, then

---

[17] In particular, I use the DW-NOMINATE Score of the primary sponsor. Using, alternatively, the median sponsor from the set of all cosponsors does not affect the results reported here.

[18] It is the case, though, that the results reported here remain if the two sets of bills are combined. However, by linking Senate bills with Senate ideology and House bills with House ideology, the estimated relationships are theoretically clearer.

[19] I transform the public mood variable by multiplying by -1, in order that higher values of this measure indicate a more conservative public; lower values indicate a more liberal

as the public becomes more conservative, the median Court-curber should also become more conservative.

The third key concept is the degree of ideological divergence between the Court and Congress. I create measures: *House Conservatism$_t$* and *Senate Conservatism$_t$*, which are equal to the conservatism of the House of Representatives and the Senate relative to the Court, respectively.[20] In particular, as the median member of the House or the Senate becomes more conservative than the median member of the Court, the relevant (House or Senate) measure becomes larger. As the median member of the chamber becomes more liberal than the median member of the Court, this measure becomes smaller.[21] The model predicts that as the Court becomes more liberal, relative to Congress, the median Court-curbing sponsor should become more conservative. Having divided the bills into House bills and Senate bills, I employ each of these two measures as a predictor for each of the relevant sets of bills.

Next, Hypothesis 3 predicts an interactive relationship between these two variables. That is, ideological divergence between the Court and Congress should attenuate the correlation between public opinion and Court-curbing ideology. Thus, I include an interaction between *Public Conservatism* and *House Conservatism$_t$* (or *Senate Conservatism$_t$*).

Finally, a key rival explanation for the determinants of Court-curbing is that Court-curbing is simply a knee-jerk reaction to the Court's ideological preferences. To account for any such effect, I include a measure of judicial conservatism. Because Court-curbing in response to judicial conservatism should be a function of the justices' decisions – not their underlying preferences – we want a measure of how liberally or conservatively the Court is deciding cases. Although a variety of such measures exist, I use here the Judicial Common Space score of the median justice. This measure identifies the relative conservatism of each justice based on his or her voting patterns and is the most widely used such measure in

public. Thus, we should expect to see a positive relationship between the public mood measure and the conservatism of the median Court-curbing sponsor.

[20] This measure is calculated as above, using the Judicial Common Space scores for the median justice on the Supreme Court and each of the House and Senate floor medians.

[21] I have estimated the models here with a variety of alternative measures, such as the closer of either the Senate or the House, the majority party median (in each chamber), the House and Senate Judiciary Committee medians, and the "pivots" (Krehbiel 1998) in Congress. The results reported here are generally robust to any of these alternative operationalizations.

the current literature. However, if the theoretical argument advanced in this book is correct, and Court-curbing is driven by public opinion, then the predictive power of this variable should be overwhelmed by the other measures of public conservatism.[22]

Empirical Model

I model the conservatism of Court-curbing as a function of these few variables using a standard OLS regression model.[23] Specifically, the conservatism of the median Court-curbing sponsor is modeled as a function of public conservatism, congressional conservatism, and judicial conservatism:

$$\text{Court-Curbing Ideology}_t = f(\text{Public Conservatism}_t, \qquad (4.3)$$
$$\text{Congressional Conservatism}_t,$$
$$\text{Court Conservatism}_t)$$

The results of this estimation are reported in Table 4.3. First, notice the positive coefficients associated with *Public Conservatism$_t$*. These coefficients indicate that as the public becomes more conservative – as it prefers more conservative policies – the typical Court-curbing sponsor becomes more conservative. What is more, the estimated coefficients from the models of Court-curbing in the House are statistically significant and more than twice the size magnitude of those from the estimation using Senate Court-curbing. This result provides direct, though mixed, support for the claim that public opinion should be a primary determinant of Court-curbing, suggesting that Court-curbing is very much a position-taking endeavor (Hypothesis 1). As the public becomes more conservative, Court-curbing – especially in the House of Representatives – also becomes more conservative. In fact, the correlation between public conservatism and House Court-curbing conservatism is quite considerable.

---

[22] Of course, it remains possible, and I do not dispute, that Court decisions may drive Court-curbing. However, my claim is that any such effect takes place only as mediated by public opinion.

[23] These data constitute time-series data. As noted above in the analysis of the number of Court-curbing bills introduced, it is important to account for any time-series dynamics in the data when specifying an empirical model. The OLS linear regression model is the standard workhorse regression model. It does require, though, a set of assumptions that can be easily violated. When those assumptions are met, however, the OLS regression model is the most efficient empirical specification one can use. In particular, diagnostics indicate that the dependent variable is stationary and that the residuals from the OLS regression are not autocorrelated. As above, specific results of the diagnostic tests and model selection are reserved to the Technical Appendix.

TABLE 4.3. *Determinants of Court-Curbing Conservatism, 1953–2008*

OLS regression coefficients (standard errors in parentheses); all continuous predictors have been normalized by centering on zero and dividing by two standard deviations

	Additive Models		Interactive Models	
	House Bills	Senate Bills	House Bills	Senate Bills
Public Conservatism$_t$	0.51***	0.22	0.52***	0.23
	(0.14)	(0.16)	(0.15)	(0.17)
House Conservatism$_t$	0.57**	–	0.62**	–
	(0.22)	–	(0.24)	–
Senate Conservatism$_t$	–	0.14	–	0.10
	–	(0.24)	–	(0.25)
Judicial Conservatism$_t$	0.24	0.28	0.34	0.21
	(0.24)	(0.26)	(0.33)	(0.30)
Public Conservatism ×	–	–	−0.21	–
House Conservatism	–	–	(0.45)	–
Public Conservatism ×	–	–	–	0.24
Senate Conservatism	–	–	–	(0.41)
Intercept	0.46***	0.29***	0.46***	0.28***
	(0.07)	(0.07)	(0.07)	(0.07)
N	53	42	53	42
R^2	0.33	0.13	0.34	0.14
DW-Statistic	1.77	1.75	1.75	1.75

*** $p \leq 0.01$;** $p \leq 0.05$;* $p \leq 0.10$ (two-tailed).

The coefficients in Table 4.3 associated with *Public Conservatism* are all about 0.5. This means that if the public becomes more conservative by about two standard deviations, we expect Court-curbing to become more conservative by about one standard deviation. That is, changes in public opinion are associated with significant swings in the ideological content of Court-curbing. More liberal Court-curbing, then, is evidence of a concurrent liberal movement in public opinion. To the extent that the justices may want to use Court-curbing to infer information about public opinion, then, knowing who has introduced Court-curbing can be a useful resource for the Court.

Second, notice that, as above, the results provide some support for the claim that Court-curbing is driven by policy disagreement between the Court and Congress. In the additive models reported in Table 4.3, we see a positive correlation between House and Senate conservatism (relative to the Court). As in the case of *Public Conservatism*, the correlation between congressional conservatism and Court-curbing conservatism is much larger in the context of House Court-curbing; it is also only statistically significant in the context of house Court-curbing. Moreover, the magnitude of the estimated coefficients associated with *House Conservatism$_t$* is substantively comparable to the magnitude of the estimated coefficients associated with *Public Conservatism$_t$*. That is, in the House, congressional and public conservatism have substantively comparable effects on the ideological tenor of Court-curbing. These findings provide additional support for Hypothesis 2, which predicts that congressional preferences will codetermine (along with public preferences) the introduction of Court-curbing. The evidence, however, is particularly stronger in the context of house Court-curbing than in the context of Senate Court-curbing. These results are suggestive of the general theme of the Conditional Self-Restraint model – although policy disagreements may induce Congress to misrepresent public opinion, those concerns will be only secondary to the position-taking incentive facing Congress. Members of Congress are primarily – if not exclusively – motivated by public opinion when introducing Court-curbing legislation.

However, the model does predict an interactive relationship between policy disagreements and public opinion (Hypothesis 3). Specifically, the model predicts that as policy disagreements between the Court and Congress become more significant (as the ideological distance between them grows), the correlation between public opinion and Court-curbing should break down. That is, as policy disagreements become larger and more significant, Congress will be willing to forsake its electoral, position-taking interests in favor of "bluffing" and misrepresenting public opinion to the Court. To test this prediction, I now reestimate the empirical model, including an interactive term between public opinion and congressional conservatism (relative to the Court). The results from this estimation are reported in the final two columns of Table 4.3. In the model of House Court-curbing, we estimate a negative coefficient on the interactive term. This indicates that ideological distance between the Court and Congress depresses the relationship between public opinion and Court-curbing. However, in the context of Senate Court-curbing, we find no such relationship, though, as noted above, there is not much statistical evidence of a relationship between either public or congressional ideology and Court-curbing.

The interactive effect is shown most clearly in Figure 4.6. We see here the predicted ideology of the median Court-curbing sponsor as a function of public conservatism, under three different conditions: a Supreme

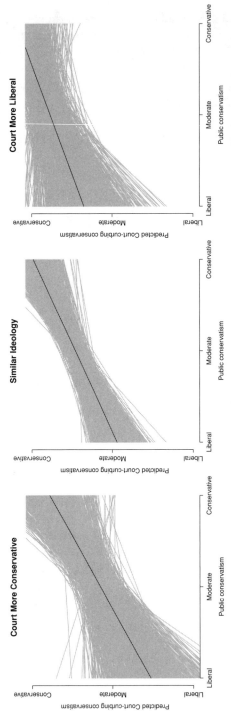

FIGURE 4.6. *Effect of public conservatism on House Court-curbing conservatism, as a function of ideological alignment between the Court and the House.* Left panel shows effect when the Court is more conservative than Congress; middle panel shows effect when the Court and Congress have similar ideologies; right panel shows effect when the Court is more liberal than Congress; grey area shows uncertainty in the estimates.

Court more conservative than the House, a Supreme Court with ideology similar to the House, and a Supreme Court more liberal than the House. The solid black line shows the point prediction using the estimates reported in Table 4.3. The grey lines show the uncertainty in this estimate using the estimated standard errors from the coefficients.[24] In the left- and right-hand panels, we see that the correlation between public opinion and Court-curbing ideology is weak. When the Court is more conservative than the House, there is a positive correlation, but the simulated correlations show a wide range of predicted relationships, with some even being negative. Indeed, the uncertainty in the point estimates shows that this correlation is not statistically meaningful – for any level of public conservatism, we would expect almost any type of Court-curbing. Similarly, when the Court is more liberal than the House, there is a positive relationship, though the uncertainty is again quite considerable, with some of the estimated relationships even being negative. Thus, for any degree of public conservatism, we would expect virtually any level of Court-curbing conservatism. By contrast, however, when the Court and Congress have similar ideological preferences (center panel), we find a positive and statistically meaningful correlation between public opinion and Court-curbing. When the public is liberal, we expect liberal members of Congress to introduce Court-curbing. When the public is conservative, we expect conservative members of Congress to introduce Court-curbing. This finding provides direct support for the interactive relationship predicted by the Conditional Self-Restraint Model (Hypothesis 3).

In particular, this interactive relationship demonstrates that when there is little ideological divergence between the Court and Congress, public opinion will be the overriding determinant of Court-curbing. However, as the degree of divergence grows, Congress will be more willing to disregard public opinion in an effort to "bluff" the Court – it will misrepresent public opinion in hopes of "tricking" the Court into exercising self-restraint. Although this finding is intuitive, it is not necessarily obvious that such a relationship should exist. It does, though, provide further insight into the nature of Court-curbing as a position-taking endeavor that can still be used to signal to the Court information about public opinion.

---

[24] Specifically, the grey lines are calculated by taking 1,000 random draws from each estimated coefficient's distribution. This simulation is performed using the sim function (Gelman and Hill 2007) in R (R Development Core Team 2009).

Finally, in the context of Senate Court-curbing, we find a similar, though statistically weaker pattern. The relationship is strongest and most statistically precise when the Court and the Senate are ideologically aligned and weakest when the Court is ideologically divergent from the Senate.[25]

Taken in conjunction, these results provide support for the claim that Court-curbing is driven by public preferences. When the public becomes more liberal, their representatives in Congress respond. Part of their response is to position-take – especially in the House. By introducing Court-curbing bills, the liberal (or conservative) members of Congress can claim that they have taken action to "rein in" the runaway activist courts. As we saw in Chapter 3, members of Congress know that Court-curbing bills can be electorally useful. Recall the legislative staffer who commented, "These issues and bills rally the base every year; they also create an issue and a constituency."[26] Given that Court-curbing seems to move with the ideological tide of public mood, then, it makes sense that the Court may think of this legislation as a credible signal about where the public stands. More liberal (conservative) Court-curbing bills indicate a more liberal (conservative) public. However, when the extent of policy disagreement between the Court and Congress becomes too large, then members of Congress will have an incentive to "bluff." As a consequence, Court-curbing will be a weaker signal about public opinion; as we saw in the theoretical analysis in Chapter 4, this may induce the Court to sometimes disregard Court-curbing. Nevertheless, if the Court has an interest in not moving too far out of line with what the public wants, as I have posited, then paying attention to Court-curbing can be an informative way of learning about the institutional bounds imposed by public opinion. What the evidence presented here suggests is that the theoretical assumption that Court-curbing is primarily a position-taking endeavor has empirical support. Moreover, the evidence presented in this chapter provides initial support for the delicate "interaction" between the Court and Congress through which congressional position-taking in front of its constituents – position-taking not directed at the Court – can nevertheless affect the Court by serving as an informative signal about public preferences.

---

[25] It is also noteworthy that when all bills are combined, the patterns look like those in the context of House Court-curbing. However, the addition of the Senate bills to the empirical models does weaken the statistical precision of the estimated relationships.

[26] Personal interview with "Staffer 2."

4.3 CONCLUSION

In this chapter, I have explored the determinants of Court-curbing in Congress. I have taken the patterns in Court-curbing sponsorship outlined in Chapter 2 and asked whether those patterns conform to the theoretical hypotheses derived in Chapter 3. In particular, I have asked whether public opinion and policy divergence between the Court and Congress are determinants of Court-curbing. In terms of both the frequency and the ideological content of Court-curbing, we have seen that public opinion is the overriding predictor of Court-curbing. We have not, however, found much evidence in support of a direct effect of policy divergence on Court-curbing. What has emerged, though, is clear evidence in support of the interactive relationship between policy divergence and public opinion. Specifically, we have seen here that increasing policy divergence between the Court and Congress attenuates the relationship between public opinion and Court-curbing. In the theoretical model developed in Chapter 3, we saw that the correlation between public support for the judiciary and Court-curbing should be strongest when the Court and Congress have similar policy views and weakest when they disagree about policy. The evidence presented here of such an interactive relationship provides empirical support for this theoretical claim.

More generally, though, the implication of the findings reported in this chapter is that Court-curbing is driven primarily by public pressure and opinion and, to a lesser extent, policy goals. Indeed, congressional responsiveness to public opinion is intuitive in light of the body's elective nature. If members of Congress want to retain their offices, then they need to be sensitive to their constituents' preferences (Mayhew 1974). Court-curbing does not, however, seem to be a knee-jerk reaction to Supreme Court decisions. Rather, legislative attacks are motivated by public perceptions about the Court and ideological divergence between the Court and Congress. This finding provides support for the claim I advance here that Court-curbing is a primarily position-taking endeavor. Moreover, the evidence presented in this chapter indicates that there is good reason for the Court to interpret Court-curbing legislation as a mediating signal of public opinion. As we saw previously, Congress uses Court-curbing as if it were a position-taking endeavor. More Court-curbing bills are associated with a decrease in public confidence in the Court; more liberal (conservative) bills indicate more liberal (conservative) policy preferences among the public. To an observer, then, Court-curbing can be an informative signal from which to learn about public opinion and the Court's legitimacy.

This finding stands on its head much of the previous scholarship on Court-curbing, which generally posits that these bills are introduced in order to "saber rattle" and intimidate the Court (Stumpf 1965; Nagel 1965; Rosenberg 1992). What we have seen here is that electoral posturing is a more likely explanation of why we observe Court-curbing. That is, as we saw in the previous chapter, although Court decisions may generate public discontent with the Court and make the Court a political issue on which legislators must position-take, those decisions do so *only to the extent that the public has an adverse reaction to the Court*. Thus, congressional responses to the Court's decisions, and Court-curbing in particular, cannot be understood as simply elite-level policy disagreements. Rather, Court-curbing is driven by public opinion about the Court, and to the extent that discontent may be policy-oriented, it is at bottom about public policy preferences, as distinct from congressional policy preferences. Moreover, this interpretation of congressional attacks on the Court makes more intuitive sense. It is easier to understand why so few Court-curbing bills are ever enacted if Court-curbing is simply a position-taking endeavor rather than a saber-rattling institutional threat.

With these lessons in hand, we now move to an investigation of the Supreme Court's reaction to Court-curbing. The question that this book sets out to ask is whether Court-curbing and institutional legitimacy are important components of the separation-of-powers model. The Conditional Self-Restraint Model predicts the conditions under which we should observe the Court responding to congressional pressure. The remainder of this book will assess the empirical support for these predictions by examining judicial responsiveness to Court-curbing in two contexts – the instance of judicial invalidations of federal laws and the ideological content of the Court's decisions.

TECHNICAL APPENDIX

In this technical appendix, I report diagnostic details regarding empirical model selection in this chapter for the analyses of both Court-curbing volume (empirical model (4.1)) and Court-curbing ideology (empirical model (4.3)).

COURT-CURBING VOLUME. First, I provide details regarding the selection of empirical model (4.1). In this specification, I model the number of Court-curbing bills introduced each year. Thus, the data constitute event-count data (i.e., data that can only take on nonnegative integer values), but they are also time-series data. Although the primary empirical model used to model event-count data is the Poisson regression model, there is an ongoing debate in the literature about the best way to treat count data that are also time-series data. The primary concern is that the data may exhibit time-series dynamics such as persistence. A persistent time series is characterized by an autocorrelation function that has a long memory; that is, shocks to the dependent variable have continuing effects for a long period of time. Even if time-series data are not persistent, they may nevertheless reflect short-term autocorrelation or cyclical dynamics. When the data exhibit such time-series dynamics, standard event count models will not be efficient; when the data, however, satisfy the assumptions of independence and equidispersion, then standard event count methods, such as the Poisson regression model, are appropriate (Cameron and Trivedi 1998, 227–8; Brandt, Williams, Fordham, and Pollins 2000).

The traditional approach to accounting for correlation among events in count data is to use a negative binomial model or a generalized event count model (King 1989). However, several recent developments in the analysis of time-series count data have identified potential deficiencies in this approach and provide the tools necessary for diagnosing these dynamics and correcting for any time-series features of the data that may complicate analysis. Among these developments are two: The Poisson Exponentially Weighted Moving Average (PEWMA) model (Brandt, Williams, Fordham, and Pollins 2000) and the Poisson Autoregressive (PAR(p)) model (Brandt, Williams, Fordham, and Pollins 2000).

To assess how best to model the data here, I have performed several diagnostic tests. First, data that suffer from serial correlation generally exhibit overdispersion; therefore, I have estimated the data as a negative binomial model and performed a likelihood-ratio test. This test indicates that, under each specification, the data exhibit overdispersion. The results of these diagnostic tests are reported in the bottom row of Table 4.1. Given these results, the Poisson regression model is inappropriate.

Next, I have evaluated the data to determine whether there is serial correlation. To test for serial correlation, a common test is to estimate the residuals from a model, where the residuals are defined as $\left(y_t - \exp\left(x_t'\hat{\beta}\right)\right)$. Then, one tests to see whether there is a correlation between the current and lagged residuals. Using this method, I have obtained the residuals from empirical model (4.1) and estimated an OLS regression model where the dependent variable is the current residual and the explanatory variable is the lagged residual. I find no correlation between the current and lagged residuals. Specifically, with the number of bills as the dependent variable, I find $\hat{\beta} = -0.17$, $p \leq 0.30$; with the number of sponsors as the dependent variable, I find $\hat{\beta} = -0.12$, $p \leq 0.46$. These statistically insignificant coefficients indicate the data are not serially correlated.

When event-count data suffer from overdispersion but are not serially correlated, then the negative binomial regression model is an appropriate empirical specification. Thus, I estimate empirical model (4.1) as a negative binomial regression model.

COURT-CURBING IDEOLOGY. I now provide details concerning the selection of a specification for empirical model (4.3). The dependent variable employed in empirical model (4.3) is a continuous variable – that is, the NOMINATE Common Space score of the median Court-curbing sponsor. For continuous variables, the OLS regression model is the workhorse empirical specification. However, OLS estimation requires a number of assumptions that are frequently violated in time-series data, such as the data used here. Thus, I perform a series of diagnostic tests to assess whether the data suffer from time-series dynamics.

The first step in assessing whether the data exhibit time-series dynamics is to determine whether the data are stationary. Data that are not stationary have a "unit root." Data with a unit root have a mean that is changing over time. Data that are not stationary will result in inconsistent estimates from an OLS regression, leading to artificially high t-statistics and spurious regression (Enders 2004, ch. 4). The most widely used test for a unit root was developed by Dickey and Fuller (1979, 1981). Here, the Dickey-Fuller test indicates that the dependent variable is stationary ($Z(t) = -5.22$, $p \leq 0.00$).

Given that the data are stationary, one next wants to know whether the data are serially correlated. One assumption required for OLS regression to be unbiased is that the expected residual in time t is uncorrelated with the residual in time $t - 1$. To assess whether there is serial correlation in the data, I perform a Durbin-Watson test. The Durbin-Watson test is a widely used method for assessing whether an OLS model yields serially correlated residuals. Here, the Durbin-Watson test indicates there is no serial correlation in the residuals from empirical model (4.3) when estimated as an OLS regression. These results are reported in the bottom row of Table 4.3. Because the data are stationary and the residuals from the OLS regression are not autocorrelated, OLS regression yields consistent and unbiased estimates and is appropriate.

5

Public Support and Judicial Review

The use of judicial review to declare legislative enactments unconstitutional is perhaps the most closely examined function of the Court. Normative inquiry into the conditions that justify the use of judicial review has given rise to both a developed theoretical discussion as well as positive empirical analysis. The normative analysis of the exercise of judicial review has been the dominant question in American constitutional theory since at least the beginning of the twentieth century and continues to interest modern constitutional theorists (Thayer 1893; Bickel 1962; Ely 1980; Whittington 1999; Eisgruber 2001). In particular, normative theorists have been concerned with the so-called countermajoritarian difficulty, which refers to the tension between democratic norms of majority rule and accountability and the power of unelected judges to have a constitutional veto over democratically enacted legislation.[1] Empirical research is more recent, at least relative to the normative scholarship. The main thrust here is to assess empirically the extent of the problem posed by the countermajoritarian difficulty. That research has examined the frequency of the Court's use of judicial review and the effect of separation-of-powers mechanisms on the Court's invalidation of majoritarian policies (Dahl 1957; Graber 1993; Segal and Westerland 2005; Whittington 2007).

Some argue the Court's power to review Acts of Congress is an essential element of the separation of powers, because it provides a mechanism for enforcing constitutional limitations on legislation. Many scholars

---

[1] As I have noted, and will make more evident in this chapter and in Chapter 7, the research in this book, while primarily positive in nature, has normative implications for the study of the countermajoritarian difficulty.

have even suggested that the Court's power to invalidate legislation is an important reinforcement of democracy. They argue the use of judicial review can stimulate debate and promote an involved citizenry (Eisgruber 2001; Peretti 1999) and that the unrestricted use of judicial review can serve a policy efficiency function (Rogers and Vanberg 2007). Critics of judicial review, on the other hand, ask why legislation that has gained the assent of Congress and the president ought to be subject to a judicial veto. For example, John Hart Ely (1980) famously argued that in order for the Court to comport with a democratic system of government, judicial power ought to be exercised only to protect the fairness of the political process and to ensure that the rights of participation are not hampered, whereas other policy choices should be left to the elected branches. Regardless of where one stands in the normative debate, it cannot be denied that by passing on the constitutionality of a federal law, the Court exercises its most fundamental power in the separation-of-powers system. Although there may be instances in which Congress may prefer for the Court to deal with difficult or complex issues (Whittington 2003, 2005; Lovell 2003; Graber 1993), the exercise of judicial review is the very definition of the "countermajoritarian" problem (Bickel 1962).

THE SEPARATION OF POWERS, JUDICIAL LEGITIMACY, AND JUDICIAL REVIEW. Despite the normative and practical significance of judicial review for the study of judicial relations with other institutions, the study of Court–Congress relations and the separation-of-powers model (as described in Chapter 1) has not focused primarily on judicial review. However, a vibrant literature has explored the influence of inter institutional politics on the use of judicial review to invalidate legislation. Perhaps most notably, Robert Dahl's (1957) influential study of judicial review generated a progeny of empirical scholarship concerned with judicial invalidations of legislation. According to Dahl, regular appointments to the Supreme Court by the president, combined with Senate confirmation, engender a system in which the Court is usually composed of members who share the views of the dominant political majority. Dahl does concede, though, that temporary lags in this relationship may occur when new coalitions come into power through realigning elections.[2] The

---

[2] Although political control of the Court may lag behind the elected branches, this lag rarely lasts longer than four years, Dahl claims, and the only times at which the disjunction between the Court and the elected branches of government is significant are those corresponding to critical, realigning elections. Realignment theory, which has its roots in Keys (1955), claims that American politics is characterized by major, swift changes American ideology. However, modern political science has been very skeptical of realignment theory (see, e.g., Mayhew 2002).

point remains, however, that, in general, normative concerns about the threat of "countermajoritarianism" may be ameliorated by the empirical reality of general ideological alignment among the branches of government (Friedman 2005).

Dahl's provocative claim has generated a significant body of research aimed at assessing whether normative concerns about judicial "countermajoritarianism" are undermined by the empirical data. Responses to, and extensions of, Dahl's analysis have been numerous. In the first critical response, Jonathan Casper (1976) criticized Dahl for focusing on the invalidation of federal legislation, to the exclusion of judicial review of state legislation. Subsequently, and using more sophisticated empirical tools, other researchers have asked whether the political process does in fact keep the judiciary ideologically aligned with the dominant governing coalition (Epstein and Segal 2005) and whether such ideological alignment minimized countermajoritarianism (Clark and Whittington 2007). While many studies assume that constitutional decisions by the Court are "final" and therefore may not be susceptible to the same separation-of-powers mechanisms as decisions grounded in nonconstitutional authority,[3] several studies in the spirit of Dahl go so far as to explicitly apply the separation-of-powers model to the case of constitutional interpretation.[4]

In this vein, students of the separation of powers have recognized that congressional hostility toward the Court may be an important component of the strategic interaction between the institutions. Noting confrontations between the branches – such as those discussed in Chapter 2 – as well as more regular patterns of interinstitutional tension, these scholars have focused on congressional hostility in its role as an institutional threat to exercise power (Segal, Westerland, and Lindquist, Forthcoming; McNollgast 1995; Rosenberg 1992). That is, the focus on congressional "saber rattling" – through either committee hearings (Segal, Westerland, and Lindquist, Forthcoming) or even Court-curbing (Rosenberg 1992) – has been primarily concerned with the potential for Congress to use its

---

[3] Indeed, the large body of separation-of-powers literature either explicitly or implicitly makes this assumption. See, for example, Gely and Spiller (1992); Spiller and Spitzer (1992); Clinton (1994); Knight and Epstein (1996); McGuire (2003).

[4] Friedman (2005) laments the lack of interdisciplinary connections between normative legal theorists and positive scholars of judicial review. Friedman also argues that the insights of positivists could have direct implications for the terms of the countermajoritarian difficulty. Notable examples include Epstein, Knight, and Martin (2001); Friedman and Harvey (2003); Segal and Westerland (2005); Harvey and Friedman (2006); and Lindquist and Solberg (2007).

constitutional powers to formally sanction the Court. For example, Friedman and Harvey (2003, 17) note, "[t]here are numerous weapons a sitting
Congress can apply against a Supreme Court deemed to be recalcitrant,
including jurisdiction stripping, budget cutting, Court packing, and even
the impeachment of Supreme Court Justices." One study has even briefly
noted the possible connection between institutional confrontations and
the Court's *legitimacy*.

> If...[Congress and the President] succeed in overriding the Court's inter-
> pretation, the Court will certainly pay a policy price...The Court also
> may bear a cost in terms of its *legitimacy*. Every override of the Court's
> interpretation will chip away at its legitimacy even if only marginally.
> *Given that the Justices' ability to achieve their policy goals hinges on
> their legitimacy, because they lack the power to enforce their decisions,
> any erosion of the Court's legitimacy is a concern.* (Epstein, Knight, and
> Martin 2001, 598 [emphasis added])

In the end, the body of research suggests Dahl may have been correct
that the dominant governing coalition does have the power to appoint
members of the Court and can potentially control the Court if in power
for long enough. However, this may not be enough to overcome the
Court's countermajoritarianism. Periods of institutional confrontation –
as well as more regular tensions between the branches – provide evidence
of systematic countermajoritarianism. In addition to the political process,
which ensures a degree of regular ideological alignment, other concerns –
in particular, institutional legitimacy – may create an incentive for judicial self-restraint and, consequently, further ameliorate concerns about
countermajoritarianism.

Because of the Court's weak institutional position, it has a special interest in maintaining and protecting its institutional legitimacy. Institutional
legitimacy is the key to overcoming the compliance problem created by
the Court's lack of enforcement powers. Congressional hostility toward
the Court, and Court-curbing in particular, are important in this respect
because they serve as *signals* to the Court about public support for the
judiciary. This chapter assesses whether this relationship creates an incentive for the Court to exercise self-restraint in its use of judicial review.

Of course, simply defining judicial review is itself a difficult task. The
first issue is to identify which type of judicial review should be examined.
The Supreme Court exercises judicial review over both federal and state
legislation, but I focus here only on judicial review of federal legislation.
There are two reasons for this focus. First, whereas there is near unanimous consent among constitutional scholars regarding the propriety of

Supreme Court review of state legislation, there has long been a significant debate among scholars over the propriety of and conditions that permit judicial review of federal legislation (see, e.g., Thayer 1893; Wechsler 1959; Bickel 1962; Ely 1980; Whittington 1999). For scholars of the countermajoritarian difficulty, it is judicial review of federal legislation that is most problematic from a normative perspective.[5] Judicial review of state legislation, therefore, is much less contentious than judicial review of federal legislation from a separation-of-powers, democratic theory perspective.

Second, I focus on judicial review of federal legislation because it is Congress that engages in Court-curbing, not the states. Although Congress is composed of the states' representatives, the states themselves are powerless to respond to the Court's decisions. In order for Congress to mount a significant response to judicial review of state legislation, there would need to be geographically widespread hostility toward the Court. Not all invalidations of state legislation are equal. The Supreme Court may invalidate a local ordinance, and its decision may have far-reaching, contentious implications. On the other hand the Supreme Court may invalidate a state statute or constitutional provision, but the decision may have minor implications that do not extend to other states. Distinguishing among decisions that affect many states and those that affect only a single state (or even just a few states) is very difficult; the Supreme Court does not identify how many states are affected by its decision, and neither does any other governmental agency.[6] Making such a distinction,

---

[5] Essentially, this is due to the widely accepted notion that because the federal government, and the federal Constitution, are supreme over the states, an invalidation of state legislation, as contrary to the federal Constitution, is not problematic. The Supreme Court, as an interpreter of the federal Constitution, may reasonably be vested with that power. This view is based in the Supremacy Clause of the U.S. Constitution, which declares the U.S. Constitution to be supreme over other laws that might be enacted. For a discussion of the Supremacy Clause's implications for judicial review, see Wechsler (1954, 1959). However, as Friedman (2002) notes, although the countermajoritarian problem was first formulated in the context of justifying judicial review, contemporary scholarship is generally focused on criticizing judicial review.

[6] This concept is difficult to handle, empirically. In order to gauge the meaning of a judicial retreat in a case involving state legislation, one would have to measure the extent of the implication of the Court's decision. That is, how does the invalidation of a state law affect other states? The invalidation of a minor local ordinance in one town may or may not have broader implications. Surely, one might qualitatively rank a series of examples, but doing so systematically is very difficult, and there is no obvious logic for how one would handle this problem. In the context of federal legislation, however, this problem is minimized because we know that the invalidation of a federal law has at least comparable implications for every jurisdiction in the country. When a state law is invalidated, though, there

though, would be critical for studying the Court's responsiveness to Court-curbing in the context of judicial review of state legislation. Nevertheless, were one able to make such a distinction, there is no reason to expect that the theoretical predictions tested here would not be borne out in the context of judicial review of state legislation.[7]

Within the context of judicial review of federal legislation, though, there is another question one must address. What is the particular judicial action in which we are interested? Studies of the effect of separation-of-powers mechanisms on judicial review have generally considered two types of dependent variables: (a) the raw number of instances of judicial review (Dahl 1957; Segal and Westerland 2005) and (b) the propensity for the Court to invalidate a given law (Harvey and Friedman 2006; Clark and Whittington 2007; Segal, Westerland, and Lindquist, Forthcoming). The type of dependent variable one chooses depends on the theoretical mechanism and substantive issue of interest. A thorough treatment of the Conditional Self-Restraint model requires analysis of both aggregate and case-level patterns of judicial review.[8]

The first analysis examines aggregate patterns in the use of judicial review by considering the number of laws held unconstitutional by the Supreme Court each year. This analysis seeks to demonstrate the relationship between congressional hostility and the frequency with which the Court uses judicial review to invalidate Acts of Congress. The aggregate analysis examines the number of laws held unconstitutional each year, from 1877 through 2004. Focusing on the aggregate pattern of judicial review is particularly helpful for two reasons. First, if the Court is fearful for its legitimacy, it need not necessarily uphold laws that it would otherwise strike down. Rather, it might instead divert its

---

is no way to determine precisely how many jurisdictions are affected. Thus, it is even harder to assess the substantive significance of an invalidation of a particular state law.

[7] Note, though, that, as we saw in Chapter 4, judicial review of state legislation is a predictor of Court-curbing, whereas judicial review of federal legislation is not. Analyzing the effect of Court-curbing on judicial review of state legislation therefore would raise significant problems of causality.

[8] Within those studies concerned with individual laws and cases, there is still even further variation in the empirical approach. Some scholars look at the probability of a law being struck down once the Supreme Court has agreed to consider a case (Clark and Whittington 2007; Segal, Westerland, and Lindquist, Forthcoming), whereas others look at the probability that any given law on the books will be struck down by the Court (Harvey and Friedman 2006). Other types of analyses have focused on the ideological implications of the Court's constitutional cases (Epstein, Knight, and Martin 2001), though such analyses are less focused on judicial review than on constitutional decision making.

attention, decline to hear a constitutional case in the first instance, and instead focus on cases that do not risk the Court's legitimacy. Thus, an analysis of the probability of a judicial invalidation at the case level might be misleading, because the cases heard during periods of hostility between the Court and Congress would be qualitatively different. Thus, we might not find any effect of Court-curbing on the use of judicial review not because the Court is not exercising self-restraint but because it is focusing instead on different cases. Second, one interpretation of the Conditional Self-Restraint model is that the Court's "decision" might be simply an indicator of how "activist" the Court is in a given year. So, we need not observe changes in the Court's individual decisions but rather a change in the broader content of the Court's decision making. So, while the Court may continue to invalidate certain laws, regardless of the intensity of public opposition and Court-curbing, it may nevertheless "scale back" and invalidate *fewer* laws.

The second analysis is case level and examines the probability that the Court strikes down a given law, once it has decided to hear a constitutional challenge to the legislation. Rather than ask whether Court-curbing affects how many laws the Court will invalidate this year, this analysis asks whether Court-curbing affects the probability of striking down a law in this case. This analysis seeks to demonstrate how the level of congressional hostility affects the Court's propensity to strike down a law that it might otherwise uphold. To do so, I examine each case in which the Supreme Court considers the constitutionality of an Act of Congress. The dependent variable will be a dichotomous measure – whether the law is invalidated or upheld.[9] Several recent studies have investigated whether separation-of-powers mechanisms affect such micro-level behavior (Segal, Westerland, and Lindquist, Forthcoming; Clark and Whittington 2007), and the analyses presented here add to this literature by explicitly testing the model of institutional hostility. Indeed, as in the aggregate analysis, there are benefits and drawbacks to the case-level analysis. The case-level analysis will allow us to more directly address the mechanism by which the Court responds to concern for its institutional legitimacy. If the

---

[9] Friedman and Harvey (2003) and Harvey and Friedman (2006) argue that the appropriate universe of observations to study is not the set of laws considered by the Court but rather the set of laws that exist and are therefore available to be invalidated by the Court. However, this approach requires that one be able to control for variation in the probability that a given law is ever the subject of litigation and therefore one that may be brought by a litigant to the Supreme Court for review – a difficult task at best.

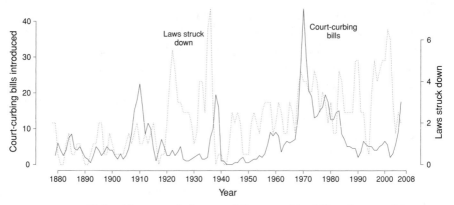

FIGURE 5.1. *Federal laws struck down and Court-curbing bills, 1877–2008* (two-year moving averages).

Court does in fact strike down fewer laws in the face of negative signals from Congress, does it do so by upholding laws it would otherwise strike down? Or, does the Court simply consider different cases?

5.1   A FIRST GLANCE

We begin by taking a first-cut look at the relationship between the exercise of judicial review and congressional hostility between 1877 and 2008.[10] Each of these analyses makes use of data covering cases where the Supreme Court has considered the constitutionality of a federal law. Common sources for these data include the list of laws held unconstitutional maintained by the Congressional Research Service ("CRS list") and the *Supreme Court Compendium* list (Epstein, Segal, Spaeth, and Walker 2007, 176–80), which is based, in part, on the CRS list. The biggest limitation of these data, though, is that they do not include instances where the Supreme Court has *upheld* a law. In order to perform a case-level analysis, I must have data that identify instances where federal laws were upheld. An original dataset compiled by Keith Whittington identifies all laws struck down by the Supreme Court as well as those upheld (Clark and Whittington 2007). These data will be the source of each of the analyses presented here.

Figure 5.1 shows the number of federal laws struck down as unconstitutional by the Supreme Court and the number of Court-curbing bills

---

[10] For reasons discussed in Chapter 2, I begin the analysis here with the year 1877.

introduced in Congress for each year.[11] In this figure we find an interesting pattern; increases in judicial review occur usually during periods of low Court-curbing. However, when Court-curbing goes up (shown in the solid line), the number of laws struck down tends to go down. This general pattern, although far from airtight evidence of judicial responsiveness, is suggestive of the hypothesized relationship between Court-curbing and judicial review.

Several specific examples can serve to better clarify the patterns in the data. Consider the late 1930s. This was the most significant era of legislative-judicial tension since Reconstruction. An active conservative Court was very busy during the early days of the New Deal, invalidating economic regulation and welfare state legislation that was central to Franklin Roosevelt's plan for recovery from the Great Depression. The invalidated legislation was generally very popular at the time. As the Court continued to aggressively invalidate federal legislation, Congress became increasingly hostile toward the Court. Court-curbing in Congress finally reached its apex in late 1936 – when the Democrats won a landslide election – and culminated in FDR's infamous Court-packing plan in early 1937. Figure 5.1 shows that following the major confrontation in 1937, the Court retreated and used its power of judicial review at the lowest level since the nineteenth century (see, for example, Wright 1942; Leuchtenberg 1969; Murphy 1972; Mason 1963). On the other hand, there also appear to be examples of times when Congress has not responded to the use of judicial review. Specifically, during both the 1920s and the late 1990s, the Court engaged in heightened use of judicial review to strike down federal laws, whereas Congress *did not respond* with Court-curbing bills. In general, judicial review during these periods was used to invalidate laws that were not supported by the dominant political majority and, as a consequence, did not result in much political reaction. During the 1990s, for example, the Supreme Court often used judicial review to overturn perceived encroachment by Congress on the sovereignty of the states. Broadly speaking, this movement did not elicit substantial political outcry.[12] In addition, the Supreme Court also intervened on behalf of the states to curtail federal efforts to limit civil liberties and criminal

---

[11] The data on Court-curbing bills come from the original data reported in Chapter 2. Recall from Chapter 2 that a Court-curbing bill is defined as a legislative proposal to limit, restrict, or otherwise remove judicial power.

[12] For example, during the 1990s, the Supreme Court intervened on behalf of state sovereignty in cases such as *Seminole Tribe of Florida v. Florida*, *Boerne v. Flores*, and *College Savings Bank v. Florida Education Expense Board*.

defendants' rights.[13] Such instances of active judicial review that are not followed by Court-curbing are instructive. They demonstrate that congressional attacks on the Court are not part of a natural cycle of increases in judicial review followed by concomitant increases in Court-curbing.[14] That is, the use of judicial review in and of itself is not sufficient to generate a political backlash through Court-curbing. More important, as we saw in Chapter 3, as opposed to the traditional separation-of-powers model, the theoretical model developed here predicts that there will be instances where the Court may act in a countermajoritarian way without provoking a legislative response – in particular, the Court may thwart majority will if it is the case that it does not engender public backlash against the Court.

The pattern of judicial responsiveness to Court-curbing appears even more strikingly when we consider case-level variation. Figure 5.2 shows the probability that the Court will strike down a law as a function of the level of Court-curbing in Congress.[15] This figure is based simply on the raw data – given all of the cases in which the Court has considered a constitutional challenge, what is the probability it will invalidate the law? As Figure 5.2 makes clear, at the lowest levels of Court-curbing, the Court invalidates laws in about 30% of those cases in which the constitutionality of a law is challenged. However, at the highest levels of Court-curbing, that figure drops to about 20%. In other words, the Court is about 50% more likely to invalidate a law in the absence of Court-curbing than in the presence of Court-curbing.

We find in these data, then, several revealing patterns. First, we see in Figure 5.1 that increases in Court-curbing are often followed by decreases in the number of laws invalidated by the Court. Moreover, we also see that increases in the use of judicial review to strike down federal laws are not necessarily met with increased Court-curbing. Providing further confirmation of the findings in Chapter 4, that pattern argues against an alternative relationship in which Court-curbing and judicial review naturally wax and wane in tandem. Second, the pattern detected in Figure 5.2 indicates that in constitutional cases, the Court is, on average,

---

[13] For example, the Supreme Court invalidated part of the Communications Decency Act in *United States v. Playboy Entertainment Group*. In *Dickerson v. United States*, the Court struck down a federal statute that sought to overturn *Miranda*–the case in which the Supreme Court declared that arrested individuals must be informed of their rights.

[14] Recall from Chapter 4 that there is not a statistically significant relationship between the number of federal laws struck down and the number of Court-curbing bills introduced.

[15] In particular, the line is a nonlinear scatterplot smoother (loess), which is a nonparametric regression estimator. The bandwidth for the loess estimator is set to 0.8.

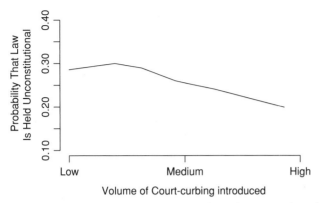

FIGURE 5.2. *Relationship between number of Court-curbing bills and the probability of a constitutional invalidation.* Lowess regression line with bandwidth set to 0.80.

less likely to invalidate a federal law when there is heightened Court-curbing than when there is little or no Court-curbing in Congress. These complementary findings are consistent with the primary claim derived from the Conditional Self-Restraint Model – an increase in Court-curbing should lead to greater judicial self-restraint. With these two preliminary findings in hand, I now turn to a statistical analysis of the relationship between Court-curbing and the use of judicial review.

5.2 STATISTICAL ANALYSES

The statistical analysis proceeds as follows. I first present a direct test of the main predictions derived from the Conditional Self-Restraint model. Does the Court respond to concerns about its legitimacy – and Court-curbing – by exercising self-restraint and using judicial review to invalidate Acts of Congress less frequently? The evidence will demonstrate a statistically significant relationship between both the Court's outlook with respect to its institutional support and the Court-curbing signals it observes in Congress and its use of judicial review. With that evidence in hand, I then demonstrate that the evidence supports Conditional Self-Restraint and is in tension with an alternative account in which the Court responds to Court-curbing because of a fear the legislation will be enacted. I show first that the Court's response to Court-curbing is not conditioned by the seriousness of Court-curbing. I then move to an analysis of the interactive hypotheses derived from the theoretical model. As we saw in Chapter 3, these interactive hypotheses run against the general intuition that follows from alternative theories of Court-curbing and judicial independence. As such, an analysis of the empirical support for those hypotheses will allow us to more rigorously assess the explanatory power of the theoretical argument advanced in this book. Finally, I test the relationship between Court-curbing and the probability of a constitutional invalidation at the case level. To the extent the analysis below demonstrates that the Court does in fact respond to Court-curbing, a question remains about the mechanism by which the responses occur. Does the Court uphold laws it might otherwise strike down? Or, does the Court shift its attention away and avoid addressing constitutional decisions? A case-level analysis will allow some insight into this question.

5.2.1   Court-Curbing and Judicial Review

Recall that the Conditional Self-Restraint model makes two main predictions about the Court's responsiveness to Court-curbing.[16] First, the model predicts that as the intensity of Court-curbing increases, the Court will exercise greater self-restraint (Hypothesis 4). This analysis asks whether an increase in Court-curbing is associated with a decrease in the number of laws held unconstitutional. Second, the model predicts that as the Court becomes increasingly pessimistic about public support for the judiciary, the Court will exercise greater self-restraint (Hypothesis 5). The analysis below asks whether decreasing public support for the judiciary is associated with fewer constitutional invalidations by the Court.

Measures of Key Variables
Before testing these predictions, I introduce the measures I will use of the key variables in the model. The measure of judicial decision making I use here is the total number of cases each year from 1877 through 2006 in which the Supreme Court invalidated, in whole or in part, an Act of Congress.[17] This measure assumes, then, that more constrained Courts

---

[16] The model also makes interactive predictions. We deal here first with the direct hypotheses and turn below to the interactive predictions.

[17] To identify the number of laws struck down each year, I reference the dataset recently compiled by Keith Whittington (Clark and Whittington 2007). Alternatively, one might use the dataset maintained by the Congressional Research Service. However, Whittington's analysis demonstrates there are notable discrepancies between the CRS list and his dataset. Generally, these discrepancies occur in the context of decisions in which a

will invalidate fewer laws than less constrained Courts. Of course, there may be instances when a constrained Court would strike down a law, but I assume that, on average, there will be a correlation between the extent to which the Court is constrained and the number of laws it will strike down. To the extent such a correlation exists, the total number of laws struck down serves as a proxy measure for the underlying concept of interest – the extent to which the Court exercises self-restraint.

The first key explanatory variable implicated by the theoretical predictions is the intensity of Court-curbing. To measure this concept, I identify the number of Court-curbing bills introduced each year in Congress, using the original data described in Chapter 2. However, the raw number of Court-curbing bills introduced each year is a less than ideal measure for several reasons. The first difficulty is that it seems unlikely that each additional Court-curbing bill introduced has a similar effect on the Court. Rather, it is most likely the case that the first few Court-curbing bills have little impact; further increases, however, will likely have a larger impact. Finally, once a given threshold has been met, it is unlikely that additional Court-curbing bills have much more of an impact. That is, the constraining effect of Court-curbing should not increase linearly in the number of Court-curbing bills; rather, there should be a difference between judicial decision making when there is little or no Court-curbing and judicial decision making when there is a lot of Court-curbing. This type of relationship describes the *logistic* function, which has an "S" shape. Thus, I transform the total number of Court-curbing bills with the logistic function, allowing the largest effect of Court-curbing to occur at a change from very few bills to many bills.[18] The second difficulty is that Court-curbing does not likely have an immediate effect on the Court's decisions. Judicial decision making is a slow process. Cases are selected for review and heard by the Court months later. After hearing a case, the Court votes on the decision and then prepares an opinion. This leads to often long lags between the time a case is selected, heard, and

---

law is invalidated "as applied" but not "on its face." Thus, although the law remains "on the books," the Court's interpretation and restriction of the law is often so strict as to prevent any reasonable application of the law. For example, the case *U.S. v. E. C. Knight*, 156 U.S. 1 (1895) does not appear on the CRS list, despite wide recognition of this case as one of the leading examples of judicial activism against congressional power.

[18] The particular transformation I use is $Court\ Curbing_t = 0.5 + (\exp(\frac{-Bills_t}{2}))^{-1}$, where $Bills_t$ is the number of Court-curbing bills introduced in year t. All of the results shown here are robust to any one of a number of operationalizations, including simply measuring the number of bills introduced or using other nonlinear transformation, such as the log of the number of bills introduced.

voted upon and the time at which the decision is handed down. In order to account for the slow process of judicial decision making and the likely lag between the introduction of Court-curbing and any noticeable change in the Court's decisions, I measure Court-curbing using the average number of bills introduced during the two preceding years.[19]

Of course, one might also measure Court-curbing by considering the number of individual legislators sponsoring Court-curbing legislation. The greater the number of individual legislators sponsoring anti-Court bills, the broader the anti-Court sentiment in Congress. However, the number of Court-curbing bills introduced and the number of unique sponsors are extremely highly correlated, suggesting that the number of Court-curbing bills is a sufficient measure to capture the breadth of anti-Court sentiment. As we saw in Chapter 4, the same factors that predict the number of Court-curbing bills introduced also predict the number of Court-curbing sponsors. Thus, we should expect these two indices to be closely related. Less systematic evidence of this relationship was presented in Chapter 2, where we saw that during periods of heightened Court-curbing activity, there is a broad geographic representation among Court-curbers. Moreover, before the mid-1930s, no cosponsorship was allowed in the Senate. Before 1967, no cosponsorship was allowed in the House; and even then cosponsorship was limited to twenty-five cosponsors per bill. It was not until 1978 that the limit on the number of cosponsors in the House was removed. The implication of these restrictions is that the number of bills introduced is institutionally constrained to be closely linked to the number of sponsors for most of the period studied here. As a consequence, the total number of Court-curbing bills introduced captures the extent of anti-Court sentiment in Congress.

The second key explanatory variable implicated by the theoretical pre-dictions is the Court's outlook about its level of public support. As we saw in the preceding chapter, however, measuring this concept is tricky. There, I proposed using public opinion polls to assess public support for the Court. The widely used item from the General Social Survey ("GSS"), which asks respondents how much "confidence" they have in the Supreme Court, is a very plausible measure of this concept. This survey is the most consistently asked survey of the American public concerning the Supreme

---

[19] Notice also that this helps account for any possible endogeneity between Court-curbing and judicial review. Whereas we saw in Chapter 4 that there does not appear to be a relationship between the instance of judicial review and Court-curbing, this operational-ization helps further prevent any possible effect.

Court that does not focus on specific decisions or recent events. Because this is the most direct measure of public opinion about the Court, I use this measure as the first measure of the Court's expectation about its public support.

In addition to this measure, I also propose here a third measure. Durr, Martin, and Wolbrecht (2000) demonstrate that a strong determinant of public support for the Court is the extent to which the ideological content of its decisions is out of line with public opinion. In their study, those authors found that an increase in the liberalism of the Court's decisions, combined with increasing conservatism in the public, is strongly associated with a decrease in public support for the Court. The same is true for increasing judicial conservatism combined with increasing public liberalism. Indeed, this is a basic feature of "diffuse" public support for courts cross-nationally – support for specific decisions is a strong determinant of diffuse support for the institution (Gibson, Caldeira, and Baird 1998). Thus, as a third measure of the Court's outlook, I adopt the variable proposed by Durr, Martin, and Wolbrecht, which is an index of the degree of divergence between public opinion and the Court's decision. To create the index, I identify how conservative or liberal the Court's decisions are in a given year; specifically, I mean normalize the percentage of decisions coded as "conservative" in the Spaeth Supreme Court Judicial Database. Then, I identify how liberal the public is in that year; to do this, I mean normalize the "public mood" variable developed by Stimson (1999).[20] Finally, I multiply these two variables together; the result is a variable that becomes increasingly large and positive as the Court becomes more conservative (or liberal) and the public becomes more liberal (or conservative).[21]

However, as we saw in Chapter 4, the use of any of these measures severely limits the scope of the analysis, as neither is available for any years before about 1953. Thus, below I present analyses using both measures, but I will then also report the results of an analysis that excludes any measure of the Court's outlook in order to consider the larger time period. Although this analysis will not allow me to test the full range of empirical predictions derived from the model, it will at least allow

---

[20] See Chapter 4 for a fuller discussion of this variable.

[21] I note here that I do not need to include in the analysis below the judicial conservatism and public liberalism variables directly. There is no theoretical prediction for these variables, and there is no reason to expect any effect from the constituent terms. Rather, the interaction itself is really a new variable, which is the central concept of interest and for which we have a theoretical prediction.

me to test the main prediction concerning the effects of Court-curbing and policy divergence on the use of judicial review. To the extent I find substantively comparable patterns in the full dataset and in the subset with public opinion controls, this will provide further reassurance of the validity of the findings reported here.

Next, the theoretical model predicts that ideological divergence between the Court and Congress should attenuate the effect of Court-curbing on the use of judicial review. Because Congress will have a greater incentive to "bluff" and misrepresent public opinion when the Court and Congress disagree about policy, the Court should be less responsive to Court-curbing when it is considered by its ideological opponents. Although many sophisticated measures of judicial and congressional ideology exist to cover a long span of time, the only measure that covers the full range of years in these data is the crude, but reasonable, measure of partisan alignment. To be sure, partisan alignment and ideological distance are not the same thing (Clark and Whittington 2007), but there is good reason to expect that it is a reasonable proxy for the underlying concept of interest. On average, Republican judges tend to be more conservative than Democratic judges; similarly, Republican legislators tend to be more conservative than Democratic legislators. Thus, I measure policy divergence between the Court and Congress with a "dummy" variable that indicates whether the Court and Congress are controlled by opposing political parties. Congress is controlled by one party if both chambers have a majority from that party; the Court is controlled by a party if a majority of the members are affiliated with that party.[22]

---

[22] To determine a justice's partisan affiliation, I rely on Epstein, Segal, Spaeth, and Walker (2007). In addition, one can also perform these analyses using more continuous measures. First, using votes cast on roll calls in Congress, as well as presidential positions on those bills, Poole and Rosenthal (1997) scale the "ideal points" of all legislators and presidents. Relying on the insight of Giles, Hettinger, and Peppers (2001), I use these ideal point estimates to infer the ideal point of each of the justices. To do this, I average the ideal points of the appointing president and each of the home-state, same-party senators, for each nominee. The essential insight here is that home-state senators provide some information about the ideological pool from which a nominee is drawn. This procedure yields an estimate of each justice's ideal point, which is comparable to congressional ideal points. Second, one might use the more sophisticated set of judicial ideal points proposed in Epstein, Martin, Segal, and Westerland (2007). These estimates are based on the justices' own voting – rather than that of their nominators. Unfortunately, though, these estimates are only available for justices serving during the latter half of the twentieth century. In any event, performing the analyses here with either of those two measures yields substantively comparable findings.

I also control for the composition of the Court. In particular, I include a set of "dummy" variables, which indicate which natural court is hearing the case. A natural court is a period of time during which the composition of the Court does not change. The inclusion of these indicator variables allows me to simultaneously control for the ideological composition of the Court – some have suggested that more conservative courts strike down more laws than more liberal courts (Segal and Westerland 2005; Clark and Whittington 2007).[23]

Finally, as in Chapter 4, I standardize all of the continuous variables by centering each on zero and dividing by two standard deviations. The consequence is that a one-unit change in any of these variables represents a two-standard-deviation change in the predictor. This allows for the continuous predictors to be on roughly the same scale as the binary predictors. With these measures in hand, I now turn to the empirical model itself.

Empirical Model

The empirical model I employ here assumes the number of federal laws held unconstitutional each year is a function of the amount of Court-curbing in Congress, public support for the Court, and policy divergence between the Court and Congress. This model is given by:

$$
\begin{aligned}
\textit{Laws Struck Down}_t = f(&\textit{Court Curbing}_{t-1}, \qquad (5.1)\\
&\textit{Public Support}_t,\\
&\textit{Court–Congress Alignment}_t,\\
&\textit{Natural Court}_t)
\end{aligned}
$$

The dependent variable in this analysis – the number of laws struck down each year – is an event count variable (i.e., it can only take on nonnegative integer values). As we saw in Chapter 4, modeling such data can be difficult. Although I reserve the technical diagnostic details to the appendix of this chapter, I note here briefly that the data do not suffer from time-series dynamics and satisfy the assumptions necessary for the Poisson regression model – the standard model for event count data. The results of this analysis are reported in Table 5.1.

---

[23] In addition, and importantly, these deterministic variables capture any time trends that may be present in the data. That is, the vector of natural court indicators allows me to nonparametrically estimate any changes in the baseline number of laws struck down by the Court, as the indicators are collinear with time. Moreover, the natural court indicators also help account for any particular idiosyncrasies that may be associated with particular courts.

TABLE 5.1. *Effect of Court-Curbing, Public Support, and Court–Congress Divergence on the Use of Judicial Review*

Poisson regression coefficients shown (standard errors in parentheses); dependent variable is number of laws invalidated in year t; natural court fixed effects included but not reported; all continuous predictors have been normalized by centering on zero and dividing by two standard deviations

	GSS Public Support Measure	Proxy Public Support Measure	No Public Support Measure
Court-curbing$_{t-1}$	-0.55^{***}	-0.48^{***}	-0.51^{***}
	(0.20)	(0.17)	(0.16)
Public Support$_t$	0.35^{**}	0.43^{**}	–
	(0.14)	(0.21)	–
Court–Congress	0.19	-0.02	-0.10
Alignment$_t$	(0.75)	(0.58)	(0.40)
Intercept	1.43^{***}	1.32^{***}	1.45^{**}
	(0.06)	(0.09)	(0.03)
N	32	52	127

$^{***}p \leq 0.01$; $^{**}p \leq 0.05$; $^{*}p \leq 0.10$ (two-tailed).

The first thing to notice here is that the coefficients associated with Court-curbing are all negative and statistically distinguishable from zero. That is, an increase in the introduction of Court-curbing bills is associated with a decrease in the number of laws held unconstitutional by the Supreme Court. This correlation provides direct support for the primary empirical prediction derived from the Conditional Self-Restraint model (Hypothesis 4). Indeed, the substantive impact that this correlation represents is considerable. The estimated coefficients predict that an increase from no Court-curbing to the introduction of ten Court-curbing bills will lead to one fewer laws per year being invalidated by the Court. Given that the Court only strikes down about two laws per year, this effect represents a substantial effect on the use of judicial review. Notably, this effect is comparable in magnitude to the pattern in the case-level data we saw previously in Figure 5.2. There, we saw that moving from no Court-curbing to "high" Court-curbing is associated with a decrease in the probability of a constitutional invalidation in a single case by about 35–50%. This evidence demonstrates a substantively considerable relationship between the introduction of Court-curbing bills and judicial self-restraint. To the extent those bills can be interpreted as *merely* signals of waning public support, then the evidence further suggests that such institutional signals about public opinion can create an incentive for judicial self-restraint.

Of course, this evidence is also consistent with an alternative account in which the Court responds to Court-curbing because it fears the enactment of the legislation. In the next analysis and again further below, I provide additional evidence that suggests responses to Court-curbing are at least partially driven by a concern for public support.

Notice next the coefficients associated with public support for the Court (both using the direct measure of public opinion and using the proxy measure). These coefficients are both positive and statistically distinguishable from zero. These results, then, indicate that as public support for the Court wanes, and as the Court's decisions become more ideologically out of line with public preferences, the Court invalidates fewer laws. To the extent these measures capture the Court's expectation about its public support, this evidence suggests that a more pessimistic Court will use judicial review less often. This finding provides direct support for the hypothesis derived from the model that more pessimistic Courts will make more constrained decisions (Hypothesis 5).

Finally, the coefficient associated with Court–Congress alignment is substantively small and statistically indistinguishable from zero in each specification. This indicates that, following the bulk of previous empirical findings, ideological divergence from Congress does not meaningfully affect the Court's decision making; there is no inherent judicial self-restraint that follows simply from the Court being ideologically opposed to Congress. Moreover, the result is in line with previous empirical results (see, e.g., Segal and Westerland 2005) and conventional wisdom that suggest traditional separation-of-powers mechanisms do not constrain the Court in the exercise of constitutional interpretation. To be sure, the theoretical model made no particular prediction about the effect of Court–Congress alignment on the use of judicial review. In fact, the only prediction it made was that the effect of Court-curbing on the use of judicial review should be conditioned on the degree of Court–Congress alignment. I turn to an analysis of that prediction later.

Not only are the findings statistically significant, but they represent a substantively considerable relationship. Over the 130-year period of study here, the Supreme Court held 284 Acts of Congress unconstitutional. The statistical results reported in Table 5.1 indicate that Court-curbing has deterred about eighty-one additional constitutional invalidations. That is, approximately 20% of the Court's exercises of judicial review have been deterred by Court-curbing legislation in Congress. Put differently, the Court's failure to respond to Court-curbing signals from Congress could have led to a 28% increase in the instances of judicial review between 1877 and 2006. Given the significance of a judicial invalidation of an Act of Congress – and the considerable political controversy that has surrounded important historical instances of judicial invalidations and judicial upholdings of federal legislation, this figure indicates a very substantial and consequential finding.

To see the impact that Court-curbing has had over time, consider Figure 5.3. Here, we see, for each decade from the 1880s through the 2000s, the total number of laws held unconstitutional by the Supreme Court and the predicted number of laws that would have been held unconstitutional had there been no relationship between Court-curbing and judicial review.[24] This figure demonstrates that in each decade since Reconstruction, the effect of Court-curbing has been considerable. Even in decades that were marked by considerable exercise of judicial review – such as the 1930s – more laws would have been held unconstitutional had there been no congressional signaling to the Court. Although this figure represents a counterfactual analysis of "what could have been," it is interesting to ask what potential developments were avoided by the use of Court-curbing to restrain the Court. If the public had been more accepting of the Court's decisions in the 1930s, what other legislation might have been blocked? Alternatively, one might ask what legislation that was invalidated might have been saved if the public had been more concerned? For example, during the 1990s, whereas the Court was invalidating some considerable federal legislation, there was little backlash from the public (see Figure 5.1 above). During the 1990s, the Supreme Court invalidated twenty-eight pieces of federal legislation. Public discontent with the Court might have preserved about ten of those laws.

This finding, then, seems to suggest that the public plays an important, if muted, role in the courtroom. The contours of public support for the Court can impose bounds on the extent to which the Court can exercise its countermajoritarian check on democratic policy making. In this sense, we find in these data a striking pattern of representation on the Court. American norms of majority rule and democracy suggest that decisions by unelected, unaccountable judges are at risk for being perceived as illegitimate and disregarded. However, to the extent that public support for the judicial institution is communicated to the Court via institutional signals from elected representatives, there is at least an indirect mechanism for

---

[24] To calculate the number of laws that would have been held unconstitutional, I estimated the effect of the Court-curbing variables each year and then added that effect to the actual number of laws struck down. I then aggregated the data by decade.

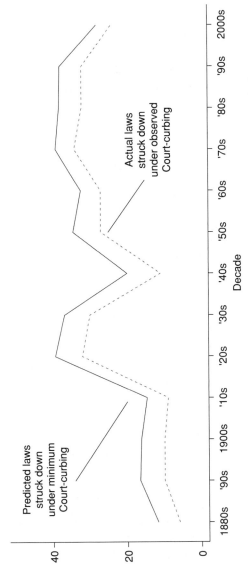

FIGURE 5.3. *Actual laws struck down each decade and predicted number of laws struck down, given no Court-curbing in Congress. Prediction derived from estimates from empirical model (5.1).*

representation on the Court. Public discontent in the 1930s can explain the Court's pull-back from its anti-New Deal activism; the lack of public discontent with the Court in the 1990s can help explain why it was so successful in invalidating federal legislation without significant consequences for its legitimacy. As I discuss in Chapter 7, this relationship may help reconcile competing goals of liberal democracy – the enforcement of constitutional protections for minorities while at the same time promoting and maintaining democratic self-government. However, before drawing any broad conclusions about the implications of this finding, I first consider alternative explanations for the patterns discovered here and demonstrate the robustness of this finding.

5.2.2   Signals about Public Support or Institutional Threats?

It is of course entirely possible that the threat of Court-curbing enactment creates an incentive for the Court to exercise self-restraint; such an effect would not be inconsistent with the Conditional Self-Restraint model. What is more, such an effect would be largely consistent with much of the evidence presented here. There is, however, evidence to suggest that a fear that the legislation will be enacted cannot wholly explain the Court's responsiveness to Court-curbing.

To begin assessing whether the Court responds to Court-curbing because it fears the legislation will be enacted or because it believes the legislation is a signal of waning public support, I have estimated an empirical model (5.1) including, in addition to the number of Court-curbing bills introduced, a measure of the seriousness of Court-curbing. Specifically, I have estimated the model including in turn the number of bills that have either received committee hearings or the number of bills reported out of committee. Although there are of course multiple stages to the legislative process, these two initial stages represent perhaps the most significant increase in the legislative "seriousness" of a proposal.[25] If the Court responds to Court-curbing only when it fears it will be enacted, then one should expect that the effect of bills that have received a hearing or made it out of committee should be larger than the effect of the total number of bills simply introduced. The results of this estimation are shown in the first column of Table 5.2. Here, I find that the effect of Court-curbing is essentially the same as shown previously although

---

[25] Alternatively, I could include the number of bills that passed at least one chamber, but there are few such examples.

TABLE 5.2. *Effect of Court-Curbing on Use of Judicial Review to Invalidate Federal Legislation, with Control for Legislative Seriousness*

Poisson regression coefficients (standard errors in parentheses); natural court fixed effects included but not shown

	Court-curbing Seriousness	Legislative Activism
Court-curbing$_{t-1}$	-0.51^{**}	-0.45^{*}
	(0.23)	(0.25)
Public Support$_t$	0.36^{***}	0.38^{***}
	(0.14)	(0.13)
Court–Congress Alignment$_t$	0.16	0.24
	(0.79)	(0.77)
Bills with Action$_{t-1}$	-0.12	–
	(0.21)	–
Total Bills Introduced$_{t-1}$	–	-0.21
	–	(0.31)
Intercept	1.42^{***}	1.35^{***}
	(0.05)	(0.16)
N	32	32

$^{***} p \leq 0.01$; $^{**} p \leq 0.05$; $^{*} p \leq 0.10$.

there is no evidence that the Court responds to the number of "serious" bills. The estimated coefficient associated with the number of bills with any legislative action is indeed negative, though it is substantively smaller than the estimated coefficient associated with all bills and is statistically indistinguishable from zero. That the number of "serious" Court-curbing bills does not seem to influence judicial behavior, while an increase in the total number of bills does predict a decrease in the use of judicial review, suggests that judicial responsiveness to Court-curbing is not conditional on the likelihood a bill will be enacted. If it were the case that the Court responds to Court-curbing out of a fear that the legislation is enacted, one would expect a differential response to bills that are more likely to be enacted than to more run-of-the-mill bills.

Finally, I have also reestimated empirical model (5.1) while including the total number of bills introduced in the previous Congress. The total number of bills introduced captures the extent of legislative activism in Congress.[26] If the Court exercises self-restraint when it fears Court-curbing legislation will be enacted, then we should expect that greater

---

[26] Alternatively, one could include the number of laws *enacted* during the previous Congress. In that case, the same results hold.

legislative activism should deter the Court from invalidating Acts of Congress. Again, we find here that the estimated effect of Court-curbing is substantively and statistically comparable to that from the main specification reported previously in Table 5.1. However, the estimated coefficient associated with the total number of bills introduced, while negative, is substantively smaller and statistically indistinguishable from zero. This finding suggests that while the Court does exercise self-restraint in the face of Court-curbing proposals, the extent of legislative activism itself does not affect the Court's decision making.

All of this discussion is not meant to suggest that the seriousness of a Court-curbing effort in Congress does not create an additional incentive for judicial self-restraint or affect the Court's decision making. Indeed, the estimated coefficients associated with the seriousness of Court-curbing and legislative activism are negative, even if they are statistically imprecise. Rather, what this is meant to suggest is that judicial responsiveness to Court-curbing cannot be explained by an account in which the Court responds only to the threat that a Court-curbing bill will be enacted. This is important because it underscores an important point – Court-curbing is a mechanism by which Congress can (possibly, credibly) communicate information to the Court about the Court's standing with the public. In sum, these two findings suggest that although a fear of enactment may be *part* of the reason why the Court responds to Court-curbing, a fear of enactment cannot explain all of the responsiveness we find here.

5.2.3   Interactive Effects

The results of the preceding statistical analyses provide direct support for the two primary predictions about judicial decision making derived from the Conditional Self-Restraint model (Hypotheses 4 and 5). However, in Chapter 3, I also derived additional, interactive hypotheses. In particular, Hypothesis 6 predicts that the Supreme Court should respond more to Court-curbing introduced by its ideological allies than its ideological opponents. Hypothesis 7 predicts that the effect of Court-curbing should be greatest when the Court is pessimistic about its diffuse support and least when the Court is more optimistic about its diffuse support.

The interactive hypotheses are particularly important predictions, because they help demonstrate the explanatory power of the theoretical model developed in this book and argue against an alternative theory of Court-curbing. Specifically, an alternative account of Court-curbing – the one implicit in previous studies of Court-curbing – holds that the consideration of these bills in Congress constrains the Court because of the threat they will actually be enacted. If that story is true, however, one would expect either that bills considered by the Court's ideological opponents would be taken more seriously by the Court, or at the very least there would be no difference in the effect of bills considered by the Court's opponents and those considered by its allies. The Court's ideological allies have a greater interest in preserving the Court's independence than its ideological opponents, because an independent Court will serve to represent the current majority's preferences in the future (Whittington 2007). Supreme Court justices benefit from life tenure, whereas elected politicians are often uncertain about their future (or at the very least the future of their governing majority). By diminishing the independence of a Supreme Court that is its ideological ally, the current majority undermines its anticipated future influence after leaving office. As a consequence, the Court's ideological allies have an incentive to not enact Court-curbing legislation that is lacking for it ideological opponents. That is, if the Court is worried the bills will actually be enacted, then when its ideological opponents control the government, the Court would likely be more concerned about threats to its institutional integrity than when the government is controlled by its ideological friends.

Similarly, the Conditional Self-Restraint Model predicts that the effect of an increase in Court-curbing will be greatest when the Court is pessimistic about its public support and least when the Court is more optimistic. This is because the Court knows that Congress may have an incentive to "bluff" about public opinion; when the Court is optimistic, it is more likely to call that bluff than when it is pessimistic. If the Court's response to Court-curbing bills is driven only by a concern the legislation will be enacted, such a conditional relationship seems less intuitive. Although it is certainly possible that such a relationship could exist, the conditional effect of Court-curbing is certainly suggestive of the public opinion communication role served by Court-curbing.

Empirical Model

This analysis employs the same empirical model as above (model (5.1)), though now includes interactions between each of (a) Court–Congress Alignment and (b) Public Support and Court-curbing. As above, the model is estimated using a Poisson regression specification.[27] The results

---

[27] An alternative approach is to divide all bills introduced into "aligned" bills and "unaligned" bills – that is, those that are introduced by individual legislators who are

are reported in Table 5.3. The first thing to notice is that in both models, the estimated coefficient associated with Court-curbing is negative and statistically significant. This means that, at the average level of Public Support, the Court responds to Court-curbing (from a same-party Congress) by invalidating fewer laws as unconstitutional. Moreover, in both models the estimated coefficient associated with Public Support is positive and statistically significant. This means that at the average level of Court-curbing, a decrease in Public Support is associated with a decrease in the number of laws struck down. The interactive specification, however, allows us to ask how Court–Congress Alignment and Public Support condition the effect of Court-curbing on the use of judicial review.

To answer this question, we turn to the interactive coefficients reported in Table 5.3. The estimated coefficients associated with the interaction between Court-curbing and Court–Congress Alignment are inconsistently signed across the two specifications (though so is the coefficient associated with Court–Congress Alignment). The estimated coefficients associated with the interaction between Court-curbing and Public Support are both negative. The substantive and statistical meaning of these estimated relationships, however, is not necessarily straightforward. Instead, it is better to evaluate these effects visually. To do this, Figure 5.4 shows the predicted number of laws that would be struck down as a function of

aligned with the Court and those legislators who are opposed to the Court, respectively. There are, to be sure, certain advantages to this approach. Specifically, a natural interpretation of the interactive hypotheses derived from the Conditional Self-Restraint model is that the ideological relationship between the Court and the bill *sponsor* is what should condition the response to Court-curbing. At the same time, there are significant limitations. First, these two measures are very strongly correlated ($r = 0.40$, $t = 3.7$). Second, dividing bills by their sponsors assumes that the conditioning effect leads the Court to care less about the opinion of people represented by their ideological foes. By conditioning the effect of Court-curbing on partisan control of Congress, the model estimated here asks whether, when the threat of enactment is less significant (when there is less incentive to enact Court-curbing), the Court responds more to Court-curbing. Nevertheless, I have also estimated a model in which Court-curbing bills are divided into those sponsored by the median justice's copartisans and those sponsored by its ideological opponents. Because of multicollinearity problems, the results are less stable. However, in nearly every specification, the estimated coefficient associated with "same-party" bills is negative, and in all models, the estimated coefficient associated with "opposite-party" bills is either positive or zero. Moreover, in the simplest models, the estimated coefficients associated with "same-party" bills are negative *and* statistically distinguishable from zero. Thus, in this alternative specification, the effect of Court-curbing bills sponsored by the Court's copartisans is, as predicted, to constrain the Court's use of judicial review. At the same time, bills sponsored by the Court's ideological opponents do not appear to constrain the Court's use of judicial review.

TABLE 5.3. *Conditional Effect of Court-Curbing on Invalidations of Acts of Congress*

Estimated Coefficients for Explanatory Variables from Interactive Version of Empirical Model (5.1); Poisson regression coefficients (standard errors in parentheses); natural court fixed effects not shown; dependent variable is total number of federal laws struck down each year; all continuous predictors have been normalized by centering on zero and dividing by two standard deviations

	GSS Public Support Measure	Proxy Public Support Measure
Court-curbing$_{t-1}$	−0.41**	−0.40***
	(0.16)	(0.08)
Public Support$_t$	0.38*	0.82***
	(0.21)	(0.31)
Court–Congress Alignment$_t$	0.30	−0.40
	(0.72)	(0.49)
Court-curbing$_{t-1}$ × Court–Congress Alignment$_t$	−0.42	0.47
	(0.50)	(0.37)
Court-curbing$_{t-1}$ × Public Support$_t$	−0.11	−1.44***
	(0.38)	(0.40)
Intercept	−0.09	1.57***
	(1.08)	(0.07)
N	32	52

*** $p \leq 0.01$; ** $p \leq 0.05$; * $p \leq 0.10$.

Court-curbing. The left panel shows the predicted number of constitutional invalidations as a function of Court-curbing both when the Court and Congress are aligned and when they are of different parties. Recall that the Conditional Self-Restraint model predicts that the Court will be more responsive to bills introduced by its ideological allies than those introduced by its ideological opponents (Hypothesis 6). We see here evidence of such a conditional effect of Court-curbing on the use of judicial review. As more bills are introduced by the Court's ideological allies, the Court responds by striking down fewer laws as unconstitutional. By contrast, bills introduced by the Court's ideological opponents have little, if any, effect on the use of judicial review. Not only does this finding support one of the more nuanced predictions derived from the model, it seems inconsistent with an alternative theory in which Court-curbing is only constraining to the extent the Court fears it will be enacted. If the Court were responding only to the threat of Court-curbing enactment, it seems unlikely that bills proposed by the Court's opponents would have so little effect, especially relative to bills introduced by the Court's

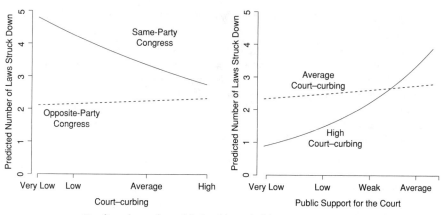

FIGURE 5.4. *Predicted number of federal laws held unconstitutional as a function of Court-curbing in Congress.* Left panel shows effect of Court-curbing for a same-party and opposite-party Congress; right panel shows predicted laws struck down as a function of public support for two levels of Court-curbing; estimates derived from model using proxy measure of public support; all other variables held at their means; natural court assumed to be final Rehnquist Court.

allies. However, in the context of the Conditional Self-Restraint model, which posits that the Court will respond to Court-curbing to the extent it is a credible signal about public support for the Court, this conditional relationship is precisely what we would expect.

At the same time, we find evidence suggesting that increases in Court-curbing have the greatest effect when the Court is pessimistic about its public support. The right-hand panel in Figure 5.4 shows the predicted number of laws that will be struck down under average Court-curbing and elevated Court-curbing, as a function of public support for the Court. We see at the left end of this figure that moving from average to elevated Court-curbing results in a considerable decrease in the number of laws struck down from just over two to less than one, a greater than 50% decrease in the use of judicial review. By contrast, at an above-average level of public support for the Court, an increase in Court-curbing is associated with a mild *increase* in the use of judicial review. Indeed, the flat relationship for average Court-curbing and the steeper relationship for elevated Court-curbing indicate that the Court is more willing to disregard Court-curbing when it is optimistic about its diffuse support.

In sum, then, these two interactive effects provide additional support for the Conditional Self-Restraint model. The interactive relationships demonstrated above, particularly the evidence that ideological divergence between the Court and Congress *attenuates* the effect of Court-curbing, seem inconsistent with the claim that the Court only responds to Court-curbing to the extent it expects such legislation to be enacted. That the Court's responsiveness to Court-curbing is conditioned by its ideological alignment with Congress and its outlook about its own legitimacy is particularly suggestive of the signaling function of Court-curbing. These two more subtle and nuanced interactive effects are directly predicted by the theory of Court-curbing as a signal about the Court's institutional legitimacy. In particular, when taken in conjunction with the main effects demonstrated above in Tables 5.1 and 5.2, the evidence paints a picture of a Court concerned for its legitimacy and learning from the political environment about how treacherous the political waters may be. The introduction of Court-curbing in Congress constrains the Court, but it is less constraining when the bills come from a less credible source – that is, a Congress that has an incentive to misrepresent public opinion. The introduction of Court-curbing is similarly less constraining when the bills do not comport with the Court's prior expectations. When the Court is very optimistic about its public support, it will be more willing to disregard those negative institutional signals; when it is less optimistic, though, Court-curbing can be particularly informative. These findings are also useful because they provide some evidence against an alternative account according to which Court-curbing is only constraining to the extent that the Court fears the legislation will be enacted. (Below, we will consider additional evidence to assess whether the threat of Court-curbing is driving judicial responsiveness to the bills.) With these results in hand, we now turn to a final statistical analysis of Court-curbing and judicial review. Specifically, we move from a yearly analysis of judicial review to a case-by-case analysis.

5.2.4 Controlling for Case-Level Effects

That the Supreme Court responds to Court-curbing by exercising self-restraint in its constitutional cases is a novel and noteworthy finding. It offers a new perspective both on institutional confrontations and, to the extent these bills can be interpreted as signals about public opinion, the role of the public in the incentives facing institutions during those confrontations. However, a question remains: Does the Court exercise self-restraint by upholding laws it would otherwise invalidate? Or, does the Court exercise self-restraint by simply choosing to hear different cases than it would otherwise? To be sure, both types of effects constitute

self-restraint on the part of the Court, and either type of behavior would
be consistent with the Conditional Self-Restraint model. Nevertheless,
the available data do allow us to parse between these two alternative
explanations. Case-level data – rather than yearly data – allow us to ask
whether the pattern of judicial responsiveness to Court-curbing holds
once we control for case-specific factors. This section presents a final
analysis that considers the Court's decisions in individual judicial review
cases.

Measurement of Key Variables

We now move from an aggregate, yearly-level analysis of the Court's use
of judicial review to a case-level analysis. Thus, I must break the measure of judicial decisions down from a yearly measure to a case-by-case
measure. In this analysis, the dependent variable is simply an indicator of
whether the Supreme Court strikes down the challenged law in a particular case or whether it upholds the law.[28] What it means to invalidate a
law, however, is not entirely clear. Indeed, one might imagine a continuum of possible judicial actions, ranging from complete deference to the
elected branches at one end to the invalidation of a statute on its face at
the other end. In between those poles, though, lie review of administrative
decisions, statutory construction, the constitutional invalidation of a law
as applied, among other forms of judicial activity. For purposes of coding,
I count all laws that are either struck down on their face or struck down
as applied as constitutional invalidations. I include both of these forms
of judicial review because the invalidation of a law as applied is often
tantamount to a facial invalidation and can often represent one of the
most consequential forms of judicial review.[29] From 1877 through 2006,
there were 1,151 cases involving constitutional challenges to a federal
law, and the Court struck down the law in question in 284 (about 25%)
of those cases.

---

[28] Specifically, the dependent variable will be a dichotomous measure, *Strike Down$_{it}$*, that
equals 1 if the Court strikes down a law in case i in year t and 0 otherwise.

[29] Of course, there are significant differences between the facial and as applied invalidation
of a law. For example, the as-applied invalidation may be more about the particular interpretation an implementing administration has put on a statute than about the
substantive content or purpose of the statute (Clark and Whittington 2007). While I
recognize these differences and appreciate their subtleties, it is beyond the scope of this
project to provide a full and careful treatment of the various forms of judicial activity; I
leave it for others to consider how the effect of Court-curbing and concerns for judicial
legitimacy might vary across the range of forms of judicial decision making.

To assess the predictions outlined in Chapter 3, I employ a set of explanatory variables similar to those used in the analyses above. First, I include the same measure of Court-curbing as used in the previous analyses. This measure necessarily induces some mismatch into the analysis – the Court-curbing variable is observed yearly, but cases are observed individually, with many occurring in each year. However, because Court-curbing cannot generally be tied to a specific case, this mismatch is essentially unavoidable. To the extent, though, we find further evidence of judicial responsiveness to Court-curbing despite this mismatch, we will be confident the effect of Court-curbing is large enough in at least some cases to evince a pattern in the aggregate data. Second, I include the various measures of the Court's outlook employed above. Specifically, I include the GSS measure of public confidence in the Court and the public-Court divergence variable. As with the Court-curbing variable, these variables are measured yearly, rather than at the case level, which necessarily introduces some mismatch between the explanation and what is being explained.

Next, I control for case-specific factors. Most important, I control for the current political majority's preferences for the law being reviewed. The variable *Congress-Law Alignment* identifies whether the current Congress is controlled by the same political party that enacted the law.[30] Thus, democratically enacted laws are "aligned" with the current Congress if the current Congress is controlled by Democrats. Laws enacted under divided government are considered to be "aligned" with future divided governments. This variable, then, serves as the analog to the Court–Congress alignment variable from above, though it is now more refined in that it is defined on a case-by-case basis. This allows for the idea that Congress may sometimes prefer that the Court invalidate a particular law – if, for example, the Court and Congress are both opposed to the legislation.[31]

---

[30] The Congress that enacted the law is assumed to be the Congress that most recently amended (or enacted) the provision in question in the given case.

[31] An interesting and compelling point has been made that sometimes it may be profitable for Congress or the president to sustain judicial review of legislation. For example, Whittington (2005) makes the point that legislative gridlock and the inertia of the status quo may mean that laws opposed by a majority (or, even a supermajority) may be too entrenched by the multiple veto points in American law-making. As a consequence, judicial invalidation of the legislation may be precisely what is needed to enable the enactment of a new law. In this sense, by dislodging the status quo from the "gridlock region" (Krehbiel 1998), the Court may actually help a legislative majority.

I also control for the degree of ideological alignment between the Court and the Congress who enacted the statute. I divide all laws being reviewed into one of three categories. The first category, *Opposite Party Law*, includes all laws that were enacted under unified government controlled by one political party and are being reviewed by a Court controlled by the opposite political party.[32] The second category, *Divided Government Law*, includes all laws enacted under divided government. The third category, *Same Party Law*, includes all laws enacted under unified government controlled by one party and being reviewed by a Court controlled by the same party. In general, one would expect that the Court would be least fond of laws in the *Opposite Party Law* category and most fond of laws in the *Same Party Law* category.

Empirical Model

The data are modeled with a logit regression model. The logit model is a standard specification for data where the dependent variable is dichotomous – here, the dependent variable can take on only one of two values: either uphold or strike down. As shown previously, I standardize all of the continuous variables by centering them on zero and dividing by two standard deviations. The Court's choice to uphold or strike down a law is modeled as a function of the variables described above as follows:

$$\text{Probability Law } i \text{ is Struck Down} = f(\textit{Court-Curbing}_{t-1}, \quad (5.2)$$
$$\textit{Court's Outlook}_t,$$
$$\textit{Opposite Party Law}_i,$$
$$\textit{Divided Government Law}_i,$$
$$\textit{Congress-Law Alignment}_i,$$
$$\textit{Court}_i)$$

To help account for variation that may be correlated across time, the standard errors are clustered on the year. The results of the estimation are shown in Table 5.4.

In each of the three models, we find a negative and statistically significant correlation between the intensity of Court-curbing in Congress and the probability the Court will hold a challenged law unconstitutional. That is, as more Court-curbing bills are introduced in Congress, the Court is less likely to hold a given law unconstitutional. Thus, at the level of

---

[32] As shown previously, the enacting party is assumed to be the party that most recently amended (or enacted) the provision of the law in question in the given case. Unified government is defined as the condition where the House of Representatives, the Senate, and the White House are all controlled by the same political party.

TABLE 5.4. *Effect of Court-Curbing on Probability of a Constitutional Invalidation*

Logit coefficients (standard errors in parentheses); dependent variable is probability the Supreme Court holds a challenged law unconstitutional; all continuous predictors have been normalized by centering on zero and dividing by two standard deviations

	GSS Public Support Measure	Proxy Public Support Measure	No Public Support Measure
Court-curbing$_{t-1}$	−0.52*	−0.52*	−0.37*
	(0.28)	(0.27)	(0.22)
Public Support$_t$	0.32	0.78**	–
	(0.35)	(0.40)	
Opposite Party Law$_i$	0.64	0.26	−0.38*
	(0.68)	(0.43)	(0.22)
Divided Government Law$_i$	0.63	0.34	−0.19
	(0.68)	(0.43)	(0.20)
Congress-Law Alignment$_i$	−0.02	0.08	−0.27
	(0.28)	(0.26)	(0.18)
Intercept	−2.48**	0.28	−1.15
	(1.03)	(1.01)	(0.41)
N	313	398	1060

*** $p \leq 0.01$; ** $p \leq 0.05$; * $p \leq 0.10$.

the individual case, while controlling for a number of case-level factors, the introduction of Court-curbing bills is associated with greater judicial restraint in the use of judicial review. This finding provides additional evidence that the mechanism by which Court-curbing influences the use of judicial review is not one in which the Court "dodges" constitutional questions. Rather, the mechanism seems to be one in which similar laws being reviewed are less likely to be invalidated when Congress has signaled waning judicial legitimacy.

The substantive significance of this effect is considerable. Of course, the raw probability that the Court will strike any given law down is very low; only about 20% of the laws reviewed by the Court are struck down. Nevertheless, the introduction of Court-curbing can explain a great deal of the variation in the Court's propensity to invalidate challenged laws. For example, using the estimates from the specification with the GSS measure of public support, holding public support at its mean, the probability that Court will strike down a same-party law that is not aligned with the sitting Congress decreases from 10% at a low level of Court-curbing (one standard deviation below the mean) to 6% at a high level of

Court-curbing (one standard deviation above the mean). This represents a 40% decrease in the probability the Court will strike the law down. This finding is notable because it suggests that Court-curbing affects the Court's decisions themselves rather than simply operating on the Court's case selection process. By holding constant the various case-specific features included in this empirical model, we can compare the predicted probability that the Court will hold unconstitutional laws with similar ideological relationships to the Court under various levels of Court-curbing. This relationship indicates that Court-curbing can influence the Court's decision in the context of a single law.

Interestingly, the relationship between public support for the Court and its use of judicial review is not as strong in this analysis as it was in the previous ones. Here, we see in Table 5.4 that each of the coefficients is positive, though only one (using the proxy measure) is statistically significant. One plausible reason for this weak relationship is that in this analysis there is the previously noted discrepancy between the dependent variable and the explanatory variables. That is, the dependent variable in this analysis is a case-by-case measure of the Court's decision; the measure of public support for the Court is, by contrast, a yearly measure. As a consequence, there is considerable variation from case-to-case within years that cannot be explained by the yearly measures – each year, some laws are upheld and some are struck down, but the measure of the Court's outlook does not change. This mismatch between the measure of the explanation and the measure of the thing being explained leads to less precise estimates of the correlations. In any event, it is notable that the estimated correlations are positive, as predicted, even if the statistical precision of the estimates is weaker.

In addition, it is noteworthy that there does not seem to be much relationship between the controls for institutional preferences over the law. In two of the three models, we estimate a positive coefficient associated with Opposite Party Law, though neither of these coefficients is statistically significant. In the third model, the estimated coefficient is incorrectly signed. In addition, the estimated coefficients associated with Divided Government Law are also inconsistently signed, and none is statistically distinguishable from zero. Together, these inconsistent and statistically weak results suggest that the Court's alignment with the law being reviewed does not affect the probability a law will be struck down.[33]

---

[33] This is consistent with Clark and Whittington (2007), who find that partisan alignment with a law is not a predictor of the Court's decision to invalidate a law.

Finally, the coefficients associated with Congress-Law Alignment are all negative, as predicted, though none is statistically distinguishable from zero and two of the three are very small in magnitude.

5.2.5 Implications

Taken together, the results of the statistical analysis provide evidence that a concern for its institutional legitimacy motivates the Supreme Court to exercise self-restraint. The statistical analysis of judicial review from 1877 through the present demonstrates that when Court-curbing bills are introduced in Congress, the justices will exercise self-restraint by attenuating their use of judicial review to invalidate federal legislation. What is more, there is considerable evidence that the reaction to Court-curbing is not driven simply by a judicial fear that the legislation will be enacted but rather by an interpretation of those bills as indicators of waning public support for the Court. The justices are able to believe the congressional signals precisely because they know those signals are motivated by constituent pressure and legislators' need to position-take on the issues of importance to their constituents. This evidence highlights the connection between public support for the Court and Court-curbing. Although previous scholars have widely recognized the importance of institutional legitimacy for the Court's efficacy, these findings highlight a complex way in which concerns about institutional legitimacy develop and are translated into incentives for judicial self-restraint. Congressional behavior, and position-taking by members of Congress in particular, serves as a useful and informative cue to the Court about public support for the Court. As "Justice C" put it in our interview, the justices are somewhat informed about the broad contours of public support for judicial discretion, but "Congress, especially the House, they really have their finger on the pulse of the public." In this way, the extent of congressional action concerning the Court mediates and communicates Congress' more refined perception of judicial legitimacy among the public. The mediation of public opinion by Congress is a notable component of the separation of powers and demonstrates a mechanism by which democratic representation on the Court takes place.

The public–Congress–Court connection demonstrated here contrasts with previous work on the separation of powers, which posits that congressional constraints on the Court are motivated by a judicial concern that divergent outcomes will lead to either policy reversal, legislative removal of jurisdiction, or other political sanctions. The evidence

presented here suggests separation-of-powers mechanisms work by holding the Court accountable, albeit indirectly, to the public. This evidence
provides good reason to reconsider the traditional separation-of-powers
model in favor of the alternative interpretation proposed in Chapter 3.
We can think of the Court as constrained by Congress out of a concern
for the Court's legitimacy as a governing institution *and only when* the
political climate is suggestive of a lack of public support for the Court.
We can therefore use the theoretical and empirical results reported in
this book to recast the separation-of-powers model as a theory of *why*
the Court should be constrained by congressional preferences and *when*
those constraints should be operative.

To be sure, the idea that congressional constraints on the Court will
operate sometimes, but not others, is not a novel claim. Proponents of the
traditional separation-of-powers model have conceded as much (Eskridge
1991*b*, 683), whereas even the most ardent supporters of the attitudinal
model have admitted that separation-of-powers mechanisms may sometimes be effective at constraining judicial behavior (Segal and Spaeth
2002, 350 n102). However, the empirical results reported here highlight a systematic pattern of conditions that gives rise to congressional
constraints on judicial behavior. Drawing on evidence that a judicial
concern for its legitimacy can give rise to sophisticated decision making
(e.g., Stephenson 2004; Vanberg 2005; Carrubba 2009; Staton 2010),
I have argued the Court's concern for its public support will give rise
to the constraints on judicial independence. This argument implicates
separation-of-powers models in a new way, because I have argued that
Congress serves an important intermediary role, communicating public
opinion to the Court. When there is a significant degree of ideological
divergence between the Court and Congress, Congress will be able to
constrain the Court only if it can successfully convince the Court that
it has lost the public's confidence. In this way, both public opinion and
institutional divergence *can*, under the right conditions, induce judicial
self-restraint.

As the empirical evidence presented in this chapter provides strong
support for this claim, students of political institutions and constitutional
checks should reconsider the mechanisms by which separation-of-powers
incentives operate. Political scientists far too often divide their attention
between (a) studies of electoral connections between elite actors and the
public and (b) elite-level interactions. However, the political world is
much more complicated than this bifurcated view would suggest, as the
public is present – at least in the background – at all levels of governmental

policy making and decision making (Erikson, MacKuen, and Stimson 2002). What may appear to be simple elite-level interactions may actually be much more complicated phenomena in which political actors are influenced by their institutions' particular designs and the ways in which their institutions are held accountable to the public – that is, the democratic features of those political insinuations. Indeed, the evidence reported in this chapter suggests that the checks and balances are much more complicated than a simple elite-level preference divergence/convergence story suggests.

5.3 AN ILLUSTRATION: THE NEW DEAL REVISITED

An illustration of congressional hostility in the context of a notable historical example serves to further illuminate the separation-of-powers mechanism posited above. This illustration, in particular, demonstrates how the theory of institutional hostility can recast our understanding of an important moment in the history of the separation-of-powers and constitutional theory.

Perhaps the most well-known example of Court-curbing is the "Court-packing plan" proposed by President Roosevelt in February 1937. The Court-packing plan ("CPP") is generally cited as the culmination of the tension between the Court and Congress that characterized the early days of the New Deal and FDR's first term in the White House. Coming just after the Democrats' landslide reelection in 1936 and shortly before the famous "switch-in-time-that-saved-nine" – a decision in which the Supreme Court reversed course and upheld Washington State's minimum wage law as constitutional – the CPP is perhaps the archetypal instance of hostility toward the Court. We can use the theoretical and empirical results reported in this book to recast the Court-packing battle and revisit the conventional wisdom about why the Court appears to have submitted to political pressure in the spring of 1937.

The CPP was designed to allow FDR to appoint several additional justices, in order that the New Deal legislative program would enjoy a solid majority of support on the Court. The legislation set up a system whereby once a justice reached a certain age, if he were to continue on the bench and not retire, the president would have the option of appointing an additional justice to the Court. The thinly veiled rationale for the legislation was that as a justice becomes too old, he is unable to keep up with the Court's busy docket, and he will need the assistance of another justice to manage his work.

THE EVENTS OF 1937. In the years preceding the CPP, the Supreme Court, led by the "Four Horsemen" (James McReynolds, George Sutherland, Willis Van Devanter, and Pierce Butler), had been very antagonistic toward FDR's New Deal economic recovery program. Embracing traditions of laissez-faire economics, the Four Horsemen, frequently joined by Justice Owen Roberts and Chief Justice Hughes, invalidated several programs that FDR and the New Deal Democrats in Congress thought were essential for recovery from the Great Depression. In 1936 alone, the Court invalidated the Agricultural Adjustment Act[34] and federal legislation regulating the coal industry.[35]

These decisions were met with considerable ire from the public. Prompted by the Supreme Court's decision on June 1, 1936, Mayor LaGuardia of New York editorialized that "[the case] serves to emphasize the need of a constitutional amendment to curb the power of the court to invalidate social and labor legislation,"[36] while *The New York Times* reported the entire text of the opinion.

Faced with a Supreme Court that was considerably out of line with the American public, Congress acted in 1935 and 1936, as it prepared to face reelection, by introducing and considering several Court-curbing measures. Two bills, H.R. 10102 and H.R. 10362, were identical to the CPP that FDR would propose in February 1937. In fact, more than twenty Court-curbing bills were introduced during the 74th Congress (1935–36), all of which were broad in nature and some of which were taken very seriously, such as H.R. 5161 (74th Congress, 1st Session), which would have set mandatory retirement ages for the justices and was approved by the House. These measures received substantial support from the public, which can be seen, for example, in letters to the editor in *The New York Times* and *The Washington Post*. Moreover, opinion polls show that a majority of the public opposed the Court's use of judicial review to invalidate Acts of Congress and thought that the Supreme Court should "be more liberal in reviewing New Deal measures."[37]

---

[34] *United States v. Butler*, 297 U.S. 1 (1936).
[35] *Carter v. Carter Coal Co.*, 298 U.S. 238 (1936).
[36] "Ruling Disappoints Leaders Here," *The New York Times*, 2 June 1936, 19.
[37] The bills H.R. 10102 (74th Congress, 2nd Session), and H.R. 10362 (74th Congress, 2nd Session), were essentially identical to the Court-packing Plan. For letters to newspaper editors reflecting public opinion, see Oswald N. Cammann, "For More Judges," letter to the editor of *The New York Times*, 4 June 1936, 22; Boris J. Friedkiss, "Protective Laws for Women," letter to the editor of *The New York Times*, 18 June 1936, 8, and S. J. Warburg, "Amendment to Constitution Urged," letter to the editor of *The Washington Post*, 8 June 1936, 8. Public opinion polls revealing public support for Court-curbing

In the midst of this political debate, the Court heard oral argument in several important New Deal cases, including another one contesting the constitutionality of a minimum wage law, the National Labor Relations Act, and the Social Security Act. In November 1936, the New Deal Democrats won a landslide election, with FDR winning every state except Maine and Vermont. In Congress, the Democrats won 334 of the 435 House seats, and the Republicans were left with only 17 of the 96 seats in the Senate. Then, on February 5, 1937, the day the Court voted on how to decide the Washington State minimum wage case, President Roosevelt announced the CPP. Ten days later, the Court heard oral argument in *N.L.R.B. v. Jones & Laughlin Steel Corp.*, a case in which the Court considered the constitutionality of the National Labor Relations Act, a key piece of the New Deal legislative program.

In the meantime, a political battle began to take place concerning the CPP (see, e.g., Pritchett 1948; Leuchtenberg 1995). The proposal was met with early opposition; its purported purpose – to help the Court catch up with its overdue caseload – was seen as a transparent attempt to conceal the overt political nature of the legislation, and from the beginning, the proposal did not garner even a bare majority of public support.[38] On March 9, 1937, FDR held a Fireside Chat – one of his well-known radio addresses to the public – in order to respond to the initial reaction to the CPP and to help build public and political support for the plan. On March 27, Chief Justice Hughes sent a letter to Congress on behalf of himself and Justices Van Devanter and Brandeis, stating that the Court was not behind on its work and that no legislative remedy was necessary to keep the Court up to date.

Two weeks later, on March 29, the Court announced its decision in *West Coast Hotel*, upholding the Washington State minimum wage law, reversing course from its earlier position on minimum wage legislation. The decision was immediately recognized as a subservient move by the Court and as an effort to appease the growing political and public discontent with the Court's antagonism to the New Deal program. Later, it

during this period include Gallup Poll, November 15–November 20, 1936. When asked if, "As a general principle would you favor limiting the power of the Supreme Court to declare acts of Congress unconstitutional?" 59% of respondents answered "Yes." When asked if, "Should the Supreme Court be more liberal in reviewing New Deal measures?" 59% of respondents also answered "Yes."

[38] Gallup poll results show that 53% of Americans opposed the legislation from the outset, and that by the end of 1937 still only 45% of Americans thought the legislation ought to be enacted.

would be dubbed the "switch-in-time-that-saved-nine," because Justice Roberts changed his position from earlier cases and sided with the Court's New Deal supporters to uphold the law. Indeed, the *Parrish* decision represented an explicit overruling of the Court's decision in *Adkins v. Children's Hospital*,[39] in which it had held that a federal minimum wage for women violated the constitution. Later that spring, the Court announced decisions upholding other key New Deal provisions, including the National Labor Relations Act and the Social Security Act. Then, in June, Justice Van Devanter retired, which created an opportunity for FDR to appoint a justice. Combined with the "Three Musketeers" – Justices Brandeis, Cardozo, and Stone – and the new jurisprudence of Justice Roberts, this appointment set the stage for the New Dealers to have a solid majority on the Court. However, the heated battle over the CPP continued. Indeed, the battle was truly "heated"; after one long debate in the Senate through the night, Senate Majority Leader Joseph Robinson, one of the leading proponents of the CPP, died in his apartment. Coupled with the Court's decisions in those key New Deal cases, Van Devanter's retirement, and growing public opposition to the legislation, the death of Senator Robinson has been cited as the end of any chance the CPP had of passing Congress (Leuchtenberg 1995).

ACCOUNTS OF THE COURT-PACKING PLAN. The debate over how to explain the Court's decisions began almost immediately in 1937 and continues to occupy legal academics and historians alike (see Kalman 2005, for a review). Accounts of the New Deal Court, the Court-packing plan, and the Court's apparent shift in 1937 have traditionally fallen into one of two camps: those called "externalist" accounts and those known as "internalist" accounts.

Externalist accounts usually attribute the Court's decisions – particularly its decision in *West Coast Hotel v. Parrish* – to political forces from outside the Court. Early analyses of the Court's decision in *Parrish* attributed the Court's change of course in the spring 1937 to FDR's Court-packing plan. The press dubbed Justice Owen Roberts' shift from the conservative wing of the Court to the liberal wing the "switch in time" that saved nine. Political scientists have noted, for example, a precipitous drop in public support for the Court before the Court-packing plan (Caldeira 1987), and many externalist historical accounts of the confrontation between FDR and the Court have attributed a causal role to the Court-packing plan (see, e.g., Wright 1942; Leuchtenberg

[39] 261 U.S. 525 (1923).

1969; Murphy 1972; Mason 1963) and the election of 1936 (see, e.g., Ackerman 1998) in explaining the Court's decisions. Indeed, on its face this claim seems very plausible. The Court made several decisions that angered the elected branches; the president announced a plan that was a not-so-well veiled attempt to remake the bench; the Court, a few months later, reversed course on some of the most important components of the New Deal legislative program.

Internalist accounts, on the other hand, attribute the Court's decisions to developments in law and jurisprudence. Internalists assert that the Court's decisions were not the product of external influences and political pressure (Friedman 1994; Cushman 1998). These narratives claim that the "switch-in-time" was merely a manifestation of doctrinal developments that had been taking place on the Court for some time before 1937. However, their most damning criticism of externalist accounts is the fact that the Court's decisions had already been made *before* the Court-packing plan was announced in 1937. Although the decisions were not announced until March 1937, the Court had made its decisions earlier that winter. Cushman (1998, 23) notes that "*Parrish* was decided six weeks, and the first Social Security case ten weeks, before the Court-packing plan was known to any but the most intimate of Roosevelt's advisors." Thus, there appears to be a significant timing problem – how could the Court have been responding to the Court-packing plan when it could not have known of the plan until well after it had reached its decisions in those key cases?

What is more, proponents of the internalist account argue that the Court could not have been responding to criticism that took place during the preceding year (White 2005, pars 33–35). These scholars suggest that criticism of the Court has been routine since the earliest days of judicial controversy – dating at least to the tenure of John Marshall – and that legislative attacks on the Court during the 1930s were not especially unique to that era. Therefore, because these scholars assume that the Court does not respond to routine criticism, there is little reason to expect the Court's decision in 1937 to be related to "routine" criticism the preceding year.

INSTITUTIONAL SIGNALING AND THE NEW DEAL. The theoretical argument advanced in this book lends some insight into the conflict between the Court and Congress over the New Deal legislative program. First, the argument here is that when faced with evidence of growing public discontent, the Court will exercise self-restraint. To be sure, an examination of the events leading up to the Court-packing plan highlights the significance of political developments that took place *before* 1937. Figure 5.5 shows a timeline of events leading up to the switch in time in March 1937. This figure shows that the political environment was much more hostile toward the Court than the traditional narrative suggests. More important, the sequence of events that took place leading up to the Court's decision suggests the Court may have reasonably been responding to political signals about the state of judicial legitimacy. The internalists may be correct that it is unlikely the Court was responding to FDR's legislative proposal when it decided *Parrish*; but, there is good reason to believe that the Court could have been responding to other political attacks on the Court.

Beginning in January 1935, Congress considered Court-curbing legislation with great frequency. Leading up to the 1936 election, many Court-curbing bills were introduced in the 74th Congress – several of which closely resemble the CPP. In the context of the theoretical argument here, these Court-curbing bills would have been early signals of public discontent with the Court. At the same time, the Court decided *United States v. Butler*,[40] in which the Court struck down the Agricultural Adjustment Act of 1933, and *Carter v. Carter Coal*,[41] in which the Court limited Congress' power to regulate coal mining. These cases were both seen as significant blows to the New Deal legislative program. Then, through the fall of 1936, culminating in the election in November, there was considerable public debate about the New Deal legislative program, as the Democrats presented themselves to the voters as "advocates of a regulated capitalism" (Ackerman 1998, 302). When they won a landslide reelection in 1936, this then served to further influence the Court's beliefs by signaling that the public was behind the New Deal and would therefore not likely tolerate future judicial frustration of the Democrats' legislative initiatives. At the same time, although FDR was reluctant to openly criticize the Court in 1936 while he was facing reelection (Leuchtenberg 1995), Congress was much more willing to take a hostile position toward the Court. Ackerman (1998) claims the 1936 election was a form of constitutional amendment (without, obviously, formal amendments) by which the public ratified the New Deal Democrats' interpretation of the Constitution and (at least implicitly) rejected the conservative jurisprudence of the Court. To be sure, weeks after the election, public opinion polls show that a majority of Americans favored legislation to limit the

[40] 297 U.S. 1 (1936).
[41] 298 U.S. 238 (1936).

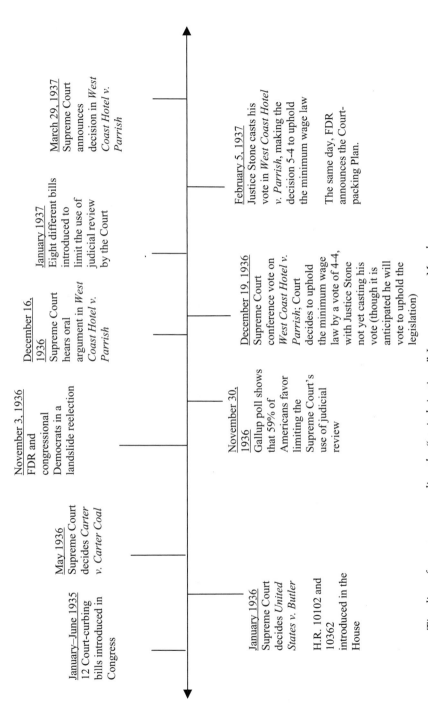

FIGURE 5.5. *Timeline of events surrounding the "switch-in-time," January 1935–March 1937.*

Supreme Court's use of judicial review and thought the Court should be more "liberal" when deciding constitutional cases. Following their reelection, as soon as they returned to Washington in January 1937, Democrats in Congress considered several measures aimed at limiting the use of judicial review.

Between the landslide reelection of the Democrats in November 1936 and their return to Washington in January 1937, the Court heard oral argument in *Parrish* and decided to uphold the Washington State minimum wage law.[42] In addition, beyond upholding the law, during the subsequent sixty years, the Court unequivocally upheld broad congressional authority to regulate the economy in the name of its power over interstate commerce; and, over the course of the following eight years, the Court would only invalidate three Acts of Congress on constitutional grounds. In this sense, the Court would exercise extreme self-restraint in the wake of its confrontation with the public and their elected representatives during the late 1930s.[43]

Although not intended to demonstrate a causal story in the context of this single example, the "switch-in-time" serves as a useful substantive illustration of the principles and mechanisms contemplated by the theoretical argument advanced here. History may have focused on the high-profile CPP, but this does not mean that *congressional* hostility toward the Court before FDR's announcement was irrelevant. Indeed, the systematic patterns described in this chapter suggest that congressional Court-curbing and hostility toward the Court *are* important.[44] Moreover, while history may have focused on the prospect of enactment of the Court-packing plan and the subsequent reversal of the Court's

[42] The vote taken in December 1936 was actually 4-4, with Justice Roberts voting to uphold the law. Justice Stone did not vote at that time, because he was unavailable. It was evident, though, how he would vote – to uphold the law – and he subsequently did cast his vote that way in February 1937.

[43] Of course, many other factors are at play in explaining the Court's reluctance to strike down federal legislation during those years. But it is noteworthy that this confrontation was followed by a period of extreme judicial self-restraint.

[44] While the president has not played a role in the theoretical or empirical work in this book, I certainly believe that executive politics may be part of the larger public-judicial connection. Indeed, research has examined the role of the president in supporting judicial independence (Whittington 2007), and there is no necessary reason to assume that the president may also convey information to the Court about public opinion. However, I have focused on Congress in large part because Congress, I believe, is most closely tied to the public and therefore offers perhaps the most carefully calibrated representation of public opinion. As I noted in Chapter 3, one Supreme Court justice even pointed out to me that "Congress, especially the House, really has its finger on the pulse of the public."

jurisprudence, the illustration here serves to highlight (a) the significance of political signals about public confidence in the Court, and (b) the incentives created by those signals for judicial self-restraint. In this example, then, we find a new interpretation of the background behind the Court-packing plan and a qualitative example to illustrate the way in which institutional signals about judicial legitimacy can operate through the separation of powers.

5.4 COURT-CURBING AND JUDICIAL REVIEW

This chapter has presented an analysis of the Supreme Court's use of judicial review to invalidate federal legislation. Specifically, I have asked whether the Court responds to Court-curbing bills introduced in Congress as institutional signals about waning public support for the Court's legitimacy. In both simple comparisons of Court-curbing and judicial review and more sophisticated statistical analyses, we find that the introduction of Court-curbing is associated with a decrease in the use of judicial review. At the same time, waning public support for the judiciary is similarly associated with a decrease in the use of judicial review. Further, we find in these data some evidence of the conditional effects of Court-curbing predicted by the Conditional Self-Restraint model. Beyond the statistical analyses, a qualitative examination of one notable instance of Court-curbing – the confrontation between New Deal Democrats and the Supreme Court during the mid-1930s – provides further insight into the public–Congress–Court connection.

Whereas judicial-congressional relations literature has previously assumed that constitutional decisions are largely immune to separation-of-powers incentives (Eskridge 1991b; Segal and Spaeth 2002), this chapter suggests otherwise. Indeed, this finding further illuminates a growing movement in separation-of-powers scholarship to empirically examine how constitutional decisions are affected by judicial-congressional relations (Epstein, Knight, and Martin 2001; Friedman and Harvey 2003; Harvey and Friedman 2006; Segal and Westerland 2005). Importantly, though, the evidence here moves the scholarly debate beyond the existing framework. By arguing that the public plays an important, if muted, role in elite-level interactions, I hope to expand the theoretical focus of separation-of-powers analyses. Recognizing the "electoral connection" at the center of congressional behavior directly implicates the public in interbranch relations. The electoral connection implies that elected officials can represent their constituents by communicating their preferences to less well connected institutions such as the judiciary. Of course, those elected officials may have, at times, an incentive to abuse their privileged positions as those most closely connected to the public. In advancing this insight, I have offered an argument that complements recent research into the relationship among the courts, the elected branches, and the public (Vanberg 2005; Staton 2010). Moreover, this recognition further highlights how democratic representation takes place in all branches of government. Although the Court may not be directly accountable to the public, that the public can nevertheless communicate to the Court the broad boundaries of legitimate judicial discretion evinces a form of representation previously unappreciated by students of judicial independence.

To the extent the analysis here demonstrates a mechanism for popular representation on the Courts, the analysis provides some insight into the so-called countermajoritarian difficulty. As I noted in Chapter 1, the countermajoritarian difficulty refers to the tension between giving unelected, unaccountable judges a virtual veto over legislation and American norms of majority rule and democracy. In Chapter 7, I will return to this theme, but it bears mentioning here that evidence of a popular constraint on the use of judicial review provides reason to further revisit the theoretical and empirical analysis of judicial countermajoritarianism.

The effect of Court-curbing legislation, however, need not be limited to only constitutional cases. While the use of judicial review is the most natural context in which to examine Court-curbing, there are other areas of judicial decision making that may also exhibit variation due to congressional hostility. If the Court perceives waning judicial legitimacy and is in fact constrained, then it may pull back from an antagonistic jurisprudence not only in its constitutional cases but more broadly in its statutory cases. For this reason, it is important not to stop the analysis of congressional hostility at the end of the Court's constitutional docket but to consider also the Court's statutory cases. The next chapter does just that.

TECHNICAL APPENDIX

Empirical model (5.1) estimated in this chapter was specified as Poisson regression models. The data used to estimate the model were both time-series and event count data. As I noted above, this type of data presents special concerns that must be addressed before choosing a specification. In this appendix, I describe the theoretical issues that arise with such data and the diagnostic steps I have taken to address those concerns.

While the primary empirical model used to model event count data is the Poisson regression model, there is an ongoing debate in the literature about the best way to treat count data that are also time-series data. The primary concern is that the data may exhibit time-series dynamics such as persistence. A persistent time series is characterized by an autocorrelation function that has a long memory; that is, shocks to the dependent variable have continuing effects for a long period of time. Even if time-series data are not persistent, they may nevertheless reflect short-term auto-correlation or cyclical dynamics. When the data exhibit such time-series dynamics, standard event count models will not be efficient; when the data, however, satisfy the assumptions of independence and equidispersion, then standard event count methods, such as the Poisson regression model, are appropriate (Cameron and Trivedi 1998, 227–8; Brandt and Williams 2000).

The traditional approach to accounting for correlation among events in count data is to use a negative binomial model or a generalized event count model (King 1989). However, several recent developments in the analysis of time-series count data have identified potential deficiencies in this approach and provide the tools necessary for diagnosing these dynamics and correcting for any time-series features of the data that may complicate analysis. Among these developments are two: the Poisson Exponentially Weighted Moving Average (PEWMA) model (Brandt and Williams 2000) and the Poisson Autoregressive (PAR(p)) model (Brandt and Williams 2001).

To assess how best to model the data here, I have performed several diagnostic tests. First, data that suffer from serial correlation generally exhibit overdispersion; therefore, I have estimated the data as a negative binomial model and performed a likelihood-ratio test. This test indicates that the data do satisfy the Poisson assumption of equidispersion ($\chi^2 = 0.12$, $p \leq 0.363$). Next, I have evaluated the data to determine whether there is serial correlation. The Portmaneau (Q) statistic indicates that the data are not serially correlated ($Q = 37.28$, $p < 0.59$). However, upon reestimating the data without the chief justice indicators, the data do exhibit serial correlation. What is more, estimating the model as a PEWMA model (or a PAR(p)) model without the chief justice fixed effects also indicates some serial correlation.[45] In both cases, though, the serial

---

[45] The PEWMA model is a structural time-series model. The structural model is characterized by two functions – a function that describes the number of events in year t as a function of the mean number of events in past years, and a transition/state function

correlation dynamics are weak. In particular, upon estimating the data as a PEWMA model, one observes $\omega = 0.86$. The parameter ω identifies the variance of the conditional mean of the dependent variable; when ω is one, then the PEWMA model is equivalent to the Poisson model (Brandt et al. 2000). Moreover, upon estimating the data as a PAR(p) model, one observes $\rho = 0.20$. The parameter ρ captures the autocorrelation of the dependent variable. Both of these parameters indicate a very low level of serial correlation. Moreover, the chief justice indicators, as evinced by the diagnostics, fully account for the weak serial correlation. Finally, I have considered the possibility that the dependent variable is a unit root. To test this, I have performed the Augmented Dickey-Fuller GLS test on the logged number of laws struck down each year. The test allows me to reject the null hypothesis of a unit root at the 1% level for any number of lags. Taken together, these diagnostics indicate that there may be a very weak level of serial correlation, which is most likely due to a shift in the number of constitutional invalidations sometime during the period of study here. Because the shift is accounted for by the chief justice indicators, a Poisson model is appropriate for the data.

that identifies the weight that past events play in determining the current number of events – as well as a conjugate prior. This state-space model is estimated using the Kalman filter. The model assumes that the observations over time are generated from a Poisson process with a mean, μ_t; the mean μ_t itself evolves over time, according to a gamma-distributed transition equation. The PAR(p) model is similar to the PEWMA model, except that rather than modeling the data as a state-space structural time series, the transition equation is replaced with a linear autoregressive process.

6

Ideological Implications of Court-Curbing

How broadly does the Supreme Court respond to Court-curbing? Is the effect of Court-curbing only to prevent laws from being held unconstitutional? Does Court-curbing affect all justices equally? What are the ideological effects of Court-curbing? In this chapter, we turn to these and other questions. The previous chapter presented the first of two systematic analyses of the consequences of Court-curbing for judicial decision making. We saw there that when it perceives waning diffuse support – as mediated by congressional position-taking – the Court exercises self-restraint and invalidates fewer laws on constitutional grounds. This chapter delves more deeply into the judicial response to Court-curbing. To do so, the analysis turns to the ideological content of the Supreme Court's decisions in statutory cases.

While it is noteworthy that congressional hostility affects the use of judicial review to invalidate laws as unconstitutional, it remains to be seen whether the effect of congressional hostility is limited to constitutional cases. There is no reason the Conditional Self-Restraint model's predictions must be limited to constitutional cases, and there are several reasons why one may expect that Court-curbing will affect the Court's decisions in statutory cases as well as constitutional cases. First, Court-curbing is not about legislative efforts to reverse Court decisions per se; rather Court-curbing is about political responsiveness to public discontent with the Court. If the Court's public support is waning, then there is no reason to believe that statutory decisions will not affect the Court's institutional legitimacy. Second, although Congress has methods other than Court-curbing with which it may respond to statutory decisions, Court-curbing is generally broad in nature – it limits a specific power, imposes a procedural requirement, or constrains the remedies or jurisdiction available to the Court, and statutory cases may be "swept up" by Court-curbing. As one former Supreme Court clerk commented, "How often, when Congress gets all upset about the Court's statutory interpretation, do they actually go back and rewrite the statute? It is easier to attack the Court than to go back and rewrite legislation."[1]

This chapter evaluates the Conditional Self-Restraint Model in the context of statutory decision making. The analysis demonstrates that there exists a strong correlation between congressional attacks on the Court and the justices' voting behavior. We also find here that although there is some variation in the extent to which *individual* justices are sensitive to Court-curbing, we find the effects of Court-curbing in the voting patterns of all justices to some degree. Taken together, these empirical findings provide direct support for the claim that a preference for institutional legitimacy can create an incentive for sophisticated decision making by the Court and that congressional attacks on the Court give rise to judicial concerns about losing public support.

6.1 STATUTORY DECISION MAKING

Modal perceptions about Court-curbing suggest that this legislation is driven by, and directed at, the Court's use of constitutional interpretation. By contrast, I argue Court-curbing is not necessarily about the type of decision the Court has made but is rather a political response to public discontent with the Court. As a consequence, there is no reason why Court-curbing must necessarily be focused on constitutional cases. Several important historical examples highlight the way in which Court-curbing legislation can be a response to statutory decision making. William Eskridge (1991*b*) demonstrates, in the context of analyzing a separation-of-powers model, the significance of civil rights disputes that arise in a statutory context (following in large part from the various Civil Rights Acts). He documents the numerous areas in which the Court invalidated racially discriminatory practices through interpretation of civil rights legislation during the latter half of the twentieth century. At the beginning of the twentieth century, the Court was similarly involved in hotly debated political issues that arose under statutory law – this time the issues involved labor relations in the newly industrialized economy. In fact, the labor injunction was one of the most salient political issues of

[1] Personal interview with "Clerk 2."

the time, representing a major piece of each party's platform in 1908 and occupying a central place in President Roosevelt's 1908 State of the Union Address. These cases were primarily statutory in nature. Several of the free-speech decisions in 1957 that motivated Court-curbing by Congress were similarly statutory in nature (Pritchett 1961; Murphy 1962).

What is more, Court-curbing may be a rational way for Congress to address an ideologically divergent Court in the context of statutory construction. Although statutory decisions may be susceptible to reversal by ordinary legislation, ordinary legislation can generally only reverse a single decision or a set of decisions in a specific, narrow legal area. Court-curbing, on the other hand, can affect judicial decision making across the board, reaching a broad set of cases. In this sense, Court-curbing can be seen as a wholesale response to a set of retail-level decisions by the Court. Even if statutory decisions are not necessarily the source of congressional hostility toward the Court, they may certainly be affected by congressional efforts to rein in the judiciary. Indeed, some evidence suggests that an interest in avoiding an institutional confrontation may create an incentive for sophisticated decision making, even in statutory cases (Hausseger and Baum 1999).

Finally, when examining the separation-of-powers model, most studies have first looked at Supreme Court decisions in cases involving statutory construction (Handberg and Hill 1980; Gely and Spiller 1990; Eskridge 1991*b*; Ferejohn and Weingast 1992; Spiller and Gely 1992; Segal 1997, 1999; Segal and Spaeth 2002).[2] Because statutory decisions can be reversed by legislative majorities through ordinary legislation, separation-of-powers theory has traditionally posited that these types of decisions should be the most likely to evince signs of congressional influence on Supreme Court decision making. This focus by political scientists on statutory construction begs the question whether the theory advanced in this book applies to statutory cases.

In addition, there are other, perhaps more substantively important reasons to examine the role of congressional pressure in statutory construction cases. First, statutory construction constitutes the largest portion of the Court's docket. Of the 7,226 cases in which a full opinion was issued by the Court during the 1953 through 2008 terms 2,508 or approximately 35% (a plurality), of them were primarily cases involving statutory construction – by far the largest single type of decision issued by

---

[2] For several notable exceptions, see Harvey and Friedman (2006), Segal and Westerland (2005), Gely and Spiller (1992).

the Court (Spaeth 2009). The next largest portion of the Court's docket during this time consisted of judicial review of state legislation (about 1,647) cases, followed by supervision of lower courts (about 797 cases), and judicial review of federal legislation (about 615 cases).

Second, statutory construction is important because the Supreme Court is often able to make important changes to public policy by interpreting statutes in a particular way. The Court's statutory jurisprudence has had significant consequences in policy areas as diverse as civil rights and environmental protection, among others.[3] Moreover, by engaging in statutory construction, the Supreme Court can avoid addressing broad constitutional questions. For example, in the case *Vermont Agency of Natural Resources v. U.S. ex rel. Stevens*,[4] the Supreme Court, through statutory construction, held that states and their agencies are not "persons" according to the definition provided in the Federal False Claims Act. The consequence of this holding was that although the Federal False Claims Act gives private citizens the right to bring suit in a federal court against any person who presents a false claim to the United States, such a right did not extend to filing a suit against a state that may have presented such a false claim. Not only did this decision allow the Court to effectuate a significant change in public policy, the use of statutory construction to reverse the lower court decision enabled the Court to avoid addressing the constitutional question whether such an action against a state would violate the Eleventh Amendment. Indeed, there are broad areas of law that became especially important during the second half of the twentieth century, such as employment discrimination and discrimination against the handicapped – which were based in statutorily created rights. Similar examples exist with respect to many other statutes, particularly those concerning torts and private rights of action.

Statutory construction is thus an important part of the Supreme Court's docket and an area of judicial decision making that may be directly affected by congressional hostility. These cases can raise important social and political issues and can be the subject of important, heated public controversies. In this chapter, we subject the empirical hypotheses derived in Chapter 3 to empirical scrutiny in the context of these cases. First, though, I briefly review the theoretical predictions. Hypothesis 4 predicts that an increase in Court-curbing should be associated

[3] Eisgruber (2007, 27) describes the breadth and significance of the Court's statutory decisions in his prescription for remedying the Supreme Court confirmation process.
[4] 259 *U.S.* 765 (2000).

with more constrained decision making. Here, I ask whether more liberal (or conservative) Court-curbing is associated with less conservative (or liberal) decision making by the Court. Hypothesis 5 predicts that as the Court becomes more pessimistic about its public support, its decision making will be more constrained. Here, I ask whether increasing public conservatism (or liberalism) is associated with increased judicial conservatism (or liberalism). The intuition here is that support for the Court decreases when the Court's decision making is out of line with public preferences (Durr, Martin, and Wolbrecht 2000). As a consequence, as the public moves in one direction, concomitant moves by the Court in the opposite direction will be associated with a loss in support for the Court. Finally, Hypotheses 6 and 7 make interactive predictions. Hypothesis 6 predicts the effect of Court-curbing will be attenuated by Court–Congress policy divergence. Hypothesis 7 predicts the effect of Court-curbing will be enhanced by a pessimistic judicial outlook. In this chapter, I present direct statistical analyses of these predictions. We begin, however, with a simple first glance at the data.

6.2 A FIRST GLANCE AT THE DATA

6.2.1 Judicial Ideology and Supreme Court Output

I begin by examining variation in the Supreme Court's liberalism between 1953 and 2008. To be sure, there is a great deal of variation in the pattern of the Supreme Court's decision making, and there are many components of that variation that we may consider. Most commonly, scholars focus on the ideological distribution of decisions in statutory cases – that is, how liberally a justice votes during a given period of time or in a particular set of cases. This focus makes sense, because the theoretical expectations generally predict that conflict between the branches will arise over ideological divergence.

The left-hand panel of Figure 6.1 plots the percent of statutory interpretation cases decided in a "liberal" direction (as coded by Spaeth 2009) each year from 1953 through 2008. I derive these data from the United States Supreme Court Judicial Database (Spaeth 2009) and restrict the cases to only those involving statutory interpretation.[5] This figure shows that there has been a conservative trend in the Court's decision making

---

[5] In the Spaeth database, these cases are identified when either AUTH_DEC, AUTH_DEC1 or AUTH_DEC2 equals 4.

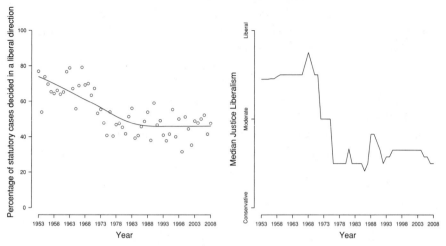

FIGURE 6.1. *Percentage of cases decided liberally and median justice liberalism, 1953–2008.* Line in left-hand panel shows a lowess regression smoother.

over the past fifty years. However, although the general trend has been toward more conservative decision making, there is additional variation from year to year that cannot necessarily be explained via traditional attitudinalism.

To explain variation in the Court's liberalism, political scientists have generally looked to the justices' personal policy preferences – or ideology. Indeed, this is the foundational lesson of the Attitudinal Model and the primary assumption on which the traditional separation-of-powers model rests. Paralleling the conservative trend in the Court's statutory decision making documented in Figure 6.1, an analysis of the ideological preferences of the justices of the Supreme Court demonstrates that the Court at the beginning of the twenty-first century is markedly more conservative in orientation than the Court of the mid-twentieth century.

The right-hand panel of Figure 6.1 shows the liberalism of the median justice on the Supreme Court during each year from 1953 through 2008.[6] The figure makes clear there has been a decidedly conservative trend on

---

[6] The justices' ideal points come from Segal and Cover (1989); commonly referred to as the Segal-Cover scores, these estimates of judicial ideology are based on preconfirmation newspaper coverage of the justice. There is, to be sure, an entire research agenda in political science concerned with measuring the ideological preferences of Supreme Court justices; this research agenda has led to the development of multiple sophisticated measures of judicial preferences. The primary distinction among various measures of judicial preferences is between those that are designed to capture what I call "primitive" preferences and those that are designed to capture what I call "induced preferences." Primitive

the Bench during the past fifty years. The conservative move in the Court's ideological composition can account for a great deal in the variation of its liberalism between 1953 and 2008. To assess how much of the variation can be explained by judicial preferences, Table 6.1 shows a regression of the percent of cases decided in a liberal direction in each year on the ideological location of the median justice and a regression of the percent of votes cast in a liberal direction by each individual justice as a function of his or her own ideology. The table makes clear that simply identifying the ideological preferences of the Court can explain a great deal of the variation in the Court's liberalism. In fact, the ideological preferences of the median justice alone can explain between about half of the variation in the Court's aggregate liberalism, whereas individual justice ideology alone can explain between a third and a half of the individual justices' liberalism. The relationship between the median and the Court's output may be much more complicated than these simple regressions allow,[7] but these results serve at least to demonstrate that merely controlling for the ideological preferences of the justices can explain a great deal of variation in the Court's output.

This finding comports with the attitudinal model's primary prediction. Moreover, this finding follows naturally from traditional separation-of-powers models; those models predict that the Court will be primarily motivated by its policy preferences – it is the degree to which its ability to pursue those preferences is attenuated by political factors about which the two schools of thought disagree.

preferences refer to those at the core of the justices' personal preferences – what she would do absent any institutional incentives. Induced preferences refer to the preferences expressed by a justice's behavior. Measures of induced preferences are generally far more methodologically sophisticated than measures of primitive preferences (see, e.g., Martin and Quinn 2002). For my purposes here, measures of induced preferences are inappropriate. These measures are based on the votes the justices cast and therefore incorporate any influences that may affect their behavior. That is, a measure of a justice's induced ideal point is really a measure of her primitive preferences plus whatever institutional forces act upon her when she casts a vote. To the extent I want to identify institutional effects on justices' votes, using these measures biases against finding those effects, as they are already captured in the measure of judicial ideology. Thus, in each of the analyses here, I use the Segal-Cover scores to measure judicial ideology. However, it is noteworthy that each of the findings remains when the analysis is replicated using the Martin-Quinn scores.

[7] Cameron and Clark (2007) demonstrate that the relationship between the Court's policy outputs and the median voter may be much more complicated than the standard median voter model of judicial decision making. To be sure, several theoretical models predict nonmedian voter outcomes (see Carrubba et al. 2007; Lax and Cameron 2007; Schwartz 1992).

TABLE 6.1. *Regressions of Supreme Court Output Liberalism on Justices' Liberalism and Congressional Conservatism*

Case-level analyses are OLS coefficients; individual-level analyses are GLS random effects coefficients (standard errors in parentheses); for individual-level models dependent variable is percent of each justice's votes coded as "liberal" by Spaeth in each year; for case-level models dependent variable is percent of case outcomes coded as "liberal" by Spaeth in each year

	Judicial Ideology		Judicial and Congressional Ideology	
	Case-Level	Justice-Level	Case-Level	Justice-Level
Judicial Liberalism	48.20	25.87	56.34	25.94
	(4.71)	(6.30)	(8.65)	(6.05)
Congressional Conservatism	–	–	−9.57	−7.37
			(8.55)	(5.11)
Constant	30.52	39.85	25.56	39.74
	(2.48)	(3.94)	(5.08)	(3.78)
R^2	0.68	0.36	0.69	0.34

Attitudinalists and proponents of the separation-of-powers model disagree, though, about the extent to which divergence between the Court and Congress affects judicial decision making. As I described this debate in Chapter 1, the attitudinalists claim that the Court is sufficiently insulated from political backlash that it need not worry about congressional preferences when it decides cases; this view has generally benefited from considerable empirical support. Although a variety of empirical specifications have been used to investigate the claim, each has asked a similar question – does congressional ideology explain any variation in judicial decision making? The final two columns of Table 6.1 report the results of a replication of the standard empirical analysis reported in the literature. The table shows the results of regressions of the Court's liberalism on judicial ideology *and* congressional ideology, where congressional ideology is measured as the median member of the House of Representatives.[8] As the figures reported in this table demonstrate, there does not appear to be any relationship between congressional preferences and the Supreme Court's output, and including congressional ideology in the regression does not in any way improve the model's ability to explain variation in

[8] The results reported here are robust to any one of a number of alternative operationalizations of congressional ideology.

judicial liberalism. (Notice the R^2 statistics in the two specifications are essentially identical.) However, the argument advanced in this book is that the Court should be responsive not to congressional preferences, per se, but rather to congressional hostility, because a hostile Congress signals a lack of judicial legitimacy.

6.2.2 Incorporating Congressional Hostility

Although Table 6.1 provides support for the received wisdom that the Court is insensitive to congressional preferences when deciding statutory cases, here I seek to incorporate the theory of institutional hostility. Figure 6.2 shows the relationship between the ideology of hostility toward the Court and the Court's behavior. The figure shows the change in each justice's liberalism in statutory cases from each year to the next as a function of the change in *who* is attacking the Court. In particular, the points in the figure show how much more liberally each justice voted from one year to the next as the median Court-curber became more conservative the previous year. When more conservative members of Congress sponsor Court-curbing legislation, liberal justices vote more conservatively. Similarly, when legislation is sponsored by more liberal members, conservative justices vote more liberally. The figure shows that liberal, moderate, and conservative justices all demonstrate a systematic relationship to Court-curbing. In particular, each group of justices exhibits a negative relationship between their liberalism and the conservatism of the Court-curbers. As the median Court-curber becomes more conservative in one year, the justices behave less liberally the following year.

To the extent that the ideological content of Court-curbing in Congress – as measured by the median Court-curbing sponsor – is indicative of the ideological motivations for public discontent for the Court, the Court's responsiveness to Court-curbing indicates an effort to moderate itself away from the policy positions that seem to have undermined public support for the Court. Although not conclusive, these data provide initial support for the claim that the Court responds to Court-curbing. However, the relationships shown in Figure 6.2 are not necessarily very strong. This is due, at least in part, to the fact that the magnitude of the Court's responsiveness to Court-curbing should be proportional to the magnitude – or intensity – of Court-curbing, which is not accounted for in this simple bivariate comparison. To capture this interactive effect, we now move to a multivariate statistical analysis of the relationship between Court-curbing and judicial decision making.

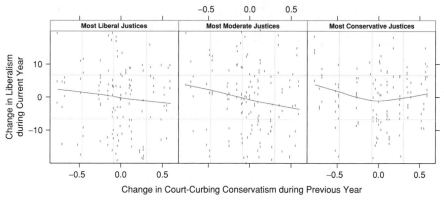

FIGURE 6.2. *Change in liberal voting and change in Court-curbing ideology,* 1953–2008.

6.3   STATISTICAL ANALYSIS

We now move to a statistical analysis of the relationship between Court-curbing and the Supreme Court's statutory liberalism. Importantly, in this chapter we switch from an analysis that focuses on the disposition of cases – the yearly and case-level analyses in Chapter 5 – to an analysis of individual justices' votes. I make this switch for two reasons. First, previous scholarship has been primarily concerned with analyzing individual justices' votes. Second, and more important, by focusing on individual justices' votes, we can more directly assess the effect of Court-curbing. That is, a focus on case outcomes might be complicated by the possibility that changes in case outcomes are due to changes in the Court's composition. By focusing on individual justices' votes, we can be more confident that any effect identified here is an effect of Court-curbing on judicial behavior. That is, in this chapter we investigate individual-level responses to Court-curbing, rather than institutional responses, which are a function of those justices serving on the Court.[9] The statistical analysis will proceed in three stages. First, I present a direct analysis of the

---

[9] The switch from aggregate-level outcomes to individual-level choices presents several advantages. First, and most important, by assessing the "within-justice" effect, an individual-level analysis can most forcefully demonstrate that Court-curbing acts to change the way the justices decide cases. The Conditional Self-Restraint model makes predictions about case outcomes, and for those predictions to be supported by the data, it must be the case that individual justices are affected, rather than that the change is taking place through turnover on the bench. Second, by moving from the aggregate- to the individual-level, we can perform more powerful tests of the available data. Indeed, the move here from aggregate-level decisions to individual-level decisions parallels the move

primary hypotheses derived in Chapter 3 (Hypotheses 4 and 5). The question asked in this analysis is whether changes in Court-curbing and public ideology are associated with changes in the liberalism of the Court's statutory decisions. Second, I present an analysis of the interactive hypotheses (Hypotheses 6 and 7). Here we ask whether Court–Congress divergence and the Court's outlook about its public support condition the effect of Court-curbing on judicial liberalism. Third, I present a final analysis that asks whether all justices respond to Court-curbing similarly and if there are any systematic patterns in the differences among justices.

6.3.1 Court-Curbing and Statutory Liberalism

Hypothesis 4 predicts that as the Court observes more negative institutional signals from Congress – as more Court-curbing is introduced – it should become more constrained in its decision making. The ideological implication of this prediction is that as more conservative members of Congress introduce more Court-curbing, the justices should vote less liberally. Hypothesis 5 predicts that as the Court becomes more pessimistic about its institutional support, it should become more constrained in its decision making. Because ideological divergence between the Court's decisions and public opinion is associated with a drop in public support for the Court (Durr, Martin, and Wolbrecht 2000), this implies that as public mood becomes more conservative, the justices should vote less liberally.

Measures of Key Variables
The first key variable in the statistical analysis is the Court's liberalism. Here, I adopt a widely used measure in political science analyses of judicial decision making – the direction of each justice's vote in each case, as coded by Spaeth's United States Supreme Court Judicial Database.[10] Spaeth applies a set of criteria whereby each justice's vote is coded as "liberal" or "conservative" by reference to which party the justice favors in his/her

---

within Chapter 4 from yearly measures of Court-curbing to individual sponsorship decisions. Thus, in the way that the individual-level analysis in Chapter 4 complemented the aggregate-level analysis, the investigation of individual justices' decisions in this chapter complements the year- and case-level analyses in the preceding chapter.

[10] McGuire et al. (2009) argue that including cases where the Supreme Court affirms lower Court decisions introduces bias into this measure and show that judicial preferences do not correlate well with dispositions in affirmances. Each of the analyses reported here is substantively insensitive to the exclusion of affirmances from the data.

vote on the disposition of the case.[11] Figure 6.1 shows the percent of case *outcomes* that are coded as liberal each year, but here we use the percent of each justice's votes that are coded as liberal.

There are several ways of measuring the interactive relationship between the intensity and ideological content of Court-curbing. Most directly, one can simply measure the ideology of Court-curbing – using perhaps the median Court-curbing sponsor – and the intensity of Court-curbing – using perhaps the number of bills introduced – and then multiply those two variables together. Using such an interactive term is very direct but introduces significant problems of collinearity and leads to a confusing interpretation of the results. On the other hand, one may divide the ideological spectrum into "bins" and count the number of bills that are introduced from that part of the ideological spectrum. Here, I adopt the latter approach and divide the ideological spectrum into four groups: liberals, conservatives, moderates from a liberal Congress, and moderates from a conservative Congress.

In particular, I create three bins. The first bin identifies the amount of Court-curbing from the liberal-most third of Congress; the second bin identifies the amount of Court-curbing from the conservative-most third of Congress. The final bin identifies the amount of Court-curbing from the middle third of Congress. A question remains, though, what directional effect Court-curbing from moderate members of Congress should have on the justices' voting. I expect, though, the effect of moderate Court-curbing will be conditioned by the Congress' general ideological disposition. Thus, I include a control for congressional conservatism and an interaction between congressional conservatism and moderate Court-curbing. The interaction allows us to assess whether moderate Court-curbing has a directional effect on the justices' votes that is conditioned by congressional ideology. The NOMINATE measures of legislators' ideal points are a widely used measure of congressional ideology. These measures, developed by Poole and Rosenthal (1997), scale each member of Congress, using their votes on roll calls.[12] To measure congressional ideology, I

---

[11] Of course, there is considerable debate about whether this measure captures the particular quantity of interest, but for my purposes here, this measure is the best available. Although there may be instances where particular votes might be coded differently, I have no reason to believe there is any systematic bias that would affect the analysis here.

[12] Although critiques of these measures have been made (see Clinton and Lapinski 2008), they are still the best measures that exist and do not necessarily introduce any bias into my analysis. Other measures, such as the ADA scores often used, are themselves

identify the median member of the House of Representatives, though I find comparable results using alternative measures of congressional conservatism. The interaction term, then, captures the conditional relationship between moderate Court-curbing and congressional ideology. When Congress is more conservative, moderate Court-curbing should push the justices in a conservative direction; when Congress is more liberal, moderate Court-curbing should push the justices in a liberal direction. Each bin is then coded as the Court-curbing variable in Chapter 5 – the logistic transformation of the previous year's Court-curbing. As in Chapter 5, this transformation allows for the largest effect of Court-curbing to occur with changes from low amounts of Court-curbing to high amounts of Court-curbing.

The second variable implicated by the theoretical predictions is the Court's outlook about its public support. As I have interpreted this previously, I will measure the Court's outlook by considering *public mood*. Durr, Martin, and Wolbrecht (2000) demonstrate that public support for the Court declines when the Court's decisions are ideologically divergent from the public's preferences. They show that when the public becomes more conservative (liberal), liberal (conservative) decision making by the Court is associated with a decrease in public approval of the Court. As a consequence, the Court should expect that its underlying level of public support should depend on the extremity of public opinion. *The more conservative the public, the more likely it will not support a liberal decision, and vice-versa.* As a proxy for the Court's outlook, I consider how liberal or conservative the public is, as measured by Stimson (1999). Stimson's estimate of public mood uses an aggregation of public opinion data each year from 1952 through the present in order to identify a common, underlying liberalism among the public, which he calls *public mood*. Figure 6.3 shows public liberalism each year, from 1953 through 2004. I adopt the logic advanced in Durr, Martin, and Wolbrecht (2000) and assume that the current public mood sets boundaries on how liberally the Court may behave without risking a loss to its institutional legitimacy.[13]

---

much more problematic as they are constructed by considering only a select few roll call votes.

[13] Specifically, I code this variable as its deviation from its mean. This transformation is simply a linear transformation of the public mood measure and therefore does not change the statistical results in any way. I adopt the transformation because it makes the variable easily interpretable – that is, negative values indicate more conservative public and positive values indicate more liberal public, relative to the average over time. In addition, I note that this transformation comports with existing scholarship on public opinion and the Court (see, e.g., Durr, Martin, and Wolbrecht 2000).

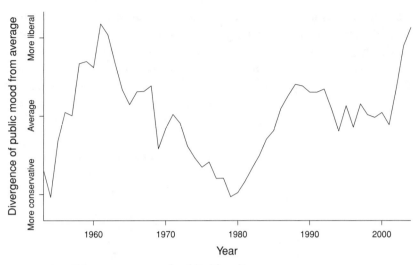

FIGURE 6.3. *Stimson measure of public liberalism, 1953–2004.*

Finally, to control for judicial liberalism, the empirical model includes
the measure of judicial liberalism described above (recall this is the measure based on preconfirmation newspaper coverage of the nominee).

Empirical Model

The data I use here provide two sources of variation that we can explore.
In particular, the data are "panel data," which means that we observe
a group of individuals – the justices – regularly over time. Thus, we
can exploit both cross-sectional and temporal variation to identify the
effect of Court-curbing on the justices. In the final analysis below, I allow
each justice to have his or her own response to Court-curbing. However,
to keep things simple, we begin with a simple analysis that assumes
each justice responds to Court-curbing similarly. Thus, I employ a simple
empirical model as follows,

$$\text{Percent Liberal}_{jt} = f(\text{Liberal Bills}_{t-1}, \qquad (6.1)$$
$$\text{Conservative Bills}_{t-1},$$
$$\text{Moderate Bills}_{t-1},$$
$$\text{Congressional Conservatism}_t,$$
$$\text{Public Mood}_t,$$
$$\text{Judicial Conservatism}_j)$$

TABLE 6.2. *Effect of Court-Curbing Intensity and Ideology on Justices' Statutory Liberalism, 1953–2008*

GLS random-effects and fixed-effects coefficients (standard errors in parentheses); dependent variable is percent of votes in a "liberal" direction by justice j in year t in all statutory cases, as coded by Spaeth (2009)

	Random Effects	Fixed Effects
Liberal Court-curbing	1.72*	1.77*
	(1.02)	(1.01)
Conservative Court-curbing	0.20	0.41
	(1.77)	(1.84)
Moderate Court-curbing	−1.97	−2.46
	(1.91)	(2.02)
Moderate Court-curbing ×	−5.00*	−5.42*
Congressional Conservatism	(2.81)	(2.77)
Congressional Conservatism	0.31	0.49
	(1.57)	(1.59)
Public Liberalism	3.86***	3.88***
	(1.30)	(1.29)
Judicial Liberalism	20.91***	–
	(4.01)	–
Intercept	52.32***	53.49***
	(1.95)	(0.35)
N	422	422
σ_μ	10.15	14.66
ρ	0.58	0.74

*** $p \leq 0.01$** $p \leq 0.05$;* $p \leq 0.10$.

I estimate the model both using what are known as "random effects" and "fixed effects." Random effects allow for differences among the justices without assuming those differences are constant over time. Fixed effects allow for differences among the justices and assume those differences are constant. The fixed effects therefore subsume all time-invariant features associated with each justice, including his or her liberalism. Thus, in the model with fixed effects, we cannot include the Segal-Cover measure of judicial liberalism, because it is necessarily incorporated into the estimated fixed effect. Further diagnostics are reported in the appendix to this chapter. The results from this estimation are shown in Table 6.2.

Notice first that we estimate a positive and statistically significant coefficient associated with the volume of liberal Court-curbing bills. That is, as more Court-curbing bills are introduced in Congress by liberal members of Congress, the justices vote more liberally. This finding provides direct support for the claim that the justices adjust their decisions in response to institutional signals of waning public support for the Court (Hypothesis 4). By contrast, however, the model estimates a positive – but substantively small and statistically insignificant – coefficient associated with conservative Court-curbing. This estimate suggests the justices do *not* respond to Court-curbing from the conservative wing of Congress. Finally, however, consider the estimates associated with moderate Court-curbing. The estimated coefficient associated with moderate Court-curbing is negative, though it is not statistically significant. The estimated coefficient associated with the interaction of moderate Court-curbing and congressional conservatism is negative and statistically significant, indicating that the effect of moderate Court-curbing depends on congressional ideology. Because the model interacts moderate Court-curbing with congressional conservatism, we cannot directly interpret the coefficient associated with moderate Court-curbing. Rather, we must interpret the effect of moderate Court-curbing *conditional on congressional conservatism.* This is best done visually, as in Figure 6.4. Here we see the effect of moderate Court-curbing with the introduction of a few bills, some bills, and a lot of bills. When moderate members of Congress introduce Court-curbing, the justices vote more liberally when Congress is liberal and more conservatively when Congress is conservative. Indeed, the magnitude of this effect is quite substantial; moving from a liberal Congress to a conservative Congress, moderate Court-curbing can move the predicted percentage liberal for a given justice by about 10%. Again, this finding provides considerable support for the primary claim that the justices will respond to the intensity and ideological orientation of Court-curbing in Congress. What is more, it is important to note that these data are individual level; the effects here are detected at the justice level and therefore cannot be attributed to composition change on the Court. Rather, these effects are driven by variation within individual justices' voting patterns.

Next, notice the positive and statistically significant estimates for the coefficients associated with public liberalism. This indicates that, all else being held equal, as the public becomes more liberal, the justices vote more liberally. Although such a relationship has been documented elsewhere (Erikson, MacKuen, and Stimson 2002, 311–6; Mishler and Sheehan 1993; Mishler and Sheehan 1996), the interpretation I put on this finding is different. This correlation is consistent with the claim that the justices worry about losing public support; Durr, Martin, and Wolbrecht (2000) demonstrate that ideological divergence between the public and the Court's decisions is associated with decreases in public support

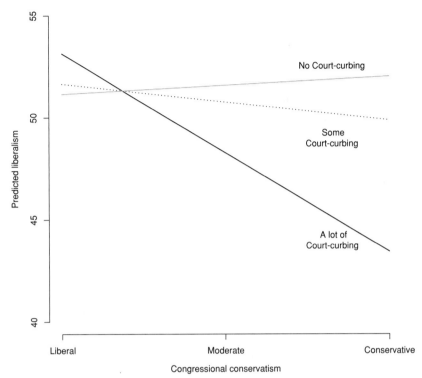

FIGURE 6.4. *Effect of moderate Court-curbing bills on judicial liberalism in statutory cases.* Lines show predicted percentage of votes cast in a liberal direction; judicial liberalism and public mood held at their mean; no liberal or conservative Court-curbing.

for the Court. If the justices worry about losing their diffuse, institutional support, then they will have an incentive to vote more liberally (conservatively) when the public becomes more liberal (conservative). The correlation estimated in this model is consistent with that account.

Finally, consider the estimated coefficients associated with judicial liberalism and congressional conservatism. With respect to judicial liberalism, the estimated coefficient is positive and statistically significant. More liberal justices vote more liberally than their more conservative colleagues. This finding is not surprising, though it is important to note that the result widely documented in the literature holds here. With respect to congressional conservatism, the coefficient is also positive and statistically significant. The standard separation-of-powers model, however, predicts a negative coefficient – as Congress becomes more conservative, the justices should vote less liberally. Thus, following most of the empirical findings in the literature, these data do not provide any support for the standard separation-of-powers model, though it is also important to note this control variable is not in and of itself a direct test of that theory. I merely note the finding is inconsistent with the general class of models. Moreover, because the model interacts congressional conservatism with moderate Court-curbing, this coefficient represents the correlation between congressional conservatism and the justices' liberalism *only* when there is no moderate Court-curbing.

Interpretation

To illustrate the magnitude of the effect of Court-curbing and public mood on the justices, Figure 6.5 shows the predicted percent of votes that will be cast in a liberal direction by justices with the same Segal-Cover scores as Justices Antonin Scalia and Ruth Bader Ginsburg, under varying types of Court-curbing and public mood.[14] In the top row of Figure 6.5, we see the predicted liberalism for "Justice Scalia" (solid line) compared with "Justice Ginsburg" (dotted line). The top-left panel shows the predicted liberalism for both, assuming no Court-curbing in Congress and average public mood. As we move to the next panel to the right, we see the predicted liberalism for "Justice Scalia" (again in the solid line) when public mood is relatively liberal.[15] As this panel makes clear, we expect "Justice Scalia" to cast a larger proportion of his votes in a liberal direction when the public mood is very liberal than when public mood is average. Now, moving to the next panel to the right, we see the predicted liberalism for "Justice Scalia" when there is average public mood but *liberal Court-curbing*.[16] As this panel makes clear, we expect much more liberal voting from "Justice Scalia" when there is liberal Court-curbing than when there is no Court-curbing. Finally, we move to the farthest-right panel in the top row. Here, we see the predicted liberalism for "Justice Scalia" when there is both a liberal public mood and liberal Court-curbing. As this panel demonstrates, under these conditions, we expect "Justice Scalia" to vote similarly to the baseline "Justice Ginsburg."

The bottom row of Figure 6.5, on the other hand, shows the effect of Court-curbing and public mood on a justice like Justice Ginsburg. Here, a similar pattern emerges. Under "normal" conditions – that is, no

---

[14] I refer to these hypothetical justices as "Justice Scalia" and "Justice Ginsburg" for the sake of sensationalism.

[15] I assume public mood moves twenty units in a liberal direction in the Stimson scale.

[16] I assume there are fifteen liberal Court-curbing bills and fifteen moderated Court-curbing bills from a liberal Congress.

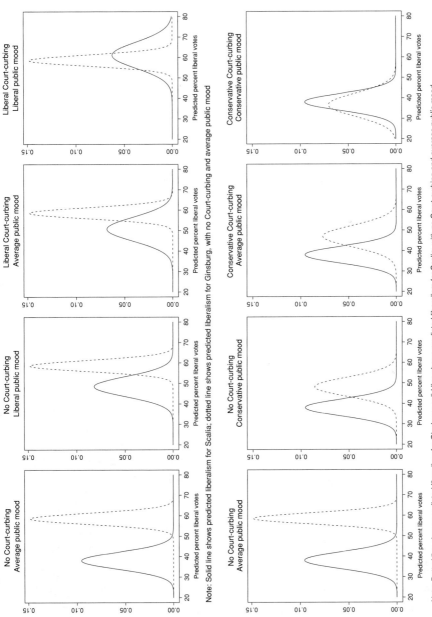

FIGURE 6.5. *Predicted percent of votes cast in a liberal direction by Scalia and Ginsburg, under different levels of Court-curbing and public mood.* Estimates derived from empirical model (6.1).

225

Court-curbing and average public mood – we see in the bottom-left panel that "Justice Ginsburg" (now the solid line) votes much more liberally than "Justice Scalia" (now, the dotted line). However, as the public becomes increasingly conservative, the next panel to the right shows that we expect much more conservative decision making from "Justice Ginsburg." In the next panel to the right, we see, in turn, that "Justice Ginsburg" votes even more conservatively when there is conservative Court-curbing and average public mood. Finally, in the bottom-right panel, we see that when there is a conservative public mood and conservative Court-curbing, we expect "Justice Ginsburg" to vote similarly to the baseline "Justice Scalia."

Notice finally that the magnitude of these predicted effects is very close to the magnitude detected in Figure 6.2 above. There, we saw that a one-unit change in the conservatism of Court-curbing in Congress is associated with a decrease in the proportion of votes cast in a liberal direction of about 10–15%. Here, we see that going from no Court-curbing to liberal Court-curbing moves the predicted percent liberal for "Justice Scalia" from 35% to about 50% – an increase of 15%. Similarly, we see that a change from no Court-curbing to conservative Court-curbing predicts a change in percent liberal by "Justice Ginsburg" from about 50% to about 40%.

This finding suggests that Court-curbing can have a substantial effect on how the justices vote. We expect two justices with ideological preferences similar to Justices Scalia and Ginsburg to behave very differently – as we see in the left-most column of Figure 6.5. However, given sufficient Court-curbing – and/or swings in public mood – we expect those two justices to vote much more similarly in statutory cases. This finding provides direct support for the two main predictions about judicial responsiveness to Court-curbing (Hypotheses 4 and 5). That the justices respond to these institutional signals – and concern for their institutional legitimacy – provides new insight into the relationship between the Court and the public. It also suggests a form of mediated, or indirect, representation on the Court. Albeit self-enforced by the justices, the Court does seem to be cognizant of its weak institutional position and the need to maintain its legitimacy.

6.3.2   An Interactive Model

The preceding analysis indicates that the ideological content and intensity of Court-curbing in Congress is associated with variation in the liberalism of individual justices' votes. However, as in Chapter 5, we can explore the empirical implications of the Conditional Self-Restraint model in greater detail. Specifically, we can use the data here to assess the interactive hypotheses. Recall that Hypothesis 6 predicts that the effect of Court-curbing will be attenuated by ideological divergence between the Court and Congress; Hypothesis 7 predicts that the effect of Court-curbing will be exacerbated by a pessimistic judicial outlook. This analysis treats each of these hypotheses in turn.

Measurement of Key Variables

In this analysis, we are confronted with a significant measurement problem. How do we measure ideological divergence between justices and Congress? An ideal measure of this concept, as we have already seen, would be an indicator of the precise degree of divergence between each justice's preferred policy and Congress' preferred policy. To do this, one might measure the distance between a justice's ideal point in some ideological space and Congress' ideal point (however that may be defined) in the same ideological space. Although a set of measures that places justices and Congress in a common space exists (Epstein, Martin, Segal, and Westerland 2007), these scores are problematic for my purposes here. Specifically, because those scores incorporate information about justices' votes, they are inappropriate to use as predictors of the justices' votes. Unfortunately, this means we lack a useful common scale on which we can measure divergence between justices and Congress. Moreover, even if we could measure ideological divergence on a common scale, we would then have to interact that measure of divergence with the various measures of Court-curbing, which themselves already involve interactions. This would significantly complicate the empirical model and interpretation of the results.

To overcome this difficulty, I propose a less sophisticated, though reasonable, alternative. Specifically, I divide justices and congresses into "liberal" and "conservative" justices and congresses. To do so, I align all justices according to their Segal-Cover score and all congresses according to the DW-NOMINATE score of the median House member. Justices more liberal than the (global) median justice are considered "liberal"; justices more conservative than the median justice are considered "conservative"; thus, a Court may be composed entirely of "conservative" or "liberal" justices. Because the time period under investigation here covers a period of both relatively liberal and conservative justices, this rule divides the justices in a way that comports with conventional expectations about which justices are to the left and which justices are to the right. Similarly, congresses more liberal or conservative than the (global) median congress are coded as "liberal" and "conservative" congresses, respectively. Each justice is therefore coded as a "liberal" justice or a "conservative" justice; each Congress is similarly coded as a "liberal" congress or a "conservative" congress. I then define a "judicial-congressional divergence" the case where a "liberal" justice faces a "conservative" Congress, or vice-versa. Using this rule, I divide the sample into justice-years where there is judicial-congressional divergence and those where there is not judicial-congressional divergence. Hypothesis 6 predicts stronger correlations between Court-curbing and judicial liberalism in the years without judicial-congressional divergence than in the years with judicial-congressional divergence.

A second measurement problem arises in the context of the Court's outlook. Hypothesis 7 predicts the effect of Court-curbing will be exacerbated by a pessimistic judicial outlook. An ideal strategy, therefore, would be to measure precisely how optimistic or pessimistic the Court is and interact that measurement with the Court-curbing variables. Such a measure, as we saw in Chapters 4 and 5, is difficult to come by. Moreover, introducing interactions among all of these variables would severely complicate the empirical model. Thus, I opt for an alternative measurement strategy. Recall from Chapters 4 and 5 that a good measure of judicial pessimism is the General Social Survey item that asks Americans how much confidence they have in the Supreme Court. Although this measure was problematic in the earlier analyses because it limited the number of observations we could use in the analysis, here that problem is not as bad because we have nine observations for each year (one for each justice). As in the case of judicial-congressional divergence, however, interacting this measure with each of the Court-curbing measures introduces additional complications into the statistical analysis. Thus, I adopt a similar approach and divide the observations into two sets – those with an optimistic Court and those with a pessimistic Court. Optimistic Courts are defined as those where the proportion of Americans saying they have "hardly any" confidence in the Court is more than one standard deviation above the mean; otherwise, the Court is labeled "optimistic."[17] Below I will estimate the empirical model on each of these sets of

---

[17] The average proportion of Americans saying they had "hardly any" confidence in the Supreme Court was 14.6%.

TABLE 6.3. *Effect of Court-Curbing Intensity and Ideology on Justices' Statutory Liberalism, 1953–2008*

Sample split by justice Congress alignment and judicial optimism; standardized GLS random-effects coefficients shown (standard errors in parentheses); dependent variable is percent of votes in a "liberal" direction by justice j in year t in all statutory cases, as coded by Spaeth (2009)

	Results by Justice-Congress Alignment		Results by Judicial Optimism	
	Aligned	Not Aligned	Optimistic	Pessimistic
Liberal Court-curbing	1.17	− 2.15	3.82***	2.02
	(1.09)	(1.59)	(1.01)	(2.25)
Conservative Court-curbing	0.31	− 2.33	7.97***	− 2.19
	(1.76)	(3.33)	(1.84)	(1.68)
Moderate Court-curbing	− 2.02	− 2.18	− 2.77	− 1.95
	(2.37)	(2.57)	(2.07)	(1.24)
Moderate Court-curbing × Congressional Conservatism	− 10.86***	− 9.60	− 0.28	− 11.39**
	(3.69)	(6.92)	(2.99)	(5.41)
Congressional Conservatism	1.71	− 8.31**	0.42	3.95*
	(2.69)	(3.38)	(1.22)	(2.31)
Public Liberalism	3.01**	6.54***	2.09	3.84**
	(1.67)	(2.46)	(1.37)	(1.97)
Judicial Liberalism	26.37***	24.25***	17.78***	22.86***
	(5.54)	(4.03)	(3.78)	(4.47)
Intercept	50.07***	53.89***	50.19***	50.62***
	(2.31)	(2.39)	(2.33)	(2.52)
N	227	195	222	200
σ_μ	12.01	10.86	7.82	9.76
ρ	0.59	0.59	0.49	0.55

$***\, p \leq 0.01;\ **\, p \leq 0.05;\ *\, p \leq 0.10$

observations. Hypothesis 7 predicts stronger effects when the Court is pessimistic than when it is optimistic.

An Empirical Model

With these measures in hand, I reestimate empirical model (6.1) from above on each of these subsamples. First, I estimate the model, dividing the sample by judicial-congressional alignment. The results are shown in the first two columns of estimates in Table 6.3. The first column of results shows the estimates for justices aligned with the current Congress; the second, justices not aligned with the current Congress. Recall that Hypothesis 6 predicts the effects of Court-curbing should be stronger when Court-curbing is introduced by a justice's ideological allies. These results provide mild evidence in support of this claim. The estimated coefficient associated with liberal Court-curbing is positive, as predicted for "aligned" justices, and it is negative for "not aligned" justices, suggesting the justices respond as predicted to liberal bills introduced by their allies but not those bills introduced by divergent Congresses. The difference between these two effects, however, is not itself statistically significant. By contrast, the estimated coefficients associated with conservative Court-curbing suggest that the justices respond more to conservative bills introduced by their ideological opponents than to those introduced by their ideological allies. The estimated coefficient associated with conservative Court-curbing is negative, as predicted, for "not aligned" justices and positive for "aligned" justices. Again, however, the difference between the two effects is not itself statistically significant.

Notice next the effect of moderate Court-curbing (and the interaction between moderate Court-curbing and congressional conservatism). Here, we estimate a statistically significant relationship between the interaction term and judicial liberalism, as predicted, for "aligned" justices. The effect of this interaction is not statistically significant for "not aligned" justices. The estimates coefficients themselves, however, are nearly identical in magnitude and are not statistically distinguishable from each other. Thus, while we have a more precise estimate of the effect of moderate Court-curbing on "aligned" justices, the evidence does not suggest the effect is attenuated by ideological divergence from Congress.

What, then, does this tell us? First, the statistical analysis provides weak evidence, if any, in support of the interactive relationship predicted by Hypothesis 6. As opposed to Chapter 5, where we found strong support for the conditioning effect of judicial-congressional alignment on Court-curbing, the evidence here is much weaker. The estimated coefficients shown in Table 6.3 provide some suggestive evidence, but nothing conclusive. Of course, the method I have used here to distinguish the two subsets of data is not very sophisticated. Nonetheless, these results do not provide very strong evidence in support of the interactive predictions derived from the Conditional Self-Restraint Model. We can only take away from this analysis what is at best mixed evidence from a limited test of the prediction. We have not been able to demonstrate with these data conclusive evidence of an attenuation of the effect of Court-curbing by judicial-congressional divergence.

The final two columns of results in Table 6.3 show the estimates from dividing the justices into "optimistic" and "pessimistic" observations. These results provide, again, mixed evidence in support of the interactive prediction that the justices will be (weakly) less likely to respond to Court-curbing when they are optimistic about their level of public support (Hypothesis 7). First, we see that optimistic justices vote more liberally when both liberal *and conservative* Court-curbing bills are introduced. However, the difference in the effect of liberal Court-curbing across pessimistic and optimistic justices is not statistically significant. By contrast, we estimate a negative, though statistically insignificant effect of conservative Court-curbing for pessimistic justices. Importantly, this effect, while statistically noisy, *is* distinguishable from the (positive) effect estimated for optimistic justices. Although it is difficult to read too much into this finding, it is noteworthy that the effect of conservative Court-curbing is opposite of the predicted effect for optimistic justices and in the predicted direction for pessimistic justices. This (statistically meaningful) difference is suggestive of the conditioning effect of the Court's expectation about its level of public support.

Next, we find that the effect of the interaction between moderate Court-curbing and congressional conservatism is correctly signed and statistically significant for pessimistic justices and substantively small and statistically insignificant for optimistic justices. Indeed, the difference between these two effects *is* itself statistically significant. That is, the effect of moderate Court-curbing is larger when the justices are pessimistic about their public support than when they are optimistic. This finding provides the clearest support for the interactive predictions of the Conditional Self-Restraint model in the context of statutory decision making.

Taken together, these findings provide some mild support for Hypothesis 7, which predicts that the effect of Court-curbing and the Court's responsiveness to institutional signals will be strongest when the Court has a pessimistic outlook regarding its public support. Although perhaps weaker evidence than we found in the analysis of the Court's use of judicial review, these findings are at least suggestive. They provide reason to believe that the Court, in an effort to protect its legitimacy and avoid overstepping the boundaries of discretion that are acceptable to the American people, does in fact pay attention to indicators of diffuse support for the judiciary. Moreover, these results take us one step further by demonstrating that the effects of Court-curbing seem to operate on justices themselves, as opposed to the institution, through the replacement of justices or some other mechanism. Individual justices themselves seem to be responsive to the introduction of Court-curbing in Congress.

6.3.3 Exploring Differences among Justices

Until now, I have assumed that all justices respond similarly to Court-curbing. However, one might expect that there are in fact differences in the extent to which justices respond to Court-curbing. If this is so, one might ask whether there are systematic patterns in such differences. Do certain *types* of justices respond more to Court-curbing? Do only justices from a certain era respond to Court-curbing? Or, are responses to Court-curbing comparable across all justices? A final statistical analysis considers any such differences. Using the same data I have been using throughout this chapter, I directly assess the differences among the justices.

An Empirical Model

As noted already, the data I use in this chapter are panel data; they consist of repeated observations of multiple justices. More advanced empirical modeling techniques allow for the effect of a particular variable of interest to vary across the observational units – for the estimated correlation between Court-curbing and statutory liberalism to be different for each justice. One such technique is an empirical model known as a "random slopes" model. The random slopes model assumes there is an average correlation between Court-curbing and the dependent variable – statutory liberalism – but that the actual relationship may vary across justices. One can think of the model as estimating a correlation between Court-curbing and statutory liberalism and then estimating a "shift" in the slope for each justice.[18]

Of course, a random slopes model is slightly more complicated than the more standard panel models used in the two analyses above. As a consequence, here I simplify the measures of Court-curbing in order to ease interpretation of the results. Rather than divide all Court-curbing into "bins," here I simply identify the amount of Court-curbing and the median Court-curbing sponsor's conservatism (as measured in NOMI-NATE space). I then interact those two variables – higher values indicate a lot of conservative Court-curbing; lower values indicate a lot of liberal Court-curbing. I estimate a random slopes model in which each coefficient for the interaction is allowed to be different for each justice.

Interpretation

For each justice, we estimate a negative slope – more Court-curbing from a more conservative Congress is associated with less liberal voting.

[18] Further technical details, however, are reserved to the appendix to this chapter.

However, as one might suspect, the magnitude of this effect varies considerably across justices. Figure 6.6 shows the effect for each justice. Each row in this figure shows the estimated slope for each justice in black, along with the uncertainty in the estimate.[19] Because the slopes involve an interaction, we must interpret the effect of Court-curbing conservatism conditional on a level of Court-curbing; here I assume that ten Court-curbing bills have been introduced (as we saw in Chapter 2, ten Court-curbing bills is at the low end of a heightened period of Court-curbing). The justices are sorted in this figure by the magnitude of the estimated effect of Court-curbing. As one can readily see here, there is considerable variation in the correlation between Court-curbing and each justice's statutory liberalism. At one end of the spectrum are Warren and Blackmun, whose voting is most strongly correlated with Court-curbing. At the other end of the spectrum are O'Connor, Fortas, and Burger, whose voting is least correlated with Court-curbing.

The substantive magnitude of these effects is indeed considerable. The estimated slope shown for each justice corresponds to the predicted change in each justice's liberalism with a one-unit change in the conservatism of the median Court-curbing sponsor. This is about the difference between Democratic and Republican Court-curbing. So, for example, we see that moving from a Democratic to a Republican Court-curbing movement predicts that Justice Blackmun would cast about 8.5% more of his votes in a conservative direction. However, Blackmun is at the high end of responsiveness. The effect for an average justice is about 4–5%. What is more, the magnitude of this effect is exacerbated by larger moves in Court-curbing conservatism or increases in the intensity of Court-curbing (recall we are assuming ten Court-curbing bills have been introduced). Because the slope involves an interaction with Court-curbing, introducing more Court-curbing bills increases the magnitude of the effect.

What distinguishes justices who respond more strongly to Court-curbing from those who respond less strongly? It is hard to know. The magnitude of the relationships between Court-curbing and voting are not correlated with the justices', ideology or their relative extremism/moderateness. Nor is it correlated with time – the tenures of Burger and Blackmun overlap considerably, though they exhibit opposite degrees

---

[19] Specifically, I simulated the estimated slope 1,000 times, by taking a random draw from the estimated average "fixed" effect and a draw from the estimated modeled, justice-specific "random" slope. This process incorporates the uncertainty in the estimates as measured by the standard deviation in each estimate. I then take the 95th and 50th percentile from those 1,000 random draws.

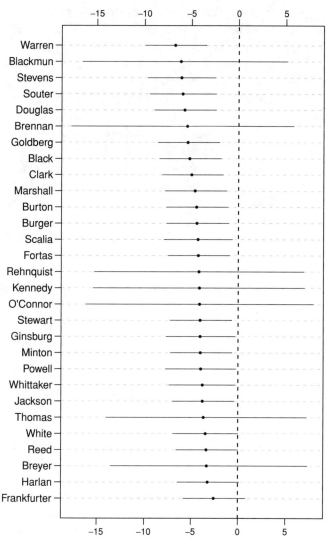

Estimated effect of Court-curbing conservatism
on justice's statutory liberalism

FIGURE 6.6. *Correlation between Court-curbing and each justice's vote, as estimated by random slopes model.* Points show point estimates of estimated effect;
bars show 5th and 95th percentile of empirical uncertainty in the estimate; effects
assume ten Court-curbing bills have been introduced.

of responsiveness. What, then, may explain the differences in responsiveness? It is most likely idiosyncratic. We do see, though, certain justices where we might expect them in the range of responsiveness. Justice Blackmun, for example, is widely known to have been sensitive to public opinion; he is one of the most responsive justices to Court-curbing. Justice O'Connor – who was very independent-minded – and Justice Fortas – who was not on the bench for a very long time – are at the other end, exhibiting very little responsiveness to Court-curbing. In the end, then, although we generally find a pattern that comports with popular expectations, there do not appear to be any systematic patterns that predict which types of justices will be more or less responsive to Court-curbing.

It is interesting to note, moreover, that this division of justices differs substantially from the list of justices that Mishler and Sheehan (1996) claim are susceptible to influence from public opinion. Specifically, they claim that Justices Stevens, White, Stewart, Marshall, Brennan, Powell, and O'Connor are susceptible to public opinion. The analysis here, on the other hand, reveals a contrasting pattern. Whereas Mishler and Sheehan identify seven justices whom they claim are susceptible to public opinion, the analysis summarized in Figure 6.6 suggests that all justices respond to popularly motivated institutional signals of waning judicial legitimacy. Although some justices respond more strongly than others, my analysis suggests comparable levels of responsiveness for all justices. Thus, whereas Mishler and Sheehan posit that individual justices respond directly to public opinion and find moderate support for their hypothesis with respect to seven justices, the analysis I have presented provides evidence to suggest that variation in individual justices' behavior is related not necessarily directly to public opinion but rather to public opinion *as mediated by representation in Congress*. What is more, it appears that a majority of the justices since 1953 have responded to congressional hostility. These findings can be interpreted to lend considerable support to the notion that the Supreme Court will have an incentive to engage in sophisticated behavior when it perceives political risk.

6.3.4 Discussion

Taken in conjunction, these three statistical tests run against the existing empirical findings in the literature. In *The Supreme Court and the Attitudinal Model Revisited*, Segal and Spaeth (2002, 349) provide extensive evidence that the Supreme Court "ignore[s] legislative preferences" and cite numerous other studies that have reached similar conclusions. What these critiques of separation-of-powers models have failed to recognize, though, is that the best explanation of judicial decision making cannot possibly take a "black-or-white" view of the model – either justices are constrained or they are not. Rather, the best explanation should demonstrate the conditions under which the Court is constrained. Indeed, even Segal and Spaeth have been willing to concede that the conditions may sometimes be right for the Court to be constrained by congressional preferences but assert that those conditions arise with extreme rarity.[20] Although they are focused, as most other scholars have been, on the exercise of congressional authority to institutionally constrain the Court, the general point remains that when the Court actually fears some adverse consequence from continued divergence from popular will, it will have an incentive to exercise self-restraint.[21]

In an effort to more systematically identify when the Court expects an adverse consequence from divergence from popular will, and what that consequence may be, I have argued that the introduction of Court-curbing legislation in Congress can explain why the Court may sometimes exercise self-restraint and why it may at other times appear to sincerely follow its own preferences. The justices may respond to Court-curbing because they fear the legislation will be enacted or because the legislation represents a signal of waning public support for the Court. Of course, the position-taking motivations behind Court-curbing demonstrated in Chapter 4 and the various patterns demonstrated here and in Chapter 5 suggest that Court-curbing is about more than legislative threats. Rather, there seems to be evidence that Court-curbing is interpreted by the Court as a signal that it is too far out of line with the broad contours of public support for the judiciary. The Court, as a consequence, will move in the direction of its antagonists, in order to minimize the loss of institutional support among the public. Recall the comments made by several legal elites about the relationship among congressional hostility, public support, and the Court's independence:

> *Justice B*: We know if there is a lot of public interest. We have to be careful not to reach too far.

---

[20] Segal and Spaeth (2002, 350 n120) observe, "If and when Congress ever mounts a clear and imminent threat to the Court's institutional policy-making powers, then and only then will the Court respond and back down. But given the extraordinary difficulty of striking at the Court's powers such times will be rare, indeed."

[21] It is in this way that the attitudinal model is actually a model of strategic behavior – the attitudinal model simply assumes that the expected adverse consequences from disregarding congressional will are sufficiently negligible that they cannot create an incentive for sophisticated decision making by the Court.

Clerk 2: Think about the memos from the *Brown* case [referring to intracourt bargaining in *Brown v. Board of Education*]. People like Felix Frankfurter were trying to find a way to make a decision that would attract popular support and would be enforced by the president and Congress.

Clerk 5: They are concerned with how they are perceived by the public. The justices are aware that they have no purse and no sword. They are very careful not to screw it up; they are very aware of how the public views the Court... The public is willing to accept decisions that are overwhelmingly unpopular because of faith in the Court.

In fact, the analysis here demonstrates a strong correlation between the justices' voting patterns and congressional attacks on the Court. The evidence indicates that as more conservative (or liberal) members of Congress engage in Court-curbing attacks on the judiciary, the justices move in a conservative (or liberal) direction (at least in statutory cases). The magnitude of this effect, moreover, is significant enough to move a justice with policy preferences similar to those of Justice Ginsburg so far in the conservative direction that her decisions would look more like those of a justice with ideological preferences similar to those of Justice Scalia. Still further, as we saw in Chapter 5, the data also provide support for the regime-dependent hypotheses, which predict that when the Court becomes sufficiently pessimistic and faces an ideologically divergent Congress, then the justices will have an incentive to exercise self-restraint, regardless of whether or not there is Court-curbing. These findings further highlight the interactive relationship between Court-curbing, public support for the judiciary, and the Court's exercise of self-restraint. In this way, the findings from the statistical analyses reveal that the broad contours of public support for the Court can impose limitations on judicial independence and discretion. When the Court is worried about its legitimacy and public support – when it observes institutional signals of waning support for the judiciary – it will have an incentive to pull back from its ideological stance in favor of a more popular view. In this way, congressional attacks on the Court limit judicial independence insofar as they serve to communicate public discontent with the Court.

In particular, the strong claim that the justices of the Supreme Court are not sensitive to changes in extrajudicial political forces does not seem to withstand the alternative theoretical and empirical conception offered here. In his analysis of Supreme Court statutory decision making, Segal (1997) claims that when pitted against each other, the attitudinal model's explanatory power clearly overwhelms "strategic" accounts. Segal's hypothesis follows the general hypotheses described previously that motivate separation of powers analyses: justices fear policy reversal. However, by re-conceptualizing the causal mechanism that motivates sophisticated behavior – the Court's concern for institutional legitimacy – the preceding analysis demonstrates that the constitutional system, including the checks and balances and the electoral connection between Congress and the public, can create incentives for sophisticated judicial decision making.

This view of the Court, as an institution responsive to concerns for its public support, via institutional signals it receives from Congress, stands in stark contrast to previous theories of judicial-legislative relations. The role that the public plays, implicitly, and the Court's preferences for institutional legitimacy construe the causal mechanisms that drive the constitutional checks and balances in a way that is related but different from a world in which Congress and the Court only care about policy outcomes. While the separation-of-powers literature has been primarily focused on whether institutional checks and balances can constrain judicial independence, the argument advanced here is that institutions may constrain the Court, but only when they do so at the behest of public will. Whether or not this is normatively desirable remains to be seen and is beyond the scope of this study. Nevertheless, that the constitutional system of checks and balances seems to incorporate democratic representation is an important lesson in the positive study of American political institutions.

6.4   AN ILLUSTRATION: SCHOOL BUSING

To further place into context the relationship among public opinion, congressional criticism of the Court, and judicial decision making, I now turn to a second historical example. During the late twentieth century, particularly the 1970s and early 1980s, the use of forced busing to integrate public schools was perhaps one of the most controversial areas of judicial involvement in the political arena. Here I provide an account of the major developments in public sentiment, congressional action, and judicial responses. This account helps illustrate the public–Congress–Court interaction I have highlighted throughout this book.

6.4.1   *Brown*, Race, and Schools

In perhaps one of the most widely known Supreme Court decisions in American history, the Supreme Court declared in *Brown v. Board of*

Education that segregating public school students by race violates the Constitution. The aftermath of *Brown* has been widely studied and documented. Scholars have examined the reluctance of political and judicial actors to enforce the Court's decision and the slow pace with which desegregation took place. One area of particular interest is the variety of judicial remedies that were used during the ensuring two decades to achieve racial integration in the public schools.

During the first fifteen years following *Brown*, desegregation of public schools took place at a very slow pace.[22] Southern school districts either refused to comply with the decision outright or developed integration policies that were at best thinly veiled efforts to maintain the status quo. The Supreme Court, for its part, did very little to compel compliance with *Brown*. During this period, the court only heard a few cases dealing with integration of public schools. In perhaps the most well known among these cases, *Cooper v. Aaron* (1958), the Court reaffirmed its decision in *Brown* and declared unequivocally that state officials were bound to comply with the Court's decision. That case arose from a dispute in Arkansas, where the state government, led by Governor Orval Faubus, resisted *Brown* and argued that state actors were not bound by Supreme Court decisions. A unanimous Court declared that its decisions were in fact binding on state officials. In a concurring opinion, Justice Frankfurter also noted that public disdain for a Court decision was not sufficient justification for disregarding the Court's decisions. Interestingly, the spirit of *Cooper v. Aaron* reveals an attempt by the Court to draw explicitly on its diffuse support.[23]

Perhaps because of the near collision between the Court's decision and the extent to which it was being respected in the South, the Court continued to avoid questions dealing with school integration over the following

---

[22] Rosenberg (1991) provides an excellent discussion of the slow pace at which schools were desegregated. In his analysis of the Court's power to effect social change, Rosenberg claims that the Court is inherently limited by the political environment in which it operates – specifically the incentives for compliance that exist within the government and among the public. In a separate, but related, analysis, Keynes and Miller (1989) analyze the congressional response to the Court's involvement in school integration. As I do here, they attribute much of the congressional response to the Court's move toward race-based integration plans. They, however, focus on Court-curbing – jurisdiction-stripping in particular – as an elite-level interaction, minimizing the role of the public.

[23] In *Cooper v. Aaron*, the Court also famously made an unequivocal claim to the supreme authority to interpret the Constitution. This is often viewed as the twentieth-century reaffirmation of the Court's declaration in *Marbury v. Madison* that the Court has the final word on questions of constitutional meaning.

decade. In 1963, though, the Court did revisit the issue. However, in this instance, the Court noted an important limitation on what states *could do* to enforce *Brown*. Specifically, the Court decided in *Goss v. Board of Education* that race-based plans for integration would not pass constitutional muster. In a brief opinion for a unanimous Court, Justice Tom C. Clark wrote, "Classifications based on race for purposes of transfers between public schools, as here, violate the Equal Protection Clause of the Fourteenth Amendment."[24] To be sure, the plan overturned in *Goss* was one that clearly sought to perpetuate segregation, rather than end it, but the Court's decision seemed to draw a line in the sand – the Court would not allow race to be used to either further or eradicate segregation. In the parlance of affirmative action debates, integration plans would have to be race-blind. Indeed, early reaction to the decision raised questions among some about race-based plans being used in the north to promote integration (rather than impede it, as in the South).[25]

6.4.2   Race-Based Remedies and Political Backlash

Only five years later, however, the Court took a turn that would lead to a heated confrontation between the public and the Court that would last fifteen years. By the spring of 1968, public opinion about integration was becoming more favorable. In September 1966, a Gallup public opinion poll asked Americans whether they thought the Johnson Administration was "pushing integration too fast, or not fast enough." Fifty-two percent of the respondents said the Administration was pushing integration too fast, whereas only 10% said not fast enough and 29% said "about right." However, when asked the same question in April 1968, only 39% of respondents said too fast, whereas 21% said not fast enough, and 25% said about right. At that time, on April 3, the Supreme Court heard oral argument in *Green v. County School Board of New Kent County* (1968). The case asked the Court to decide whether a "freedom of choice plan," under which students could choose which of two schools to attend, satisfied the spirit of *Brown*, when the system led to de facto segregation, as whites all chose one school and blacks, out of fear of retaliation, all

[24] *Goss v. Board of Education*, 373 U.S. 683, 687.
[25] For example, in the front-page story covering the decision in *The New York Times*, Anthony Lewis commented on the potential problems the Court's race-neutral criterion could cause for plans that used race in the North to integrate schools. Anthony Lewis, "Pupil Transfers to Divide Races Voided by Court," *The New York Times*, June 4, 1963, p1.

chose the other school. Writing for a unanimous Court, Justice William Brennan declared that the plan, which was in letter race-neutral, was insufficient to effectuate integration. As Keynes and Miller (1989, 209) observe, "[f]or the first time, the Supreme Court explicitly required *effective* desegregation measures."

Green marked the beginning of a new era in judicial involvement in segregation. The Court signaled its willingness to force state officials to achieve integration; no longer could they create race-neutral plans and allow citizens to use them to self-segregate. The state would be responsible for enforcing integration. This move, however, did not in and of itself cause any discernible public backlash. In February 1970, for example, a Harris public opinion poll found that 48% of Americans approved of the Court's declaration that segregated public schools must become integrated "without further delay." However, *Green* did pave the way for another decision that would engender considerable public backlash. In 1971, the Court decided in *Swann v. Charlotte-Mecklenburg Board of Education* that federal courts had the power to order forced busing to integrate public schools. Writing for an again unanimous Court, Chief Justice Warren Burger conceded that the primary responsibility for integration lies with the local school boards but also claimed that given local failure, the use of race-based forced busing to achieve integration was not outside of the scope of remedial powers held by federal district courts. Two years later, the Court found, for the first time, evidence of segregation in a Northern city. In *Keyes v. School District No. 1* (1973)[26] the Court found that even absent a statutorily constructed racially segregated school system, "statutory dual system" – school system segregated by race according to law – the courts may conclude there exists a dual system if the government has carried out "a systematic program of segregation."[27] Together, these decisions marked an important growth in the powers and aggressiveness of the Courts to enforce integration.

Public reaction was swift and forceful. A Gallup public opinion poll taken in August 1971 found that 94% of Americans had heard about the use of busing the integrate schools. Of those polled, the survey also found that 73% opposed the use of busing to integrate schools. Two months later, that figure had only grown – 77% of Americans opposed busing. The following summer, 71% of Americans said they were "totally opposed to busing children for the purpose of achieving racial balance

---

[26] 413 U.S. 189 (1973).
[27] *Keyes v. School District No. 1*, 413 U.S. 189, 201 (1973).

in the schools."[28] Moreover, the public did not hesitate to let the Court know it was displeased with the use of busing to integrate schools. For example, Justice Brennan received volumes of hate mail about his decision to allow forced busing and was the subject of editorials (which he read and kept). Beyond such direct communications, the justices also witnessed sustained public outcry. Citizens demonstrated outside of the Supreme Court building and on the grounds of the Capitol across the street, and the justices' attention was drawn to the demonstrations. For example, in a letter to each of them, Representaitve Carroll Hubbard, from the 1st District of Kentucky, advised the justices of a planned demonstration the following Saturday by her constituents against school busing and inviting them to attend the demonstration.[29]

During the ensuing years, the Court retrenched a bit; it held in a series of cases that busing orders must be narrowly contained to the specific areas in which there was a history of de jure segregation. In *Milliken v. Bradley* (1974), *Austin Independent School District v. United States* (1976), and *Dayton Board of Education v. Brinkman* (1977) (*Dayton I*), the Court repeatedly declared that busing students across school districts or among towns without a history of segregation was too broad and violated the equal protection clause of the Constitution. At the same time, despite public opposition to busing, the fervor of the opposition was not very strong. Only about five Court-curbing bills were introduced in Congress between 1971 and 1975, four of which came from extremely conservative Republicans. Thus, despite the unpopularity of busing, the Court's retrenchment and refusal to push too hard on the issue minimized the extent to which the public pushed for a full-blown congressional assault on the Court. Indeed, public opinion polls suggest that although

---

[28] Survey by Gallup Organization, August 27–August 30, 1971. Retrieved December 15, 2008, from the iPOLL Databank, The Roper Center for Public Opinion Research, University of Connecticut. <http://www.ropercenter.uconn.edu/ipoll.html>. Survey by Gallup Organization, October 8–October 11, 1971. Retrieved December 15, 2008, from the iPOLL Databank, The Roper Center for Public Opinion Research, University of Connecticut. <http://www.ropercenter.uconn.edu/ipoll.html>. Survey by Time and Daniel Yankelovich, Inc., July 24–August 11, 1972. Retrieved December 15, 2008, from the iPOLL Databank, The Roper Center for Public Opinion Research, University of Connecticut. <http://www.ropercenter.uconn.edu/ipoll.html>.

[29] The Papers of William J. Brennan, Library of Congress, Box I:203, contain much of this mail. The October 20, 1975, letter from Representative Carroll Hubbard to the justices can be found in The Papers of Harry A. Blackmun, Box 1375, Folder 6, Congressional Matters, 1970–1978, Manuscript Division, Library of Congress.

support for a constitutional amendment to ban forced busing received considerable support, it could not attract a majority.[30]

Just a few years later, however, the Court expanded the scope of busing as a remedial tool for the courts. In *Dayton Board of Education v. Brinkman* (1979) (*Dayton II*) and *Columbus Board of Education v. Penick* (1979), the Court lowered the standards that must be met to determine that busing would be appropriate and expanded the types of busing plans that would pass constitutional muster. Importantly, the Court reversed course from its earlier stance and decided that the courts could order busing that would encompass jurisdictions without de jure segregation but where segregation had been in place at the time of *Brown*. The Court's decisions in these cases marked the breaking point. Public outcry was vociferous, and their elected representatives responded in turn. Opposition to busing remained strong, with 75% of Americans opposing the practice.[31] More to the point, support for a constitutional amendment to ban forced busing grew to a strong majority – 61% of Americans now favored an amendment, up from 49% only two years earlier.[32] To be sure, twenty-six Court-curbing bills were introduced in Congress between 1979 and 1980, and this would only mark the beginning of the confrontation. At a time when the Court was already suffering because of its decisions prohibiting school prayer and legalizing abortion, school busing was just another in a series of salient policy issues on which the Court was out of line with the American public.

The salience of the unpopular decisions by the Court drew it into the presidential campaign of 1980. The conservative movement was gaining ground in the electoral arena, and its ideological agenda was taking shape.[33] Conservatives continued to oppose abortion, as they had in 1976, though the Court became a more central focus for Republican politicians. Teles (2008) documents the rise of the conservative legal movement and shows that by this point the conservatives had begun to

[30] Only 49% of respondents said they favored such an amendment. Survey by Time and Yankelovich, Skelly & White, March, 1977. Retrieved December 15, 2008, from the iPOLL Databank, The Roper Center for Public Opinion Research, University of Connecticut. <http://www.ropercenter.uconn.edu/ipoll.html>.

[31] Survey by *Los Angeles Times*, November 9–November 13, 1980. Retrieved December 15, 2008, from the iPOLL Databank, The Roper Center for Public Opinion Research, University of Connecticut. <http://www.ropercenter.uconn.edu/ipoll.html>.

[32] Survey by H & R Block and Roper Organization, May 5–May 12, 1979. Retrieved December 15, 2008, from the iPOLL Databank, The Roper Center for Public Opinion Research, University of Connecticut. <http://www.ropercenter.uconn.edu/ipoll.html>.

[33] For analysis of the conservative intellectual movement, see Nash (1996).

develop a coherent ideological program that was prepared to make significant advances in the legal academy and on the bench. The Court's
position on busing provided them with an additional agenda item. The
Republican platform in 1980 reiterated its position on abortion from
the 1976 platform but added its opposition to busing and racial quotas
(Stephenson 1999, 202). In December 1980, under considerable public
pressure, Congress attached an amendment to the Department of Justice's
FY 1981 appropriations bill that would preclude the DOJ from litigat-
ing cases to enforce busing orders, though it was vetoed by lame-duck
President Jimmy Carter during his last weeks in office. The antibusing
legislation was removed and the legislation subsequently enacted. However, at the same time, public opinion was turning against the Court,
with upward of 80% of the public supporting a constitutional amendment to prohibit the Court from ordering busing to integrate schools, and
the debate over school busing certainly did not go away. What is more,
Congress during this period was also actively assailing the Court for its
decisions on school prayer and abortion (see, e.g., Keynes and Miller
1989).

6.4.3   Judicial Retrenchment

It was in this climate that the Court began to pull back on busing. In part,
the Court refused to hear some of the most intensely watched busing cases.
In a memorandum shortly after *Penick* was decided, Harry Blackmun was
advised by his clerk Bill McDaniel that the Court should deny certiorari
in several important busing cases.

> These cases – involving Wilmington, Minneapolis, Austin, and Louis-
> ville – are among the most important desegregation cases in the country.
> They have attracted a lot of attention, have been in litigation for years,
> and are hotly debated. It would be a safe bet that at least some members
> of the Conference will be anxious to see them granted, in hopes, perhaps,
> of repairing the "damage" done this Term by the *Dayton* and *Columbus*
> cases.[34]

The Court declined to hear those cases.

The Court's careful side-stepping and moderation, however, did not
undo the "damage" the Court had brought upon itself in the arena of
public opinion. The anti-Court movement gained new strength, which

---

[34] Memorandum from Bill McDaniel, Jr., to Mr. Justice Blackmun, June 19, 1979, Papers
of Harry A. Blackmun, Library of Congress, Box 295, Folder 8.

was only strengthened in Washington by the election of Ronald Reagan as president and the Republican take over of the Senate. The Court was becoming a central target of the conservative movement, and front-page newspaper stories document the focus on school busing.[35] During the first three weeks of the 97th Congress, no fewer than fifteen Court-curbing bills were introduced, among which most were concerned with either busing or abortion. Jesse Helms led the battle in the Senate, whereas public discourse became more heated and contentious, with figures such as law professor Robert Bork speaking out against the Court. In May 1981, the Constitution and Courts Subcommittee of the Senate Judiciary Committee held hearings on legislation that would have taken away from the courts jurisdiction over busing-related cases. On June 16, Jesse Helms proposed an Amendment 69 to the Department of Justice's appropriations bill, S. 951, which would preclude the DOJ from enforcing mandatory busing of public school students. Three days later, he proposed an additional amendment, Amendment 96, with the same intent. All of a sudden, Democrats who had been working to overcome Republican filibusters during the 96th Congress found themselves leading filibusters with the help of a few moderate Republicans (see, Weicker and Sussman 1995, 130). This development reflects, to some extent, a significant shift in public opinion and political power toward conservatism during the late 1970s and early 1980s. To be sure, as we saw in Figure 6.3, the public was much more conservative during those years than it was at any other period between 1950 and 2000.

Despite growing public conservatism, though, there was some elite-level resistance to the anti-Court movement in Congress. On June 30, 1981, a bipartisan group of twelve Senators wrote an open letter to the Senate, denouncing the attacks on the Courts.[36] Law professors similarly editorialized in the newspapers against legislative efforts to sanction the Court.[37] Amid all of this, Democrats in the Senate led filibusters and

---

[35] See, for example, Dudley Clendinen, "Rulings on School Integration Key Target for Conservatives," *The New York Times*, May 17, 1982, A1.

[36] See, for example, "Attempt to Limit Courts is Assailed," *The New York Times*, 1 July 1981, A17. The senators signing the open letter were Daniel Patrick Moynihan (D-NY), Bill Bradley (D-NJ), Lowell Weicker (R-CT), Edward Kennedy (D-MA), Mark Hattfield (R-OR), Charles Mathias, Jr. (R-MD), George Mitchell (D-ME), Spark Matsunaga (D-HI), Charles Percy (R-IL), John Chaffee (R-RI), Gary Hart (D-CO), and Arlen Specter (R-PA).

[37] For example, Howard Fink, a law professor from Ohio State University, editorialized in *The New York Times* that jurisdiction stripping over the busing issue could have negative consequences for the political economy and property rights (Fink 1981).

public campaigns against the Court-curbing legislation. Several "maverick" Republicans such as Lowell Weicker of Connecticut and Charles Mathias, Jr., of Maryland led a filibuster against the Helms Amendments. Indeed, Mathias (1982) even wrote an essay in the *Annals of the American Academy of Political and Social Science* denouncing the attacks on the Court.

Ultimately, after five votes, cloture was invoked in the debate over Amendment 96 on September 16, by a vote of 61-36, and the amendment was agreed to by a vote of 60-39.[38] In December, the Senate invoked cloture on Helms Amendment 69, and agreed to the amendment by a vote of 64-35. In March 1982, the appropriations bill passed the Senate by a vote of 57-37, with both antibusing amendments, and in May, President Reagan formally endorsed jurisdiction-stripping legislation to prohibit the Court from ordering school busing. It appeared as though this time the Republicans, in control of the Senate and the White House, were going to have their way with the Court, either through jurisdiction stripping or some other measure.

Three months later, on the last day of its October 1981 Term, June 30, 1982, the Supreme Court announced decisions in two key busing decisions, *Crawford v. Board of Education* and *Washington v. Seattle School District No. 1*. Although not a full-scale reversal of policy, *Crawford* represented an important moderation of the Court's policy. As one clerk from the Court when these cases were decided recalled,

> Marshall had become not just in the permanent minority but oftentimes the minority of one. Brennan, who was a shrewd political operative... built a coalition [in the *Crawford* and *Washington* cases], surprisingly, that would save the Seattle thing, but to do that we had to give up *Crawford*. And, Marshall would not go for that. Marshall believed there was a wholesale retrenchment going on over civil rights and was determined to be the last man standing. *He was quite aware that the country had changed, that the politicians had changed, and he was aware of Reagan....* It affected him by making him both sad and mad. But it wasn't so much in the way that it changed anything he was doing except to make him even more determined to dissent in every case he thought he needed to dissent in. He didn't think it was possible to broker a kind of political compromise on the Court that would save these issues. But, of course, the change was producing a conservative majority.[39]

[38] Recorded Vote No. 257.
[39] Personal interview with "Clerk 2" (emphasis added).

The decisions were immediately received by the public as a careful equivocation by the Court and a refusal to make an explicit decision one way or the other. Articles and editorials in the *New York Times*, the *Wall Street Journal*, and the *Washington Post* alike all commented on the careful equivocation in the Court's opinions. The Court's decisions in the two cases reflected, in the words of the *Wall Street Journal*, a policy position "full of hypocrisies large and small."[40] This equivocation represented the Court's effort to slowly pull back from its earlier position in the face of public animosity toward the Court. Indeed, there is direct evidence that the justices explicitly acknowledged Congress' hostility toward the Court over this issue. In a memo to Justice Harry Blackmun, his clerk wrote of the Court-curbing bills in Congress regarding jurisdiction over school busing:

> If Congress removes the power of the federal courts to order busing to redress constitutional violations – and if it is upheld in doing so – Proposition 1 [the California state law being challenged] will have the effect of imposing the same restrictions on the California courts. Yet the states may not restrict the power of their own courts of general jurisdiction to vindicate constitutional rights. And it seems that some court – state or federal – must remain open to redress violations of federal constitutional rights. Obviously the issue will not arise until Congress actually passes and the Court upholds one of these jurisdictional statutes. *But the issue is significant enough that the Court probably should explicitly reserve the question.*[41]

Thus, in light of Congress' hostility toward the Court and its efforts to prohibit the Court from ordering school busing, Justice Blackmun's clerk advised him that the Court should explicitly avoid deciding whether the State of California could prohibit its own courts from ordering busing. What is more, as the courts receded from their stance on school busing, public support for the Court-curbing legislation waned. By the time the Supreme Court handed down its decision in June 1982, public opinion polls were finding less popular support for the jurisdiction-stripping legislation. In a pattern similar to that of the New Deal and the Court-packing plan, public discontent with the Court's position on a key issue – here, school busing – was translated into elite criticism of the Court. Observing these institutional signals, the Court became aware of its waning institutional legitimacy. In part as a consequence, the Court pulled

---

[40] "Fine Tuning the Machine," *Wall Street Journal*, July 12, 1982, 18.
[41] Memorandum from CAR to HAB, 3/19/1982, Papers of Harry A. Blackmun, Library of Congress, Box 357, Folder 9 (emphasis added).

back and exercised some degree of deference to the elected branches on the issue; following that deference, public support for reining in the courts dissipated. In a pattern remarkably similar to that from the New Deal confrontation and the Court-packing Plan, public opposition to busing remained high – about 71% of Americans opposed the practice – whereas support for the Helms amendment fell – only 41% of Americans supported the law.[42]

The internal Court memoranda and the comments by Court insiders suggest that the Court may have rendered very different decisions in its school busing cases in the early 1980s if there had not been such heated public and political opposition. The Court observed strong public discontent both directly (through hate mail and demonstrations) as well as indirectly, through congressional attacks on the Court. These observations by the Court indicate that by pushing too far on the busing issue, the Court would risk losing public support. Clearly, the justices (save, perhaps, Marshall – the lone dissenter in the California case) were concerned about rendering a decision that would be publicly and politically rejected, which would have inflicted considerable harm on the Court's public image and institutional prestige. What is more, over the course of the following years, the Court very carefully moderated its position on busing, to the point where Sanford Levinson notes that by the late 1980s, the Court had effectively diffused the controversy itself by rendering the point moot (Levinson and McCloskey 2000, 209–11). It is notable that the Court's decisions in *Crawford* and *Washington* represent an important change in the Court's jurisprudence that is independent of personnel change on the Court. In fact, between the decisions in *Dayton* and *Penick* and the decisions in those two cases, only the moderate Justice O'Connor was appointed to the Court (replacing the moderate Justice Powell).

Chief Justice Burger, for the remainder of his tenure, would be sure to keep the justices up to date on legislative activity concerning the Court, particularly on Court-curbing legislation. The papers of Justices Harry Blackmun, William Brennan, and Thurgood Marshall all contain memoranda from the Chief Justice summarizing Court-curbing legislation and

---

[42] See, Survey by National Opinion Research Center, University of Chicago, February 1983. Retrieved December 15, 2008, from the iPOLL Databank, The Roper Center for Public Opinion Research, University of Connecticut. <http://www.ropercenter.uconn.edu/ipoll.html>. Survey by Louis Harris & Associates, February 12–February 17, 1982. Retrieved December 15, 2008, from the iPOLL Databank, The Roper Center for Public Opinion Research, University of Connecticut. <http://www.ropercenter.uconn.edu/ipoll.html>.

other legislative action relevant to the Court. These memoranda suggest that the Court is indeed aware of Court-curbing legislation and is sensitive to its implications for legislative-judicial relations.[43]

The pattern detected here is indeed very familiar. As in 1937, the Court's unpopular decisions engendered public discontent; in response the Court was drawn into electoral politics, and members of Congress reacted by introducing and pushing for Court-curbing legislation. Some elites voiced opposition to the Court-curbing, but the justices ultimately backed down. Following the judicial retrenchment, public opposition to the Court's policies remained, but support for the legislation waned. The point had been made, and the Court had retreated. This example shows very clearly how the Court may have an incentive to be mindful of congressional and public preferences when it makes decisions in salient policy areas. Although Court-curbing played a central role in the Court's decision to moderate itself in the busing cases during the 1980s, there was considerable Court-curbing activity during the 1970s that did not seem to affect the Court. However, with the Republican takeover of the Senate (and the White House, too), the Court suddenly became very aware of the political peril that would follow from further antagonizing the states. This case, then, provides a useful illustration for understanding congressional hostility and the effect of political confrontations on the Court's jurisprudence. As public confidence in the Court decreased from 1979 through 1982, Congress engaged in increased Court-curbing, and the Court ultimately made a strategic retreat in the busing cases. Indeed, once there was sufficient ideological divergence between the Court and the elected branches (with the election of a Republican Senate and president in 1980), and the public mood became much more conservative (recall from Figure 6.3 that the years between 1979 and 1982 witnessed a marked shift toward conservatism among the American public), the Court had good reason to expect that a divergent decision would not be respected by the public or political actors. With the increase in Court-curbing and ideological divergence between the Court and the public around 1980, the argument advanced here is that the Court would have had an incentive to exercise self-restraint in the busing cases in the early 1980s. This is precisely what happened, and the archival evidence suggests that these concerns were indeed central in the Court's decision-calculus (both in the cases it did decide and those cases it chose not to hear).

---

[43] Consider also congressional hearings on FDR's Court-packing plan in 1937, in which testimony was given by members of the Court.

6.5   CONCLUSIONS AND CAVEATS

The evidence presented in this chapter suggests the effect of Court-curbing and judicial concerns for institutional legitimacy extends beyond the context of constitutional interpretation. Indeed, the analyses above reveal a systematic relationship between institutional signals from Congress and the ideological content of the Court's statutory decisions. This is particularly notable in light of the extensive effort that scholars have invested in identifying any relationship between congressional *preferences* and the Court's statutory decisions. However, as I noted in Chapter 1, the previous scholarship has focus on the claim that the Supreme Court ought to respond to the general policy preferences of Congress (e.g., Marks 1989; Ferejohn and Shipan 1990; Gely and Spiller 1990; Eskridge 1991*b*) – or at least its preferences in specific policy areas (Hansford and Damore 2000) – because it fears the policy consequences of a statutory reversal. Following recent scholarship (Vanberg 2005; Staton 2010), I have argued instead that the causal mechanism that explains sophisticated behavior is actually a concern for institutional legitimacy and public prestige. Specifically, the data demonstrate that Court-curbing in Congress is associated with variation in Supreme Court statutory construction. The analyses above reveal that when the members of Congress engage in political attacks on the Court, they signal public discontent with the Court, and the Court reacts by deviating from its preferred jurisprudential course in favor of an ideological direction more preferred by the faction that is discontented by the Court. In this way, the argument and evidence presented here highlight the role of democratic representation in the constitutional checks and balances.

Of course, one should bear in mind two caveats when interpreting the consequences of these findings. First, this analysis does not control for the fact that the Supreme Court generally has discretionary jurisdiction and can choose which cases it will decide. As a consequence, one may expect that control over its docket should affect the degree to which the justices are susceptible to congressional hostility, because the Court can always use its passive virtues (Bickel 1962) to avoid the "hot-button" issues. However, the bias introduced by this possible effect runs against the predictions and findings reported here; that is, one should expect that docket effects should only strengthen the role of attitudinal forces in the face of congressional preferences. That is, conservative justices, if they are strictly driven by their own ideological preferences, should be more likely to take cases that allow them to reverse liberal lower court decisions, and liberal justices should be more likely to take cases that allow them to reverse conservative lower court decisions. Indeed, there is a great deal of empirical and theoretical evidence suggesting that the justices prefer to accept cases that they would like to reverse (Segal and Spaeth 2002, ch. 6; Boucher and Segal 1995). Therefore, one would expect that any docket effect would be parallel to variation in the Supreme Court's ideological preferences.

Second, and perhaps more troubling, the analysis here does not allow me to control for variation across policy areas. Court-curbing is frequently provoked by specific policy issues – such as school busing and prayer in the 1970s and 1980s or economic regulation in the 1930s. However, Court-curbing legislation, as we saw in Chapters 2 and 4, is almost always very broad in nature. It is therefore very difficult to systematically identify the policy issues at which Court-curbing legislation is directed. Moreover, there is no necessary reason to expect that the Court may, in general, try to "lie low" when Congress is particularly hostile and may respond to congressional hostility by making decisions in various policy areas that will help appease the public discontent with the Court's jurisprudence. In any event, the analysis does not control for variation across policy areas and still finds a relationship in the Court's aggregate behavior. This finding suggests that either the effect of congressional hostility is a blanket effect across all of the Court's decisions or that it is much larger than identified here, but only in the specific policy areas that are highlighted at any given time. With the evidence offered here, however, we cannot distinguish between those two possible conclusions.

As noted at the outset of this chapter, statutory construction is the most frequent and perhaps most important action taken by the Supreme Court. The evidence here suggests that the Supreme Court's decision making in statutory cases is affected by the ideological orientation and volume of anti-Court activity in Congress. This finding provides a new and important insight into the separation powers. The claim advanced in this book is that the separation of powers must be understood not in terms of individual institutions strategically deviating from their preferred policies in light of the preferences of other institutions. Rather, the system of separated powers and checks and balances creates incentives for individual institutions to deviate from their preferred policies only when the political environment itself is treacherous. In the relationship under investigation here, this claim implies that the Court should not seek to appease Congress unless it believes that politically divergent decisions will be rejected by the public and elected elites.

By positioning itself as hostile toward the Court through the introduction of Court-curbing legislation, Congress is able to signal information about the Court's level of public support and the political consequences that will follow if the Court continues to run against popular opinion. The evidence presented here reveals that the Court responds to Congress' positioning by adjusting its decision making toward the preferences of the anti-Court advocates in Congress.

TECHNICAL APPENDIX

In this appendix, I provide details on the selection of the empirical specifications used in this chapter. The data used in each of the analyses are cross-sectional time-series (or panel) data – observations for individual justices across time. Perhaps the most important structural issue with these panel data is the possibility of heteroskedasticity, or dissimilarity in the variance of the error disturbances for each justice. Heteroskedasticity violates a fundamental assumption of pooled regression (Frees 2004). Indeed, the data here are heteroskedastic across individuals. Because of this heteroskedasticity, a panel data model is necessary – either a random-effects or fixed-effects model, in order to account for this cross-sectional variation. A second difficulty that may arise with panel data is serial correlation within individuals. Serial correlation would indicate that not only is there variation in the disturbances across justices, but the disturbances for each justice are correlated across time. Fortunately, Durbin-Watson tests indicate that serial correlation is not a problem in these data. The results of this test are shown in Table 6.4.

Given that the data are heteroskedastic but not serially correlated, the widely used random- and fixed-effects models are appropriate for the data. The only remaining issue to be addressed is whether the fixed- and random-effects models yield consistent estimates of the model's parameters. Deciding whether to use a fixed-effects or a random-effects model is one of the most vexing and ubiquitously debated issues when modeling panel data. When both models yield consistent results, the random-effects model is preferable because it is more efficient. The Hausman test indicates that the estimates from both models are consistent. Therefore, the first two models estimated in this chapter include random, or modeled, effects. However, I also present the results of a fixed-effects model, which nonparametrically estimates all time-invariant heterogeneity among the justices, including underlying ideological preferences.

TABLE 6.4. *Durbin-Watson Statistics for Individual Justices*

Justice	Durbin-Watson Statistic	Justice	Durbin-Watson Statistic
Black	$DW(3, 18) = 1.20^*$	Marshall	$DW(3, 25) = 1.66^*$
Blackmun	$DW(3, 25) = 1.83^*$	Minton	NA
Brennan	$DW(3, 35) = 2.03^*$	O'Connor	$DW(3, 24) = 2.50^*$
Breyer	$DW(3, 11) = 2.51^*$	Powell	$DW(3, 16) = 2.01^*$
Burger	$DW(3, 18) = 1.30^\dagger$	Reed	$DW(3, 4) = 1.19^*$
Burton	$DW(3, 15) = 1.49^\dagger$	Rehnquist	$DW(3, 33) = 2.48^*$
Clark	$DW(3, 14) = 1.55^*$	Scalia	$DW(3, 19) = 1.79^*$
Douglas	$DW(3, 21) = 1.39^\dagger$	Souter	$DW(3, 15) = 1.53^\dagger$
Fortas	$DW(3, 5) = 1.99^*$	Stevens	$DW(3, 29) = 1.60^*$
Frankfurter	$DW(3, 9) = 1.36^\dagger$	Stewart	$DW(3, 24) = 2.28^*$
Ginsburg	$DW(3, 12) = 2.14^*$	Thomas	$DW(3, 14) = 2.41^*$
Goldberg	$DW(3, 4) = 2.22^*$	Warren	$DW(3, 16) = 1.87^*$
Harlan	$DW(3, 17) = 1.91^*$	White	$DW(3, 32) = 1.33^\dagger$
Jackson	NA	Whittaker	$DW(3, 6) = 1.89^*$
Kennedy	$DW(3, 17) = 2.83^*$		

†test is inconclusive; * test indicates no serial correlation; NA insufficient observations.

The third empirical model presented in this chapter is a "random slopes" model. In this model, random, or modeled, effects are included for each justice, as in the main empirical model. However, in this case, the slope on Court-curbing ideology is allowed to vary by justice. As I noted in the chapter, the inclusion of each of the "bins" of Court-curbing complicates the model; as a consequence, I simplify the specification by including a single measure of Court-curbing ideology – the ideal point of the median Court-curbing sponsor. Formally, the model estimated is as follows:

$$\text{Percent Liberal}_{jt} = \alpha + \beta_1 SC_j + \beta_2 CCID_t$$
$$+ \beta_3 Bills_t + \beta_4 (CCID_t \times Bills_t)$$
$$+ \gamma_j^{justice} (CCID_t \times Bills_t)$$
$$+ \alpha_j^{justice} + \varepsilon_j t$$

where SC_j is the Segal-Cover score of justice j, $CCID_t$ is the NOMI-NATE score of the median Court-curbing sponsor in year t, and $Bills_t$ is the number of Court-curbing bills introduced in year t. The parameter $\alpha_j^{justice}$ captures the justice-specific intercept shift for justice j, and the parameter $\gamma_j^{justice}$ captures the justice-specific shift in the slope on the interaction term for justice j. Formally, these random effects are modeled as follows:

$$\alpha^{justice} \sim N\left(0, \sigma^2_{justice}\right)$$
$$\gamma^{justice} \sim N\left(0, \sigma^2_{\gamma}\right)$$

The slopes reported in Figure 6.6 are given by $\beta_2 + \beta_4 \times Bills_t + \gamma_j \times Bills_t$.

7

The Limits of Judicial Independence

7.1 UNDERSTANDING JUDICIAL INDEPENDENCE

The political insulation of its judges has been a source of both pride and criticism for the American federal judiciary. On one hand, independent, politically insulated judges are able to make decisions that are on their face more legitimate than decisions that appear to have been manipulated by politicians or other powerful elites. This is precisely the problem that undermines the integrity of the judicial systems of several other nations, especially those of Eastern Europe. On the other hand, the independence and insulation of our federal judges has caused concern among democratic theorists who recognize a tension between American norms of democracy and majority rule and the great powers held by unelected, unaccountable judges. These sources of pride and criticism beg the question: how independent are these judges? What constraints on their discretion and decision making exist? Is the system we have normatively desirable? In this book, I have tried to offer an answer to the first two of these questions. Here, I offer some concluding remarks on the implications of the findings reported here and speculate about the answer to the third and final question – is the system I have described a good one or a bad one?

7.1.1 Court-Curbing as Position-Taking

The arguments and evidence offered in this book offer insights into the relationship between the public and elite behavior – specifically, I have sought to demonstrate that congressional attacks on the Court can be interpreted as institutional signals about public opinion. Although there has not previously been a systematic study of Court-curbing and its consequences for judicial decision making over a long period of time, Court-curbing has been far from an ignored topic among students of Court–Congress relations. Almost uniformly, however, previous scholarship on Court-curbing has focused on its function as an institutional threat and an attempt to exercise congressional power to "rein in" judicial power. For this reason, studies of Court-curbing have sought to illustrate the conditions that predict legislative success of Court-curbing and whether judicial responses to Court-curbing are related to those conditions.

By contrast, I have argued that Court-curbing legislation is not usually introduced with the intention of being enacted and removing judicial power. Rather, Court-curbing is usually introduced as a position-taking effort. By position-taking, I mean members of Congress primarily engage in Court-curbing in order to publicly stake a position on the Court and enable themselves to claim credit for having introduced legislation, even if they believe that legislation will never be enacted. Members of Congress, who must regularly stand for reelection in order to keep their jobs, have an interest in advertising their positions and taking stances on the issues about which they care (Mayhew 1974). Sponsoring legislation, such as Court-curbing, can be a very effective way to position-take. Members of Congress can easily inform their constituents that they have made an effort to "rein in" the Courts by pointing out the legislation they have sponsored. Recall a comment made by a legislative staffer whom I interviewed: "These bills are great because they rally the base each year; they create a constituency."

At the same time, legislators do not have to take credit for the failure of Court-curbing legislation, because their constituents know that they alone are not able to enact legislation. Indeed, it may even be in a member's interest to leave a Court-curbing effort unfinished, as she can use that as an issue during her next campaign. A member can take credit for introducing the bill but blame the complexities of congressional decision making for the failure to enact the bill. As Richard Fenno famously observed, "Members of Congress run for Congress by running against Congress" (1978, 168). What is more, the types of legislative efforts that are most likely to be enacted are precisely those that would not attract much attention or garner much electoral benefit for a legislator. For example, "Congressman A" described to me a very detailed, technical Court-curbing episode that took place in his home state. This episode, which he described as "surgical" was indeed effective at altering the judiciary's power in a particular substantive area. In this case, a piece of narrowly tailored legislation was enacted that precluded one specific remedy from the state courts' toolbox in cases involving public education. However, it did not garner much media attention and does not in any way resemble the Court-curbing legislation he often sponsors in Congress. When I asked him why he thought the "surgical" approach was successful while his regular efforts in Congress never even receive a committee hearing, he said, "The way to get the courts is with a scalpel, not a B-2 bomber." When I then asked him why he uses the "B-2 bomber" so often, he said "The B-2 bomber gets a lot of attention; people notice. The scalpel does not get any attention."

It is the electoral connection, then, that gives meaning to Court-curbing bills; the incentive to engage in political posturing allows the Court to infer from these proposals that the Court is losing popularity among the public. It is worth noting that this function of Court-curbing, and this interpretation of position-taking is in some tension with modal perceptions of position-taking, though it does not in any way contradict what scholars often mean when they use the term "position-taking." Specifically, scholars often use position-taking to refer to pure posturing that may have no policy consequences. What I have demonstrated is that such posturing can in fact lead to policy consequences. By introducing Court-curbing bills, members of Congress can position-take, and that activity can serve as an informative signal to the Court about its level of legitimacy among the public. This function of position-taking – its informative value to other elites – represents an advancement in how scholars think about Court-curbing and position-taking more generally.

More to the point, the position-taking function of Court-curbing provides a richer, more nuanced depth to the limits of judicial independence I have outlined here. Not only is the Court sensitive to an incentive to protect its institutional legitimacy and responsive to criticism of the Court, but because of the electoral connection explaining the introduction of Court-curbing bills, the justices can credibly believe that these bills are in fact accurate signals of waning public support for the Court. By tying the congressional preference for Court-curbing to public opinion, the justices know that the introduction of these bills must be an indicator that the public has sided with Congress over the Court.[1] Thus, an important

---

[1] It may be tempting to view a Court-curbing bill that has been introduced but never seen the light of a committee room as a "failure." However, interpreted as a position-taking endeavor, such a bill may very well be a success. For, the only purpose that the

component of the limits of judicial independence is that the Court will exercise self-restraint when the public is united with its elected representatives in opposition to the Court.

7.1.2 The Separation-of-Powers Model Reconsidered

The public–Congress–Court connection points directly to a second, related implication of the arguments, and evidence presented here concerns the separation-of-powers model of judicial decision making and independence. As we saw in Chapter 1, the dominant (political science) model for studying judicial independence is the separation-of-powers model. This model posits that the Supreme Court's discretion will be limited, especially in statutory cases, by its expectations about what Congress will do in response to a decision. If the Court expects a congressional reversal of its decision, then it will have an incentive to moderate itself and pick a policy it believes to be immune from a congressional override. While myriad iterations of this model have been advanced, empirical support for this primary prediction has been mixed at best.

I have adopted, by contrast, an alternative conception of the incentives facing the Court – one that relies not solely on judicial preferences over policy outcomes. In the spirit of a growing literature in the study of judicial independence, I have claimed that the Court has a preference for protecting its institutional legitimacy. Legitimacy is valuable for courts for a number of reasons, not least among which is the notion that courts can use their legitimacy to overcome enforcement dilemmas. As Vanberg (2005) observed in his groundbreaking study of the German Constitutional Court, judicial legitimacy can bolster the Court's institutional strength. Because officials charged with enforcing judicial decisions are usually elected, they must make decisions that can be justified to their constituents. Disregarding judicial decisions seen as legitimate by the public can endanger an elected official's job security and thereby force his or her hand, compelling compliance with a decision the official might otherwise be inclined to disregard. Indeed, the value of institutional legitimacy for judicial efficacy is an idea that has recently been increasingly incorporated into studies of judicial independence (Stephenson 2004; Vanberg 2005; Carrubba 2009; Staton 2010).

---

bill seeks to serve is to provide an opportunity for a member of Congress to voice his constituents' opposition to the Court. To the extent that the bills have any substantive effect on the Court, the proposed legislation achieves even more than it needs to in order to be considered successful.

What this book contributes to the study of judicial legitimacy and the separation-of-powers is an understanding of how institutional interactions between an elected body – here, Congress – and the Court can influence the Court's beliefs about its legitimacy with the public. The electoral connection between legislators and their constituents implies that the Court can, under the right conditions, infer public opinion from congressional behavior. Of course, this possibility can give rise to an incentive for members of Congress to misrepresent public opinion, if they believe they can "trick" the Court into making decisions preferred by Congress. The existing research considering how public support for the judiciary affects the balance of power between courts and elected branches has not considered the implications of the elected branches' informational advantage over the courts in matters of public opinion (Stephenson 2004; Vanberg 2005; Staton 2010). The dynamic considered in this book highlights a feature of the separation-of-powers system previously unappreciated – elected officials may be able to manipulate the Court's independence by leveraging their informational advantage about public opinion to influence the Court's perception about its institutional legitimacy.

The implications of this research, then, for the separation-of-powers model are considerable. Rather than focus simply on policy disagreement and ask whether changes in congressional preferences are associated with changes in judicial policy outputs, scholars should consider the political system more broadly and ask how congressional (and executive) alignment with public and judicial preferences affect the performance of policy making institutions. Indeed, what most previous separation-of-powers models lack is a condition that can explain and predict when the Court should be constrained and when the Court should be unconstrained. As others have argued, and as I have suggested in this book, differential public congruence with judicial and congressional preferences is one such condition. In this way, the Conditional Self-Restraint model represents an advancement of the separation-of-powers literature.[2] It is in

---

[2] I want to make clear I believe my argument is a rejection of neither the traditional separation-of-powers model nor of the attitudinal model. Rather, we may use the theory posited here to reconcile some of the divergent findings reported in the literature. As I described in Chapter 1, the bulk of the systematic empirical evidence does not lend much support to the separation-of-powers model. However, several studies have documented episodes of behavior that can best – or perhaps only – be interpreted as judicial deference to the legislature (Pritchett 1961; Murphy 1962; Keynes and Miller 1989; Leuchtenberg 1995; Hansford and Damore 2000). Because the previous scholarship has largely assumed that the Court either does or does not respond to separation-of-powers mechanisms routinely, that scholarship has been unable to explain this discrepancy; however, the Conditional Self-Restraint Model can.

this advancement that we begin to find an answer to the questions motivating this book – how independent is the Supreme Court from political
pressure and what constraints on its discretion may exist? This study
contributes to the growing evidence that an institutional concern for protecting judicial integrity and legitimacy is a consequential constraint on
judicial independence.

7.1.3   Courts in the Macropolity

These findings – that the Court will exercise self-restraint when it fears
losing institutional legitimacy and that unified public and political opposition to the Court can engender that fear – bring us to the primary
lesson. The Court is interwoven into the macropolity, and because of
its weak institutional position, the broad contours of public support
for the institution impose limits on judicial power and discretion. A
related implication of the relationships documented in the preceding
chapters concerns the Court's relationship to the "macropolity." The
macropolity refers to the connection among the public and governing institutions – the common trends in preferences and policy. In the
foundational volume on this topic, Erikson, MacKuen, and Stimson
(2002) demonstrate that there exists some evidence of a correlation
between public mood and the ideological content of the Court's decisions. Indeed, research has examined and documented evidence of a relationship between public opinion and judicial decision making (Stimson,
MacKuen, and Erikson 1995; Mishler and Sheehan 1993, 1996; Marshall 1989b). Generally, these studies conclude that increases in public
liberalism (or conservatism) are associated with increases in judicial liberalism (or conservatism). In the words of Mr. Dooley, "No matter whether
the Constitution follows the flag or not, the Supreme Court follows the
election returns."

By contrast, I have argued that judicial responsiveness to public opinion does not occur directly by the Supreme Court "following the election
returns." Rather, I have argued that the public plays a subtle, but important, role in the courtroom. Because the Court relies on political will in
order to be an efficacious governing institution, it is important that the
Court act within the (generally broad) contours of public opinion. Because
the Court is more insulated from the public than are other institutions –
in particular, Congress – the Court learns from institutional signals to
which it can attribute meaning about public support for the judiciary.
In this way, the influence of public opinion on the Court is mediated

by elected representatives, who can serve to communicate the breadth and depth of public discontent with the Court. That complex interaction brings together the judiciary, the elected branches of government – specifically, Congress – and the public. What is more, the argument advanced here brings together the macro polity with separation-of-powers theory, which is generally regarded as an elite-level interaction in which the public does not participate.

7.1.4 A Countermajoritarian Court?

The Court's connection to the macropolity uncovered in the preceding chapters brings us back to one of the primary questions motivating this book. The defining issue of constitutional theory for the past century is the so-called countermajoritarian problem. This "problem" refers to the difficulty of reconciling the power of an unelected, unaccountable body of life-appointed judges to declare majority-enacted legislation unconstitutional – and thereby veto the legislation – with American notions of majority rule and democracy. This tension in the American constitutional system has inspired a variety of normative theories of constitutional interpretation. Some theorists have proposed methods of constitutional interpretation that purport not to offend principles of majoritarianism and to comport with constitutional democracy (Thayer 1893; Llewellyn 1934; Wechsler 1959; Whittington 1999). Others have offered criteria for limiting the Court's involvement in "political" questions (Bickel 1962; Ely 1980). Another strand of normative theorists, by contrast have proposed that either the Court should be free to involve itself in politics through the act of constitutional interpretation (Eisgruber 2001; Peretti 1999) or that the Constitution should be "taken away" from the courts (Kramer 2004; Tushnet 2000, 2003). The countermajoritarian problem has even been the inspiration for foundational empirical work on judicial review and judicial independence (Dahl 1957). Although empirical scholarship on the countermajoritarian problem has direct implications for normative debates, the most fruitful connections between empirical and normative inquires have yet to be made (Friedman 2005).

As a step in that direction, the research reported in this book sheds some light on the normative debate. In particular, judicial self-restraint in the face of institutional signals from democratically-elected bodies may potentially ameliorate concerns with the countermajoritarian difficulty. The evidence offered in the preceding chapters suggests the Court does exercise self-restraint when it receives signals that it is going beyond the boundaries imposed by public support.[3] Although the justices who sit on the Supreme Court may not be directly accountable through elections, their institution is designed in such a way that they have an incentive to maintain a base of public support. This institutional design gives rise to a relationship, described above, in which the broad contours of public opinion can shape and direct judicial decision making.

In this way, the Court's incentive to protect its institutional legitimacy in order to overcome compliance with its decisions gives rise to an interesting equilibrium of judicial power that can more easily be reconciled with democratic theory. The Court may use its power to thwart majoritarian will, but it may only do so within the broad contours of public support. Put differently, the Court may undermine majority rule, but it will only do so to the extent that can be supported by a critical mass of the public. This balance between judicial power and judicial self-restraint allows for both judicial power enforcement and constitutional commitments as well as democratic limitations on judicial power. However, it remains an open question the extent to which such an institutional design promotes or hinders a normatively desirable judicial function.

Regardless of its normative implications, though, the implications of this research for the countermajoritarian difficulty bring us face-to-face with my final answer to the two positive questions motivating this work. The limits of judicial independence are those imposed by the polity. Judicial discretion exists to the extent there is sufficient public support for judicial independence. The Court need not have a majority on its side. That requirement in fact would seem to completely undermine the claim that courts can (at least potentially) enforce constitutional limits on government. Rather, the Court must have a sufficient base of support – what we have called here legitimacy – in order to exercise its powers. When constitutional rights are to be invoked, they must be done so in a manner that is not entirely anathema to the American polity. Thus, constitutional meaning may change not necessarily through formal amendment but possibly through the evolution of interpretations supported by a critical mass of the American people. Within the contours of those limits, the Court remains free to exercise its discretion. Interestingly, though, the Court's wide discretion is derived from its unwillingness not to abuse that discretion or overstep the bounds set by the people.

The Court's balancing of legitimacy and discretion brings me back to a subtle point I mentioned in Chapter 1 and to which I now return. The

---

[3] Others have similarly noted that popular constraints on judicial power can help reconcile the countermajoritarian difficulty (e.g., Friedman 2009).

Court's legitimacy and power lies in its image as an apolitical institution that interprets and applies law absent any political constraints. However, in order to maintain that legitimacy, the Court must engage in a deeply political behavior in which it identifies and recognizes precisely those political constraints the freedom from which bestows upon it legitimacy. These are the limits of judicial independence and what I call the *politics–legitimacy paradox*.

7.1.5 Institutions and Commitment

The findings reported in this book also have direct implications for the study of courts as integral components of the institutional matrix of prosperity and liberty. A central problem in creating a limited government – particularly a society in which property and individual rights are protected – is establishing an institution to enforce commitments. In fact, the problem of making credible commitments is a pervasive problem in society, and independent courts have been proposed as a means to that end.

The problem may be stated thusly: in order to protect individual and property rights, there must be a mechanism to bind individuals and government to commitments they have made from which they will have an interest in defecting (Shepsle 1991). In any transaction that takes place in a sequence there is always a risk that the last mover will have an incentive to "cheat." When you purchase a book online and then wait for it to be mailed to you, what compels the online retailer to mail you the book for which you have already paid? One answer is: courts. Independent courts provide a mechanism for individuals to enforce contractual agreements. The enforcement of contractual agreements by courts thus allows greater efficiency in economic transactions, which could be costlier without an independent arbiter to enforce the terms of the transaction. Some evidence has explicitly linked judicial independence and economic growth empirically (e.g., La Porta et al. 2004). What is more, the independent enforcement of commitments need not be limited to private economic transactions; courts can enforce commitments made between the government and the governed (Barro 2000; Weingast 1997). More generally, the creation of institutions that create veto points in policy making, such as courts, lessens fears among private actors that the government will make opportunistic changes in policy (North and Weingast 1989).[4]

---

4 David Stasavage (2002) argues, by contrast, that the creation of independent institutions is neither necessary nor sufficient to provide such protection. Rather, the structure of partisan coalitions in society needs to be considered in conjunction with institutional structures.

Independent courts are an important part of that separation-of-powers scheme.

That judicial independence is limited by diffuse popular support for the courts highlights an important constraint on their institutional capacity to solve the problem of making credible commitments. It also underscores the politics–legitimacy paradox. Courts are intended (among other things) to protect property and contractual rights, in part by acting as an independent veto player. However, putting them in a position to perform that function sets them up to potentially incur institutional damage that could very well undermine their very efficacy. The full implications of this tension remain to be explored, but the argument I have advanced certainly points to an incompatibility between the purpose and the practice of a judicial resolution to the problem of credible commitments.

7.1.6   Designing a Good Court

All of this brings us to the third and final question outlined above: is this a normatively desirable system? To answer this question, we must first outline the virtues and vices of an independent judiciary. Independent judiciaries have several virtues that have been well documented in the literature. Independent judiciaries are better situated than their less independent counterparts to enforce constitutional rights against popular majorities and thereby correct perceived injustices.[5] Independent judiciaries are associated with greater economic freedom and growth, because they provide mechanisms whereby investors and citizens can ensure their property against appropriation (La Porta et al. 2004). Indeed, judicial independence has long been recognized by constitutional theorists as a critical element of limited government (Locke 2003 [1690]; Montesquieu 1991 [1748]) and was a substantial consideration for the Framers of the American Constitution (Madison, Hamilton, and Jay 1788). Critics of strong judicial independence – often confusing judicial independence with judicial review – charge that the Court "undermines the rule of law, permitting the judges to substitute result-oriented adjudication for the rule of the Constitution" (Wolfe 1994, 11). Indeed, the general spirit of any criticism of judicial independence is really a criticism of judicial review, which are necessarily two distinct concepts.

The question, then, is really whether the limits of judicial independence are not so great as to undermine the virtues of an independent judiciary

---

[5] See, for example, McCann (1986); Neely (1981); Hochschild (1984).

while sufficiently strong to avoid the risk of abusive judicial power. The answer to this question is certainly beyond the scope of this book, but there are some suggestive lessons we might note. First, the limits of judicial independence do not preclude the active use of judicial review to enforce constitutional rights. By strategically exercising self-restraint, the Court is able to maintain a reservoir of good will that enables it to act when there is a question of great import. Self-restraint, though, means that the Court cannot become a dictator. Unlimited judicial power is a serious concern – in a world of unchecked judicial authority, who guards the guardians? Thus, we find here evidence of a delicate balance in which the Court is able to draw upon its legitimacy in times of great consequence, but the limited reservoir of good will means that it cannot charge forward in the constant name of judicial legitimacy. Recall the comment made by Clerk 8, "the Court is going to spend its capital if it is on a major issue of social justice; however, if the cost is going to be too high, then the Court will 'knuckle under.'" It would seem, at least on its face, that this balance of judicial power and judicial independence at least creates the conditions for a normatively desirable judicial institution. However, the full implications of the institutional limits and incentives described here have yet to be fully explored.

7.2 THE ROAD AHEAD

7.2.1 Questions Unanswered

Despite these lessons drawn from the findings reported in this book, there are limitations on what we can learn from the evidence and caveats that one should bear in mind when interpreting the findings. First, the Conditional Self-Restraint model posited two possible functions that Court-curbing may serve. On one hand, Court-curbing may simply serve a position-taking interest for legislators seeking electoral benefits; on the other hand, Court-curbing may operate to further politicize the Court and erode judicial legitimacy. Unfortunately, regardless of which mechanism is at work, the theoretical model yields the same predictions, and we cannot therefore distinguish between these two mechanisms with the observational data used here. There is, to be sure, some anecdotal evidence to suggest that both mechanisms may be at work (as contemplated by Model 3 in Chapter 3). In particular, recall the comment by one congressional staffer that "[t]hese ... bills rally the base every year; they also create an issue and a constituency."[6] Moreover, recent experimental research indicates that when citizens learn a decision was either made by a close majority or in conflict with previous precedent, they are less likely to support that decision (Zink, Spriggs, and Scott 2009). Future scholars should be encouraged to continue this line of inquiry and further press on this unresolved question.

Second, this research does not address the process of case selection. As noted in Chapter 5, it may be the case that the Court responds to Court-curbing and concerns about its institutional legitimacy by actually changing how it decides cases or, alternatively, by shifting its attention and its docket to less salient or contentious areas of the law. Because the focus of the research here has been on the Court's decisions in cases – and because of a lack of extensive data on the case selection process – I have been unable to assess definitively whether the Court adjusts its decisions, its docket, or some combination of both. Some of the evidence in Chapters 5 and 6 – specifically the case- and justice-level analyses – suggests that the effect of Court-curbing exists above any potential case selection effect. However, it is not possible to answer this question definitively with the data at hand. Regardless of which mechanism is at work, though, the implications of the empirical findings reported in this book do not change. The Court, motivated by an interest to protect its institutional legitimacy, responds to institutional signals about its standing with the public.

Third, this book has focused exclusively on congressional communication of public discontent. However, the president can also play a vital role in communicating (and leading) public opinion.[7] Because the president represents a national constituency, his statements on the Court may be more significant in that they might reflect a deeper, broader discontent with the Court. Presidential criticism of the Court may be a stronger signal that the Court has already gone too far and must more immediately exercise self-restraint. For example, following its decision in *Citizens United v. Federal Election Commission*, President Obama criticized the Supreme Court several times for striking down limitations on corporate and union expenditures on campaigns. In doing so, he called for a congressional response to the decision. Most saliently, the president criticized the Court during his State of the Union Address, while six of the nine justices sat

---

[6] Personal interview with Staffer 2.

[7] Scholarship on presidential agenda-setting has examined how the president may use the bully pulpit to rally public opinion and press his legislative agenda (Canes-Wrone 2006).

in the front of the House Chamber. There was a loud and forceful positive reaction to Obama's criticism from those sitting immediately around the justices. Justice Alito subtly mouthed "that's not true" in reaction to Obama's critique of the case, which drew considerable attention from the media. Surely, this experience served to signal to the Court that there was political and public discontent with the decision. By ignoring the president in this study, I do not mean to suggest these functions are not important or potentially consequential. Indeed, this seems a particularly appealing avenue for future research.

Finally, as I noted in Chapter 1, while Court-curbing bills are the focus of this book, it is certainly possible that the Court learns from other types of institutional signals. Court-curbing bills are, I believe, the primary institutional signal that conveys information to the Court about its public legitimacy. As I have noted, Court-curbing bills are very salient to the Court. Moreover, Court-curbing bills are the primary way in which members of Congress respond to constituent pressure to "rein in" the Courts. However, as I have also noted, the justices are political people and they live (usually) in the Washington, DC, area. They, like all elites, are well aware of developments in politics and current affairs. For example, newspapers – including editorials – are sources of information about reactions to the Court's decisions. In addition, other sources, such as law review articles, hearings by professional organizations – such as the American Bar Foundation – and other interactions with legal interest groups with which the justices are involved may all provide additional information to the Court about reactions to its decisions. In the end, though, the evidence demonstrates that Court-curbing is at least one component of the signals that the Court observes about its legitimacy. To the extent that other contextual signals are also operative, though, this does not necessarily undermine the argument advanced here; it simply serves to suggest a more nuanced political world in which the separation of powers operates.

7.2.2 The Separation of Powers and Judicial Legitimacy

The retirement of Justice Sandra Day O'Connor and her replacement by Samuel Alito in 2005 ushered in the first Supreme Court in American history on which not a single member has ever held elective office – either legislative or executive. To the extent that professional judges are different than individuals who have experience as elected politicians, this might suggest that the relationship between the public and the Court may be different today than previously. Perhaps we are entering a period in which the Court will relate differently to the public. Perhaps judges without experience standing for election to retain their jobs will be less sensitive to the institutional need for public support. Or, perhaps a Court staffed by only professional judges will have a less sanguine view of the Court as a political institution and will be more protective of the Court's prestige as a legal body.

On the other hand, perhaps the particular biographies of the individuals occupying the bench will have no effect on the Court's relationship to the public. As I have argued, the Court's reliance on public support and judicial legitimacy is a feature of the institution inherent in the nature of a judiciary. The institution itself motivates the justices to strategically protect the Court. Of course, while the evidence offered here supports this claim, it cannot rule out the possibility that the institutional design of the Court could give rise to other types of Court–Congress–public relations. Perhaps future scholarship may make use of a comparative perspective to assess the effect of varying the institutional design of courts. In any event, though, it is important to note that the question of whether the incentives created by the judicial institutions in the United States are the unique incentives that may be generated by this design.

Indeed, this question could become particularly relevant, if, as the analysis in Chapter 2 suggests, we are entering a new period of heightened conflict between the public and the Court. With the Democratic takeover of Congress in 2006 and the White House in 2008, there have been signs of growing liberal discontent with the relatively conservative Supreme Court.[8] To be sure, there is some evidence to suggest that public support for the Court is waning. During the summer of 2007, *The New York Times* and *The Washington Post* both ran stories about growing interest

---

[8] Oddly, though, until only recently, public discontent has been coming most fervently from the political right in an era where the Supreme Court is fairly conservative from a historical perspective. The "Religious Right" has made the judiciary a key component of its political activity, focusing on judicial involvement in policy areas such as abortion and homosexual equality. Conservative politicians hoping for national support from the right end of the political spectrum are routinely called upon to denounce unpopular court decisions and to promise to appoint conservative justices who would oppose abortion and homosexual equality. For example, during the October 8, 2004, debate between President George W. Bush and Senator John Kerry – in advance of the November 2004 election – George Bush, now famously, voiced his opposition to the *Dred Scott* case, a case decided in 1857 affirming the legal status of slaves as property. Political pundits soon thereafter observed that *Dred Scott* is a code word among the religious right for *Roe v. Wade*, the Supreme Court decision in 1973 prohibiting state bans on abortion, which is so reviled by the conservative movement.

group pressure, from the political left, for Congress to consider Court-curbing. These stories also reported evidence from then-recent public opinion polls to suggest that public support for the judiciary is declining. A survey conducted by the Pew Research Center in 2007 revealed that 29% of Americans had either a "somewhat unfavorable" or a "very unfavorable" opinion of the Supreme Court, compared with only 21% who gave the same response in January 2001 (just weeks after the divisive decision in *Bush v. Gore*).

How the Court will respond to growing liberal opposition remains to be seen. However, my analysis here suggests a period of relative judicial self-restraint, and anecdotal evidence points in that direction. On October 22, 2007, *Time Magazine* ran a cover story entitled, "Does the Supreme Court Still Matter?" The story noted that the Supreme Court, under the leadership of Chief Justice Roberts, is hearing very few cases, and those that it does hear seem to be less controversial in subject matter than those often decided by the Rehnquist Court. It is, of course, still early in the Roberts Court, and it is not necessarily true that every Term of the Court offers the opportunity to rule on cases like *Brown v. Board of Education*. Nevertheless, if the Court is in fact being sensitive to the increasing political discontent with the Court – discontent coming from both ends of the political spectrum – then perhaps this trend in the Court's docket can be attributed, at least in part, to a wariness among the justices about ruling on hotly debated issues. Perhaps the justices are worried about undermining the Court's legitimacy by making decisions that will be soundly rejected by one half of the public or the other.

Finally, I conclude by commenting on perhaps the most significant contribution of this study. I have observed at several points that the relationship among the Court, Congress, and the public contemplated by the argument in this book suggests a way in which we may reconcile two competing goals of liberal constitutional democracy. On one hand, democratic theory contends that majority rule is essential to legitimate government. On the other hand, the principles of constitutionally limited government contend that proper limitations must be enforced on majority rule in order to protect fundamental liberties and freedoms for everyone. It is clear that these two goals may at times be in tension with each other. The solution to this tension proposed by many constitutional orders – including the United States – is to vest power in the courts to exercise a constitutional veto over majoritarian policy making. As the debates of American constitutional theory during the past century make clear, this solution is not necessarily fool-proof. Potential judicial overreaching can raise questions about the propriety of a judicial check over democratic policy making. However, if the courts do indeed exercise self-restraint in order to remain within the broad contours of public support, then perhaps the judicial veto is in some sense compatible with majority rule. In a way similar to the supermajority rules of the Senate, the Court may act as a conservative force in American politics. On the other hand, the Court may also act as a supermajoritarian progressive force. Either way, though, to the extent that the Court is limited by the public through self-restraint, the Court cannot be viewed as an inherently undemocratic institution. But, it is still the public's responsibility to remain vigilant and enforce its sovereignty over the courts. If not, then they do so at the risk of constitutionally limited government, including constitutionally limited courts.

APPENDIX A

Elite Interview Methodology

This research has benefited greatly from interviews I have had with Supreme Court justices, former law clerks, members of Congress, congressional staff, and interest group activists. Access to these elites is not easily granted, and when it is gained, a heavy responsibility lies with the researcher to promote a high degree of professionalism, as he represents the academic community to these individuals. In order to maintain a high level of professionalism, to protect the interests of my interview subjects, and to ensure that they may continue to be willing to speak with members of the academic community in the future, I have adopted a set of conventions that guide the use of interview evidence in this book. In this appendix, I describe the interview process – gaining access, conducting interviews, and following up from interviews – as well as the conventions I have adopted for the use of these interviews in my research.

A.1 METHOD

The method of conducting interviews is an art, not a science. Interview methodology involves gaining access, preparing for and conducting interviews, and post-interview follow-up.

A.1.1 Gaining Access

Different types of individuals vary in how they may be best contacted and how willing they are to grant access for an interview. Supreme Court justices, for example, have widely available contact information, though the only practical way to contact them is through the mail. These individuals, however, generally do not grant access to academics or the public. In December 2006, I wrote a letter to each current Supreme Court justice and the one living retired justice, Sandra Day O'Connor. Several justices replied relatively quickly, within a few weeks, whereas others took much longer to reply. Three justices granted me an interview, six declined to participate in my research, and one justice never replied to my letter. One justice who declined to participate was kind enough to send along a note with a copy of a speech that justice had given with some relevance to my research topic.

Former law clerks, on the other hand, are much more difficult to identify, though they are generally more willing to grant access for an interview. The process of identifying former law clerks is necessarily piecemeal. I identified several former clerks by searching Web pages of major law schools and law firms, reading through individuals' biographies to identify anyone who served as a clerk on the Supreme Court. I also identified several clerks through the process of interviewing other clerks. For example, during an interview with one clerk, s/he may have commented that I should contact person X, who would be interested in this topic or have something more to contribute.

Between December 2006 and January 2007, I contacted more than twenty former law clerks and interviewed ten of them. I initially sent a standard letter to each former clerk for whom I could identify a mailing address. Most responded within a few weeks; some never responded. After a few weeks, I followed up my initial letter with an e-mail to those for whom I could identify an e-mail address. Among those to whom I sent an e-mail, all but one agreed to an interview.

Identifying members of Congress and their contact information is extremely easy. These individuals are highly public figures, and their Web pages always contain contact information for their Washington, DC, offices as well as district offices. Moreover, they are oftentimes very willing to speak with students and academics, though their busy schedules often preclude any opportunity to actually meet and speak with them. I identified approximately twenty members of Congress who had either sponsored Court-curbing legislation, served on the Judiciary Committee, or were in some way active with respect to judicial issues. I sent each of these legislators a letter in December 2006 and followed up on that letter during early January 2007. Although I was only able to schedule a meeting with two legislators, many others indicated a willingness to speak. Oftentimes, it proved easier to meet with staff members than to meet with the legislators themselves.

In particular, I contacted six congressional staffers, including legislative assistants (LAs) to members and committee staffers. To identify staffers, I searched the Congressional Staff Directory for the names and phone numbers of committee staff and legislative assistants. Several interviews were conducted over the telephone and some were conducted in Washington, DC. Before traveling to Washington, I made appointments with several staffers, and while there, I was on several occasions directed by one interviewee to visit another staffer. For example, during one interview, an LA told me that there was one staffer in another member's office who would be interested in speaking with me and would have much to say. I was able to simply show up at that staffer's office, and we spent fifteen minutes talking.

A.1.2 Preparing and Conducting Interviews

To prepare for the interviews, I first agreed on a set of conditions and parameters for the interviews. In each case, I promised the interview subjects, following my initial request, that the interviews would remain anonymous. I also promised each subject that I would not audiotape the interviews and that I would not ask questions about specific cases or events that they may have experienced in connection with their employment on the Court.

I developed a list of topics that I thought appropriate for the interviews. My primary method was to determine which questions it was most important to have the interview subject answer. I made sure to design questions that would tap into the interview subjects' general impressions on the main themes of the research. The interviews were intended to be exploratory in nature, and I wanted to ensure that the interview subjects would provide candid opinions about the relationship between the Court and (a) the public and (b) Congress. The list of topics and questions was offered to the interview subjects in advance. Two of the three Supreme Court justices asked for the list of topics and questions. Each of the former law clerks declined to see the questions in advance.

I interviewed three Supreme Court justices and ten former law clerks. Interviews with each of the Supreme Court justices took place in the justice's chambers. Each interview lasted between thirty minutes and one hour. Among the justices I interviewed, there was variation in partisan affiliation and length of tenure. I interviewed two members of Congress, one of whom I interviewed in person in his Washington, DC, office, and the other of whom I interviewed over the telephone while he was at home in his constituency. The in-person interview lasted twenty minutes, while the telephone interview lasted approximately fifteen minutes. Neither of the members was a member of the Judiciary Committee, though both have sponsored Court-curbing legislation. Moreover, both have sponsored Court-curbing legislation that has come to a final vote on the floor as well as legislation that has never received a committee hearing. One member had only been in Congress for two terms, whereas the other was a relatively senior member.

Interviews with nine of the ten law clerks were conducted over the telephone; one was conducted in person. These interviews ranged from twenty to sixty minutes in duration, with the modal interview lasting approximately thirty-five minutes. Within the set of clerks I interviewed, there was great variation across most dimensions. The clerks represent a wide range of time on the Court, with one clerk having worked at the Court during the 1950s and one clerk having been on the Court as recently as the early 2000s. The clerks I interviewed worked for justices who may be considered liberal and justices who may be considered conservative; they worked for female and male justices; they came from varying law schools and now work in various professions, including academics, government, and private practice. Some of the former clerks currently maintain an active practice before the Supreme Court. Perhaps most interesting, all of these clerks agreed in great detail with respect to their impressions about the Court's relationship to public opinion and Court-curbing, despite the many other differences in their experiences.

Finally, among the congressional staffers I interviewed, there was considerable variation in partisan affiliation and length of service. For example, one legislative assistant had been an LA for quite a while but was new to the judiciary component of her member's staff. At least two of the staffers with whom I spoke had law degrees, and at least one had only an undergraduate bachelor's degree. Another staffer had been working on the Judiciary Committee of her chamber for more than twenty years. Of these six interviews, three took place in person in their Washington, DC, offices. The remaining three took place over the telephone. Interviews with staffers ranged from about fifteen minutes in duration to approximately half an hour.

A.1.3 Post-interview Follow-Up

At the conclusion of each interview, I offered each subject an opportunity to review my notes to check for the accuracy of my impressions. I advised each subject that, upon request, I would provide a full list of all quotations that would be used in any research. Several of the interview subjects reviewed my research notes, and a few chose to edit my quotations. I also offered to provide each interview subject with a list of any and all publications that may result from the interview research.

A.2 CONVENTIONS

In many cases, as a condition of the interview, I have promised anonymity to the interview subject. In particular, Supreme Court justices and former clerks from the Court have all been promised anonymity as well as other congressional staff members. In all instances, I have chosen to report interviews anonymously. This decision comes after much consideration. To be sure, there are strong reasons both for and against the use of anonymous interviews in scholarly work. Perhaps most significant, the standards of scientific inquiry require the fullest possible disclosure of the source of empirical evidence. However, at the same time, because of the sensitivity of the subject matter discussed with my interview subjects and the norms of confidentiality that permeate the judicial branch, confidentiality is the only way to ensure my interview subjects would speak candidly.

In order to help protect the identity of those who have agreed to participate in an interview, I will uniformly refer to Supreme Court justices as "he" and former clerks as "she;" Supreme Court justices will be referred to as "Justice A," "Justice B," and so forth, whereas former clerks will be referred to as "Clerk 1," "Clerk 2," and so forth. "Justice A" will remain "Justice A" throughout the book; the same convention applies to all pseudonyms assigned to anonymous interviewees.

In addition, I adopt the following rules regarding quotations from interviews. Because most of my interviewees preferred that I not use any audiotaping equipment, I was obliged to take shorthand notes during the interviews. As a consequence, quotations very closely reflect the spirit of an individual interviewee's statements but may not be exact word-for-word quotations. When possible, I have been able to provide interview subjects with a list of exact quotations that I have planned to use and allowed the subject to edit or revise any quotation that he or she believes does not best represent his or her comments.

Court-Curbing Bills, 1877–2008

TABLE B.1. *Court-Curbing Bills Introduced in Congress, 1877–2008*

Bill	Date Sponsored	Congress	Sponsor	Type of Legislation
H.R. 2713	1/28/1878	45	Butler	Misc
S. 908	3/12/1878	45	Kernan	Statute – Jurisdiction
H.R. 4027	3/25/1878	45	Stephens	Statute – Procedure
S. 1319	5/25/1878	45	Christianey	Statute – Jurisdiction
S. 1127	12/4/1878	45	Garland	Statute – Jurisdiction
S. 322	4/1/1879	46	Williams	Statute – Jurisdiction
H.R. 666	4/21/1879	46	McMillan	Statute – Judicial Review
H.R. 421	4/21/1879	46	Herbert	Statute – Jurisdiction
S. 509	4/28/1879	46	Davis (IL)	Statute – Jurisdiction
S. 216	5/26/1879	46	Whyte	Statute – Jurisdiction
S. 274	5/31/1879	46	Whyte	Statute – Jurisdiction
H.R. 1801	5/6/1879	46	Bragg	Statute – Procedure
H.R. 6496	12/6/1880	46	Springer	Statute – Composition
H.R. 6807	1/25/1881	46	Geddes	Misc
S. 2098	1/25/1881	46	Davis (IL)	Statute – Procedure
S. 814	1/12/1882	47	Edmunds	Statute – Procedure
H.R. 141	12/13/1881	47	Thomas	Statute – Procedure
H.R. 865	12/16/1881	47	Manning	Statute – Procedure
H.R. 3556	1/30/1882	47	Oates	Statute – Procedure
S. 59	4/25/1882	47	George	Amendment – Jurisdiction
S. 2184	12/4/1882	47	Voorhees	Statute – Judicial Review
S. 2343	1/11/1883	47	Farley	Statute – Procedure
H.Res. 316	1/15/1883	47	Dibrell	Statute – Procedure
H.R. 7591	2/15/1883	47	Jacobs	Statute – Procedure
H.R. 7519	2/5/1883	47	Walker	Statute – Procedure

Bill	Date Sponsored	Congress	Sponsor	Type of Legislation
S. 1848	5/5/1883	47	George	Statute – Composition
S. 1846	5/5/1883	47	Morgan	Statute – Procedure
S. 309	12/5/1883	48	Garland	Statute – Procedure
S. 432	12/6/1883	48	Call	Statute – Procedure
H.R. 241	12/10/1883	48	Thomas	Statute – Procedure
H.R. 1107	12/11/1883	48	Scales	Misc
H.Res. 51	12/11/1883	48		Amendment – Composition
H.R. 1956	1/7/1884	48	Wood	Statute – Judicial Review
H.R. 2784	1/8/1884	48	R. Warner	Statute – Composition
H.R. 2833	1/8/1884	48	Culberson	Statute – Procedure
H.R. 3072	1/14/1884	48	Oates	Statute – Procedure
S. 1560	2/15/1884	48	Manderson	Statute – Procedure
H.R. 5884	5/10/1884	48	Holmes	Statute – Procedure
H.R. 7988	1/19/1885	48	Morrill	Statute – Judicial Review
S. 140	12/8/1885	49	Manderson	Statute – Procedure
S. 439	12/10/1885	49	Voorhees	Statute – Procedure
S. 873	1/5/1886	49	Call	Statute – Composition
H.R. 2487	1/6/1886	49	Crain	Statute – Composition
H.R. 2488	1/6/1886	49	Crain	Statute – Composition
H.R. 4458	1/26/1886	49	Townshend	Statute – Judicial Review
H.R. 4909	2/1/1886	49	Hepburn	Statute – Composition
S. 273	12/12/1887	50	Vest	Statute – Judicial Review
S. 240	12/12/1887	50	Call	Statute – Procedure
S. 191	12/12/1887	50	Manderson	Statute – Procedure
S. 636	12/13/1887	50	Reagan	Statute – Procedure
S. 799	12/15/1887	50	Call	Statute – Procedure
H.R. 1873	1/4/1888	50	Culberson	Statute – Judicial Review
H.R. 11396	9/10/1888	50	Henderson (NC)	Statute – Procedure
S. 45	12/4/1889	51		Statute – Composition
S. 25	12/4/1889	51		Statute – Procedure
H.R. 9887	4/29/1890	51	Stewart (GA)	Statute – Judicial Review
H.R. 8	1/5/1892	52	Oates	Statute – Composition
H.R. 456	1/7/1892	52	Culberson	Statute – Judicial Review
H.R. 565	1/7/1892	52	Henderson (NC)	Statute – Procedure
H.R. 5980	2/15/1892	52	Chipman	Statute – Judicial Review
S. 3293	6/20/1892	52	Sanders	Statute – Judicial Review
S. 40	8/8/1893	53	Vest	Statute – Jurisdiction
H.R. 3131	9/15/1893	53	Oates	Statute – Procedure
H.R. 1892	9/6/1893	53	Culberson	Statute – Jurisdiction
H.Res. 72	10/10/1893	53	Mercer	Amendment – Composition
H.R. 4295	10/31/1893	53	Bailey	Statute – Composition
S. 1563	2/5/1894	53	Allen	Statute – Remedy

(continued)

TABLE B.I *(continued)*

Bill	Date Sponsored	Congress	Sponsor	Type of Legislation
H.R. 5755	2/12/1894	53	Culberson	Statute – Jurisdiction
H.R. 6528	4/2/1894	53	Tucker	Statute – Jurisdiction
S. 2774	2/16/1895	53	Vilas	Statute – Jurisdiction
H.R. 318	12/6/1895	54	Bailey	Statute – Composition
S. 1448	1/9/1896	54	Vilas	Statute – Jurisdiction
H.R. 4700	1/23/1896	54	Culberson	Statute – Jurisdiction
S. 1729	1/23/1896	54	Call	Statute – Jurisdiction
H.R. 5565	2/5/1896	54	Cooke (IL)	Statute – Composition
H.R. 7042	3/9/1896	54	Little	Statute – Composition
H.R. 9925	1/9/1897	54	Jones	Statute – Procedure
S. 3643	2/3/1897	54	Nelson	Misc
S. 200	2/16/1897	55	Thuston	Statute – Composition
S. 33	3/16/1897	55	Berry	Statute – Jurisdiction
H.R. 2593	4/3/1897	55	Jones (VA)	Statute – Procedure
S. 2999	1/5/1898	55	Nelson	Statute – Procedure
S.Res. 79	1/10/1898	55	Butler	Amendment – Composition
H.R. 7941	2/9/1898	55	Burke (TX)	Statute – Jurisdiction
H.R. 3359	12/11/1899	56	Burke (TX)	Statute – Jurisdiction
S.Res. 47	12/20/1899	56	Butler	Amendment – Composition
H.R. 1080	12/5/1899	56	Moon (PA)	Statute – Jurisdiction
H.R. 1081	12/5/1899	56	Moon (PA)	Statute – Jurisdiction
H.J.Res. 36	12/5/1899	56	Cooper (TX)	Amendment – Composition
H.R. 109	12/2/1901	57	Overstreet	Statute – Jurisdiction
H.R. 2018	12/3/1901	57	Woods	Statute – Jurisdiction
H.J.Res. 77	12/13/1901	57	Cooper (TX)	Amendment – Composition
H.R. 13286	4/2/1902	57	Woods	Statute – Jurisdiction
H.R. 14840	6/3/1902	57	Woods	Statute – Jurisdiction
S. 6628	12/16/1902	57	Patterson	Statute – Jurisdiction
S. 3540	1/18/1904	58	Clay	Statute – Jurisdiction
H.J.Res. 93	1/27/1904	58	Russell	Amendment – Composition
H.J.Res. 92	1/27/1904	58	Russell	Amendment – Jurisdiction
H.R. 16299	12/12/1904	58	Lacey	Statute – Composition
H.R. 16452	12/13/1904	58	Watson	Statute – Composition
H.R. 17996	12/19/1905	58	Heflin	Statute – Composition
H.R. 437	12/4/1905	59	Stephens (TX)	Statute – Jurisdiction
H.R. 4503	12/6/1905	59	Gillespie	Misc
H.R. 9327	12/19/1905	59	Gillbert (IN)	Statute – Remedy
H.R. 13386	1/29/1906	59	James	Statute – Jurisdiction
S. 3801	1/29/1906	59	Patterson	Statute – Jurisdiction
H.R. 18943	2/3/1906	59	Randell (TX)	Statute – Procedure
H.R. 14971	2/15/1906	59	Moon (PA)	Misc
H.R. 15721	2/26/1906	59	Garrett	Statute – Jurisdiction

Bill	Date Sponsored	Congress	Sponsor	Type of Legislation
H.R. 15720	2/26/1906	59	Garrett	Statute – Jurisdiction
H.R. 17794	4/5/1906	59	Hughes	Statute – Jurisdiction
H.R. 17835	4/6/1906	59	De Armond	Statute – Jurisdiction
H.R. 17883	4/7/1906	59	Parker	Statute – Jurisdiction
H.R. 17976	4/10/1906	59	Henry (TX)	Statute – Remedy
H.R. 18171	4/13/1906	59	Pearre	Statute – Remedy
H.R. 18446	4/20/1906	59	Pearre	Statute – Remedy
H.R. 18752	4/28/1906	59	Pearre	Statute – Remedy
H.R. 24124	1/14/1907	59	De Armond	Statute – Composition
H.J.Res. 250	1/22/1907	59	Russell	Amendment – Judicial Review
H.J.Res. 226	1/24/1907	59	Lamar	Amendment – Composition
H.J.Res. 248	2/20/1907	59	Kitchin	Amendment – Composition
H.J.Res. 249	2/22/1907	59	Russell	Amendment – Composition
H.R. 94	12/2/1907	60		Misc
H.R. 69	12/2/1907	60	Henry (TX)	Statute – Remedy
H.J.Res. 15	12/2/1907	60	Russell (TX)	Amendment – Composition
H.J.Res. 27	12/2/1907	60	Cooper (TX)	Amendment – Composition
H.R. 3947	12/3/1907	60	Garrett	Statute – Jurisdiction
H.R. 3948	12/3/1907	60	Garrett	Statute – Jurisdiction
H.R. 3918	12/3/1907	60	De Armond	Statute – Jurisdiction
H.R. 4000	12/3/1907	60	Hardwick	Misc
H.J.Res. 42	12/5/1907	60	Kitchin	Amendment – Composition
H.J.Res. 50	12/9/1907	60	Lamar	Amendment – Composition
H.R. 7636	12/12/1907	60	Clayton	Statute – Remedy
H.R. 9195	12/16/1907	60	Henry (TX)	Statute – Remedy
H.R. 14275	1/7/1908	60	Hackney	Statute – Remedy
H.R. 13830	1/15/1908	60	Randell (TX)	Statute – Composition
H.R. 14372	1/17/1908	60	Hackney	Statute – Remedy
H.R. 15944	1/31/1908	60	Thomas (NC)	Statute – Remedy
H.R. 16758	2/10/1908	60	Patterson (SC)	Statute – Remedy
H.R. 17137	2/14/1908	60	Rodenberg	Misc
H.R. 20823	4/6/1908	60	Small	Statute – Remedy
H.R. 21359	4/20/1908	60	Payne	Statute – Remedy
H.R. 21454	4/20/1908	60	Chaney	Statute – Remedy
H.R. 21358	4/20/1908	60	Sterling	Statute – Remedy
H.R. 21539	4/20/1908	60	Boyd	Statute – Remedy
H.R. 21769	5/4/1908	60	Caulfield	Statute – Composition
H.R. 21629	5/4/1908	60	Boynge	Statute – Remedy
H.R. 21991	5/12/1908	60	Beall (TX)	Statute – Procedure
H.R. 22032	5/12/1908	60	Reynolds	Statute – Remedy
H.R. 21989	5/12/1908	60	Beall (TX)	Statute – Remedy
H.R. 22010	5/12/1908	60	Hepburn	Statute – Remedy
H.R. 22298	12/7/1908	60	Young	Statute – Remedy

(*continued*)

TABLE B.1 *(continued)*

Bill	Date Sponsored	Congress	Sponsor	Type of Legislation
H.R. 24781	12/19/1908	60	Hubbard (WV)	Statute – Remedy
H.R. 25821	1/11/1909	60	Howell (UT)	Statute – Jurisdiction
H.R. 26300	1/15/1909	60	Madison	Statute – Remedy
H.R. 26609	1/19/1909	60	Cox (IN)	Statute – Remedy
H.R. 21814	5/11/1909	60	Caulfield	Misc
H.R. 2174	3/18/1909	61		Statute – Judicial Review
H.R. 2107	3/18/1909	61	Kitchin	Statute – Jurisdiction
H.R. 2725	3/19/1909	61	Garrett	Statute – Jurisdiction
H.R. 2724	3/19/1909	61	Garrett	Statute – Jurisdiction
H.R. 3058	3/19/1909	61	Wilson (PA)	Statute – Jurisdiction
H.R. 3667	3/22/1909	61	Gardner (NJ)	Statute – Procedure
H.R. 4324	3/24/1909	61		Statute – Judicial Review
H.R. 4329	3/24/1909	61		Statute – Jurisdiction
H.R. 5179	3/26/1909	61	Richardson	Statute – Procedure
H.R. 6035	3/30/1909	61	Madison	Statute – Remedy
H.R. 7528	4/12/1909	61	Hardwick	Statute – Remedy
H.R. 9766	5/17/1909	61	Kendall	Statute – Remedy
H.R. 11775	6/20/1909	61	Randell (TX)	Statute – Composition
H.R. 10890	6/21/1909	61	Young (MI)	Statute – Remedy
H.R. 12176	8/3/1909	61	Henry (TX)	Statute – Remedy
H.R. 12182	8/3/1909	61	Henry (TX)	Statute – Remedy
H.R. 15411	12/5/1909	61	Kitchin	Statute – Jurisdiction
H.R. 15412	12/5/1909	61	Kitchin	Statute – Jurisdiction
H.J.Res. 80	12/10/1909	61	Russell	Amendment – Composition
H.J.Res. 81	12/10/1909	61	Russell	Amendment – Jurisdiction
H.R. 14577	12/14/1909	61	Thomas (KY)	Statute – Jurisdiction
S. 4138	12/16/1909	61	Jones	Statute – Procedure
H.R. 19281	1/25/1910	61	Alexander (NY)	Statute – Jurisdiction
S. 6657	2/21/1910	61	Clay	Statute – Jurisdiction
H.R. 22326	3/4/1910	61	Parker	Statute – Jurisdiction
H.R. 24065	4/5/1910	61	Dickinson	Statute – Jurisdiction
H.R. 24318	4/9/1910	61	Randell (TX)	Statute – Composition
H.R. 30143	12/21/1910	61	Stephens (TX)	Statute – Judicial Review
H.R. 31165	1/11/1911	61	Moon (PA)	Misc
H.R. 2892	4/10/1911	62	Dickinson	Statute – Judicial Review
H.J.Res. 45	4/10/1911	62	Raker	Amendment – Jurisdiction
H.J.Res. 44	4/10/1911	62	Raker	Amendment – Jurisdiction
H.R. 5148	4/14/1911	62	Wilson (PA)	Amendment – Judicial Review
H.R. 5604	4/17/1911	62	Thomas	Statute – Judicial Review
H.J.Res. 149	8/10/1911	62	Madison	Amendment – Composition
S. 3222	8/14/1911	62	Bourne	Statute – Judicial Review
H.R. 14003	8/22/1911	62	Garrett	Statute – Judicial Review

Bill	Date Sponsored	Congress	Sponsor	Type of Legislation
H.R. 14004	8/22/1911	62	Garrett	Statute – Judicial Review
H.R. 14005	8/22/1911	62	Garrett	Statute – Judicial Review
H.J.Res. 214	1/17/1912	62	Jackson	Amendment – Composition
H.J.Res. 227	1/24/1912	62	Lafferty	Amendment – Composition
H.J.Res. 246	2/20/1912	62	Dickinson	Amendment – Composition
H.J.Res. 270	3/14/1912	62	Neely	Amendment – Composition
H.R. 22771	4/2/1912	62	Taylor (CO)	Statute – Composition
H.J.Res. 290	4/6/1912	62	Neely	Amendment – Composition
S. 6266	4/11/1912	62	Bacon	Statute – Judicial Review
S.J.Res. 109	5/21/1912	62	Crawford	Amendment – Composition
H.J.Res. 336	7/10/1912	62	Dickinson	Amendment – Composition
H.J.Res. 345	8/2/1912	62	Hull	Amendment – Composition
S.J.Res. 130	8/5/1912	62	Ashurst	Amendment – Composition
S.J.Res. 142	12/5/1912	62	Bristow	Amendment – Judicial Review
S. 8007	1/7/1913	62	Tillman	Misc
S. 8116	1/15/1913	62	Gore	Statute – Composition
H.J.Res. 26	4/7/1913	63	Lafferty	Amendment – Composition
S.J.Res. 6	4/7/1913	63	Reed	Amendment – Composition
S. 747	4/12/1913	63	Tillman	Statute – Procedure
S.J.Res. 19	4/15/1913	63	Crawford	Amendment – Composition
H.R. 7028	7/22/1913	63	Rupley	Statute – Composition
H.R. 9839	12/4/1913	63	Seldomridge	Statute – Jurisdiction
H.R. 10946	1/31/1914	63	McCoy	Statute – Procedure
H.J.Res. 12	12/6/1915	64	Dickinson	Amendment – Composition
H.J.Res. 113	1/20/1916	64	Taggart	Amendment – Composition
S. 5734	4/24/1916	64	Overman	Amendment – Procedure
S. 5758	4/26/1916	64	Pittman	Statute – Composition
S. 6226	5/31/1916	64	Hughes	Statute – Composition
S.J.Res. 142	6/13/1916	64	Thomas	Amendment – Composition
S.J.Res. 168	8/18/1916	64	Sheppard	Amendment – Composition
S. 7322	12/13/1916	64	Nelson	Statute – Jurisdiction
S.J.Res. 195	1/11/1917	64	Owen	Statute – Judicial Review
S.J.Res. 193	1/18/1917	64	Owen	Statute – Judicial Review
S.J.Res. 217	2/26/1917	64	Owen	Statute – Judicial Review
S.J.Res. 220	3/2/1917	64	Owen	Statute – Judicial Review
S.J.Res. 7	4/4/1917	65	Owen	Resolutions
H.J.Res. 39	4/5/1917	65	Hayden	Amendment – Judicial Review
S. 2916	9/25/1917	65	Johnson (CA)	Statute – Jurisdiction
S. 137	3/7/1918	65	Myers	Amendment – Composition
H.J.Res. 264	3/12/1918	65	Welty	Amendment – Composition
H.R. 13157	11/21/1918	65	Dillon	Misc
S.J.Res. 58	6/23/1919	66	Sheppard	Amendment – Composition

(continued)

TABLE B.I *(continued)*

Bill	Date Sponsored	Congress	Sponsor	Type of Legislation
S. 2880	8/23/1919	66	Norris	Statute – Composition
H.R. 13310	3/27/1920	66	Brand	Statute – Composition
H.R. 13945	5/5/1920	66	Brand	Statute – Composition
S. 5042	2/24/1921	66	Dial	Statute – Procedure
S.J.Res. 173		66	LaFollette	Amendment – Composition
H.R. 3190	4/14/1921	67	Brand	Statute – Composition
H.R. 14209	2/5/1923	67	Woodruff	Statute – Judicial Review
S. 4483	2/5/1923	67	Borah	Statute – Judicial Review
H.R. 697	12/5/1923	68	Woodruff	Statute – Judicial Review
H.R. 721	12/5/1923	68	LaGuardia	Statute – Judicial Review
H.R. 441	12/5/1923	68	Brand (GA)	Statute – Composition
H.R. 2910	12/10/1923	68	Thomas (KY)	Misc
S. 1297	12/15/1923	68	Borah	Statute – Judicial Review
H.R. 6993	2/14/1924	68	Keller	Statute – Procedure
S. 2595	2/22/1924	68	Johnson (MN)	Statute – Procedure
S.J.Res. 93	3/10/1924	68	Dill	Amendment – Composition
H.R. 6762	1/5/1926	69	Woodruff	Statute – Judicial Review
S.J.Res. 103	4/19/1926	69	Dill	Amendment – Composition
S. 2206	1/4/1928	70	Norris	Statute – Composition
H.R. 9050	1/10/1928	70	Graham	Statute – Composition
H.R. 9488	1/17/1928	70	Brand	Statute – Composition
H.R. 135	4/15/1929	71	LaGuardia	Misc
S.J.Res. 126	1/6/1930	71	Dill	Amendment – Composition
H.R. 8963	1/22/1930	71	Brand	Statute – Composition
S.J.Res. 162	4/1/1930	71	Brookhart	Statute – Jurisdiction
S.Res. 258	4/30/1930	71	Walsh	Resolutions
H.R. 16344	1/19/1931	72	Graham	Statute – Composition
S.J.Res. 52	12/15/1931	72	Dill	Amendment – Composition
S.J.Res. 107	2/17/1932	72	Dill	Amendment – Composition
H.J.Res. 144	4/4/1933	73	Swank	Amendment – Composition
S.J.Res. 58	5/29/1933	73	Dill	Amendment – Composition
H.R. 6204	1/3/1934	73	Ramsay	Statute – Jurisdiction
S. 3529	4/26/1934	73	McKellar	Statute – Composition
H.R. 93	1/3/1935	74	Ramsay	Statute – Jurisdiction
H.R. 5161	3/6/1935	74	Sumners (TX)	Statute – Composition
H.R. 7782	4/29/1935	74	Sumners (TX)	Statute – Composition
H.R. 7911	5/6/1935	74	Sumners (TX)	Statute – Composition
H.J.Res. 277	5/7/1935	74	Ramsay	Amendment – Judicial Review
S. 3211	5/13/1935	74	LaFollette	Amendment – Procedure
S.J.Res. 149	5/13/1935	74	Norris	Amendment – Judicial Review
H.J.Res. 287	5/14/1935	74	Dobbins	Amendment – Judicial Review
H.R. 8100	5/16/1935	74	Crosser (OH)	Statute – Judicial Review

Bill	Date Sponsored	Congress	Sponsor	Type of Legislation
H.R. 8123	5/17/1935	74	Young	Statute – Judicial Review
H.J.Res. 296	5/20/1935	74	Knute Hill	Amendment – Judicial Review
H.R. 8309	6/3/1935	74	Cross (TX)	Statute – Jurisdiction
H.J.Res. 317	6/7/1935	74	Tolan	Amendment – Judicial Review
H.R. 10102	1/10/1936	74	Quinn	Statute – Composition
S. 3739	1/16/1936	74	Norbeck	Statute – Judicial Review
S.J.Res. 208	1/16/1936	74	Lewis	Statute – Procedure
H.R. 10362	1/17/1936	74	Lundeen	Statute – Composition
H.R. 10315	1/19/1936	74	Sisson	Statute – Jurisdiction
H.J.Res. 509	3/3/1936	74	Buckler	Amendment – Judicial Review
H.J.Res. 565	4/9/1936	74	Zioncheck	Amendment – Judicial Review
H.R. 44	1/5/1937	75	Ramsay	Statute – Judicial Review
H.R. 50	1/5/1937	75	Ramsay	Statute – Judicial Review
H.R. 2284	1/8/1937	75	Faddis	Statute – Judicial Review
H.R. 2265	1/8/1937	75	Walter	Statute – Judicial Review
S. 437	1/8/1937	75	Pope	Statute – Judicial Review
S. 1098	1/26/1937	75	Gillette	Statute – Judicial Review
H.R. 3895	1/28/1937	75	Teigan	Statute – Judicial Review
H.R. 3895	1/28/1937	75	Teigan	Statute – Judicial Review
S. 1276	2/1/1937	75	Gillette	Statute – Judicial Review
H.R. 4279	2/3/1937	75	Coffee (WA)	Statute – Judicial Review
H.R. 4417	2/5/1937	75	Maverick	Statute – Composition
S. 1378	2/5/1937	75	Lundeen	Statute – Composition
S. 1392	2/8/1937	75	Ashurst	Statute – Composition
H.R. 5172	3/1/1937	75	O'Connor (MT)	Statute – Judicial Review
H.J.Res. 265	3/8/1937	75	Treadway	Amendment – Composition
H.R. 5485	3/9/1937	75	Fish	Statute – Judicial Review
H.J.Res. 276	3/11/1937	75	Fish	Amendment – Judicial Review
S.J.Res. 98	3/11/1937	75	O'Mahoney	Amendment – Judicial Review
S.J.Res. 100	3/12/1937	75	Andrews	Amendment – Composition
S. 1890	3/15/1937	75	Norris	Statute – Judicial Review
H.J.Res. 293	3/24/1937	75	Bulwinkle	Amendment – Composition
S.J.Res. 118	3/29/1937	75	Bilbo	Amendment – Judicial Review
H.J.Res. 303	3/30/1937	75	Case (SD)	Amendment – Composition
H.J.Res. 333	4/22/1937	75	Fish	Amendment – Judicial Review
S. 2352	5/6/1937	75	Andrews	Statute – Composition
S.J.Res. 143	5/6/1937	75	McAdoo	Amendment – Composition
H.R. 7154	5/20/1937	75	Gray	Statute – Judicial Review
H.J.Res. 373	5/20/1937	75	Gray (Indiana)	Amendment – Composition
H.J.Res. 383	5/27/1937	75	Gearhart	Amendment – Composition
H.R. 7765	7/6/1937	75	Vinson	Statute – Composition
H.R. 8053	7/29/1937	75	McFarlane	Statute – Composition

(continued)

TABLE B.I *(continued)*

Bill	Date Sponsored	Congress	Sponsor	Type of Legislation
S.J.Res. 217	8/20/1937	75	Connally	Amendment – Composition
H.J.Res. 22	1/3/1939	76	Daly	Amendment – Composition
S.J.Res. 14	1/4/1939	76	Andrews	Amendment – Composition
H.R. 4372	3/9/1944	78	Welchel (GA)	Statute – Procedure
S. 2135	4/30/1946	79	Bridges	Misc
S.J.Res. 167	6/18/1946	79	Eastland and Bridges	Amendment – Composition
S.J.Res. 188	8/2/1946	79	Andrews	Amendment – Procedure
H.J.Res. 105	2/3/1947	80	Smith (WI)	Amendment – Composition
H.J.Res. 86	1/13/1949	81	Smith (WI)	Amendment – Composition
H.R. 8940	6/26/1950	81	Combs	Statute – Procedure
H.J.Res. 64	1/4/1951	82	Smith (WI)	Amendment – Composition
H.R. 2424	1/6/1951	82	Wilson (TX)	Statute – Procedure
S.J.Res. 154	5/13/1952	82	Butler (MD)	Amendment – Composition
H.R. 642	1/3/1953	83	Wilson (TX)	Statute – Procedure
H.J.Res. 91	1/6/1953	83	Smith (WI)	Amendment – Composition
S.J.Res. 44	2/16/1953	83	Butler (MD)	Amendment – Composition
H.J.Res. 194	2/18/1953	83	Miller (MD)	Amendment – Composition
H.R. 3701	2/7/1955	84	Rivers	Statute – Jurisdiction
H.R. 3769	2/8/1955	84	Forrester	Statute – Jurisdiction
S. 1011	2/9/1955	84	Johnston (SC)	Statute – Jurisdiction
S. 1016	2/9/1955	84	Thurmond	Statute – Jurisdiction
S.J.Res. 45	2/15/1955	84	Butler	Amendment – Composition
H.J.Res. 227	2/22/1955	84	Miller (MD)	Amendment – Composition
H.R. 8906	1/30/1956	84	Matthews	Statute – Jurisdiction
S.J.Res. 168	5/9/1956	84	Long	Amendment – Composition
H.R. 11600	6/5/1956	84	Huddleston	Statute – Judicial Review
H.R. 11795	6/14/1956	84	Vinson	Statute – Judicial Review
H.R. 11847	6/19/1956	84	Sikes	Statute – Judicial Review
H.R. 463	1/3/1957	85	Smith (MS)	Statute – Judicial Review
H.R. 692	1/3/1957	85	Huddleston	Statute – Judicial Review
H.R. 175	1/3/1957	85	Forrester	Statute – Jurisdiction
H.R. 1228	1/3/1957	85	Rivers	Statute – Jurisdiction
S.J.Res. 9	1/7/1957	85	Long	Amendment – Composition
S.J.Res. 114	6/24/1957	85	Eastland and Johnston (SC)	Amendment – Composition
H.J.Res. 388	6/25/1957	85	Smith (WI)	Amendment – Composition
S. 2401	6/26/1957	85	Thurmond	Statute – Jurisdiction
H.J.Res. 415	7/1/1957	85	Herlong	Amendment – Composition
H.J.Res. 403	7/11/1957	85	Abernethy	Amendment – Composition
H.J.Res. 407	7/15/1957	85	Whitten	Amendment – Composition
S. 2646	7/26/1957	85	Jenner	Statute – Jurisdiction
H.R. 9207	8/9/1957	85	St. George	Statute – Jurisdiction

Bill	Date Sponsored	Congress	Sponsor	Type of Legislation
H.J.Res. 536	2/10/1958	85	Long	Amendment – Composition
H.R. 10775	2/16/1958	85	Colmer	Statute – Jurisdiction
H.R. 13857	8/22/1958	85	Abbitt	Amendment – Judicial Review
H.R. 659	1/7/1959	86	Smith (MS)	Statute – Judicial Review
H.R. 1133	1/7/1959	86	Huddleston	Statute – Judicial Review
H.R. 634	1/7/1959	86	St. George	Statute – Jurisdiction
H.R. 486	1/7/1959	86	Colmer	Statute – Jurisdiction
H.J.Res. 32	1/7/1959	86	Abernathy	Amendment – Composition
H.R. 1939	1/9/1959	86	Rivers (SC)	Statute – Jurisdiction
S.J.Res. 7	1/9/1959	86	Johnston (SC)	Amendment – Composition
H.J.Res. 136	1/12/1959	86	Whitener	Amendment – Composition
S.J.Res. 18	1/20/1959	86	Long	Amendment – Composition
H.J.Res. 201	1/29/1959	86	Sikes	Amendment – Judicial Review
H.R. 4659	2/17/1959	86	Tuck	Statute – Judicial Review
H.R. 4565	2/17/1959	86	Abbitt	Statute – Judicial Review
S. 1593	4/7/1959	86	Talmadge	Statute – Jurisdiction
H.R. 6639	4/27/1959	86	Casey	Statute – Composition
H.J.Res. 453	7/6/1959	86	Brooks (LA)	Amendment – Composition
H.J.Res. 700	5/6/1960	86	Devine	Amendment – Judicial Review
H.R. 654	1/3/1961	87	Colmer	Statute – Judicial Review
H.R. 404	1/3/1961	87	Huddleston	Statute – Judicial Review
H.R. 756	1/3/1961	87	St. George	Statute – Jurisdiction
S. 412	1/13/1961	87	Talmadge and Ellender	Statute – Jurisdiction
H.J.Res. 141	1/16/1961	87	Brooks (LA)	Amendment – Composition
H.R. 5789	3/21/1961	87	Rogers (TX)	Statute – Procedure
H.R. 10992	3/28/1962	87	Tuck	Statute – Remedy
H.R. 10965	3/28/1962	87	Abbitt	Statute – Remedy
H.J.Res. 772	6/28/1962	87	Chelf	Amendment – Judicial Review
H.J.Res. 790	6/29/1962	87	St. George	Amendment – Judicial Review
H.R. 12389	7/2/1962	87	Rivers (SC)	Statute – Jurisdiction
H.R. 356	1/9/1963	88	Huddleston	Statute – Judicial Review
H.R. 121	1/9/1963	88	Rogers (TX)	Statute – Procedure
H.J.Res. 59	1/9/1963	88	St. George	Amendment – Judicial Review
H.R. 1771	1/14/1963	88	Colmer	Statute – Jurisdiction
H.R. 3213	1/31/1963	88	Sikes	Statute – Remedy
H.R. 4063	2/21/1963	88	Rogers (TX)	Statute – Procedure
S. 1683	6/6/1963	88	Eastland	Statute – Jurisdiction
H.J.Res. 537	7/1/1963	88	Saylor	Amendment – Judicial Review
H.R. 11077	4/29/1964	88	Winstead	Statute – Judicial Review
H.R. 11381	5/26/1964	88	Abbitt	Statute – Remedy
H.J.Res. 1158	8/14/1964	88	Pucinski	Amendment – Composition

(continued)

TABLE B.1 *(continued)*

Bill	Date Sponsored	Congress	Sponsor	Type of Legislation
H.J.Res. 1163	8/19/1964	88	Chelf	Amendment – Composition
H.R. 887	1/4/1965	89	Rogers (TX)	Statute – Procedure
H.R. 536	1/4/1965	89	Rogers (TX)	Statute – Procedure
H.R. 712	1/4/1965	89	Abernathy	Statute – Remedy
H.J.Res. 7	1/4/1965	89	Chelf	Amendment – Composition
H.J.Res. 84	1/4/1965	89	Pucinski	Amendment – Composition
H.R. 1584	1/5/1965	89	Tuck	Statute – Remedy
H.R. 1586	1/5/1965	89	Waggoner	Statute – Remedy
H.R. 2400	1/12/1965	89	Colmer	Statute – Remedy
H.R. 6621	3/23/1965	89	Dorn	Statute – Remedy
H.J.Res. 1124	4/26/1966	89	Cabell	Amendment – Judicial Review
H.J.Res. 1139	5/9/1966	89	Mize	Amendment – Judicial Review
H.J.Res. 1168	6/14/1966	89	Devine	Amendment – Judicial Review
H.R. 16329	7/19/1966	89	Sweeney	Misc
H.R. 18403	10/17/1966	89	Randall	Misc
H.R. 395	1/10/1967	90	Colmer	Statute – Jurisdiction
H.J.Res. 32	1/10/1967	90	Chamberlain	Amendment – Composition
H.J.Res. 104	1/10/1967	90	Waggoner	Amendment – Composition
H.J.Res. 147	1/16/1967	90	Whitten	Amendment – Composition
H.J.Res. 173	1/18/1967	90	Younger	Amendment – Judicial Review
S.J.Res. 22	1/23/1967	90	Ervin	Statute – Jurisdiction
H.R. 6529	3/2/1967	90	Rarick	Amendment – Judicial Review
H.J.Res. 384	3/2/1967	90	Rarick	Amendment – Judicial Review
S. 1194	3/7/1967	90	Ervin	Statute – Jurisdiction
H.Con.Res. 269	3/8/1967	90	King (NY)	Resolutions
H.R. 6944	3/9/1967	90	Patman	Statute – Jurisdiction
H.J.Res. 418	3/9/1967	90	Saylor	Amendment – Judicial Review
H.J.Res. 443	3/16/1967	90	Devine	Amendment – Judicial Review
H.J.Res. 466	3/22/1967	90	Bevill	Amendment – Composition
H.J.Res. 607	6/6/1967	90	King (NY)	Amendment – Judicial Review
H.R. 11007	6/20/1967	90	Erlenborn	Statute – Judicial Review
H.J.Res. 738	7/24/1967	90	Hutchinson	Amendment – Composition
H.Con.Res. 504	9/12/1967	90	Duncan	Resolutions
H.R. 12992	9/19/1967	90	Hungate	Statute – Procedure
H.J.Res. 841	9/21/1967	90	Rarick	Amendment – Composition
H.R. 13978	11/13/1967	90	Blackburn	Statute – Jurisdiction
H.J.Res. 988	1/22/1968	90	Mize	Amendment – Judicial Review
H.J.Res. 996	1/23/1968	90	Edwards (Al)	Amendment – Judicial Review
H.J.Res. 997	1/23/1968	90	Eshleman	Amendment – Composition
H.J.Res. 1038	2/1/1968	90	Long (LA)	Amendment – Composition
H.J.Res. 1094	2/15/1968	90	Rarick	Amendment – Composition
H.R. 15556	2/26/1968	90	Taylor	Statute – Jurisdiction

Bill	Date Sponsored	Congress	Sponsor	Type of Legislation
H.J.Res. 1126	2/26/1968	90	Taylor	Amendment – Composition
S. 3061	2/29/1968	90	Tydings	Statute – Composition
H.J.Res. 1149	3/5/1968	90	Rogers (FL)	Amendment – Judicial Review
H.J.Res. 1172	3/14/1968	90	Pool	Amendment – Judicial Review
H.R. 16106	3/20/1968	90	Scott	Statute – Jurisdiction
H.R. 16365	4/1/1968	90	Rarick	Statute – Judicial Review
H.J.Res. 1220	4/4/1968	90	Fountain	Amendment – Composition
H.J.Res. 1279	5/22/1968	90	Edwards (Al)	Misc
H.J.Res. 1282	5/23/1968	90	Nichols	Amendment – Composition
H.R. 17741	6/10/1968	90	Pool	Statute – Jurisdiction
H.R. 18103	6/25/1968	90	Abbitt	Statute – Jurisdiction
H.J.Res. 1369	6/26/1968	90	Teague (Tex)	Amendment – Judicial Review
H.J.Res. 1373	6/27/1968	90	Gardner	Amendment – Composition
H.J.Res. 1374	6/27/1968	90	Gurney	Amendment – Composition
H.J.Res. 1370	6/27/1968	90	Blackburn	Amendment – Composition
H.J.Res. 1386	7/3/1968	90	Thompson (GA)	Statute – Composition
H.J.Res. 1387	7/8/1968	90	Adair	Amendment – Composition
H.J.Res. 1399	7/10/1968	90	Gurney	Amendment – Judicial Review
H.J.Res. 1401	7/10/1968	90	Lennon	Amendment – Composition
H.J.Res. 1407	7/11/1968	90	Rogers (FL)	Amendment – Composition
H.R. 18703	7/18/1968	90	Railsback	Statute – Composition
H.J.Res. 1418	7/24/1968	90	Gardner	Amendment – Composition
H.J.Res. 1426	7/29/1968	90	Scott	Amendment – Composition
H.J.Res. 1439	8/2/1968	90	Winn	Amendment – Composition
H.J.Res. 1448	9/10/1968	90	Abbitt	Amendment – Composition
H.J.Res. 1456	9/12/1968	90	Randall	Amendment – Composition
H.J.Res. 1469	10/10/1968	90	Betts	Amendment – Judicial Review
H.J.Res. 1469	10/10/1968	90	Betts	Amendment – Judicial Review
H.R. 1317	1/3/1969	91	Rarick	Statute – Judicial Review
H.R. 1024	1/3/1969	91	Colmer	Statute – Judicial Review
H.R. 1331	1/3/1969	91	Rarick	Statute – Judicial Review
H.R. 855	1/3/1969	91	Minshall	Statute – Jurisdiction
H.J.Res. 82	1/3/1969	91	Saylor	Amendment – Judicial Review
H.J.Res. 168	1/3/1969	91	Sikes	Amendment – Judicial Review
H.J.Res. 68	1/3/1969	91	Rarick	Amendment – Composition
H.J.Res. 124	1/3/1969	91	Bevill	Amendment – Composition
H.J.Res. 71	1/3/1969	91	Rarick	Amendment – Composition
H.J.Res. 103	1/3/1969	91	Abbitt	Amendment – Composition
H.J.Res. 101	1/3/1969	91	Whitten	Amendment – Composition
H.J.Res. 66	1/3/1969	91	Randall	Amendment – Composition
H.J.Res. 133	1/3/1969	91	Chamberlain	Amendment – Composition
H.J.Res. 45	1/3/1969	91	Hutchinson	Amendment – Composition

(continued)

TABLE B.1 *(continued)*

Bill	Date Sponsored	Congress	Sponsor	Type of Legislation
H.J.Res. 155	1/3/1969	91	Lennon	Amendment – Composition
H.J.Res. 86	1/3/1969	91	Sikes	Amendment – Composition
H.J.Res. 125	1/3/1969	91	Bevill	Amendment – Composition
H.J.Res. 193	1/7/1969	91	Cabell	Amendment – Judicial Review
H.J.Res. 242	1/13/1969	91	Roberts	Amendment – Composition
H.J.Res. 297	1/23/1969	91	Teague (TX)	Amendment – Composition
H.J.Res. 331	1/29/1969	91	Skubitz	Amendment – Composition
H.J.Res. 471	2/19/1969	91	Scott	Amendment – Composition
H.R. 7507	2/24/1969	91	Railsback	Statute – Composition
H.R. 7782	2/26/1969	91	Thompson (GA)	Statute – Composition
H.R. 7739	2/26/1969	91	Mathias	Statute – Composition
H.R. 8014	3/3/1969	91	"Railsback, et al."	Statute – Composition
H.R. 8930	3/13/1969	91	Edwards (Al)	Statute – Composition
H.R. 8960	3/13/1969	91	McClure	Statute – Composition
H.J.Res. 557	3/17/1969	91	Nichols	Amendment – Judicial Review
H.J.Res. 558	3/17/1969	91	Nichols	Amendment – Composition
H.J.Res. 671	4/23/1969	91	Clark	Amendment – Judicial Review
H.J.Res. 693	4/30/1969	91	Long (LA)	Amendment – Composition
H.R. 10903	5/5/1969	91	Springer	Statute – Remedy
H.R. 10962	5/6/1969	91	Hastings	Statute – Remedy
H.R. 10985	5/6/1969	91	Sikes	Statute – Remedy
H.J.Res. 700	5/6/1969	91	Devine	Amendment – Judicial Review
H.R. 11021	5/7/1969	91	Fuqua	Statute – Remedy
H.R. 11034	5/7/1969	91	McMillan	Statute – Remedy
H.R. 11008	5/7/1969	91	Cederberg	Statute – Remedy
H.R. 11124	5/12/1969	91	Carter	Statute – Remedy
H.R. 11383	5/15/1969	91	Waggoner	Statute – Remedy
H.J.Res. 720	5/15/1969	91	Daniel (VA)	Amendment – Composition
H.R. 11431	5/19/1969	91	Williams	Statute – Remedy
H.J.Res. 723	5/19/1969	91	Dickinson	Amendment – Composition
H.R. 11447	5/20/1969	91	Cleveland	Statute – Remedy
H.J.Res. 730	5/20/1969	91	Eshleman	Amendment – Composition
H.J.Res. 741	5/22/1969	91	Pollock	Amendment – Composition
H.R. 11715	5/27/1969	91	Harvey	Statute – Remedy
H.J.Res. 768	6/5/1969	91	Watson	Amendment – Composition
H.J.Res. 774	6/11/1969	91	Duncan	Amendment – Judicial Review
S.J.Res. 125	6/19/1969	91	Eastland	Statute – Jurisdiction
H.J.Res. 796	6/25/1969	91	Dorn	Amendment – Composition
H.J.Res. 817	7/15/1969	91	Wydler	Amendment – Composition
H.J.Res. 1047	1/20/1970	91	Bennett	Amendment – Composition
H.J.Res. 1074	2/3/1970	91	Andrews (AL)	Amendment – Judicial Review
H.J.Res. 1075	2/3/1970	91	Andrews (AL)	Amendment – Composition

Bill	Date Sponsored	Congress	Sponsor	Type of Legislation
H.J.Res. 1087	2/19/1970	91	Brinkley	Amendment – Composition
H.R. 16161	2/24/1970	91	Wiggins	Statute – Procedure
H.J.Res. 1252	6/9/1970	91	Chappell	Amendment – Composition
H.Res. 1213	9/17/1970	91	Cramer	Resolutions
H.R. 390	1/22/1971	92	Rarick	Statute – Judicial Review
H.R. 373	1/22/1971	92	Rarick	Statute – Judicial Review
H.R. 1255	1/22/1971	92	Colmer	Statute – Judicial Review
H.R. 136	1/22/1971	92	Edwards (AL)	Statute – Composition
H.R. 1473	1/22/1971	92	Minshall	Statute – Jurisdiction
H.Res. 135	1/22/1971	92	Sikes	Resolutions
H.J.Res. 148	1/22/1971	92	Randall	Amendment – Judicial Review
H.J.Res. 38	1/22/1971	92	Bevill	Amendment – Composition
H.J.Res. 39	1/22/1971	92	Bevill	Amendment – Composition
H.J.Res. 63	1/22/1971	92	Edwards (AL)	Amendment – Composition
H.J.Res. 82	1/22/1971	92	Fuqua	Amendment – Composition
H.J.Res. 149	1/22/1971	92	Randall	Amendment – Composition
H.J.Res. 52	1/22/1971	92	Chamberlain	Amendment – Composition
H.J.Res. 152	1/22/1971	92	Rarick	Amendment – Composition
H.J.Res. 31	1/22/1971	92	Bennett	Amendment – Composition
H.J.Res. 165	1/22/1971	92	Roberts	Amendment – Composition
H.J.Res. 177	1/22/1971	92	Sikes	Amendment – Procedure
S. 385	1/28/1971	92	Gurney	Statute – Remedy
H.R. 3111	2/1/1971	92	Collier	Statute – Remedy
H.J.Res. 293	2/4/1971	92	Teague (TX)	Amendment – Judicial Review
H.J.Res. 294	2/4/1971	92	Teague (TX)	Amendment – Composition
S.J.Res. 38	2/11/1971	92	Allen	Amendment – Composition
H.R. 4773	2/22/1971	92	Wiggins	Statute – Composition
H.J.Res. 437	3/3/1971	92	Long (LA)	Amendment – Composition
H.J.Res. 442	3/8/1971	92	Abbitt	Amendment – Composition
H.J.Res. 448	3/9/1971	92	Whitten	Misc
H.R. 6379	3/18/1971	92	Hagan	Statute – Jurisdiction
H.R. 6501	3/22/1971	92	Schmitz	Statute – Jurisdiction
S. 1553	4/15/1971	92	Hollings	Statute – Procedure
H.J.Res. 574	4/27/1971	92	G. Andrews (AL)	Amendment – Judicial Review
H.J.Res. 575	4/27/1971	92	G. Andrews (AL)	Amendment – Composition
H.R. 10614	9/13/1971	92	Schmitz	Statute – Remedy
H.J.Res. 866	9/14/1971	92	Chappell	Amendment – Composition
H.J.Res. 865	9/14/1971	92	Chappell	Statute – Composition
H.R. 12527	1/20/1972	92	Schmitz	Statute – Jurisdiction
H.J.Res. 1120	3/20/1972	92	Teague (TX)	Amendment – Composition
H.J.Res. 1177	4/25/1972	92	Seiberling	Amendment – Composition
H.J.Res. 1247	6/29/1972	92	Saylor	Amendment – Judicial Review

(*continued*)

TABLE B.1 *(continued)*

Bill	Date Sponsored	Congress	Sponsor	Type of Legislation
H.R. 955	1/3/1973	93	Rarick	Statute – Judicial Review
H.R. 81	1/3/1973	93	Archer	Statute – Jurisdiction
H.J.Res. 113	1/3/1973	93	Saylor	Amendment – Judicial Review
H.J.Res. 60	1/3/1973	93	Bennett	Statute – Judicial Review
H.R. 1391	1/5/1973	93	Edwards (AL)	Statute – Composition
H.J.Res. 130	1/6/1973	93	Bevill	Amendment – Composition
H.J.Res. 149	1/9/1973	93	Rarick	Amendment – Composition
S.J.Res. 13	1/9/1973	93	Byrd (VA)	Amendment – Composition
S.J.Res. 16	1/11/1973	93	Scott (VA)	Amendment – Composition
H.J.Res. 199	1/18/1973	93	Brinkley	Amendment – Composition
H.R. 3324	1/30/1973	93	Wiggins	Statute – Composition
H.J.Res. 323	2/7/1973	93	Teague (TX)	Amendment – Judicial Review
H.J.Res. 324	2/7/1973	93	Teague (TX)	Amendment – Composition
H.J.Res. 326	2/7/1973	93	Teague (TX)	Amendment – Composition
H.J.Res. 325	2/7/1973	93	Teague (TX)	Amendment – Composition
H.J.Res. 461	3/26/1973	93	Broomfield	Amendment – Composition
H.J.Res. 475	4/3/1973	93	W.C. Daniel	Amendment – Composition
H.J.Res. 477	4/3/1973	93	Sikes	Amendment – Procedure
H.J.Res. 511	4/16/1973	93	Sikes	Amendment – Composition
H.J.Res. 583	5/30/1973	93	Archer	Amendment – Composition
H.R. 9044	6/28/1973	93	Gunter	Statute – Remedy
S. 2455	7/20/1973	93	Tunney	Statute – Composition
H.R. 1133	1/14/1974	93	Waggoner	Statute – Jurisdiction
H.R. 14337	4/24/1974	93	Crane	Statute – Jurisdiction
H.R. 14336	4/24/1974	93	Crane	Statute – Jurisdiction
S. 3981	9/11/1974	93	Helms	Statute – Jurisdiction
H.R. 17147	10/8/1974	93	Flood	Statute – Jurisdiction
H.R. 523	1/14/1975	94	Holt	Statute – Jurisdiction
H.J.Res. 84	1/14/1975	94	Teague (TX)	Amendment – Judicial Review
H.J.Res. 88	1/14/1975	94	Teague (TX)	Amendment – Composition
H.J.Res. 86	1/14/1975	94	Teague (TX)	Amendment – Composition
H.J.Res. 75	1/14/1975	94	Pettis	Amendment – Composition
H.J.Res. 87	1/14/1975	94	Teague (Tex)	Amendment – Composition
H.J.Res. 44	1/14/1975	94	Downing	Amendment – Composition
H.J.Res. 16	1/14/1975	94	Robinson	Amendment – Composition
H.R. 1515	1/16/1975	94	Dingell	Statute – Jurisdiction
H.R. 1678	1/20/1975	94	Flood	Statute – Jurisdiction
S. 283	1/21/1975	94	Helms	Statute – Jurisdiction
H.R. 1971	1/23/1975	94	Quillen	Statute – Jurisdiction
S.J.Res. 14	1/23/1975	94	Scott (VA)	Amendment – Composition
S.J.Res. 16	1/27/1975	94	Byrd (VA)	Amendment – Composition
H.J.Res. 164	1/29/1975	94	Whitten	Amendment – Composition

Bill	Date Sponsored	Congress	Sponsor	Type of Legislation
H.J.Res. 169	1/29/1975	94	Whitten	Misc
H.R. 2414	1/30/1975	94	Ashbrook	Statute – Jurisdiction
H.R. 2509	1/31/1975	94	Bevill	Statute – Jurisdiction
H.R. 4811	3/12/1975	94	Wampler	Statute – Jurisdiction
S. 1295	3/21/1975	94	Roth	Statute – Jurisdiction
H.R. 5658	4/7/1975	94	Crane	Statute – Jurisdiction
H.J.Res. 390	4/15/1975	94	Brinkley	Amendment – Composition
H.J.Res. 417	4/29/1975	94	Broomfield	Amendment – Composition
H.R. 9806	9/24/1975	94	Crane	Statute – Remedy
H.J.Res. 669	9/24/1975	94	Snyder	Amendment – Composition
H.J.Res. 851	3/4/1976	94	Broyhill	Statute – Composition
S.J.Res. 175	3/4/1976	94	Allen	Amendment – Composition
H.J.Res. 868	3/16/1976	94	Jacobs	Amendment – Composition
H.J.Res. 921	4/13/1976	94	Milford	Statute – Composition
H.R. 15169	8/10/1976	94	Paul	Statute – Jurisdiction
H.J.Res. 1079	8/30/1976	94	Ketchum	Amendment – Composition
H.R. 15502	9/9/1976	94	Kemp	Statute – Jurisdiction
H.R. 154	1/4/1977	95	Ashbrook	Statute – Jurisdiction
H.R. 391	1/4/1977	95	Holt	Statute – Jurisdiction
H.R. 1159	1/4/1977	95	Quillen	Statute – Jurisdiction
H.R. 392	1/4/1977	95	Holt	Statute – Remedy
H.R. 1178	1/4/1977	95	Roberts	Statute – Remedy
H.R. 153	1/4/1977	95	Ashbrook	Statute – Remedy
H.R. 1350	1/4/1977	95	Teague (TX)	Statute – Remedy
H.R. 1111	1/4/1977	95	O'Brien	Statute – Remedy
H.R. 1351	1/4/1977	95	Teague (TX)	Statute – Remedy
H.R. 1353	1/4/1977	95	Teague (TX)	Statute – Remedy
H.Res. 26	1/4/1977	95	Conte	Resolutions
H.Res. 66	1/4/1977	95	Roe	Resolutions
H.J.Res. 7	1/4/1977	95	Robinson	Amendment – Composition
H.J.Res. 16	1/4/1977	95	Brinkley	Amendment – Composition
H.R. 1914	1/13/1977	95	Waggoner	Statute – Jurisdiction
H.J.Res. 223	2/1/1977	95	Robinson	Amendment – Composition
S.J.Res. 19	2/1/1977	95	Byrd (VA)	Amendment – Composition
H.R. 3956	2/23/1977	95	Snyder	Statute – Remedy
H.R. 3955	2/23/1977	95	Snyder	Statute – Remedy
H.J.Res. 279	2/23/1977	95	Snyder	Amendment – Composition
H.J.Res. 270	2/23/1977	95	Broomfield	Amendment – Composition
S.J.Res. 31	3/1/1977	95	Scott	Amendment – Composition
H.R. 4273	3/2/1977	95	Crane	Statute – Jurisdiction
H.R. 4274	3/2/1977	95	Crane	Statute – Remedy
H.R. 4479	3/3/1977	95	McDonald	Statute – Remedy

(*continued*)

TABLE B.1 *(continued)*

Bill	Date Sponsored	Congress	Sponsor	Type of Legislation
H.R. 5703	3/29/1977	95	Shipley	Statute – Jurisdiction
H.R. 6596	4/25/1977	95	Evans (DE)	Statute – Remedy
H.J.Res. 414	4/25/1977	95	White	Amendment – Jurisdiction
S. 1467	5/5/1977	95	Roth	Statute – Jurisdiction
H.R. 7422	5/25/1977	95	Dickinson	Statute – Remedy
H.J.Res. 543	7/12/1977	95	Jacobs	Amendment – Composition
S.J.Res. 76	7/21/1977	95	Roth	Amendment – Composition
S. 2573	2/23/1978	95	Helms	Statute – Jurisdiction
S. 2989	4/25/1978	95	Helms	Misc
H.R. 13677	8/1/1978	95	Flowers	Misc
H.R. 446	1/15/1979	96	Holt	Statute – Jurisdiction
H.J.Res. 77	1/15/1979	96	Robinson	Amendment – Composition
H.R. 993	1/18/1979	96	P. Crane	Statute – Jurisdiction
H.R. 1082	1/18/1979	96	Quillen	Statute – Jurisdiction
H.R. 992	1/18/1979	96	P. Crane	Statute – Remedy
S.Res. 160	1/24/1979	96	Quayle	Amendment – Composition
H.J.Res. 188	2/5/1979	96	J. Edwards	Amendment – Composition
H.J.Res. 191	2/8/1979	96	Applegate	Amendment – Composition
S. 438	2/21/1979	96	Helms	Statute – Jurisdiction
H.J.Res. 315	5/1/1979	96	Jacobs	Amendment – Composition
H.R. 4109	5/16/1979	96	Dornan	Statute – Judicial Review
H.R. 4111	5/16/1979	96	Dornan	Statute – Judicial Review
H.R. 4110	5/16/1979	96	Dornan	Statute – Procedure
H.R. 4200	5/23/1979	96	Dornan	Statute – Procedure
H.R. 4200	5/23/1979	96	Dornan	Statute – Procedure
H.J.Res. 1102	8/1/1979	96	Flowers	Amendment – Composition
S. 1808	9/24/1979	96	Laxalt	Statute – Jurisdiction
H.J.Res. 318	10/12/1979	96	Brinkley	Amendment – Composition
S.J.Res. 110	10/12/1979	96	Boren	Amendment – Composition
S. 2070	11/30/1979	96	W. Roth	Statute – Jurisdiction
H.R. 6028	12/4/1979	96	Symms	Statute – Jurisdiction
H.J.Res. 465	12/13/1979	96	Hyde	Amendment – Composition
H.J.Res. 482	1/23/1980	96	Rousselot	Amendment – Composition
H.J.Res. 491	1/30/1980	96	Paul	Amendment – Composition
H.R. 7445	5/22/1980	96	Symms	Statute – Jurisdiction
H.R. 311	1/5/1981	97	Hansen	Statute – Jurisdiction
H.R. 72	1/5/1981	97	Ashbrook	Statute – Jurisdiction
H.R. 73	1/5/1981	97	Ashbrook	Statute – Jurisdiction
H.R. 340	1/5/1981	97	Holt	Statute – Jurisdiction
H.R. 408	1/5/1981	97	Quillen	Statute – Jurisdiction
H.J.Res. 60	1/5/1981	97	Robinson	Amendment – Composition
H.J.Res. 8	1/5/1981	97	Applegate	Amendment – Composition

Bill	Date Sponsored	Congress	Sponsor	Type of Legislation
H.R. 761	1/6/1981	97	McDonald	Statute – Remedy
H.R. 867	1/16/1981	97	Crane	Statute – Jurisdiction
H.R. 869	1/16/1981	97	Crane	Statute – Remedy
H.R. 900	1/19/1981	97	Hyde	Statute – Jurisdiction
S. 158	1/19/1981	97	Helms	Statute – Jurisdiction
H.R. 1079	1/22/1981	97	Hinson	Statute – Remedy
S.J.Res. 21	1/27/1981	97	Boren	Amendment – Composition
S.J.Res. 24	1/29/1981	97	Durenberger	Amendment – Composition
S. 481	2/16/1981	97	Helms	Statute – Jurisdiction
H.R. 2047	2/24/1981	97	Moore	Statute – Remedy
S. 528	2/24/1981	97	Johnston	Statute – Remedy
H.R. 2347	3/5/1981	97	Crane	Statute – Jurisdiction
H.R. 2365	3/9/1981	97	Evans	Statute – Jurisdiction
H.R. 2791	3/24/1981	97	Evans	Statute – Jurisdiction
S. 1005	4/27/1981	97	Helms	Statute – Remedy
H.R. 4756	10/15/1981	97	Dowdy	Statute – Jurisdiction
H.R. 5183	12/11/1981	97	Dornan	Statute – Judicial Review
H.R. 5182	12/11/1981	97	Dornan	Statute – Judicial Review
H.R. 5181	12/11/1981	97	Dornan	Statute – Procedure
H.J.Res. 419	3/3/1982	97	Clinger	Amendment – Composition
H.J.Res. 451	3/31/1982	97	A. Smith	Amendment – Composition
H.J.Res. 570	8/12/1982	97	Fuqua	Amendment – Composition
S. 3018	10/1/1982	97	East	Statute – Jurisdiction
H.R. 183	1/3/1983	98	Holt	Statute – Jurisdiction
H.R. 253	1/3/1983	98	Quillen	Statute – Jurisdiction
H.R. 158	1/3/1983	98	Hansen	Statute – Remedy
H.J.Res. 17	1/3/1983	98	Fuqua	Amendment – Composition
H.J.Res. 28	1/3/1983	98	Hansen	Amendment – Remedy
H.R. 520	1/6/1983	98	Crane	Statute – Jurisdiction
H.R. 523	1/6/1983	98	Crane	Statute – Jurisdiction
H.R. 525	1/6/1983	98	Crane	Statute – Jurisdiction
H.R. 521	1/6/1983	98	Crane	Statute – Remedy
H.J.Res. 144	2/15/1983	98	Jacobs	Amendment – Composition
S.J.Res. 39	2/22/1983	98	Boren	Amendment – Composition
S. 784	3/11/1983	98	Helms	Statute – Jurisdiction
H.J.Res. 252	4/28/1983	98	Corcoran	Amendment – Composition
H.J.Res. 651	9/25/1984	98	Volkmer	Amendment – Remedy
H.R. 79	1/3/1985	99	Crane	Statute – Jurisdiction
H.R. 80	1/3/1985	99	Crane	Statute – Jurisdiction
H.R. 81	1/3/1985	99	Crane	Statute – Remedy
S. 47	1/3/1985	99	Helms	Statute – Jurisdiction
H.J.Res. 56	1/3/1985	99	Fuqua	Amendment – Composition

(*continued*)

TABLE B.I *(continued)*

Bill	Date Sponsored	Congress	Sponsor	Type of Legislation
H.J.Res. 30	1/3/1985	99	Jacobs	Amendment – Composition
S.J.Res. 30	1/24/1985	99	Boren	Amendment – Composition
H.R. 1211	2/21/1985	99	Gaydos	Statute – Remedy
H.J.Res. 403	10/1/1985	99	Dorman	Amendment – Judicial Review
H.J.Res. 557	3/10/1986	99	Dorgan	Amendment – Composition
H.R. 103	1/6/1987	100	Crane	Statute – Jurisdiction
H.R. 104	1/6/1987	100	Crane	Statute – Jurisdiction
H.R. 160	1/6/1987	100	Gaydos	Statute – Remedy
H.R. 105	1/6/1987	100	Crane	Statute – Remedy
S. 213	1/6/1987	100	Helms	Statute – Jurisdiction
H.J.Res. 71	1/7/1987	100	Jacobs	Amendment – Composition
H.J.Res. 177	3/10/1987	100	Dorgan	Amendment – Composition
H.J.Res. 325	6/25/1987	100	Applegate	Amendment – Composition
S. 2001	1/25/1988	100	Helms	Statute – Jurisdiction
H.J.Res. 15	1/3/1989	101	Jacobs	Amendment – Composition
H.J.Res. 66	1/4/1989	101	Applegate	Amendment – Composition
S.Res. 151	6/22/1989	101	Mitchell	Misc
S. 2106	2/8/1990	101	Thurmond	Statute – Composition
S.J.Res. 295	4/20/1990	101	Danforth	Amendment – Remedy
H.J.Res. 564	5/7/1990	101	Clay	Amendment – Remedy
H.J.Res. 560	5/21/1990	101	Thomas	Amendment – Remedy
H.J.Res. 71	1/11/1991	102	Fields	Amendment – Composition
H.J.Res. 74	1/11/1991	102	Sensebrenner	Amendment – Composition
S. 77	1/14/1991	102	Helms	Statute – Judicial Review
S. 135	1/14/1991	102	Thurmond	Statute – Composition
H.J.Res. 85	1/22/1991	102	Applegate	Amendment – Composition
H.J.Res. 119	2/6/1991	102	Jacobs	Amendment – Composition
H.J.Res. 192	3/19/1991	102	Coleman	Amendment – Remedy
S. 1818	10/8/1991	102	Hatch	Statute – Composition
H.J.Res. 382	11/25/1991	102	English	Amendment – Composition
H.J.Res. 554	9/24/1992	102	DeFazio	Amendment – Composition
S.J.Res. 345	10/2/1992	102	Danforth	Amendment – Remedy
H.J.Res. 5	1/5/1993	103	Applegate	Amendment – Composition
H.J.Res. 40	1/5/1993	103	Sensebrenner	Amendment – Composition
H.J.Res. 59	1/6/1993	103	Fields (TX)	Amendment – Composition
S. 46	1/21/1993	103	Thurmond	Statute – Composition
H.J.Res. 73	1/26/1993	103	Jacobs	Amendment – Composition
S. 620	3/18/1993	103	Riegle	Misc
H.R. 1480	3/25/1993	103	Sangmeister	Statute – Composition
H.J.Res. 277	10/14/1993	103	English	Amendment – Composition
H.J.Res. 324	2/10/1994	103	Sarpalius	Amendment – Composition
S. 2147	5/24/1994	103	DeConcini	Statute – Procedure

Bill	Date Sponsored	Congress	Sponsor	Type of Legislation
S. 52	1/4/1995	104	Helms	Statute – Composition
H.J.Res. 63	1/24/1995	104	Fields	Amendment – Composition
H.R. 1170	3/8/1995	104	Bono	Statute – Judicial Review
H.R. 1624	5/12/1995	104	Dornan (CA)	Statute – Jurisdiction
H.R. 1958	6/29/1995	104	Dornan (CA)	Statute – Jurisdiction
H.R. 2087	7/20/1995	104	Stockman (TX)	Statute – Jurisdiction
H.J.Res. 160	2/16/1996	104	Hayes (LA)	Amendment – Composition
H.R. 3100	3/14/1996	104	Manzullo (IL)	Statute – Remedy
S. 33	1/21/1997	105	Thurmond	Statute – Composition
S. 42	1/21/1997	105	Helms (NC)	Statute – Jurisdiction
H.R. 1027	3/13/1997	105	Paxon (NY)	Statute – Judicial Review
H.R. 1170	3/20/1997	105	Bono (CA)	Statute – Judicial Review
H.R. 1252	4/9/1997	105	Hyde (IL)	Statute – Judicial Review
H.R. 1280	4/10/1997	105	Chabot (OH)	Misc
S.J.Res. 26	4/23/1997	105	Smith (NH)	Amendment – Composition
H.J.Res. 77	5/7/1997	105	Hefley	Amendment – Composition
H.R. 3182	2/11/1998	105	Manzullo	Statute – Remedy
H.J.Res. 110	2/11/1998	105	Manzullo	Amendment – Remedy
H.Res. 591	10/9/1998	105	Meeks	Misc
S. 40	1/19/1999	106	Helms	Misc
H.R. 111	3/11/1999	106	Meeks	Misc
H.R. 1281	3/25/1999	106	Chabot	Misc
S. 16	3/25/1999	106	Smith (NH)	Amendment – Composition
S. 721	3/25/1999	106	Grassley	Misc
S.J.Res. 99	3/25/1999	106	Smith (NH)	Amendment – Composition
H.J.Res. 59	6/17/1999	106	Manzullo	Amendment – Remedy
H.Con.Res. 142	6/23/1999	106	Stearns	Resolutions
H.Con.Res. 377	7/19/1999	106	Kaptur	Resolutions
H.Con.Res. 199	10/19/1999	106	Bonilla	Resolutions
S. 3086	9/21/2000	106	Specter	Misc
S. 191	1/25/2001	107	Feingold	Statute – Jurisdiction
S. 986	6/5/2001	107	Grassley	Misc
H.R. 2519	7/17/2001	107	Chabot	Misc
H.Res. 466	6/26/2002	107	Israel	Resolutions
H.Con.Res. 428	6/26/2002	107	Hilleary	Resolutions
H.R. 5101	7/11/2002	107	Hefley	Other
H.R. 118	1/7/2003	108	Hefley	Other
S. 554	3/6/2003	108	Grassley	Misc
H.Res. 132	3/6/2003	108	Ose	Resolution
H.R. 2028	5/8/2003	108	Akin	Statute – Jurisdiction
H.R. 2155	5/20/2003	108	Chabot	Misc
H.R. 3313	10/16/2003	108	Hostettler	Statute – Jurisdiction

(*continued*)

TABLE B.1 *(continued)*

Bill	Date Sponsored	Congress	Sponsor	Type of Legislation
H.Res. 446	11/18/2003	108	Ryun	Resolution
H.Res. 468	11/21/2003	108	Graves	Resolution
H.R. 3799	2/11/2004	108	Aderholt	Statute – Jurisdiction
S. 2082	2/12/2004	108	Shelby	Statute – Jurisdiction
H.R. 3893	3/4/2004	108	Paul	Statute – Jurisdiction
H.R. 3920	3/9/2004	108	Lewis (KY)	Statute – Judicial Review
H.Res. 568	3/17/2004	108	Feeney	Resolution
H.R. 4118	4/1/2004	108	Paul (TX)	Resolution
S. 2323	4/20/2004	108	Shelby (AL)	Statute – Jurisdiction
S.Con.Res. 130	7/21/2004	108	Hatch	Resolution
H.R. 4892	7/22/2004	108	Istook	Statute – Jurisdiction
H.Con.Res. 478	7/22/2004	108	Coble	Resolution
H.Con.Res. 52	2/9/2005	109	Sullivan	Resolution
H.R. 776	2/10/2005	109	Paul	Statute – Jurisdiction
H.Res. 97	2/15/2005	109	Feeney	Resolution
H.R. 1100	3/3/2005	109	Hostettler	Statute – Jurisdiction
H.R. 1070	3/3/2005	109	Aderholt	Statute – Jurisdiction
S. 520	3/3/2005	109	Shelby (AL)	Statute – Jurisdiction
H.R. 1658	4/14/2005	109	Paul	Resolution
H.Res. 214	4/14/2005	109	King (IA)	Resolution
S. 829	4/18/2005	109	Grassley	Resolution
S. 1046	5/17/2005	109	Kyl	Statute – Jurisdiction
H.R. 2422	5/18/2005	109	Chabot	Misc
H.Res. 311	6/9/2005	109	Delauro	Resolution
H.Res. 340	6/24/2005	109	Gingrey	Resolution
H.Con.Res. 194	6/26/2005	109	Melancon	Resolution
H.R. 3073	6/27/2005	109	Lewis (KY)	Statute – Judicial Review
H.R. 3631	7/29/2005	109	Hefley	Resolution
S.Res. 243	9/15/2005	109	Talent	Resolution
H.Con.Res. 245	9/15/2005	109	Issa	Resolution
H.Res. 453	9/20/2005	109	McCotter	Resolution
S. 1768	9/26/2005	109	Specter (PA)	Misc
H.Con.Res. 253	9/27/2005	109	Bonilla	Resolution
H.R. 4379	11/17/2005	109	Paul (TX)	Statute – Jurisdiction
H.R. 4364	11/17/2005	109	Barrett	Statute – Jurisdiction
H.R. 4380	11/17/2005	109	Poe	Misc
H.R. 4576	12/16/2005	109	Pickering	Statute – Jurisdiction
H.Con.Res. 333	2/1/2006	109	Kaptur	Other
H.R. 5151	4/6/2006	109	Nadler	Resolution
S. 2593	4/6/2006	109	Boxer	Resolution
H.J.Res. 84	4/27/2006	109	Akin	Resolution
H.R. 5295	5/4/2006	109	Davis	Other

Bill	Date Sponsored	Congress	Sponsor	Type of Legislation
H.R. 5528	6/6/2006	109	Cannon	Statute – Jurisdiction
H.R. 5739	6/29/2006	109	Paul	Statute – Jurisdiction
S. 2389	7/20/2006	109	Akin	Statute – Jurisdiction
S. 3731	7/26/2006	109	Specter	Resolution
S. 4009	9/29/2006	109	Menendez	Other
S. 4051	11/14/2006	109	Specter	Resolution
S.J.Res. 6	1/4/2007	110	Kaptur (OH)	Other
H.R. 300	1/5/2007	110	Paul (TX)	Jurisdiction
H.J.Res. 9	1/5/2007	110	Emerson (MO)	Other
H.J.Res. 11	1/5/2007	110	Emerson (MO)	Other
H.J.Res. 12	1/11/2007	110	Murtha (PA)	Other
H.J.Res. 13	1/11/2007	110	Murtha (PA)	Other
S. 352	1/22/2007	110	Grassley (IA)	Misc
S. 344	1/22/2007	110	Specter (PA)	Misc
H.R. 699	1/29/2007	110	Akin (MO)	Jurisdiction
H.R. 724	1/30/2007	110	Burton (IN)	Jurisdiction
H.J.Res. 22	2/6/2007	110	Lungren (CA)	Other
H.J.Res. 31	2/13/2007	110	Jackson (IL)	Other
H.R. 1094	2/15/2007	110	Paul (TX)	Misc
H.J.Res. 38	2/27/2007	110	Platts (PA)	Other
H.R. 1299	3/1/2007	110	Poe	Misc
H.R. 2104	5/2/2007	110	Barrett (SC)	Misc
H.R. 2128	5/3/2007	110	Chabot (OH)	Misc
H.Res. 372	5/3/2007	110	Feeney (FL)	Misc
H.R. 2594	6/6/2007	110	Paul (TX)	Misc
H.R. 2898	6/28/2007	110	Akin (MO)	Composition
H.R. 5514	2/28/2008	110	Cannon	Jurisdiction
H.Res. 1076	4/3/2008	110	McKeon (CA)	Misc
S.Res. 572	5/21/2008	110	Dole	Other
H.Res. 1264	6/11/2008	110	Gingrey	Misc
S.Res. 626	7/25/2008	110	Vitter	Misc

Bibliography

Abraham, Henry J. 1999. *Justices, Presidents, and Senators: A History of the U.S. Supreme Court Appointments from Washington to Clinton*. Lanham, MD: Rowman & Littlefield Publishers, Inc.

Achen, Christopher H. 1977. "Measuring Representation: Perils of the Correlation Coefficient." *American Journal of Political Science* 21(4):805–15.

Achen, Christopher H. 1978. "Measuring Representation." *American Journal of Political Science* 22(3):475–510.

Ackerman, Bruce. 1998. *We the People 2: Transformations*. Cambridge, MA: Belknap.

Adamany, David. 1973. "Law and Society: Legitimacy, Realigning Elections, and the Supreme Court." *Wisconsin Law Review* 1973(3):790–846.

Alivizatos, Nicos. 1995. Judges as Veto Players. In *Parliaments and Majority Rule in Western Europe*, ed. Herbert Doring. New York: St. Martin's Press.

Ansolabehere, Stephen, James M. Snyder, Jr. and Charles Stewart III. 2001. "Candidate Positioning in U.S. House Elections." *American Journal of Political Science* 45(1):136–59.

Barro, Robert. 2000. Democracy and the Rule of Law. In *Governing for Prosperity*, ed. Bruce Bueno de Mesquita and Hilton Root. New Haven, CT: Yale University Press pp. 209–31.

Bartels, Larry M. 1991. "Constituency Opinion and Congressional Policy Making: The Reagan Defense Buildup." *American Political Science Review* 85(2):457–74.

Baum, Lawrence. 2007. *Judges and Their Audiences: A Perspective on Judicial Behavior*. Princeton, NJ: Princeton University Press.

Bell, Lauren C. and Kevin M. Scott. 2006. "Policy Statements or Symbolic Politics? Explaining Congressional Court-Limiting Attempts." *Judicature* 89(4):196–201.

Bensel, Richard F. 2000. *The Political Economy of American Industrialization, 1877–1900*. New York: Cambridge University Press.

Bickel, Alexander M. 1962. *The Least Dangerous Branch: The Supreme Court at the Bar of Politics*. New Haven, CT: Yale University Press.

Boucher, Robert L., Jr. and Jeffrey A. Segal. 1995. "Supreme Court Justices as Strategic Decision Makers: Aggressive Grants and Defensive Denials on the Vinson Court." *Journal of Politics* 57(3):824–37.

Brandt, Patrick T. and John T. Williams. 2001. "A Linear Poisson Autoregressive Model: The Poisson AR(p) Model." *Political Analysis* 9(2):164–84.

Brandt, Patrick T., John T. Williams, Benjamin Fordham, and Brian Pollins. 2000. "Dynamic Modeling for Persistent Event-Count Time Series." *American Journal of Political Science* 44(4):823–43.

Breyer, Stephen. 2006. "Fair and Independent Courts: A Conference on the State of the Judiciary." Transcript of Remarks by Stephen Breyer. Georgetown Law Center, Washington, DC, September 28, 2006.

Burbank, Stephen B. and Barry Friedman, eds. 2002. *Judicial Independence at the Crossroads: An Interdisciplinary Approach*. Thousand Oaks, CA: Sage Publications.

Burton, Harold H., J. 1955. "Two Significant Decisions: *Ex Parte Milligan* and *Ex Parte McCardle*." *American Bar Association Journal* (2).

Cain, Bruce, John Ferejohn and Morris Fiorina. 1987. *The Personal Vote: Constituency Service and Electoral Independence*. Cambridge, MA: Harvard University Press.

Caldeira, Gregory A. 1986. "Neither the Purse Nor the Sword: Dynamics of Public Confidence in the Supreme Court." *The American Political Science Review* 80(4):1209–26.

Caldeira, Gregory A. 1987. "Public Opinion and the U.S. Supreme Court: FDR's Court-Packing Plan." *The American Political Science Review* 81(4):1139–53.

Caldeira, Gregory A. and James L. Gibson. 1992. "The Etiology of Public Support for the Supreme Court." *American Journal of Political Science* 36(3):635–64.

Caldeira, Gregory A. and James L. Gibson. 1995. "The Legitimacy of the Court of Justice in the European Union: Models of Institutional Support." *American Political Science Review* 89(2):356–76.

Cameron, A. Colin and Pravin K. Trivedi. 1998. *Regression Analysis of Count Data*. New York: Cambridge University Press.

Cameron, Charles M. and Tom S. Clark. 2007. "Is the Median Justice Really King? Micro-Theories and the Macro-Politics of the U.S. Supreme Court, 1952–2004." Presented at the Annual Meeting of the American Political Science Association.

Cameron, Charles M., Jeffrey A. Segal and Donald R. Songer. 2000. "Strategic Auditing in a Political Hierarchy: An Informational Model of the Supreme Court's Certiorari Decisions." *American Political Science Review* 94:101–16.

Canes-Wrone, Brandice. 2006. *Who Leads Whom? Presidents, Policy, and the Public*. Chicago: University of Chicago Press.

Canes-Wrone, Brandice, David W. Brady and John F. Cogan. 2002. "Out of Step, Out of Office: Electoral Accountability and House Members' Voting." *American Political Science Review* 96(1):127–40.

Carrubba, Clifford J. 2003. "The European Court of Justice, Democracy, and Enlargement." *European Union Politics* 4(1):75–100.

Carrubba, Clifford J. 2005. "Courts and Compliance in International Regulatory Regimes." *Journal of Politics* 67(3):669–89.

Carrubba, Clifford J. 2009. "A Model of the Endogenous Development of Judicial Institutions in Federal and International Systems." *Journal of Politics* 71(1):55–69.

Carrubba, Clifford J., Barry Friedman, Andrew Martin and Georg Vanberg. 2007. "Does the Median Justice Control the Content of Supreme Court Opinions?" Presented at the Conference on Empirical Legal Studies.

Casey, Gregory. 1976. "Popular Perceptions of Supreme Court Rulings." *American Politics Quarterly* 4(1):3–45.

Casper, Jonathan D. 1976. "The Supreme Court and National Policy Making." *The American Political Science Review* 70(1):50–63.

Clark, John A. and Kevin T. McGuire. 1996. "Congress, the Supreme Court, and the Flag." *Political Research Quarterly* 49(4):771–81.

Clark, Tom S. and Benjamin Lauderdale. Forthcoming. "Locating Supreme Court Opinions in Doctrine Space." *American Journal of Political Science.*

Clark, Tom S. and Keith E. Whittington. 2007. "Judicial Review of Acts of Congress, 1790–2006." Paper presented at the 2006 meeting of the Midwest Political Science Association, Chicago, IL.

Clinton, Joshua D. and John Lapinski. 2008. "Laws and Roll Calls in the U.S. Congress, 1891–1994." *Legislative Studies Quarterly* 33(4):511–42.

Clinton, Robert Lowry. 1994. "Game Theory, Legal History, and the Origins of Judicial Review: A Revisionist Anaylsis of Marbury v. Madison." *American Journal of Political Science* 38:285–302.

Commission on Separation of Powers and Judicial Independence. 1997. An Independent Judiciary. Technical report American Bar Association Washington, DC.

Cox, Gary W. and Matthew D. McCubbins. 1993. *Legislative Leviathan: Party Government in the House.* New York: Cambridge University Press.

Cross, Frank N. and Blake J. Nelson. 2001. "Strategic Institutional Effects on Supreme Court Decisionmaking." *Northwestern University Law Review* 95(4):1437–93.

Cushman, Barry. 1998. *Rethinking the New Deal Court.* New York: Oxford University Press.

Dahl, Robert. 1957. "Decision-Making in a Democracy: The Supreme Court as National Policy-Maker." *Journal of Public Law* 6(2):279–95.

Denzau, Arthur T. and Robert J. Mackay. 1983. "Gatekeeping and Monopoly Power of Committees: An Analysis of Sincere and Sophisticated Behavior." *American Journal of Political Science* 27(4):740–61.

Devins, Neal. 2006. "Should the Supreme Court Fear Congress?" *Minnesota Law Review* 90(5):1337–62.

Dickey, David and Wayne A. Fuller. 1979. "Distribution of the Estimates for Autoregressive Time Series with a Unit Root." *Journal of the American Statistical Association* 74(366):427–31.

Dickey, David and Wayne A. Fuller. 1981. "Likelihood Ration Statistics for Autoregressive Time Series with a Unit Root." *Econometrica* 49(4):1057–72.

Dolbeare, Kenneth M. and Phillip E. Hammond. 1968. "The Political Party Basis of Attitudes toward the Supreme Court." *Public Opinion Quarterly* 37(1):16–30.

Durr, Robert H., Andrew D. Martin and Christina Wolbrecht. 2000. "Ideological Divergence and Public Support for the Supreme Court." *American Journal of Political Science* 44(4):768–76.

Easton, David. 1965. *A Systems Analysis of Political Life*. New York: Wiley.

Eisgruber, Christopher L. 2001. *Constitutional Self-Government*. Cambridge, MA: Harvard University Press.

Eisgruber, Christopher L. 2007. *The Next Justice*. Princeton, NJ: Princeton University Press.

Ely, John Hart. 1980. *Democracy and Distrust: A Theory of Judicial Review*. Cambridge, MA: Harvard University Press.

Enders, Walter. 2004. *Applied Econometric Time Series*. 2nd ed. Hoboken, NJ: John Wiley & Sons, Inc.

Epstein, Lee and Jack Knight. 1998. *The Choices Justices Make*. Washington, DC: CQ Press.

Epstein, Lee, Jack Knight and Andrew D. Martin. 2001. "The Supreme Court as a Strategic National Policymaker." *Emory Law Journal* 50(2):583–611.

Epstein, Lee, Andrew D. Martin, Jeffrey A. Segal and Chad Westerland. 2007. "The Judicial Common Space." *Journal of Law Economics & Organization* 23(2):303–325.

Epstein, Lee and Jeffrey A. Segal. 2005. *Advice and Consent: The Politics of Judicial Appointments*. New York: Oxford University Press.

Epstein, Lee, Jeffrey A. Segal, Harold J. Spaeth and Thomas G. Walker. 2007. *The Supreme Court Compendium: Data, Decisions and Developments*. 4th ed. Washington, DC: Congressional Quarterly, Inc.

Erikson, Robert S. 1978. "Constituency Opinion and Congressional Behavior: A Reeexamination of the Miller-Srokes Representation Data." *American Journal of Political Science* 22(3):511–35.

Erikson, Robert S., Michael B. MacKuen and James A. Stimson. 2002. *The Macro Polity*. New York: Cambridge University Press.

Erikson, Robert S., Gerald C. Wright and John P. McIver. 1993. *Statehouse Democracy: Public Opinion and Policy in the American States*. New York: Cambridge University Press.

Eskridge, William N., Jr. 1991*a*. "Overriding Supreme Court Statutory Interpretation Decisions." *Yale Law Journal* 101(1):331–455.

Eskridge, William N., Jr. 1991*b*. "Reneging on History? Playing the Court/Congress/President Civil Rights Game." *California Law Review* 79(2):613–84.

Fenno, Richard F., Jr. 1973. *Congressmen in Committees*. Boston, MA: Little, Brown.

Fenno, Richard F., Jr. 1978. *Home Style: House Members in Their Districts*. New York: Longman.

Ferejohn, John. 1999. "Independent Judges, Dependent Judiciary." *Southern California Law Review* 72(1):353–84.

Ferejohn, John and Charles Shipan. 1990. "Congressional Influence on Bureaucracy." *Journal of Law, Economics & Organization* 6(Special Issue):1–20.

Ferejohn, John and Barry Weingast. 1992. "The Limitation of Statutes: Strategic Statutory Interpretation." *Georgetown Law Journal* 80(3):565–82.

Fink, Howard P. 1981. "Undoing the High Court." *The New York Times*, July 17, A23.

Fiorina, Morris P. 1974. *Representatives, Roll Calls, and Constituencies*. Lexington, MA: Lexington Books.

Fiorina, Morris P. 1977. *Congress: Keystone of the Washington Establishment*. New Haven, CT: Yale University Press.

Frankfurter, Felix and Nathan Greene. 1963. *The Labor Injunction*. Gloucester, MA: P. Smith.

Frees, Edward W. 2004. *Longitudinal and Panel Data: Analysis and Applications in the Social Sciences*. New York: Cambridge University Press.

Friedman, Barry. 2002. "The Birth of an Academic Obsession: The History of the Countermajoritarian Difficulty, Part Five." *Yale Law Journal* 112(2):153–259.

Friedman, Barry. 2005. "The Politics of Judicial Review." *Texas Law Review* 84:257–337.

Friedman, Barry. 2009. *The Will of the People: How Public Opinion Has Influenced the Supreme Court and Shaped the Meaning of the Constitution*. New York: Farrar, Straus and Giroux.

Friedman, Barry and Anna L. Harvey. 2003. "Electing the Supreme Court." *Indiana Law Journal* 78(1):123–51.

Friedman, Richard. 1994. "Switching Time and Other Thought Experiments: The Hughes Court and Constitutional Transformation." *University of Pennsylvania Law Review* 142(1994):1891–1984.

Gelman, Andrew. 2008. "Scaling Regression Inputs by Dividing by Two Standard Deviations." *Statistics in Medicine* 27(15):2865–73.

Gelman, Andrew and Jennifer Hill. 2007. *Data Analysis Using Regression and Multilevel/Hierarchical Models*. Cambridge: Cambridge University Press.

Gely, Rafael and Pablo T. Spiller. 1990. "A Rational Choice Theory of Supreme Court Statutory Decisions with Applications to the Farm and City Cases." *Journal of Law, Economics, and Organization* 6:263–300.

Gely, Rafael and Pablo T. Spiller. 1992. "The Political Economy of Supreme Court Constitutional Decisions: The Case of Roosevelt's Court-Packing Plan." *International Review of Law and Economics* 12(1):45–67.

Gibson, James L. 2008. "Challenges to the Impartiality of State Supreme Courts: Legitimacy Theory and 'New Style' Judicial Campaigns." *American Political Science Review* 102(1):59–75.

Gibson, James L. and Gregory A. Caldeira. 1995. "The Legitimacy of Transnational Legal Institutions: Compliance, Support, and the European Court of Justice." *American Journal of Political Science* 39(2):459–89.

Gibson, James L. and Gregory A. Caldeira. 1998. "Changes in the Legitimacy of the European Court of Justice: A Post-Maastricht Analysis." *British Journal of Political Science* 28(1):63–91.

Gibson, James L. and Gregory A. Caldeira. 2003. "Defenders of Democracy? Legitimacy, Popular Acceptance, and the South African Constitutional Court." *Journal of Politics* 65(1):1–30.

Gibson, James L. and Gregory A. Caldeira. 2009. *Citizens, Courts, and Confirmations*. Princeton, NJ: Princeton University Press.

Gibson, James L., Gregory A. Caldeira and Vanessa Baird. 1998. "On the Legitimacy of National High Courts." *American Political Science Review* 92(3):343–58.

Gibson, James L., Gregory A. Caldeira and Lester Kenyatta Spence. 2003. "Measuring Attitudes toward the United States Supreme Court." *American Journal of Political Science* 47(2):354–67.

Giles, Michael W., Virginia A. Hettinger and Todd Peppers. 2001. "Picking Federal Judges: A Note on Policy and Partisan Selection Agendas." *Political Research Quarterly* 54:623–41.

Ginsburg, Ruth Bader. 2006. "Judicial Independence: The Situation of the U.S. Federal Judiciary." *Nebraska Law Review* 85(1):1–14.

Goffman, Erving. 1959. *The Presentation of Self in Everyday Life*. New York: Doubleday.

Gompers, Samuel. 1984. *[1925]*. *Seventy Years of Life and Labor: An Autobiography*. Ithaca, NY: ILR Press.

Graber, Mark. 1993. "The Non-Majoritarian Problem: Legislative Deference to the Judiciary." *Studies in American Political Development* 7(1):35.

Gregory, Charles Noble. 1898. "Government by Injunction." *Harvard Law Review* 11(8):487–511.

Grosskopf, Anke and Jeffery J. Mondak. 1998. "Do Attitudes toward Specific Supreme Court Decisions Matter? The Impact of Webster and Texas v. Johnson on Public Confidence in the Supreme Court." *Political Research Quarterly* 51(3):633–54.

Grossman, Joel B. 1984. "Judicial Legitimacy and the Role of Courts: Shapiro's *Courts*." *American Bar Foundation Research Journal* 9(1):214–22.

Handberg, Roger and Harold F. Hill. 1980. "Court Curbing, Court Reversals, and Judicial Review: The Supreme Court versus Congress." *Law and Society Review* 14(2):309–22.

Hansford, Thomas G. and David F. Damore. 2000. "Congressional Preferences, Perceptions of Threat, and Supreme Court Decision Making." *American Politics Quarterly* 28(4):490–510.

Harvey, Anna and Barry Friedman. 2006. "The Limits of Judicial Independence: The Supreme Courts Constitutional Rulings, 1987–2000." *Legislative Studies Quarterly* 31(4):533–62.

Hattam, Victoria C. 1993. *Labor Visions and State Power: The Origins of Business Unionism in the United States*. Princeton, NJ: Princeton University Press.

Hausmaninger, Herbert. 1995. "Towards a New Russian Constitutional Court." *Cornell International Law Journal* 28(2):349–86.

Hausseger, Lori and Lawrence Baum. 1999. "Inviting Congressional Action: A Study of Supreme Court Motivations in Statutory Interpretation." *American Journal of Political Science* 43(1):162–85.

Helmke, Gretchen. 2002. "The Logic of Strategic Defection: Judicial Decision-Making in Argentina under Dictatorship and Democracy." *American Political Science Review* 96(2):291–303.

Henschen, Beth. 1983. "Statutory Interpretations of the Supreme Court." *American Political Science Review* 11(3):441–58.

Hettinger, Virginia and Christopher Zorn. 2005. "Explaining the Incidence and Timing of Congressional Responses to the U.S. Supreme Court." *Legislative Studies Quarterly* 30(1):5–28.

Highton, Benjamin and Michael S. Rocca. 2005. "Beyond the Roll-Call Arena: The Determinants of Position Taking in Congress." *Political Research Quarterly* 58(2):303–16.

Hochschild, Jennifer L. 1984. *The New American Dilemma*. New Haven, CT: Yale University Press.

Hoekstra, Valerie J. 2000. "The Supreme Court and Local Public Opinion." *American Political Science Review* 94(1):89–100.

Hoekstra, Valerie J. 2003. *Public Reaction to Supreme Court Decisions*. New York: Cambridge University Press.

Iaryczower, Matías, Pablo T. Spiller and Mariano Tommasi. 2002. "Judicial Independence in Unstable Environments, Argentina 1935–1998." *American Journal of Political Science* 46(4):699–716.

Ignagni, Joseph and James Meernik. 1994. "Explaining Congressional Attempts to Reverse Supreme Court Decisions." *Political Research Quarterly* 47(2):353–71.

Jaros, Dean and Robert Roper. 1980. "The U.S. Supreme Court Myth: Myth, Diffuse Support, Specific Support, and Legitimacy." *American Politics Quarterly* 8(1):85–105.

Johnson, Charles A. and Bradley C. Canon. 1984. *Judicial Policies: Implementation and Impact*. Washington, DC: Congressional Quarterly Press.

Kalman, Laura. 2005. "The Constitution, the Supreme Court, and the New Deal." *American Historical Review* 110(4):1052–80.

Kersch, Ken I. 2004. *Constructing Civil Liberties: Discontinuities in the Development of American Constitutional Law*. New York: Cambridge University Press.

Key, V. O. 1955. "A Theory of Critical Elections." *Journal of Politics* 17(1):3–18.

Keynes, Edward and Randall K. Miller. 1989. *The Court vs. Congress: Prayer, Busing, and Abortion*. Durham, NC: Duke University Press.

King, Gary. 1989. "Event Count Models for International Relations: Generalizations and Applications." *International Studies Quarterly* 33(2):123–47.

Klein, David and Darby Morrisroe. 1999. "The Prestige and Influence of Individual Judges on the U.S. Courts of Appeals." *Journal of Legal Studies* 28(2):371–92.

Knight, Jack and Lee Epstein. 1996. "On the Struggle for Judicial Supremacy." *Law & Society Review* 30(1):87–130.

Kramer, Larry D. 2004. *The People Themselves*. New York: Oxford University Press.

Krehbiel, Keith. 1998. *Pivotal Politics: A Theory of U.S. Lawmaking*. Chicago: University of Chicago Press.

Kutler, Stanley I. 1968. *Judicial Power and Reconstruction Politics*. Chicago: University of Chicago Press.

Landes, William M. and Richard A. Posner. 1975. "The Independent Judiciary in an Interest-Group Perspective." *Journal of Law and Economics* 18(3):875–901.

La Porta, Rafael, Florencio Lopez-de Silanes, Cristian Pop-Eleches and Andrei Shleifer. 2004. "Judicial Checks and Balances." *Journal of Political Economy* 112(2):445–70.

Lasser, William. 1988. *The Limits of Judicial Power: The Supreme Court in American Politics*. Chapel Hill, NC: University of North Carolina Press.

Lax, Jeffrey R. and Charles M. Cameron. 2007. "Bargaining and Opinion Assignment on the U.S. Supreme Court." *Journal of Law, Economics, and Organization* 23(2):276–302.

Lax, Jeffrey R. and Justin H. Phillips. 2009. "How Should We Estimate Public Opinion in the States?" *American Journal of Political Science* 53(1):107–21.

Leary, Mark R. 1996. *Self Presentation: Impression Management and Interpersonal Behavior*. Boulder, CO: Westview Press.

Leary, Mark R. 2007. "Motivational and Emotional Aspects of the Self." *Annual Review of Psychology* 58:317–44.

Leuchtenberg, William E. 1969. Franklin D. Roosevelt's Supreme Court "Packing" Plan. In *Essays on the New Deal*, ed. Harold M. Hollingsworth and William F. Holmes. Austin, TX: University of Texas Press.

Leuchtenberg, William E. 1995. *The Supreme Court Reborn: The Constitutional Revolution in the Age of Roosevelt*. New York: Oxford University Press.

Levinson, Sanford and Robert G. McCloskey. 2000. *The American Supreme Court*. 3 ed. Chicago: University of Chicago Press.

Lindquist, Stefanie A. and Rorie Spill Solberg. 2007. "Judicial Review in the Burger and Rehnquist Courts." *Political Research Quarterly* 60(1):71–90.

Llewellyn, Karl N. 1934. "On The Constitution as an Institution." *Columbia Law Review* 34(1):1–40.

Locke, John. 2003 [1690]. The Second Treatise of Government. In *Two Treatises of Government*, ed. Peter Laslett. New York: Cambridge University Press.

Lovell, George I. 2003. *Legislative Deferrals: Statutory Ambiguity, Judicial Power, and American Democracy*. New York: Cambridge University Press.

Maltzman, Forrest, James F. Spriggs and Paul J. Wahlbeck. 2000. *Crafting Law on the Supreme Court: The Collegial Game*. New York: Cambridge University Press.

Marks, Brian A. 1989. "A Model of Judicial Influence on Congressional Policymaking: *Grove City College v. Bell*." Ph.D. dissertation, Washington University.

Marshall, Thomas R. 1989a. "Policymaking and the Modern Court: When Do Supreme Court Rulings Prevail?" *The Western Political Quarterly* 42(4):493–507.

Marshall, Thomas R. 1989b. *Public Opinion and the Supreme Court*. Boston: Unwin Hyman.

Marshall, Thomas R. 2004. "Public Opinion Leadership and the Rehnquist Court." Paper delivered at the annual meeting of the Midwest Political Science Association, Chicago, IL.

Martin, Andrew D. 2001. "Congressional Decision Making and the Separation of Powers." *American Political Science Review* 95(2):361–78.

Martin, Andrew D. and Kevin M. Quinn. 2002. "Dynamic Ideal Point Estimation Via Markov Chain Monte Carlo for the U.S. Supreme Court, 1953–1999." *Political Analysis* 10(2):134–53.

Mason, Alpheus Thomas. 1956. *Harlan Fiske Stone: Pillar of the Law.* New York: Viking Press.

Mason, Alpheus Thomas. 1963. *The Supreme Court: Palladium of Freedom.* Ann Arbor, MI: University of Michigan Press.

Mathias, Charles McCurdy, Jr. 1982. "The Federal Courts Under Seige." *Annals of the American Academy of Political and Social Science* 462:–33.

Mayhew, David E. 1974. *Congress: The Electoral Connection.* New Haven, CT: Yale University Press.

Mayhew, David E. 2002. *Electoral Realignments: A Critique of an American Genre.* New Haven, CT: Yale University Press.

McCann, Michael. 1986. *Taking Reform Seriously: Perspectives on Public Interest Liberalism.* Ithaca, NY: Cornell University Press.

McCarty, Nolan, Keith T. Poole and Howard Rosenthal. 2006. *Polarized America: The Dance of Political Ideology and Unequal Riches.* Cambridge, MA: MIT Press.

McGuire, Kevin T. 2003. "The Constitution, The Supreme Court, and the Macropolity." Paper presented at the Annual Meeting of the Midwest Political Science Association, Chicago, IL.

McGuire, Kevin T. and James A. Stimson. 2004. "The Least Dangerous Branch Revisited: New Evidence on Supreme Court Responsiveness to Public Preferences." *Journal of Politics* 66(4):1018–35.

McGuire, Kevin T., Georg Vanberg, Charles E. Smith, Jr. and Gregory A. Caldeira. 2009. "Measuring Policy Content on the U.S. Supreme Court." *Journal of Politics* 71(4).

McNollgast. 1995. "Politics and the Courts: A Positive Theory of Judicial Doctrine and the Rule of Law." *Southern California Law Review* 68:1631–89.

Meernik, James and Joseph Ignagni. 1997. "Judicial Review and Coordinate Construction of the Constitution." *American Journal of Political Science* 41(2):447–67.

Miller, Warren E. and Donald E. Stokes. 1963. "Constituency Influence in Congress." *American Political Science Review* 57(1):45–56.

Mishler, William and Reginald S. Sheehan. 1993. "The Supreme Court as a Countermajoritarian Institution? The Impact of Public Opinion on Supreme Court Decisions." *American Political Science Review* 87(1):87–101.

Mishler, William and Reginald S. Sheehan. 1996. "Public Opinion, the Attitudinal Model, and Supreme Court Decision Making: A Micro-Analytic Perspective." *Journal of Politics* 58(1):169–200.

Mondak, Jeffery J. 1994. "Policy Legitimacy and the Supreme Court: The Sources and Contexts of Legitimation." *Political Research Quarterly* 47(3):675–92.

Mondak, Jeffery J. and Shannon Ishiyama Smithey. 1997. "The Dynamics of Public Support for the Supreme Court." *Journal of Politics* 59(4):1114–42.

Montesquieu, Charles de Secondat. 1991 [1748]. *The Spirit of the Laws.* Littleton, CO: Rothman.

Murphy, Paul L. 1972. *The Constitution in Crisis Times, 1918–1969.* New York: HarperCollins.

Murphy, Walter F. 1962. *Congress and the Court.* Chicago: University of Chicago Press.

Murphy, Walter F. 1964. *Elements of Judicial Strategy.* Chicago: University of Chicago Press.

Murphy, Walter F. and Joseph Tanenhaus. 1990. "Publicity, Public Opinion, and the Supreme Court." *Northwestern University Law Review* 84(4):985–1023.

Nagel, Stuart S. 1965. "Court-Curbing Periods in American History." *Vanderbilt Law Review* 18(3):925–44.

Nash, George H. 1996. *The Conservative Intellectual Movement in America.* Wilmington, DE: Intercollegiate Studies Institute.

Neely, Richard. 1981. *How Courts Govern America.* New Haven, CT: Yale University Press.

Nelson, William E. 2000. *Marbury v. Madison: The Origins and Legacy of Judicial Review.* Lawrence: University Press of Kansas.

North, Douglas and Barry Weingast. 1989. "Constitutions and Commitment: The Evolution of Institutions Governing Public Choice in Seventeenth Century England." *Journal of Economic History* 49:803–32.

O'Connor, Sandra Day. 2006a. "Fair and Independent Courts: A Conference on the State of the Judiciary." Transcript of Remarks by Sandra Day O'Connor. Georgetown Law Center, Washington, DC, September 28, 2006.

O'Connor, Sandra Day. 2006b. "The Threat to Judicial Independence." *The Wall Street Journal*, September 27, A18.

Park, David K., Andrew Gelman and Joseph Bafumi. 2005. State Level Opinions from National Surveys: Poststratification Using Multilevel Logistic Regression. In *Public Opinion in State Politics*, ed. Jeffrey E. Cohen. Stanford, CA: Stanford University Press pp. 209–28.

Parker, Glenn R. and Roger H. Davidson. 1979. "Why Do Americans Love Their Congressmen So Much More Than Their Congress?" *Legislative Studies Quarterly* 4:53–61.

Paschal, Richard A. 1992. "The Continuing Colloquy: Congress and the Finality of the Supreme Court." *Journal of Law and Politics* 8(1):142–226.

Peretti, Terri Jennings. 1999. *In Defense of a Political Court.* Princeton, NJ: Princeton University Press.

Perry, H.W., Jr. 1991. *Deciding to Decide: Agenda Setting in the United States Supreme Court.* Cambridge, MA: Harvard University Press.

Pickerill, J. Mitchell. 2004. *Constitutional Deliberation in Congress: The Impact of Judicial Review in a Separated System.* Durham, NC: Duke University Press.

Poole, Keith T. 1998. "Recovering a Basic Space from a Set of Issue Scales." *American Journal of Political Science* 42:954–93.

Poole, Keith T. and Howard Rosenthal. 1997. *Congress: A Political-Economic History of Roll Call Voting.* Oxford: Oxford University Press.

Powe, Lucas A. 2000. *The Warren Court in American Politics.* Cambridge, MA: Belknap Press of Harvard University Press.

Pritchett, C. Herman. 1948. *The Roosevelt Court; A Study in Judicial Politics and Values, 1937–1947.* New York: Macmillan.

Pritchett, C. Herman. 1961. *Congress Versus the Supreme Court, 1957–1960.* Minneapolis: University of Minnesota Press.

R Development Core Team. 2009. *R: A Language and Environment for Statistical Computing.* Vienna, Austria: R Foundation for Statistical Computing. ISBN 3-900051-07-0.
URL: *http://www.R-project.org*

Ramseyer, J. Mark. 1994. "The Puzzling (In)dependence of Courts: A Comparative Approach." *Journal of Legal Studies* 23(3):721–47.

Ramseyer, J. Mark and Eric B. Rasmusen. 2001. "Why Are Japanese Judges So Conservative in Politically Charged Cases?" *American Political Science Review* 95(2):331–44.

Rehnquist, William. 2003. "Remarks of the Chief Justice." Symposium on Judicial Independence, University of Richmond T. C. Williams School of Law, March 21, 2003.

Roberts, John C., Jr. 2006. "Fair and Independent Courts: A Conference on the State of the Judiciary." Transcript of Remarks by John G. Roberts, Jr. Georgetown Law Center, Washington, DC, September 28, 2006.

Rogers, James R. 2001. "Information and Judicial Review: A Signaling Game of Legislative-Judicial Interaction." *American Journal of Political Science* 45(1):84–99.

Rogers, James R. and Georg Vanberg. 2007. "Resurrecting Lochner: A Defense of Unprincipled Judicial Activism." *Journal of Law, Economics & Organization* 23(2):442–68.

Rosenberg, Gerald N. 1991. *The Hollow Hope: Can Courts Bring about Social Change?* Chicago: University of Chicago Press.

Rosenberg, Gerald N. 1992. "Judicial Independence and the Reality of Political Power." *Review of Politics* 54(3):369–88.

Ross, William G. 1994. *A Muted Fury: Populists, Progressive, and Labor Unions Confront the Courts, 1890–1937.* Princeton, NJ: Princeton University Press.

Ross, William G. 2002. "Attacks on the Warren Court by State Officials: A Case Study of Why Court-Curbing Movements Fail." *Buffalo Law Review* 50(2):483–612.

Sala, Brian R. and James F. Spriggs III. 2004. "Designing Tests of the Supreme Court and the Separation of Powers." *Political Research Quarterly* 57(2):197–208.

Salzberger, Eli and Paul Fenn. 1999. "Judicial Independence: Some Evidence from The English Court of Appeal." *Journal of Law and Economics* 42(2):831–47.

Scheppele, Kim Lane. 1999. "The New Hungarian Constitutional Court." *East European Constitutional Review* 8(4):81–7.

Schlencker, Barry R. and Beth A. Pontari. 2000. The Strategic Control of Information: Impression Management and Self-Presentation in Daily Life. In *Psychological Perspectives on Self and Identity,* ed. Abraham Tesser, Richard B. Felson and Jerry M. Suls. Washington, DC: American Psychological Association.

Schmidhauser, John R. 1963. *Constitutional Law in the Political Process.* New York: Rand McNally.

Schwartz, Edward P. 1992. "Policy, Precedent, and Power: A Positive Theory of Supreme Court Decision-Making." *Journal of Law, Economics, & Organization* 8(2):219–52.

Segal, Jeffrey A. 1997. "Separation-of-Powers Games in the Positive Theory of Congress and Courts." *American Political Science Review* 91:28–44.

Segal, Jeffrey A. 1999. Supreme Court Deference to Congress: An Examination of the Marksist Model. In *Supreme Court Decision-Making: New Institutionalist Approaches*, ed. Cornell W. Clayton and Howard Gillman. Chicago: University of Chicago Press.

Segal, Jeffrey A. and Albert D. Cover. 1989. "Ideological Values and the Votes of U.S. Supreme Court Justices." *The American Political Science Review* 83(2):557–65.

Segal, Jeffrey A. and Harold J. Spaeth. 2002. *The Supreme Court and the Attitudinal Model Revisited*. New York: Cambridge University Press.

Segal, Jeffrey A. and Chad Westerland. 2005. "The Supreme Court, Congress, and Judicial Review." *North Carolina Law Review* 83(5):1323–52.

Segal, Jeffrey A., Chad Westerland and Stefanie A. Lindquist. Forthcoming. "Congress, the Supreme Court and Judicial Review: Testing a Constitutional Separation of Powers Model." *American Journal of Political Science*.

Shepsle, Kenneth. 1991. Discretion, Institutions, and the Problem of Government Commitment. In *Social Theory for a Changing Society*, ed. Pierre Bordieux and James S. Coleman. Boulder, CO: Westview Press pp. 245–63.

Smith, Joseph L. 1999. "Judicial Procedures as Instruments of Political Control." Ph.D. dissertation, University of Texas at Austin.

Snyder, James M., Jr. and Michael Ting. 2005. "Why Roll Calls? A Model of Position-Taking in Legislative Voting and Elections." *Journal of Law, Economics and Organization* 21(1):153–78.

Spaeth, Harold J. 2009. *United States Supreme Court Judicial Database*. URL: *http://www.as.uky.edu/polisci/ulmerproject/sctdata.htm*

Spiller, Pablo T. and Rafael Gely. 1992. "Congressional Control or Judicial Independence: The Determinants of U.S. Supreme Court Labor-Relations Decisions, 1949–1988." *Rand Journal of Economics* 23:463–92.

Spiller, Pablo T. and Matthew L. Spitzer. 1992. "Judicial Choice of Legal Doctrines." *Journal of Law, Economics, & Organization* 8(1):8–46.

Stasavage, David. 2002. "Credible Commitment in Early Modern Europe: North and Weingast Revisited." *Journal of Law, Economics & Organization* 18(1):155–86.

Staton, Jeffrey K. 2006. "Constitutional Review and the Selective Promotion of Case Results." *American Journal of Political Science* 50(1): 98–112.

Staton, Jeffrey K. 2010. *Why Do Judges Go Public? Constitutional Review and Judicial Public Relations in Mexico*. New York: Cambridge University Press.

Staton, Jeffrey K. and Georg Vanberg. 2008. "The Value of Vagueness: Delegation, Defiance, and Judicial Opinions." *American Journal of Political Science* 52(3):504–19. Working paper.

Stephenson, Donald Grier, Jr. 1999. *Campaigns & the Court*. New York: Columbia University Press.

Stephenson, Matthew C. 2004. "Court of Public Opinion: Government Accountability and Judicial Independence." *Journal of Law, Economics & Organization* 20(2):379–99.

Stimson, James A. 1991. *Public Opinion in America: Moods, Cycles, and Swings.*
Boulder, CO: Westview Press.

Stimson, James A. 1999. *Public Opinion in America: Moods, Cycles, and Swings.*
2 ed. Boulder, CO: Westview Press.

Stimson, James A., Michael B. MacKuen and Robert S. Erikson. 1995. "Dynamic
Representation." *American Political Science Review* 89(3):543–65.

Stites, Francis N. 1981. *John Marshall – Defender of the Constitution.* Boston:
Little, Brown.

Stumpf, Harry. 1965. "Congressional Responses to Supreme Court Rulings: The
Interaction of Law and Politics." *Journal of Public Law* 14(2):377–95.

Tanenhaus, Joseph and Walter F. Murphy. 1981. "Patterns of Public Support for
the Supreme Court: a Panel Study." *The Journal of Politics* 43(1):24–39.

Taylor, John B. 1992. "The Supreme Court and Political Eras: A Perspective on
Judicial Power in a Democratic Polity." *Review of Politics* 54(3):345–68.

Teles, Steven M. 2008. *The Rise of the Conservative Legal Movement.* Princeton,
NJ: Princeton University Press.

Tetlock, Philip E. and A.S.R. Manstead. 1985. "Impression Management Versus
Intrapsychic Explanations in Social Psychology: A Useful Dichotomy?" *Psychological Review* 92(1):59–77.

Thayer, James Bradley. 1893. "The Origin and Scope of the American Doctrine
of Constitutional Law." *Harvard Law Review* 7(3):129–56.

Tsebelis, George. 2000. "Veto Players and Institutional Analysis." *Governance*
13(4):441–74.

Tushnet, Mark. 2000. *Taking the Constitution Away from the Courts.* Princeton,
NJ: Princeton University Press.

Tushnet, Mark. 2003. *The New Constitutional Order.* Princeton, NJ: Princeton
University Press.

Vanberg, Georg. 2005. *The Politics of Constitutional Review in Germany.* New
York: Cambridge University Press.

Warren, Charles. 1926. *The Supreme Court in United States History.* Boston:
Little, Brown.

Wechsler, Herbert. 1954. "The Political Safeguards of Federalism: The Role of
the States in the Composition and Selection of the National Government."
Columbia Law Review 54(4):543–60.

Wechsler, Herbert. 1959. "Toward Neutral Principles of Constitutional Law."
Harvard Law Review 73(1):1–35.

Weicker, Lowell P., Jr., and Barry Sussman. 1995. *Maverick: A Life in Politics.*
New York: Little, Brown and Co.

Weingast, Barry R. 1997. "The Political Foundations of Democracy and the Rule
of Law." *American Political Science Review* 91(2):245–63.

White, G. Edward. 2005. "AHR Forum: Constitutional Change and the New
Deal: The Internalist/Externalist Debate." *The American Historical Review*
110(4).
　　URL: *http://www.historycooperative.org/journals/ahr/110.4/white.html*

Whittington, Keith E. 1999. *Constitutional Interpretation: Textual Meaning, Original Intent, and Judicial Review*. Lawrence: University Press of Kansas.

Whittington, Keith E. 2003. "Legislative Sanctions and the Strategic Environment of Judicial Review." *I-Con: The International Journal of Constitutional Law* 1(3):446–74.

Whittington, Keith E. 2005. "'Interpose Your Friendly Hand': Political Supports for the Exercise of Judicial Review by the United States Supreme Court." *American Political Science Review* 99(4):583–96.

Whittington, Keith E. 2007. *Political Foundations of Judicial Supremacy*. Princeton, NJ: Princeton University Press.

Wiecek, William I. 1969. "The Reconstruction of Federal Judicial Power, 1863–1875." *American Journal of Legal History* 13(4):333–59.

Wolfe, Christopher. 1994. *The Rise of Modern Judicial Review*. Lanham, MD: Littlefield Adams.

Wright, Benjamin F. 1942. *The Growth of American Constitutional Law*. New York: Houghton Mifflin.

Zink, James R., James F. Spriggs and John T. Scott. 2009. "Courting the Public: The Influence of Decision Attributes on Individuals Views of Court Opinions." *Journal of Politics* 71(3):909–25.

Index

Page numbers followed by *f* or *t* indicate a figure or table, respectively. Page numbers followed by n and a number refer to footnotes.

effect of Court-Congress policy
divergence on statutory decisions,
221*t*, 223–224, 227, 229–230,
229*t*

effect of Court-curbing ideology on
ideology of, 215, 215*t*, 216*f*,
221–222, 221*t*, 223*f*, 224, 225*f*

effect of Court-curbing intensity/ideology
on statutory liberalism of, 221*t*,
229–232, 229*t*, 250

effect of Court-public mood divergence
on statutory decisions, 217, 221*t*,
222–223, 224, 225*f*

effect of intense Court-curbing in
statutory cases, 217, 224, 225*f*,
226–227

effect of pessimism concerning public
support on statutory decisions, 227,
229*t*, 230–232, 235, 250

ideology of, 50, 211–215, 212*f*, 214*t*

immunity to electoral/political
accountability, 12–13

impeachment of, 13, 19, 38, 56, 77,
162

incentives for self-restraint, 7–9, 15–16,
90, 94, 96, 97, 104–106, 109–110,
113, 170–171, 176*t*, 180–182,
190–193, 191*t*, 217, 236, 266–267,
268

incentives for sophisticated decision
making, 9–13, 69n7, 194, 208, 209,
235, 237–238

individual patterns of response to
Court-curbing, 208, 216, 217, 233,
234*t*

interpretation of Court-curbing, 18, 20,
48–49, 71–80, 193–194, 236,
257–260

Judiciary Act (1801) and, 31

lack of further ambition, 13

measure of liberalism of, 217–218, 220,
227–228

number of, 39n14

ones never having been elected to office,
267–268

perceptions of Court-curbing, 71–76, 80

personal policy preferences, 211–215,
212*f*

Roosevelt's Court-Packing Plan, 28, 49,
52, 53–54, 167, 195–200, 201*t*,
202–203, 249n43

selection methods, 2, 38, 57, 160,
162

self-preservation motivations of,
70–71

switch-in-time-that-saved-nine, 53–54,
195, 197–200, 201*f*, 202–203

telephone justice and, 7

tenure of, 5, 19, 38–39, 42, 53n34

See also Supreme Court; *specific
Supreme Court judge*

judicial activism, 41, 165, 166*f*,
170–171n17, 180

Judicial Code (1911), 52

Judicial Common Space score, 133n7,
135n8, 142n14, 148

Judicial Conference of the United States,
68

judicial independence

Court-curbing as threat to, 18–21,
73–75, 194

definition of, 5

effect of breakdowns of, 5, 14–15

effect of legislative preference for, 81

judicial review and, 264–265

judicial self-restraint in face of
institutional signals and, 3–4, 6, 8–9,
63–64, 178, 180, 180*t*, 259–260, 262,
264

link to economic growth, 263–264

periods of breakdown of, 6–7, 28–29,
30–36, 53–54. *See also* desegregation;
New Deal; *specific period by date*

political pressures limiting, 7–9,
259–260. *See also* Court-curbing;
diffuse public support of Court

politics-legitimacy paradox, 21–22,
262–263, 264

position-taking function of
Court-curbing and, 257–258

preservation of, 6–7, 15–16

scholarship on, 2, 3, 5, 8, 258

switch-in-time-that-saved-nine and,
53–54, 195, 197–200, 201*f*,
202–203

unpopular decisions and. *See*
countermajoritarian difficulty

virtues/vices of, 6, 255, 264

judicial-legislative relations. *See*
Court-Congress ideological
divergence; Court-Congress relations;
Court-curbing

David Stasavage, *Public Debt and the Birth of the Democratic State: France and Great Britain, 1688–1789*

Charles Stewart III, *Budget Reform Politics: The Design of the Appropriations Process in the House of Representatives, 1865–1921*

George Tsebelis and Jeannette Money, *Bicameralism*

Georg Vanberg, *The Politics of Constitutional Review in Germany*

Nicolas van de Walle, *African Economies and the Politics of Permanent Crisis, 1979–1999*

John Waterbury, *Exposed to Innumerable Delusions: Public Enterprise and State Power in Egypt, India, Mexico, and Turkey*

David L. Weimer, ed., *The Political Economy of Property Rights: Institutional Change and Credibility in the Reform of Centrally Planned Economies*